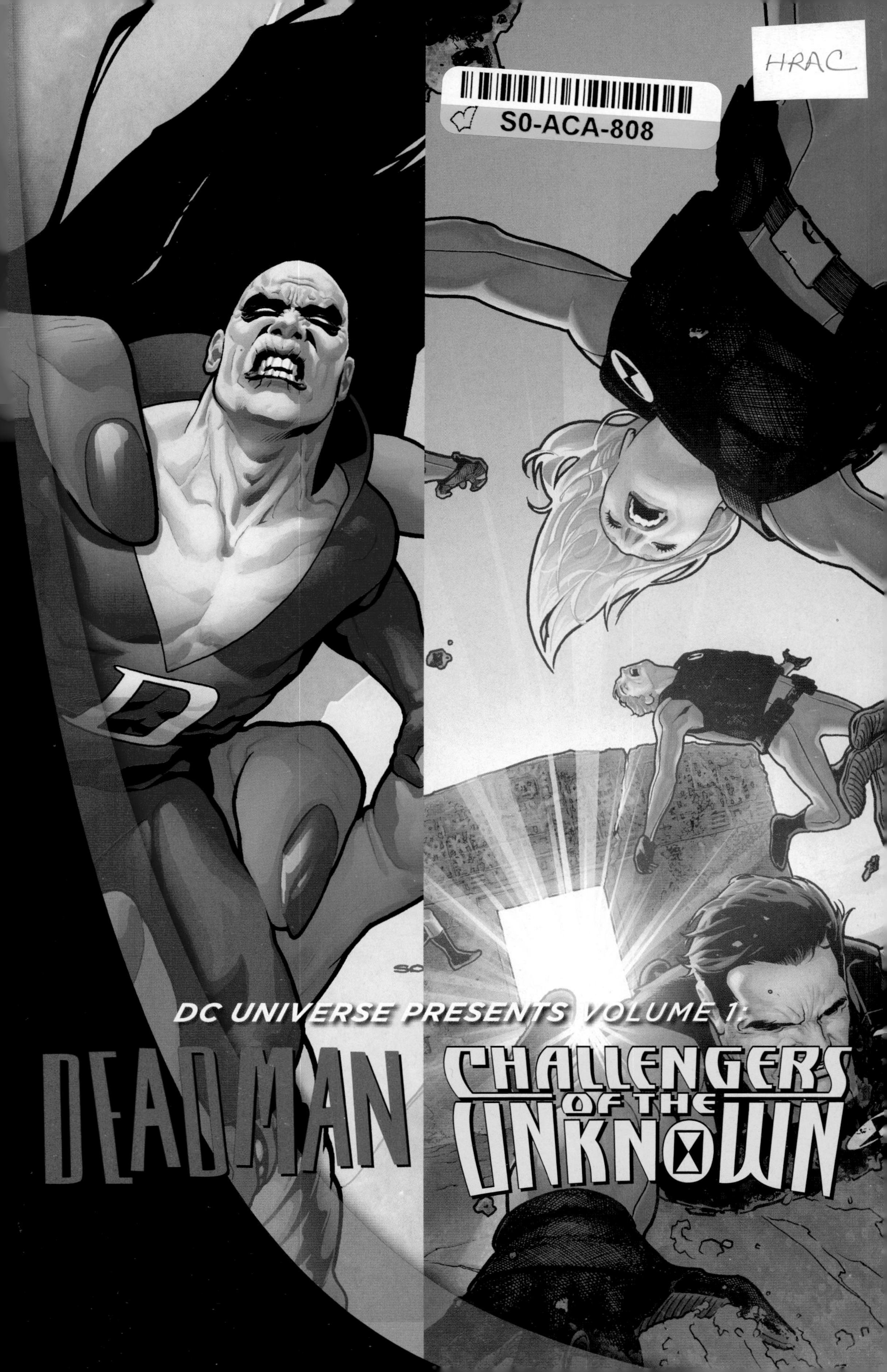
DC UNIVERSE PRESENTS VOLUME 1:
DEADMAN
CHALLENGERS OF THE UNKNOWN

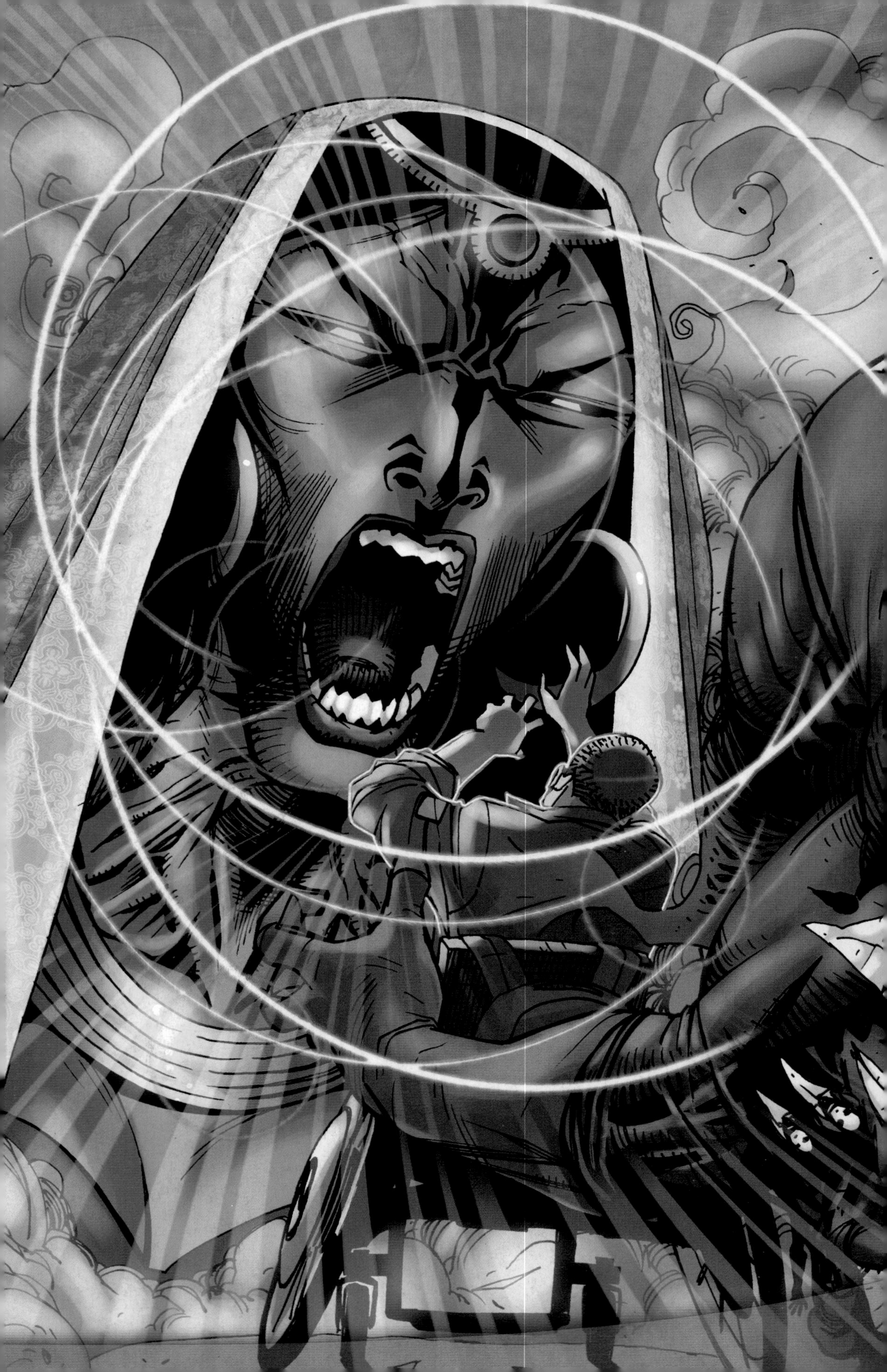

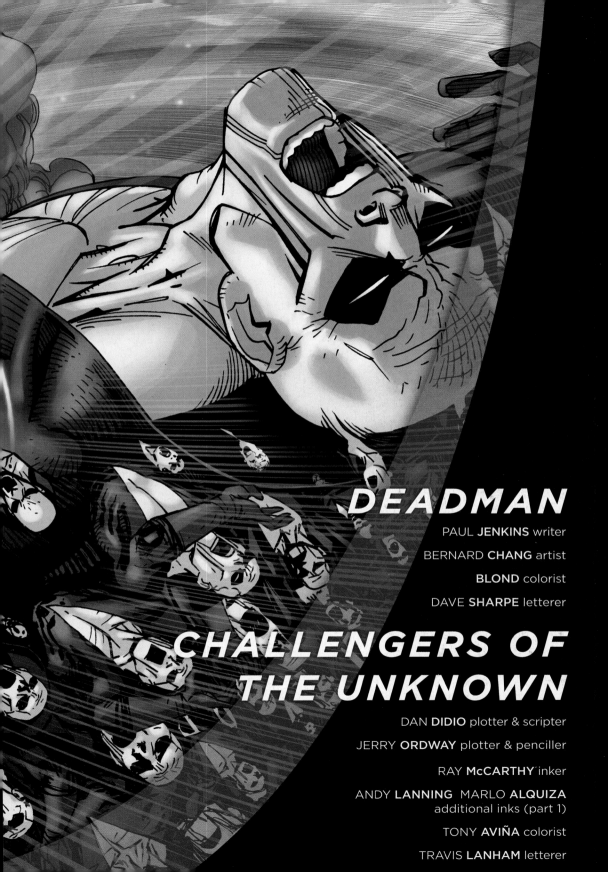

DEADMAN

PAUL **JENKINS** writer

BERNARD **CHANG** artist

BLOND colorist

DAVE **SHARPE** letterer

CHALLENGERS OF THE UNKNOWN

DAN **DIDIO** plotter & scripter

JERRY **ORDWAY** plotter & penciller

RAY **McCARTHY** inker

ANDY **LANNING** MARLO **ALQUIZA**
additional inks (part 1)

TONY **AVIÑA** colorist

TRAVIS **LANHAM** letterer

WIL MOSS Editor – Original Series ROBIN WILDMAN Editor
ROBBIN BROSTERMAN Design Director – Books ROBBIE BIEDERMAN Publication Design

BOB HARRAS VP – Editor-in-Chief

DIANE NELSON President DAN DIDIO and JIM LEE Co-Publishers
GEOFF JOHNS Chief Creative Officer
JOHN ROOD Executive VP – Sales, Marketing and Business Development
AMY GENKINS Senior VP – Business and Legal Affairs NAIRI GARDINER Senior VP – Finance
JEFF BOISON VP – Publishing Operations MARK CHIARELLO VP – Art Direction and Design
JOHN CUNNINGHAM VP – Marketing TERRI CUNNINGHAM VP – Talent Relations and Services
ALISON GILL Senior VP – Manufacturing and Operations HANK KANALZ Senior VP – Digital
JAY KOGAN VP – Business and Legal Affairs, Publishing JACK MAHAN VP – Business Affairs, Talent
NICK NAPOLITANO VP – Manufacturing Administration SUE POHJA VP – Book Sales
COURTNEY SIMMONS Senior VP – Publicity BOB WAYNE Senior VP – Sales

DC UNIVERSE PRESENTS VOLUME 1 FEATURING DEADMAN & CHALLENGERS OF THE UNKNOWN

Published by DC Comics. Cover and compilation Copyright © 2012 DC Comics. All Rights Reserved.

Originally published in single magazine form in DC UNIVERSE PRESENTS #1-8. Copyright © 2011, 2012 DC Comics. All Rights Reserved.
All characters, their distinctive likenesses and related elements featured in this publication are trademarks of DC Comics.
The stories, characters and incidents featured in this publication are entirely fictional.
DC Comics does not read or accept unsolicited ideas, stories or artwork.

DC Comics, 1700 Broadway, New York, NY 10019
A Warner Bros. Entertainment Company.
Printed by RR Donnelley, Salem, VA, USA. 10/26/12. First Printing.
978-1-4012-3716-5

Library of Congress Cataloging-in-Publication Data

Jenkins, Paul, 1965-
DC Universe presents. Volume 1, featuring Deadman & Challengers of the Unknown / Paul Jenkins, Dan
DiDio, Bernard Chang, Jerry Ordway.
p. cm.
ISBN 978-1-4012-3716-5
1. Graphic novels. I. DiDio, Dan, 1959- II. Chang, Bernard, 1972- III. Ordway, Jerry. IV. Title.
PN6728.D35334J46 2012
741.5'973—dc23
2012033193

SUSTAINABLE
FORESTRY
INITIATIVE

Certified Chain of Custody
At Least 20% Certified Forest Content
www.sfiprogram.org

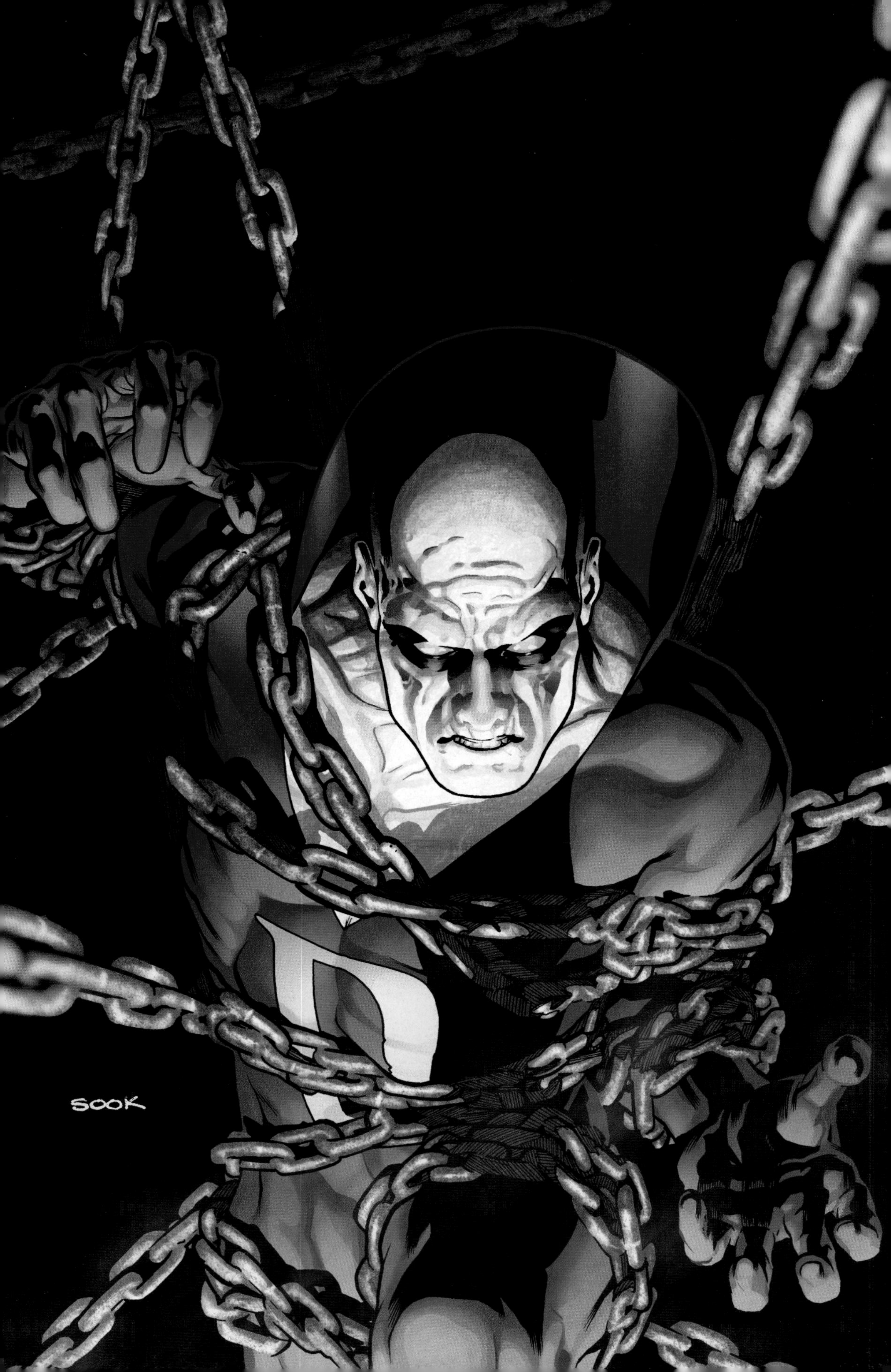
SOOK

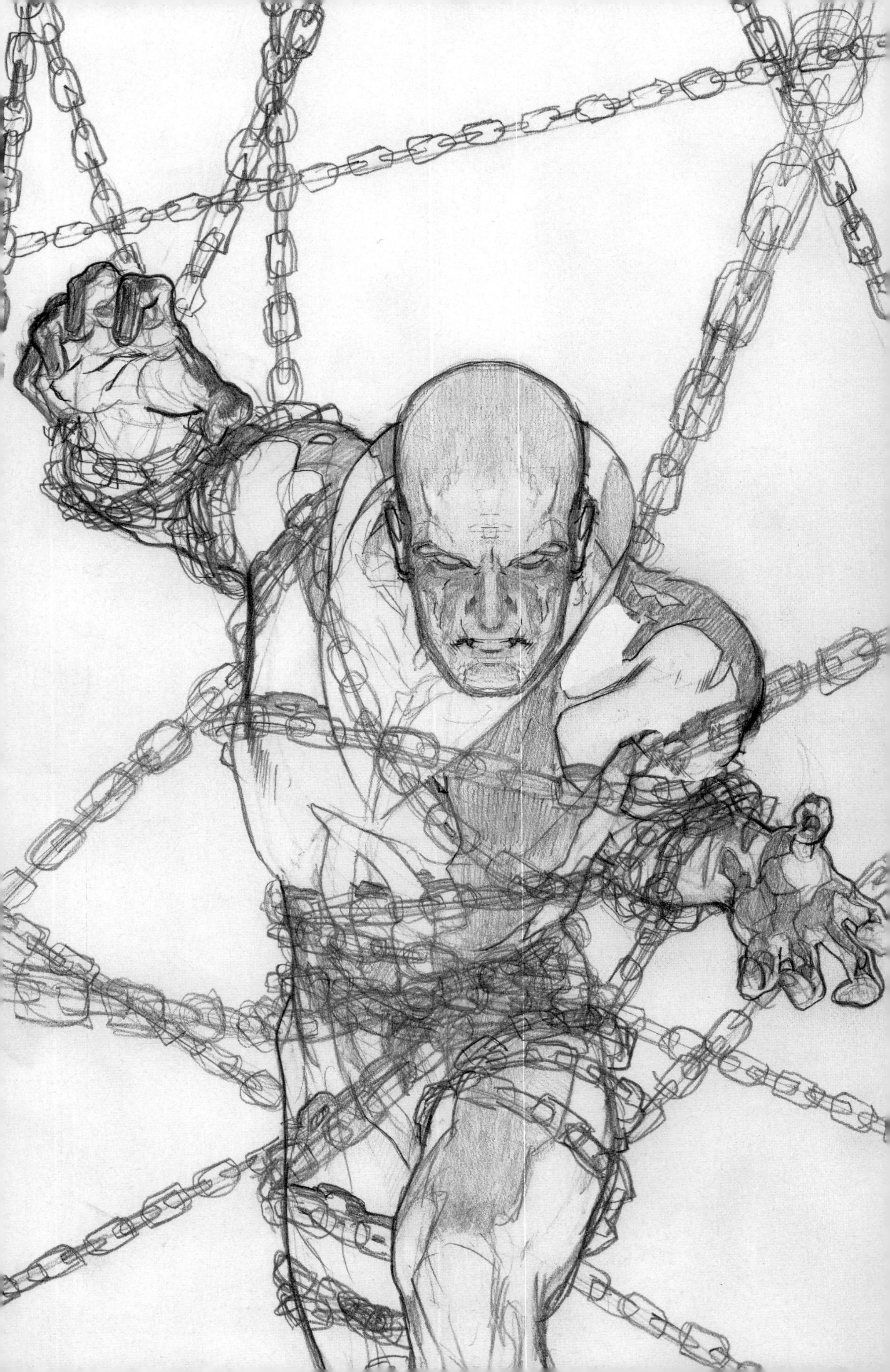

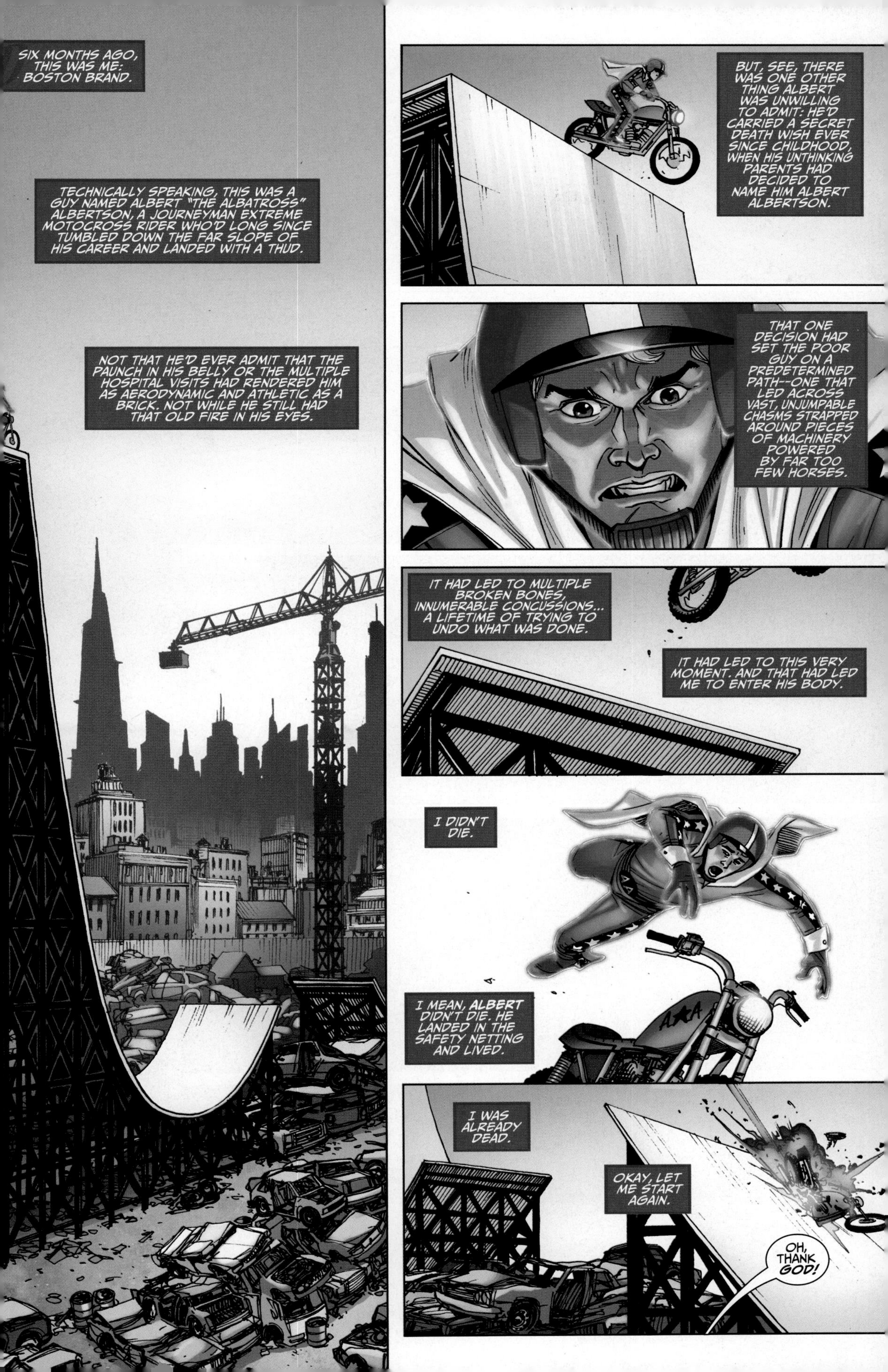
SIX MONTHS AGO, THIS WAS ME: BOSTON BRAND.
TECHNICALLY SPEAKING, THIS WAS A GUY NAMED ALBERT "THE ALBATROSS" ALBERTSON, A JOURNEYMAN EXTREME MOTOCROSS RIDER WHO'D LONG SINCE TUMBLED DOWN THE FAR SLOPE OF HIS CAREER AND LANDED WITH A THUD.
NOT THAT HE'D EVER ADMIT THAT THE PAUNCH IN HIS BELLY OR THE MULTIPLE HOSPITAL VISITS HAD RENDERED HIM AS AERODYNAMIC AND ATHLETIC AS A BRICK. NOT WHILE HE STILL HAD THAT OLD FIRE IN HIS EYES.
BUT, SEE, THERE WAS ONE OTHER THING ALBERT WAS UNWILLING TO ADMIT: HE'D CARRIED A SECRET DEATH WISH EVER SINCE CHILDHOOD, WHEN HIS UNTHINKING PARENTS HAD DECIDED TO NAME HIM ALBERT ALBERTSON.
THAT ONE DECISION HAD SET THE POOR GUY ON A PREDETERMINED PATH--ONE THAT LED ACROSS VAST, UNJUMPABLE CHASMS STRAPPED AROUND PIECES OF MACHINERY POWERED BY FAR TOO FEW HORSES.
IT HAD LED TO MULTIPLE BROKEN BONES, INNUMERABLE CONCUSSIONS... A LIFETIME OF TRYING TO UNDO WHAT WAS DONE.
IT HAD LED TO THIS VERY MOMENT. AND THAT HAD LED ME TO ENTER HIS BODY.
I DIDN'T DIE.
I MEAN, ALBERT DIDN'T DIE. HE LANDED IN THE SAFETY NETTING AND LIVED.
A★A
I WAS ALREADY DEAD.
OKAY, LET ME START AGAIN.
OH, THANK GOD!

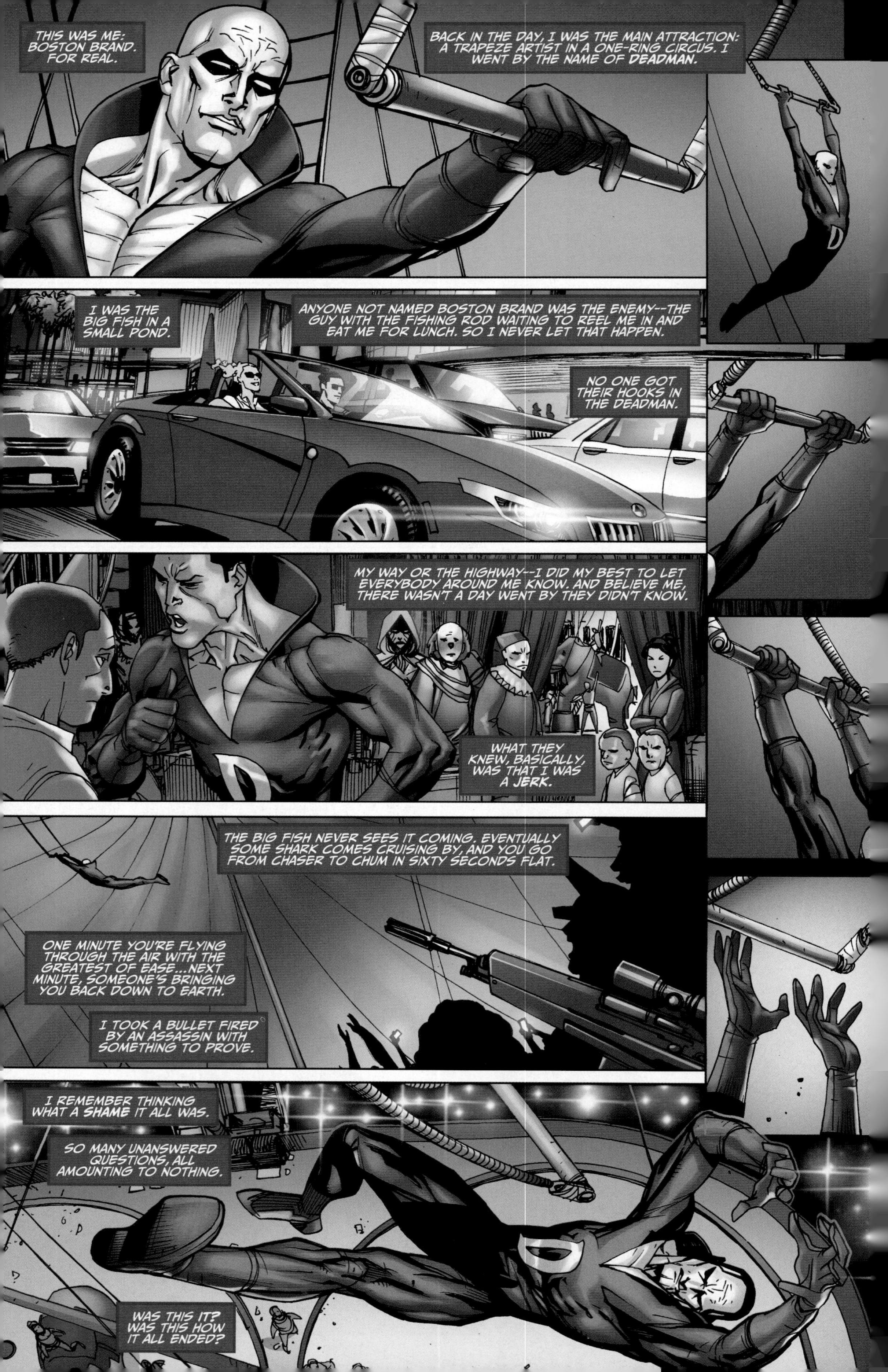
THIS WAS ME: BOSTON BRAND. FOR REAL.
BACK IN THE DAY, I WAS THE MAIN ATTRACTION: A TRAPEZE ARTIST IN A ONE-RING CIRCUS. I WENT BY THE NAME OF DEADMAN.
I WAS THE BIG FISH IN A SMALL POND.
ANYONE NOT NAMED BOSTON BRAND WAS THE ENEMY--THE GUY WITH THE FISHING ROD WAITING TO REEL ME IN AND EAT ME FOR LUNCH. SO I NEVER LET THAT HAPPEN.
NO ONE GOT THEIR HOOKS IN THE DEADMAN.
MY WAY OR THE HIGHWAY--I DID MY BEST TO LET EVERYBODY AROUND ME KNOW. AND BELIEVE ME, THERE WASN'T A DAY WENT BY THEY DIDN'T KNOW.
WHAT THEY KNEW, BASICALLY, WAS THAT I WAS A JERK.
THE BIG FISH NEVER SEES IT COMING. EVENTUALLY SOME SHARK COMES CRUISING BY, AND YOU GO FROM CHASER TO CHUM IN SIXTY SECONDS FLAT.
ONE MINUTE YOU'RE FLYING THROUGH THE AIR WITH THE GREATEST OF EASE...NEXT MINUTE, SOMEONE'S BRINGING YOU BACK DOWN TO EARTH.
I TOOK A BULLET FIRED BY AN ASSASSIN WITH SOMETHING TO PROVE.
I REMEMBER THINKING WHAT A SHAME IT ALL WAS.
SO MANY UNANSWERED QUESTIONS, ALL AMOUNTING TO NOTHING.
WAS THIS IT? WAS THIS HOW IT ALL ENDED?

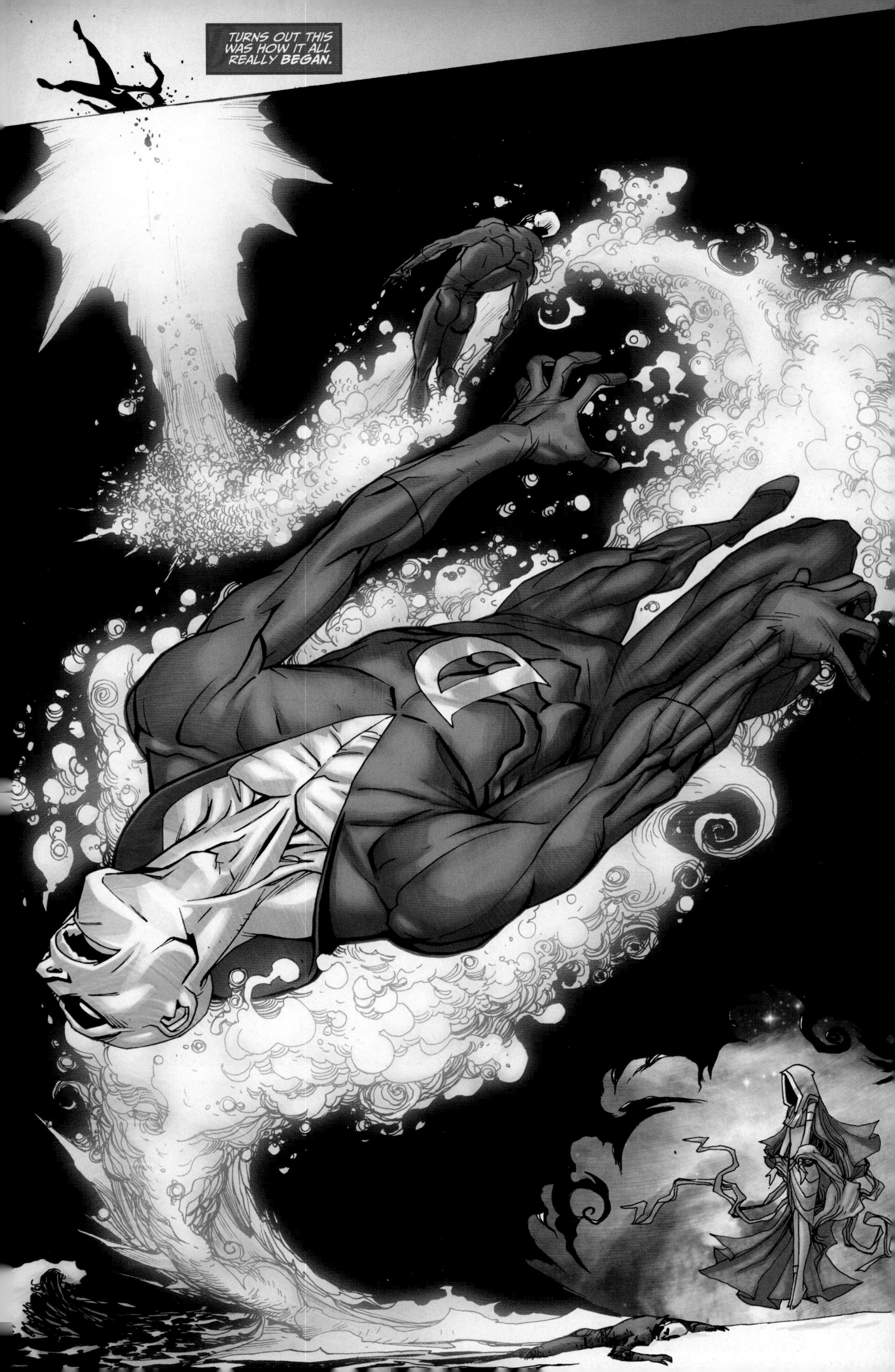
TURNS OUT THIS WAS HOW IT ALL REALLY BEGAN.

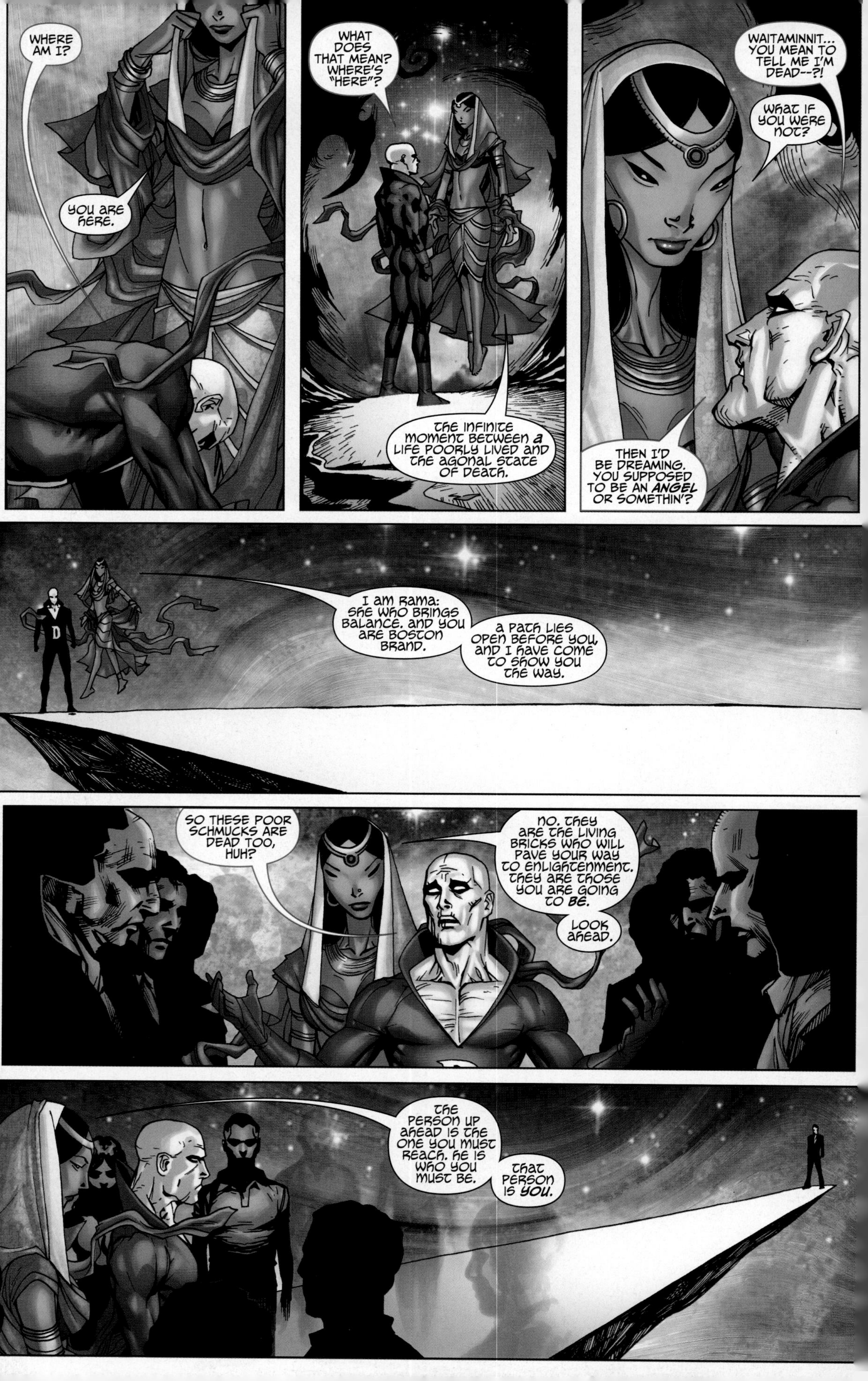
WHERE AM I?
YOU ARE HERE.
WHAT DOES THAT MEAN? WHERE'S "HERE"?
THE INFINITE MOMENT BETWEEN A LIFE POORLY LIVED AND THE AGONAL STATE OF DEATH.
WAITAMINNIT... YOU MEAN TO TELL ME I'M DEAD--?!
WHAT IF YOU WERE NOT?
THEN I'D BE DREAMING. YOU SUPPOSED TO BE AN ANGEL OR SOMETHIN'?
I AM RAMA: SHE WHO BRINGS BALANCE. AND YOU ARE BOSTON BRAND.
A PATH LIES OPEN BEFORE YOU, AND I HAVE COME TO SHOW YOU THE WAY.
SO THESE POOR SCHMUCKS ARE DEAD TOO, HUH?
NO. THEY ARE THE LIVING BRICKS WHO WILL PAVE YOUR WAY TO ENLIGHTENMENT. THEY ARE THOSE YOU ARE GOING TO BE.
LOOK AHEAD.
THE PERSON UP AHEAD IS THE ONE YOU MUST REACH. HE IS WHO YOU MUST BE.
THAT PERSON IS YOU.

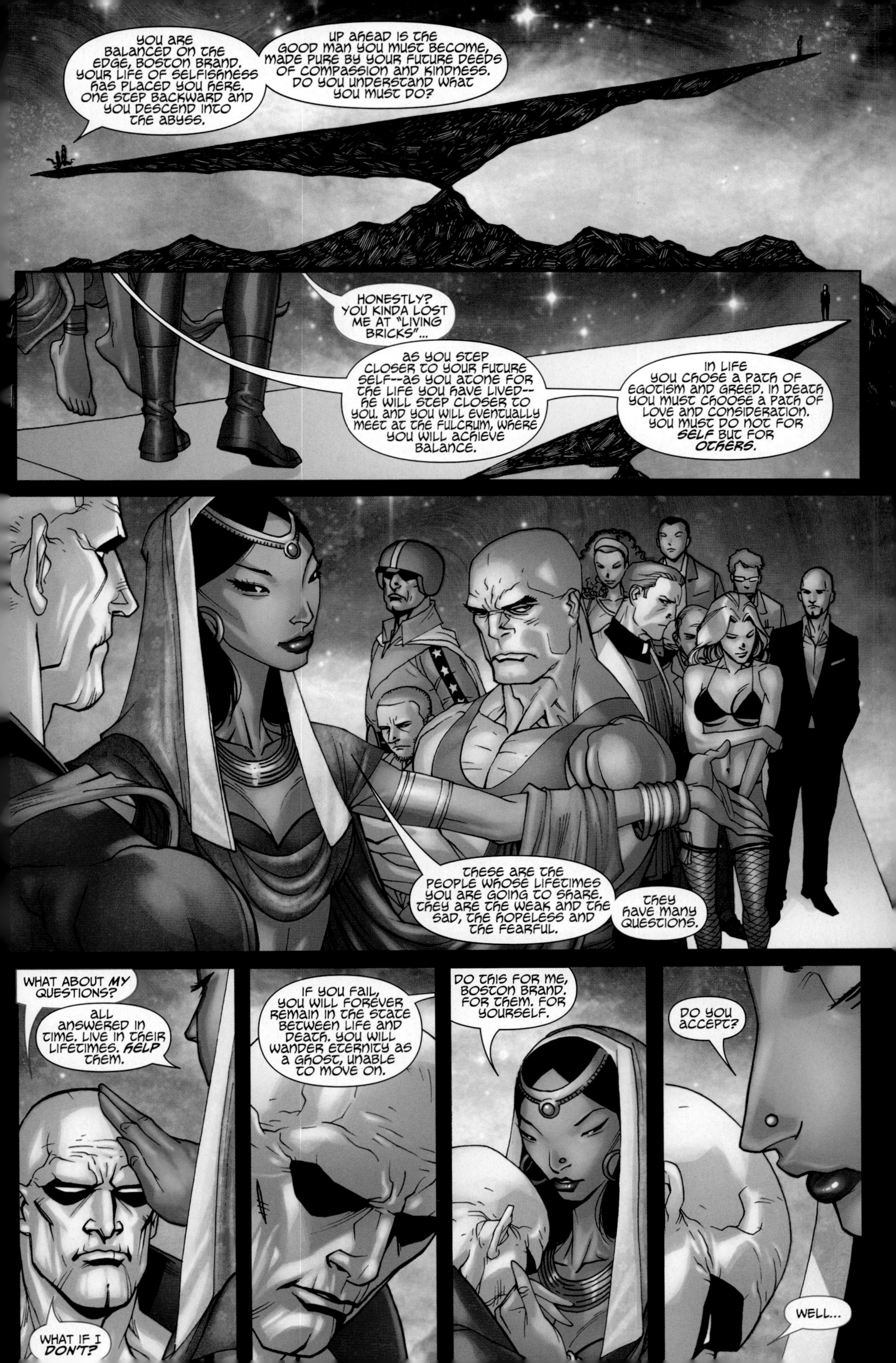
YOU ARE BALANCED ON THE EDGE, BOSTON BRAND. YOUR LIFE OF SELFISHNESS HAS PLACED YOU HERE. ONE STEP BACKWARD AND YOU DESCEND INTO THE ABYSS.
UP AHEAD IS THE GOOD MAN YOU MUST BECOME, MADE PURE BY YOUR FUTURE DEEDS OF COMPASSION AND KINDNESS. DO YOU UNDERSTAND WHAT YOU MUST DO?
HONESTLY? YOU KINDA LOST ME AT "LIVING BRICKS"...
AS YOU STEP CLOSER TO YOUR FUTURE SELF--AS YOU ATONE FOR THE LIFE YOU HAVE LIVED--HE WILL STEP CLOSER TO YOU. AND YOU WILL EVENTUALLY MEET AT THE FULCRUM, WHERE YOU WILL ACHIEVE BALANCE.
IN LIFE YOU CHOSE A PATH OF EGOTISM AND GREED. IN DEATH YOU MUST CHOOSE A PATH OF LOVE AND CONSIDERATION. YOU MUST DO NOT FOR SELF BUT FOR OTHERS.
THESE ARE THE PEOPLE WHOSE LIFETIMES YOU ARE GOING TO SHARE. THEY ARE THE WEAK AND THE SAD, THE HOPELESS AND THE FEARFUL.
THEY HAVE MANY QUESTIONS.
WHAT ABOUT MY QUESTIONS?
ALL ANSWERED IN TIME. LIVE IN THEIR LIFETIMES. HELP THEM.
WHAT IF I DON'T?
IF YOU FAIL, YOU WILL FOREVER REMAIN IN THE STATE BETWEEN LIFE AND DEATH. YOU WILL WANDER ETERNITY AS A GHOST, UNABLE TO MOVE ON.
DO THIS FOR ME, BOSTON BRAND. FOR THEM. FOR YOURSELF.
DO YOU ACCEPT?
WELL...

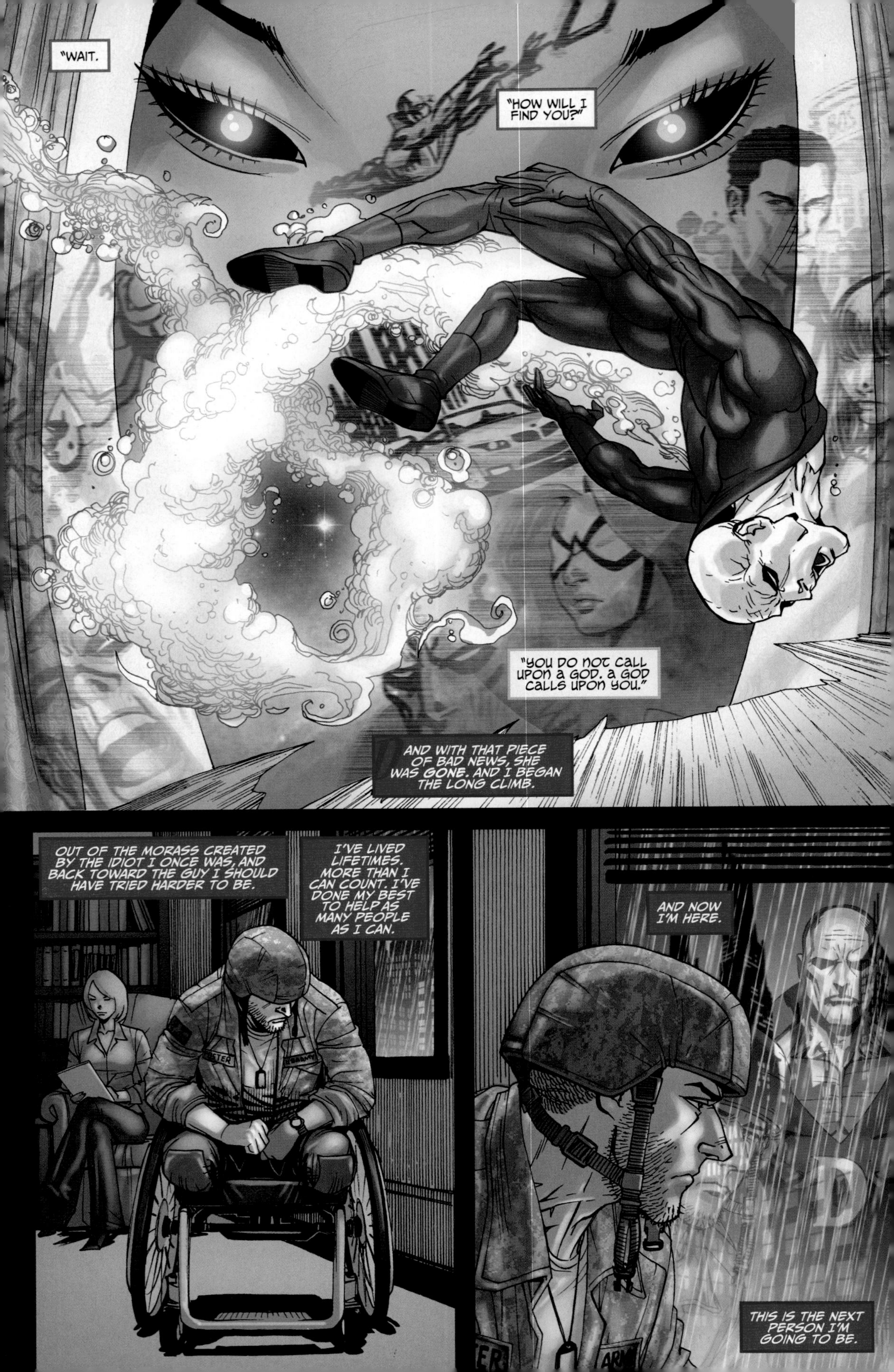
"WAIT.
"HOW WILL I FIND YOU?"
"YOU DO NOT CALL UPON A GOD. A GOD CALLS UPON YOU."
AND WITH THAT PIECE OF BAD NEWS, SHE WAS GONE. AND I BEGAN THE LONG CLIMB.
OUT OF THE MORASS CREATED BY THE IDIOT I ONCE WAS, AND BACK TOWARD THE GUY I SHOULD HAVE TRIED HARDER TO BE.
I'VE LIVED LIFETIMES. MORE THAN I CAN COUNT. I'VE DONE MY BEST TO HELP AS MANY PEOPLE AS I CAN.
AND NOW I'M HERE.
THIS IS THE NEXT PERSON I'M GOING TO BE.

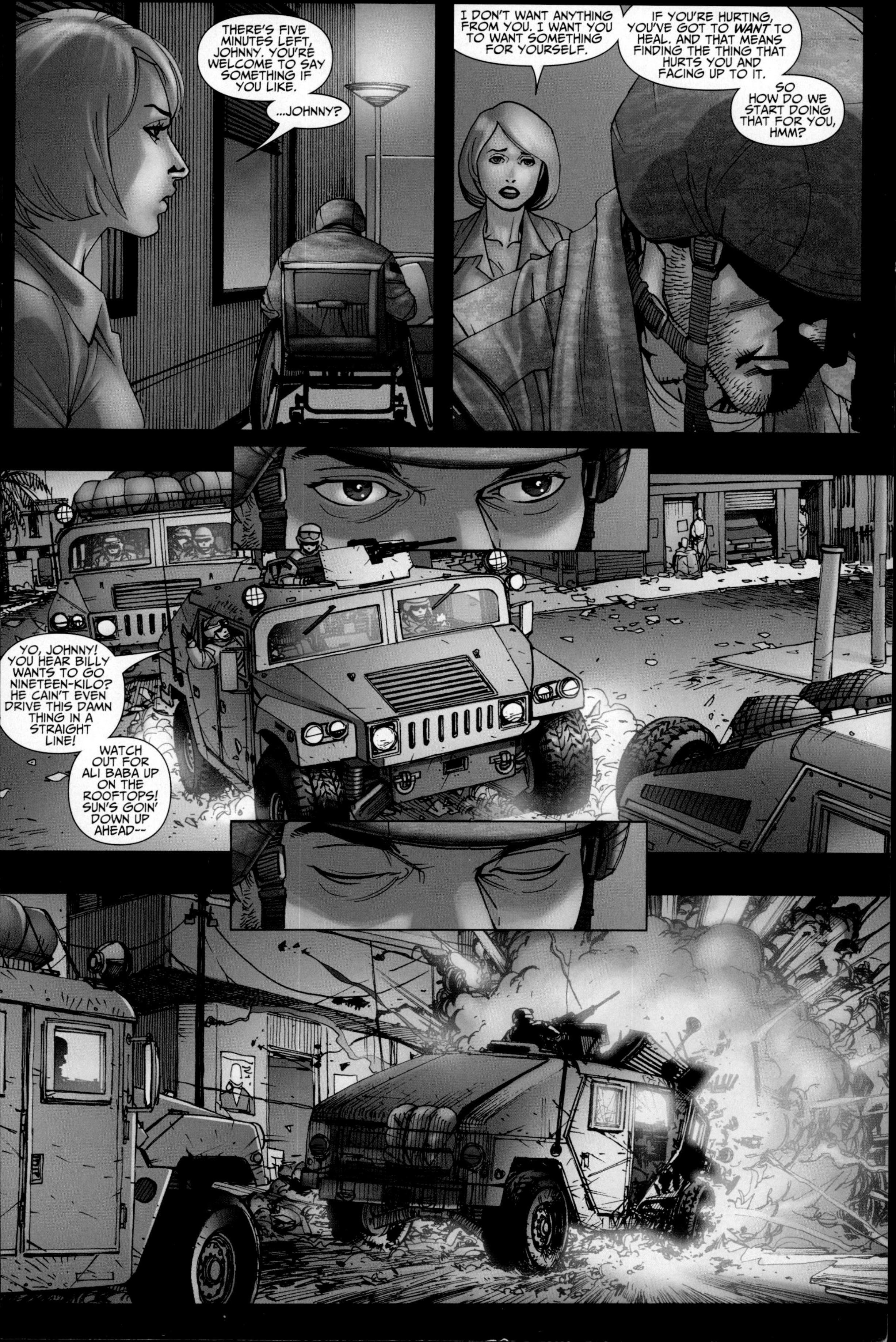
THERE'S FIVE MINUTES LEFT, JOHNNY. YOU'RE WELCOME TO SAY SOMETHING IF YOU LIKE.
...JOHNNY?
I DON'T WANT ANYTHING FROM YOU. I WANT YOU TO WANT SOMETHING FOR YOURSELF.
IF YOU'RE HURTING, YOU'VE GOT TO WANT TO HEAL. AND THAT MEANS FINDING THE THING THAT HURTS YOU AND FACING UP TO IT.
SO HOW DO WE START DOING THAT FOR YOU, HMM?
YO, JOHNNY! YOU HEAR BILLY WANTS TO GO NINETEEN-KILO? HE CAIN'T EVEN DRIVE THIS DAMN THING IN A STRAIGHT LINE!
WATCH OUT FOR ALI BABA UP ON THE ROOFTOPS! SUN'S GOIN' DOWN UP AHEAD--

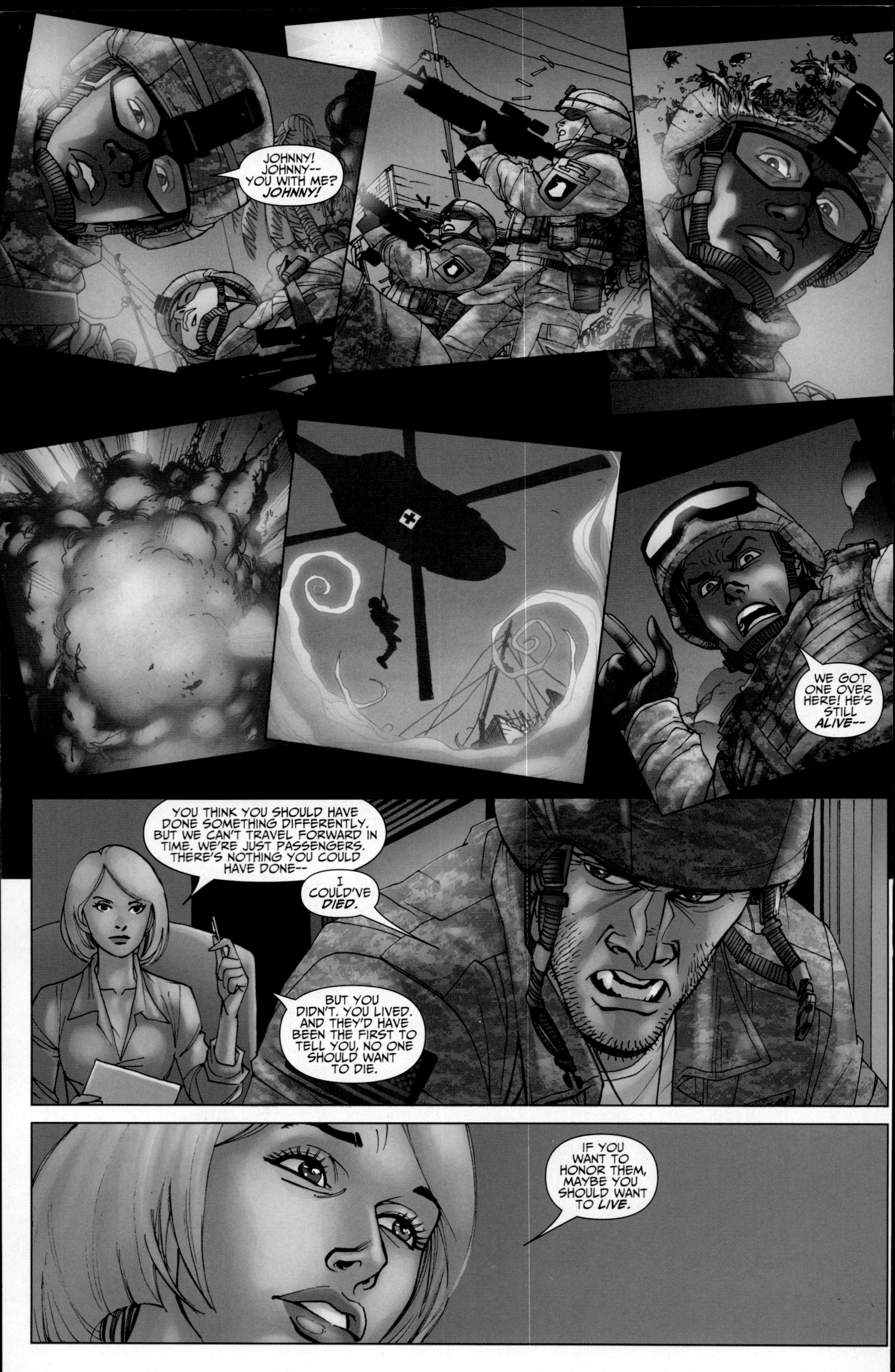

JOHNNY! JOHNNY-- YOU WITH ME? JOHNNY!
WE GOT ONE OVER HERE! HE'S STILL ALIVE--
YOU THINK YOU SHOULD HAVE DONE SOMETHING DIFFERENTLY. BUT WE CAN'T TRAVEL FORWARD IN TIME. WE'RE JUST PASSENGERS. THERE'S NOTHING YOU COULD HAVE DONE--
I COULD'VE DIED.
BUT YOU DIDN'T. YOU LIVED. AND THEY'D HAVE BEEN THE FIRST TO TELL YOU, NO ONE SHOULD WANT TO DIE.
IF YOU WANT TO HONOR THEM, MAYBE YOU SHOULD WANT TO LIVE.

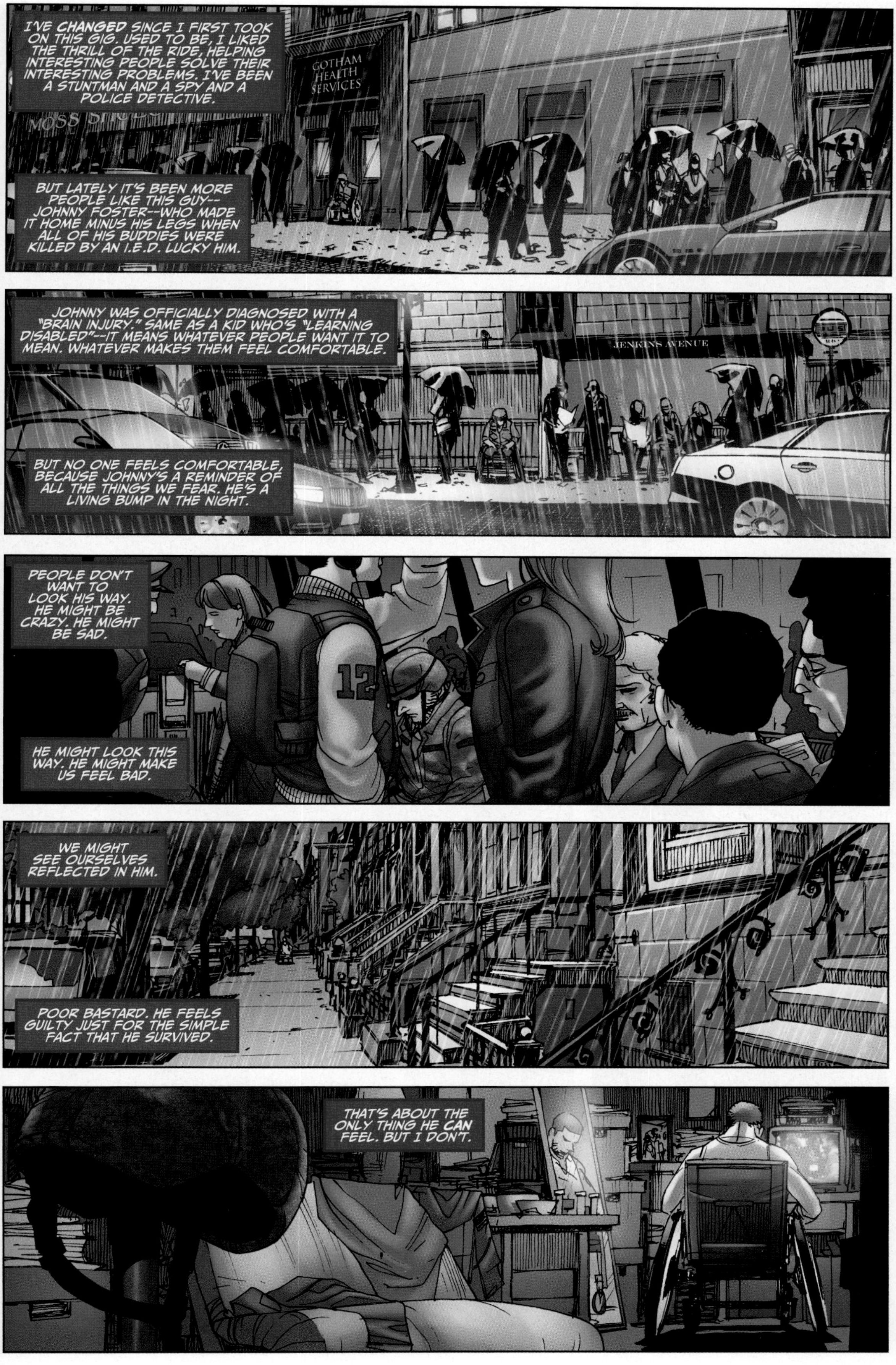
I'VE CHANGED SINCE I FIRST TOOK ON THIS GIG. USED TO BE, I LIKED THE THRILL OF THE RIDE, HELPING INTERESTING PEOPLE SOLVE THEIR INTERESTING PROBLEMS. I'VE BEEN A STUNTMAN AND A SPY AND A POLICE DETECTIVE.
GOTHAM HEALTH SERVICES
BUT LATELY IT'S BEEN MORE PEOPLE LIKE THIS GUY--JOHNNY FOSTER--WHO MADE IT HOME MINUS HIS LEGS WHEN ALL OF HIS BUDDIES WERE KILLED BY AN I.E.D. LUCKY HIM.
JOHNNY WAS OFFICIALLY DIAGNOSED WITH A "BRAIN INJURY." SAME AS A KID WHO'S "LEARNING DISABLED"--IT MEANS WHATEVER PEOPLE WANT IT TO MEAN. WHATEVER MAKES THEM FEEL COMFORTABLE.
JENKINS AVENUE
BUT NO ONE FEELS COMFORTABLE, BECAUSE JOHNNY'S A REMINDER OF ALL THE THINGS WE FEAR. HE'S A LIVING BUMP IN THE NIGHT.
PEOPLE DON'T WANT TO LOOK HIS WAY. HE MIGHT BE CRAZY. HE MIGHT BE SAD.
12
HE MIGHT LOOK THIS WAY. HE MIGHT MAKE US FEEL BAD.
WE MIGHT SEE OURSELVES REFLECTED IN HIM.
POOR BASTARD. HE FEELS GUILTY JUST FOR THE SIMPLE FACT THAT HE SURVIVED.
THAT'S ABOUT THE ONLY THING HE CAN FEEL. BUT I DON'T.

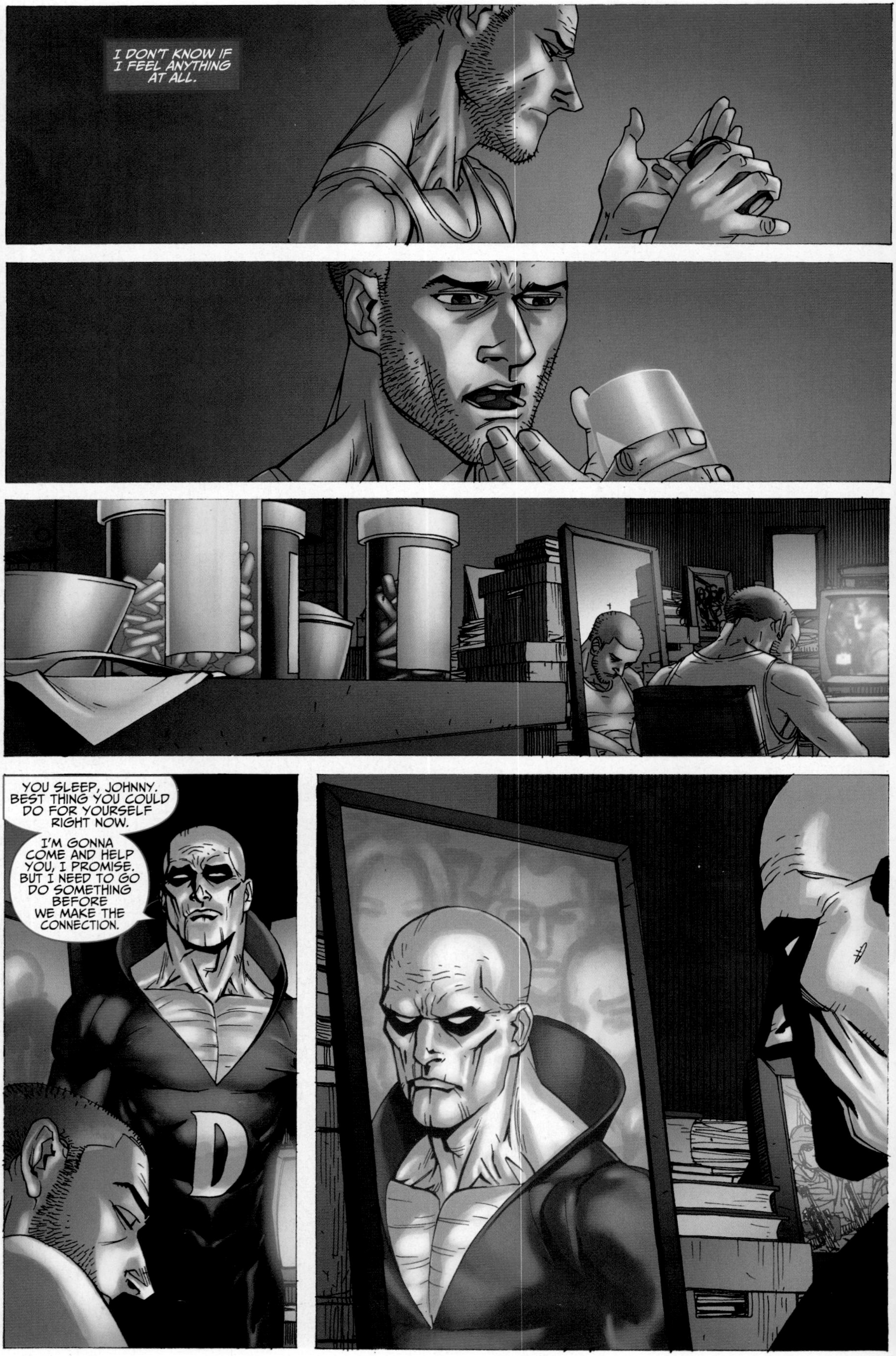
I DON'T KNOW IF I FEEL ANYTHING AT ALL.
YOU SLEEP, JOHNNY. BEST THING YOU COULD DO FOR YOURSELF RIGHT NOW.
I'M GONNA COME AND HELP YOU, I PROMISE. BUT I NEED TO GO DO SOMETHING BEFORE WE MAKE THE CONNECTION.

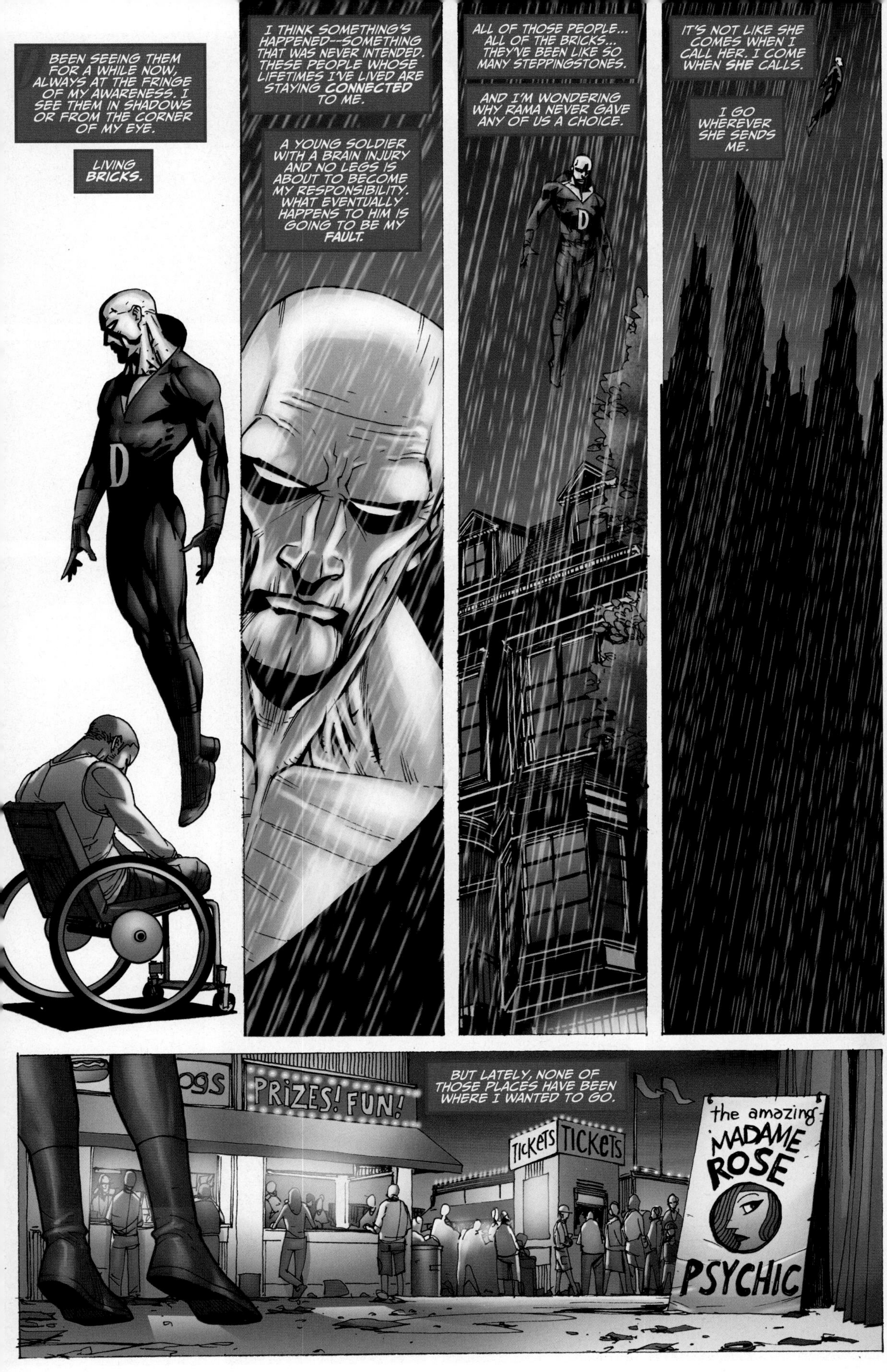
BEEN SEEING THEM FOR A WHILE NOW, ALWAYS AT THE FRINGE OF MY AWARENESS. I SEE THEM IN SHADOWS OR FROM THE CORNER OF MY EYE.
LIVING BRICKS.
I THINK SOMETHING'S HAPPENED--SOMETHING THAT WAS NEVER INTENDED. THESE PEOPLE WHOSE LIFETIMES I'VE LIVED ARE STAYING CONNECTED TO ME.
A YOUNG SOLDIER WITH A BRAIN INJURY AND NO LEGS IS ABOUT TO BECOME MY RESPONSIBILITY. WHAT EVENTUALLY HAPPENS TO HIM IS GOING TO BE MY FAULT.
ALL OF THOSE PEOPLE... ALL OF THE BRICKS... THEY'VE BEEN LIKE SO MANY STEPPINGSTONES.
AND I'M WONDERING WHY RAMA NEVER GAVE ANY OF US A CHOICE.
IT'S NOT LIKE SHE COMES WHEN I CALL HER. I COME WHEN SHE CALLS.
I GO WHEREVER SHE SENDS ME.
BUT LATELY, NONE OF THOSE PLACES HAVE BEEN WHERE I WANTED TO GO.
OGS
PRIZES! FUN!
TICKETS
TICKETS
the amazing MADAME ROSE
PSYCHIC

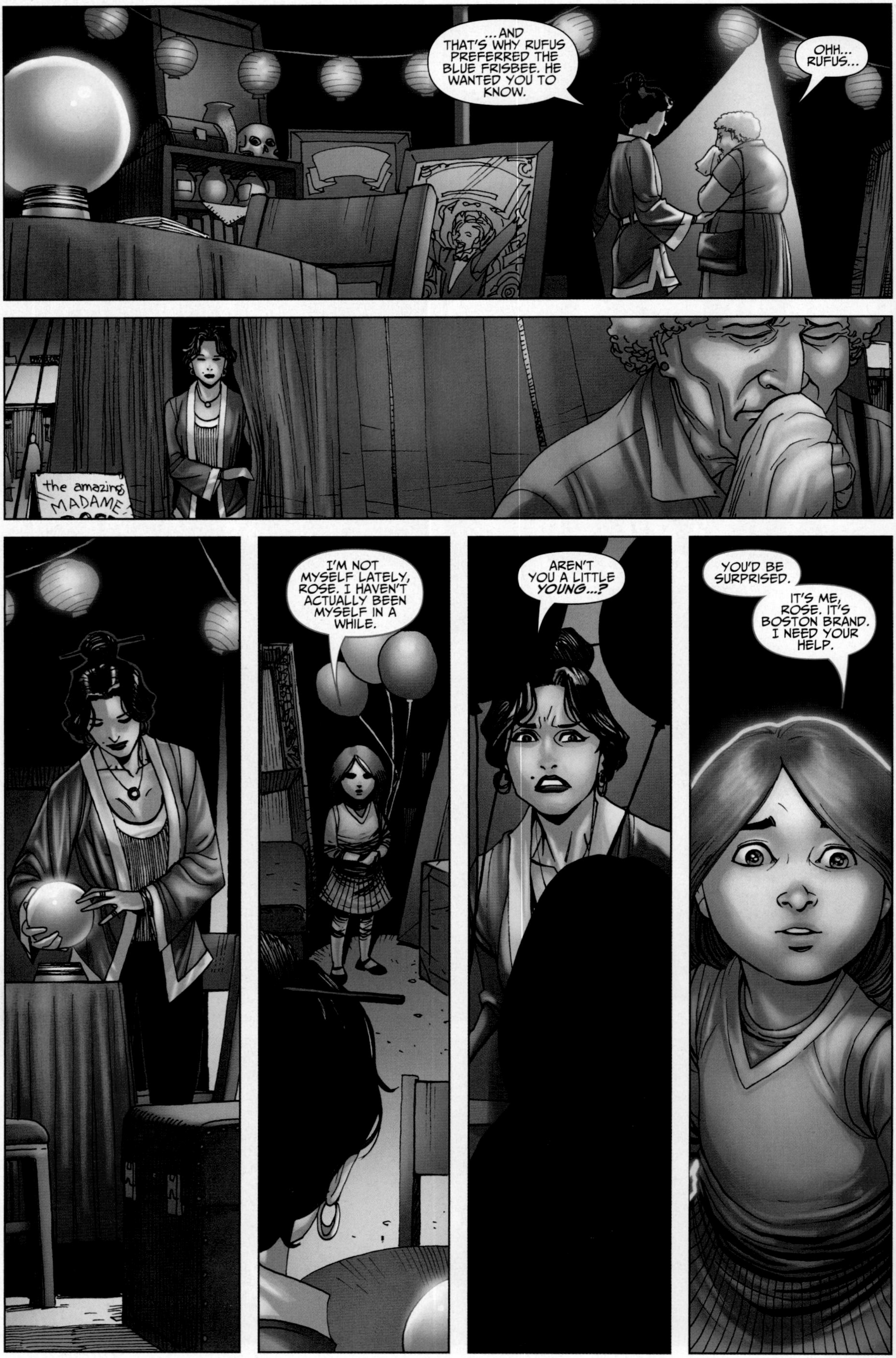
...AND THAT'S WHY RUFUS PREFERRED THE BLUE FRISBEE. HE WANTED YOU TO KNOW.
OHH... RUFUS...
the amazing MADAME
I'M NOT MYSELF LATELY, ROSE. I HAVEN'T ACTUALLY BEEN MYSELF IN A WHILE.
AREN'T YOU A LITTLE *YOUNG...?*
YOU'D BE SURPRISED.
IT'S ME, ROSE. IT'S BOSTON BRAND. I NEED YOUR HELP.

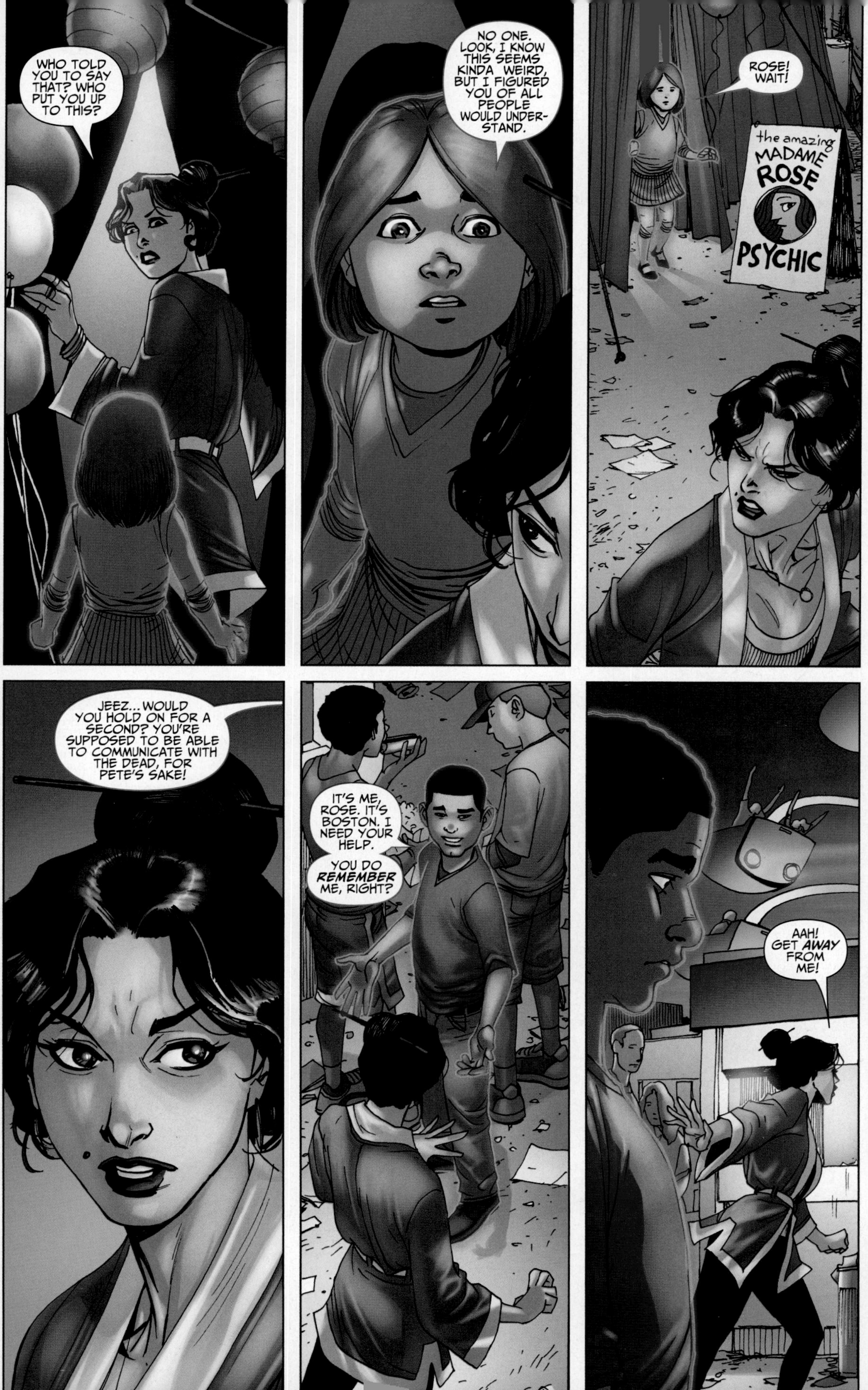
WHO TOLD YOU TO SAY THAT? WHO PUT YOU UP TO THIS?
NO ONE. LOOK, I KNOW THIS SEEMS KINDA WEIRD, BUT I FIGURED YOU OF ALL PEOPLE WOULD UNDER-STAND.
ROSE! WAIT!
the amazing MADAME ROSE PSYCHIC
JEEZ...WOULD YOU HOLD ON FOR A SECOND? YOU'RE SUPPOSED TO BE ABLE TO COMMUNICATE WITH THE DEAD, FOR PETE'S SAKE!
IT'S ME, ROSE. IT'S BOSTON. I NEED YOUR HELP.
YOU DO REMEMBER ME, RIGHT?
AAH! GET AWAY FROM ME!

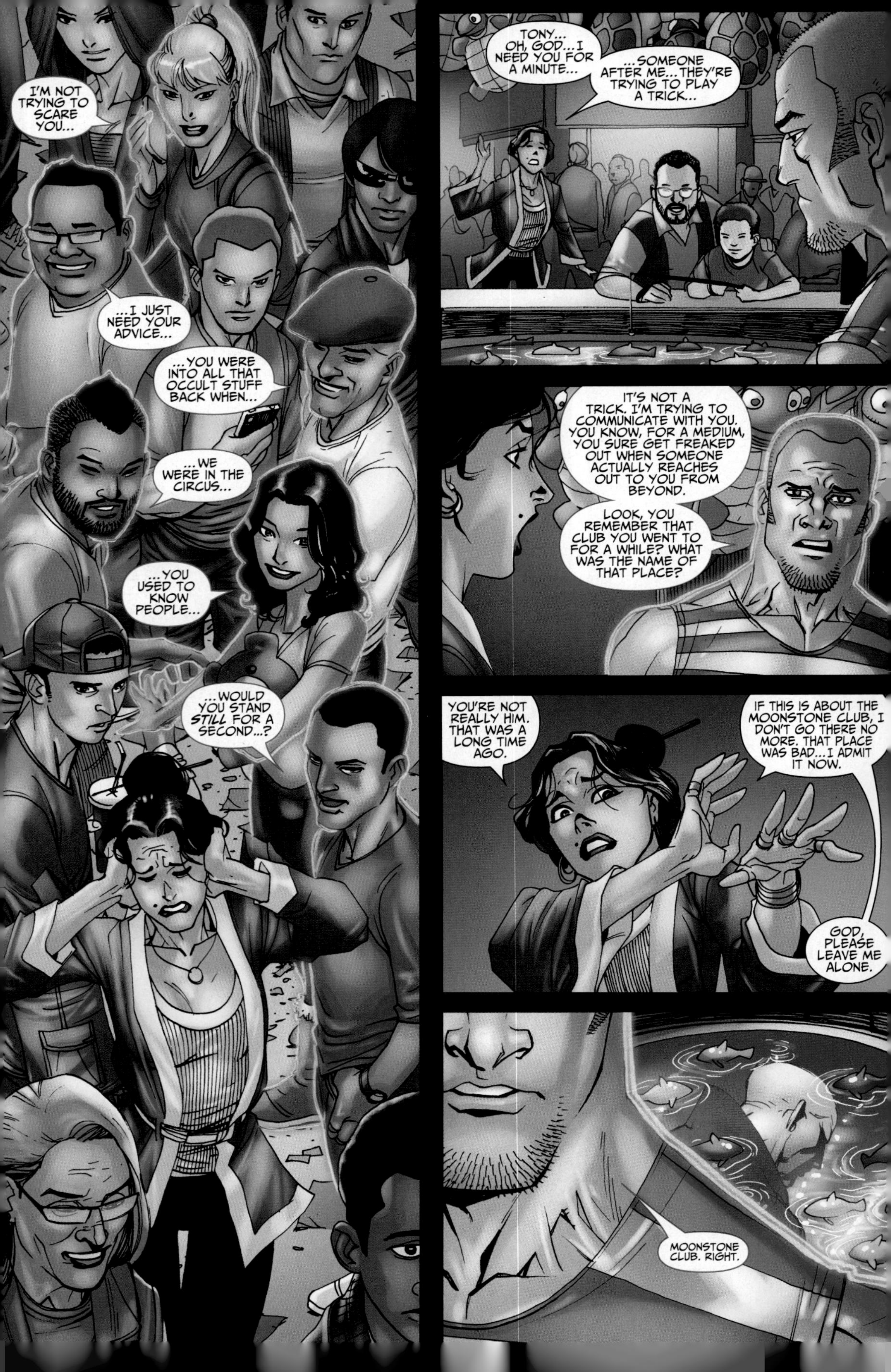
I'M NOT TRYING TO SCARE YOU...
...I JUST NEED YOUR ADVICE...
...YOU WERE INTO ALL THAT OCCULT STUFF BACK WHEN...
...WE WERE IN THE CIRCUS...
...YOU USED TO KNOW PEOPLE...
...WOULD YOU STAND STILL FOR A SECOND...?
TONY... OH, GOD... I NEED YOU FOR A MINUTE...
...SOMEONE AFTER ME... THEY'RE TRYING TO PLAY A TRICK...
IT'S NOT A TRICK. I'M TRYING TO COMMUNICATE WITH YOU. YOU KNOW, FOR A MEDIUM, YOU SURE GET FREAKED OUT WHEN SOMEONE ACTUALLY REACHES OUT TO YOU FROM BEYOND.
LOOK, YOU REMEMBER THAT CLUB YOU WENT TO FOR A WHILE? WHAT WAS THE NAME OF THAT PLACE?
YOU'RE NOT REALLY HIM. THAT WAS A LONG TIME AGO.
IF THIS IS ABOUT THE MOONSTONE CLUB, I DON'T GO THERE NO MORE. THAT PLACE WAS BAD...I ADMIT IT NOW.
GOD, PLEASE LEAVE ME ALONE.
MOONSTONE CLUB. RIGHT.

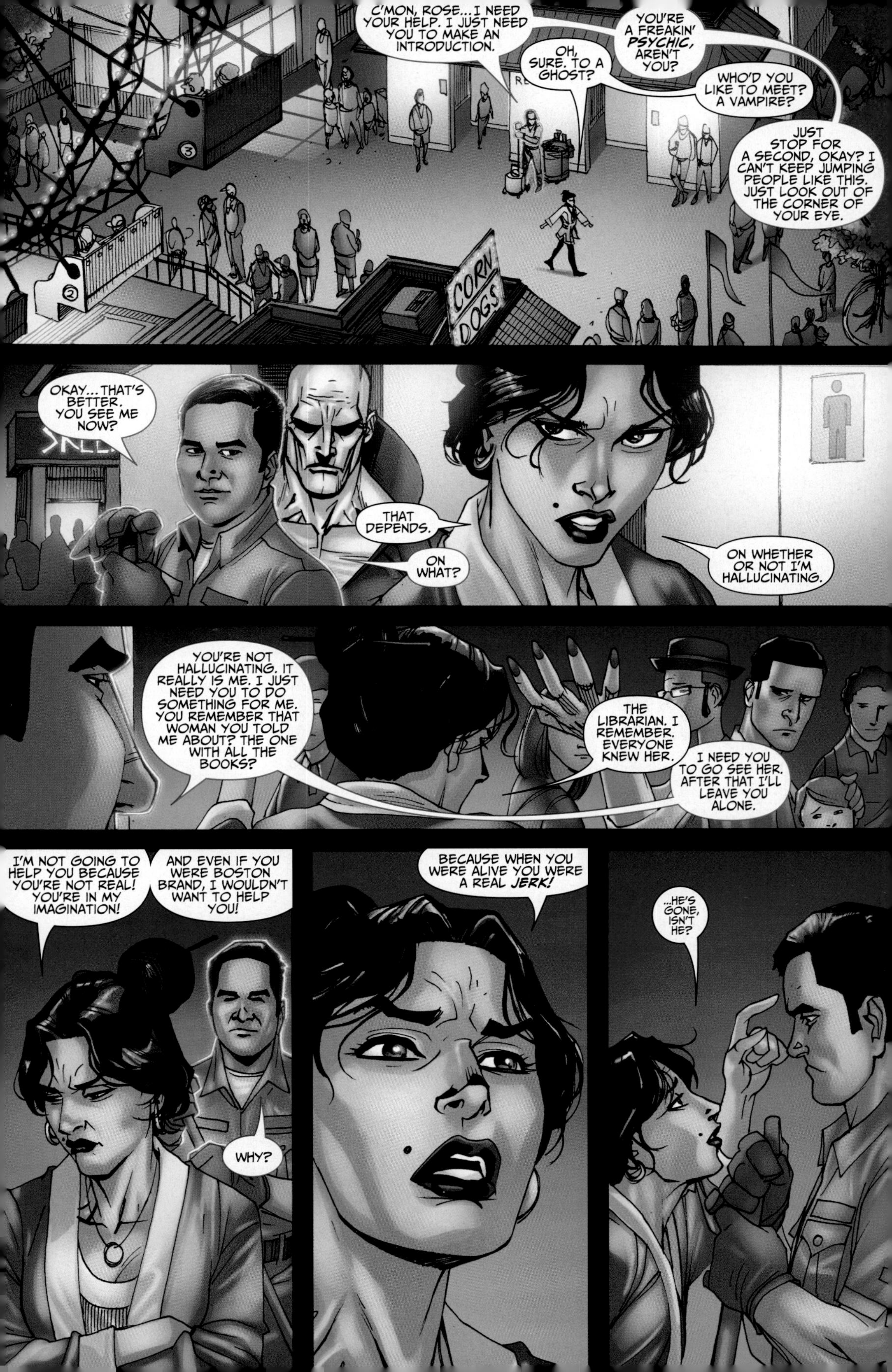
C'MON, ROSE... I NEED YOUR HELP. I JUST NEED YOU TO MAKE AN INTRODUCTION.
OH, SURE. TO A GHOST?
YOU'RE A FREAKIN' PSYCHIC, AREN'T YOU?
WHO'D YOU LIKE TO MEET? A VAMPIRE?
JUST STOP FOR A SECOND, OKAY? I CAN'T KEEP JUMPING PEOPLE LIKE THIS. JUST LOOK OUT OF THE CORNER OF YOUR EYE.
CORN DOGS
OKAY... THAT'S BETTER. YOU SEE ME NOW?
THAT DEPENDS.
ON WHAT?
ON WHETHER OR NOT I'M HALLUCINATING.
YOU'RE NOT HALLUCINATING. IT REALLY IS ME. I JUST NEED YOU TO DO SOMETHING FOR ME. YOU REMEMBER THAT WOMAN YOU TOLD ME ABOUT? THE ONE WITH ALL THE BOOKS?
THE LIBRARIAN. I REMEMBER. EVERYONE KNEW HER.
I NEED YOU TO GO SEE HER. AFTER THAT I'LL LEAVE YOU ALONE.
I'M NOT GOING TO HELP YOU BECAUSE YOU'RE NOT REAL! YOU'RE IN MY IMAGINATION!
AND EVEN IF YOU WERE BOSTON BRAND, I WOULDN'T WANT TO HELP YOU!
WHY?
BECAUSE WHEN YOU WERE ALIVE YOU WERE A REAL JERK!
...HE'S GONE, ISN'T HE?

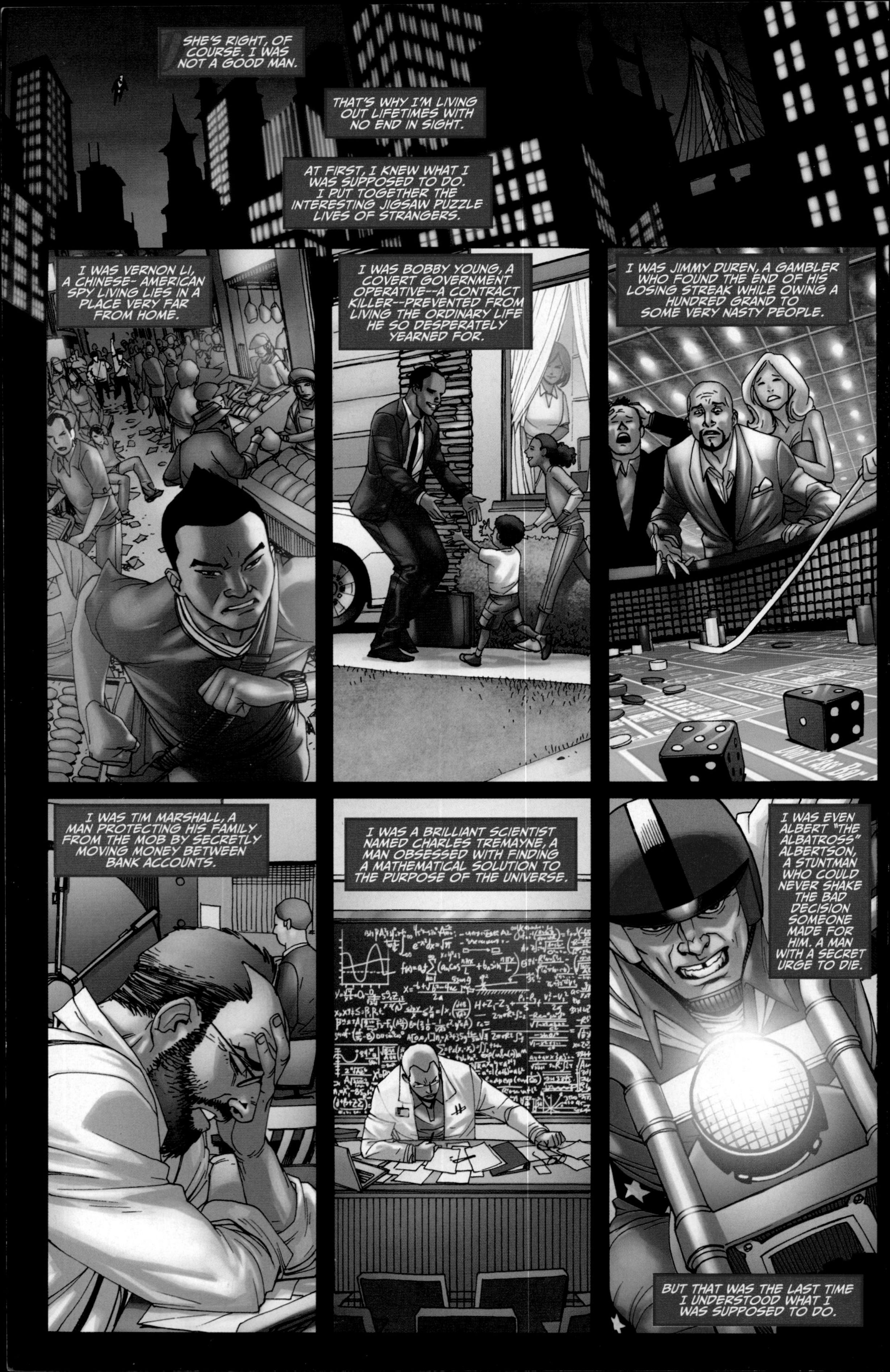
SHE'S RIGHT, OF COURSE. I WAS NOT A GOOD MAN.
THAT'S WHY I'M LIVING OUT LIFETIMES WITH NO END IN SIGHT.
AT FIRST, I KNEW WHAT I WAS SUPPOSED TO DO. I PUT TOGETHER THE INTERESTING JIGSAW PUZZLE LIVES OF STRANGERS.
I WAS VERNON LI, A CHINESE- AMERICAN SPY LIVING LIES IN A PLACE VERY FAR FROM HOME.
I WAS BOBBY YOUNG, A COVERT GOVERNMENT OPERATIVE--A CONTRACT KILLER--PREVENTED FROM LIVING THE ORDINARY LIFE HE SO DESPERATELY YEARNED FOR.
I WAS JIMMY DUREN, A GAMBLER WHO FOUND THE END OF HIS LOSING STREAK WHILE OWING A HUNDRED GRAND TO SOME VERY NASTY PEOPLE.
I WAS TIM MARSHALL, A MAN PROTECTING HIS FAMILY FROM THE MOB BY SECRETLY MOVING MONEY BETWEEN BANK ACCOUNTS.
I WAS A BRILLIANT SCIENTIST NAMED CHARLES TREMAYNE, A MAN OBSESSED WITH FINDING A MATHEMATICAL SOLUTION TO THE PURPOSE OF THE UNIVERSE.
I WAS EVEN ALBERT "THE ALBATROSS" ALBERTSON, A STUNTMAN WHO COULD NEVER SHAKE THE BAD DECISION SOMEONE MADE FOR HIM. A MAN WITH A SECRET URGE TO DIE.
BUT THAT WAS THE LAST TIME I UNDERSTOOD WHAT I WAS SUPPOSED TO DO.

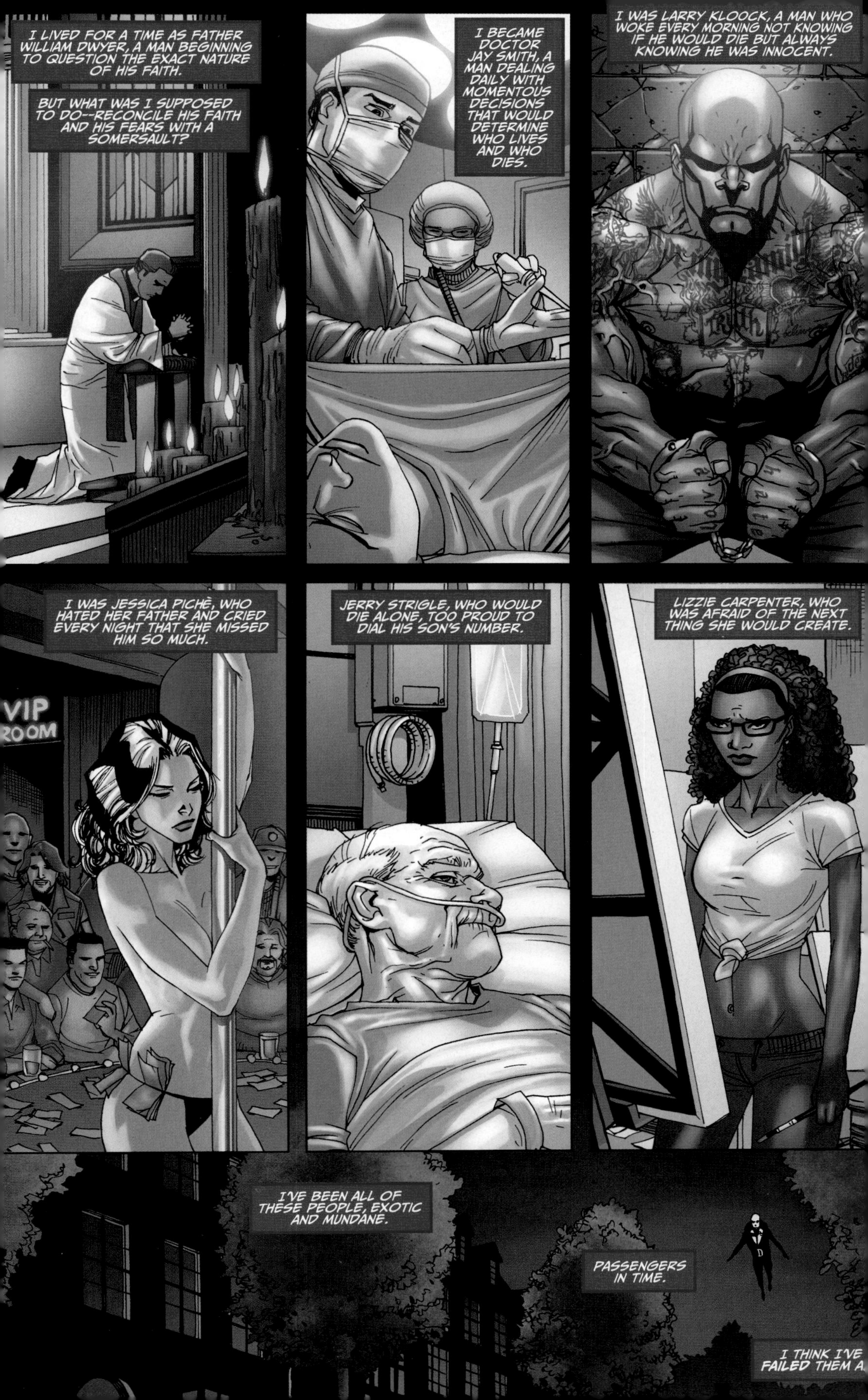
I LIVED FOR A TIME AS FATHER WILLIAM DWYER, A MAN BEGINNING TO QUESTION THE EXACT NATURE OF HIS FAITH.
BUT WHAT WAS I SUPPOSED TO DO--RECONCILE HIS FAITH AND HIS FEARS WITH A SOMERSAULT?
I BECAME DOCTOR JAY SMITH, A MAN DEALING DAILY WITH MOMENTOUS DECISIONS THAT WOULD DETERMINE WHO LIVES AND WHO DIES.
I WAS LARRY KLOOCK, A MAN WHO WOKE EVERY MORNING NOT KNOWING IF HE WOULD DIE BUT ALWAYS KNOWING HE WAS INNOCENT.
TRUTH
I WAS JESSICA PICHÈ, WHO HATED HER FATHER AND CRIED EVERY NIGHT THAT SHE MISSED HIM SO MUCH.
VIP
ROOM
JERRY STRIGLE, WHO WOULD DIE ALONE, TOO PROUD TO DIAL HIS SON'S NUMBER.
LIZZIE CARPENTER, WHO WAS AFRAID OF THE NEXT THING SHE WOULD CREATE.
I'VE BEEN ALL OF THESE PEOPLE, EXOTIC AND MUNDANE.
PASSENGERS IN TIME.
I THINK I'VE FAILED THEM A

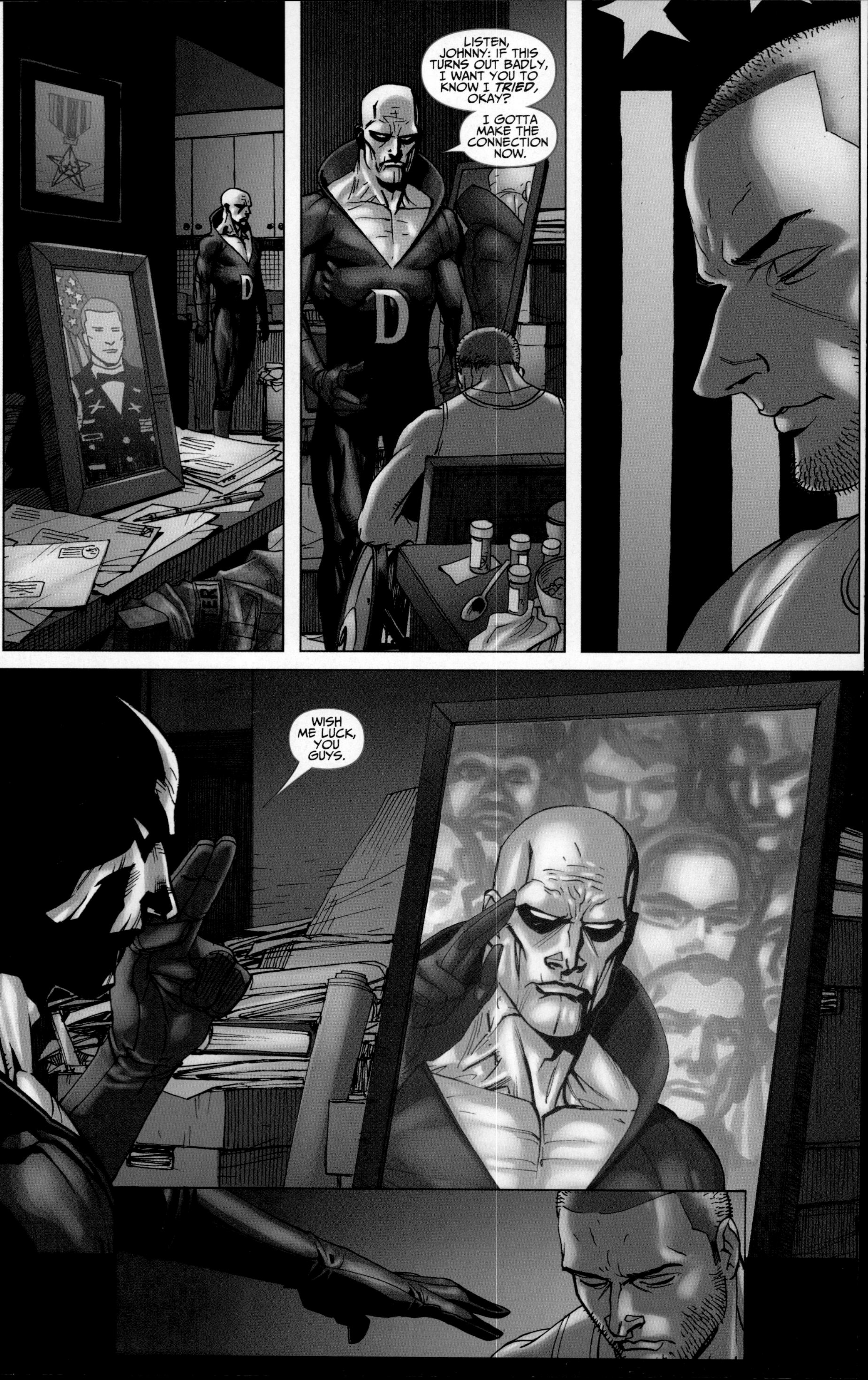
LISTEN, JOHNNY: IF THIS TURNS OUT BADLY, I WANT YOU TO KNOW I *TRIED*, OKAY?
I GOTTA MAKE THE CONNECTION NOW.
WISH ME LUCK, YOU GUYS.

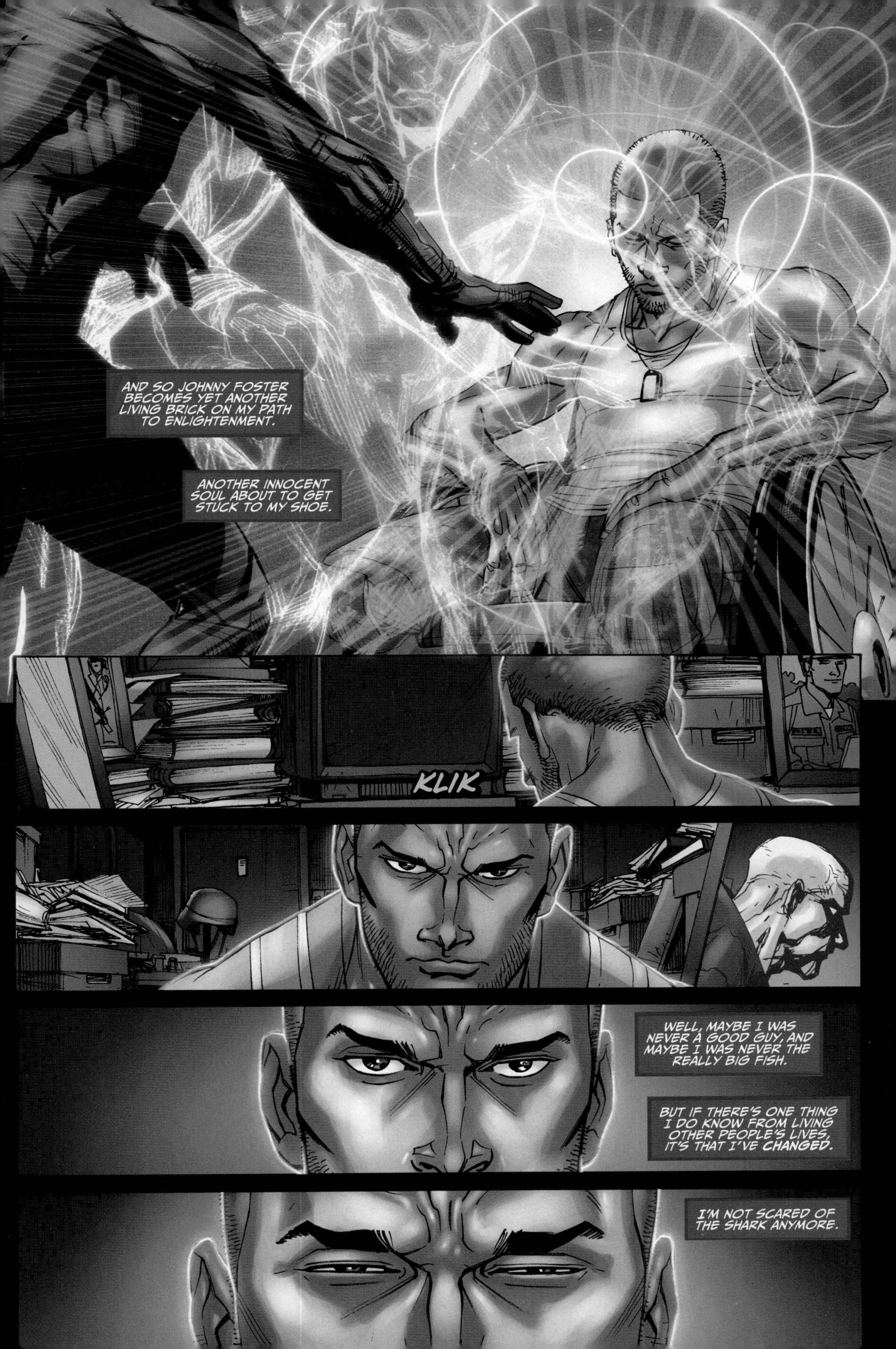
AND SO JOHNNY FOSTER BECOMES YET ANOTHER LIVING BRICK ON MY PATH TO ENLIGHTENMENT.
ANOTHER INNOCENT SOUL ABOUT TO GET STUCK TO MY SHOE.
KLIK
WELL, MAYBE I WAS NEVER A GOOD GUY, AND MAYBE I WAS NEVER THE REALLY BIG FISH.
BUT IF THERE'S ONE THING I DO KNOW FROM LIVING OTHER PEOPLE'S LIVES, IT'S THAT I'VE CHANGED.
I'M NOT SCARED OF THE SHARK ANYMORE.

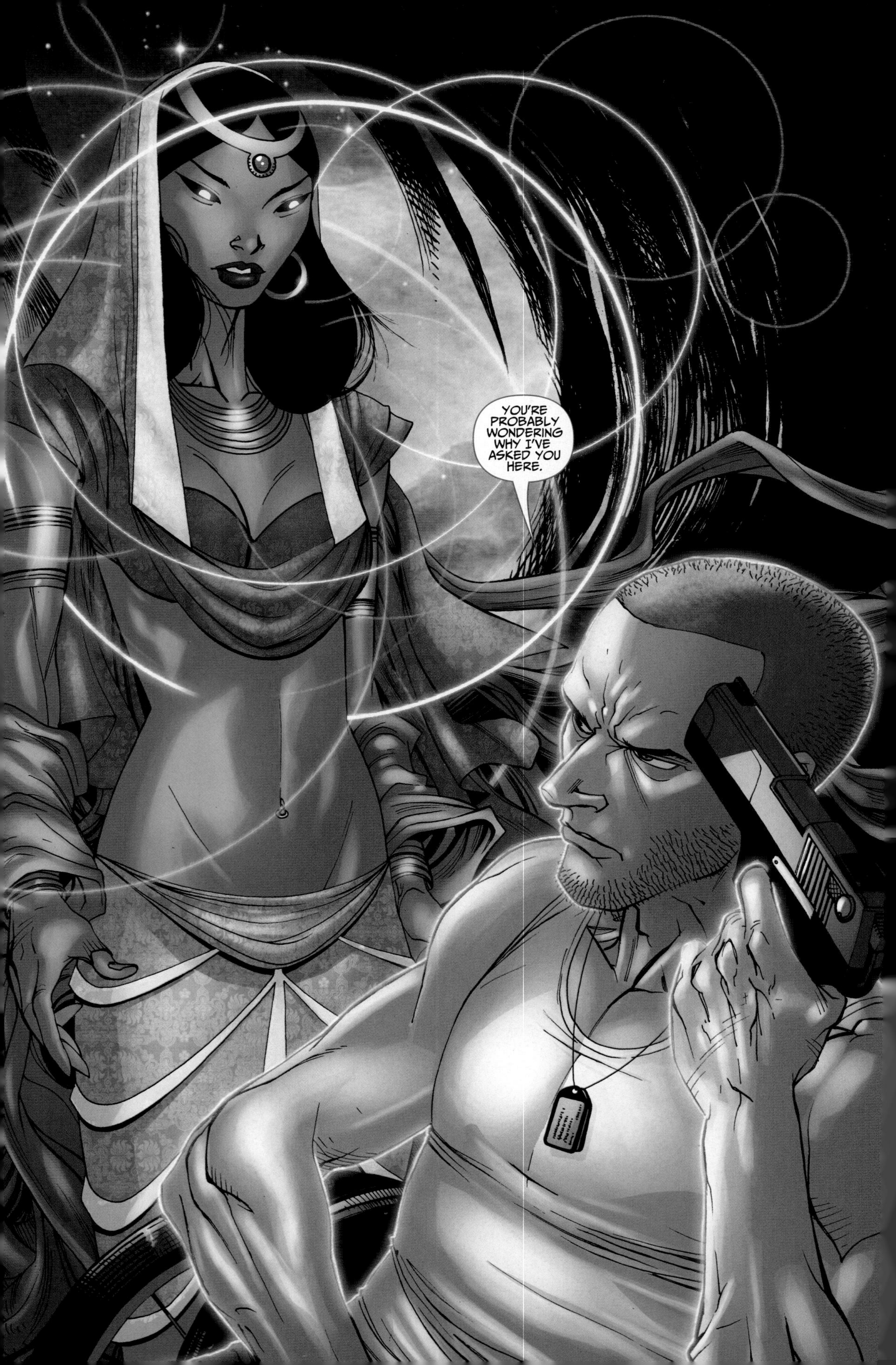
YOU'RE PROBABLY WONDERING WHY I'VE ASKED YOU HERE.

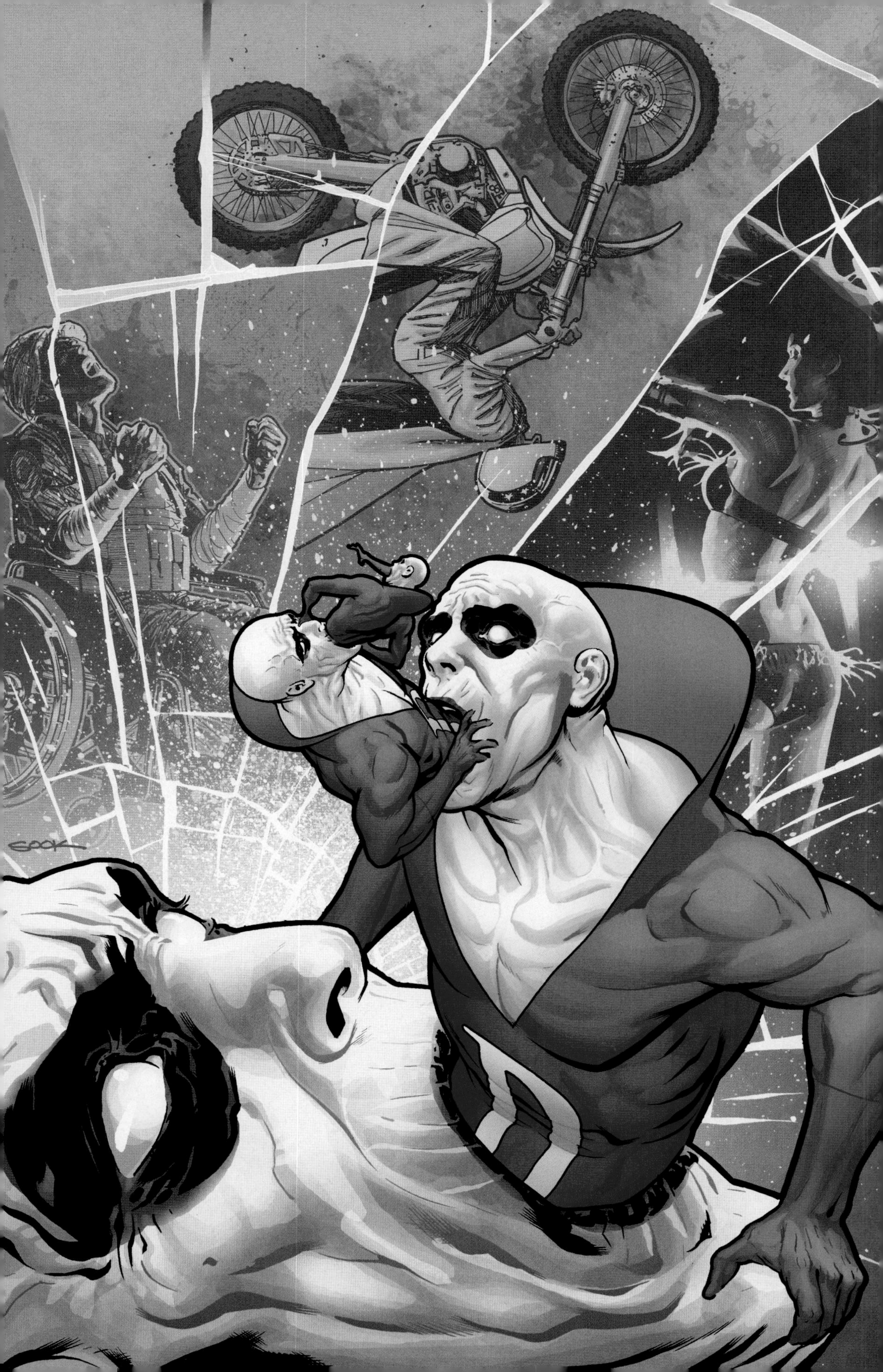
COOK

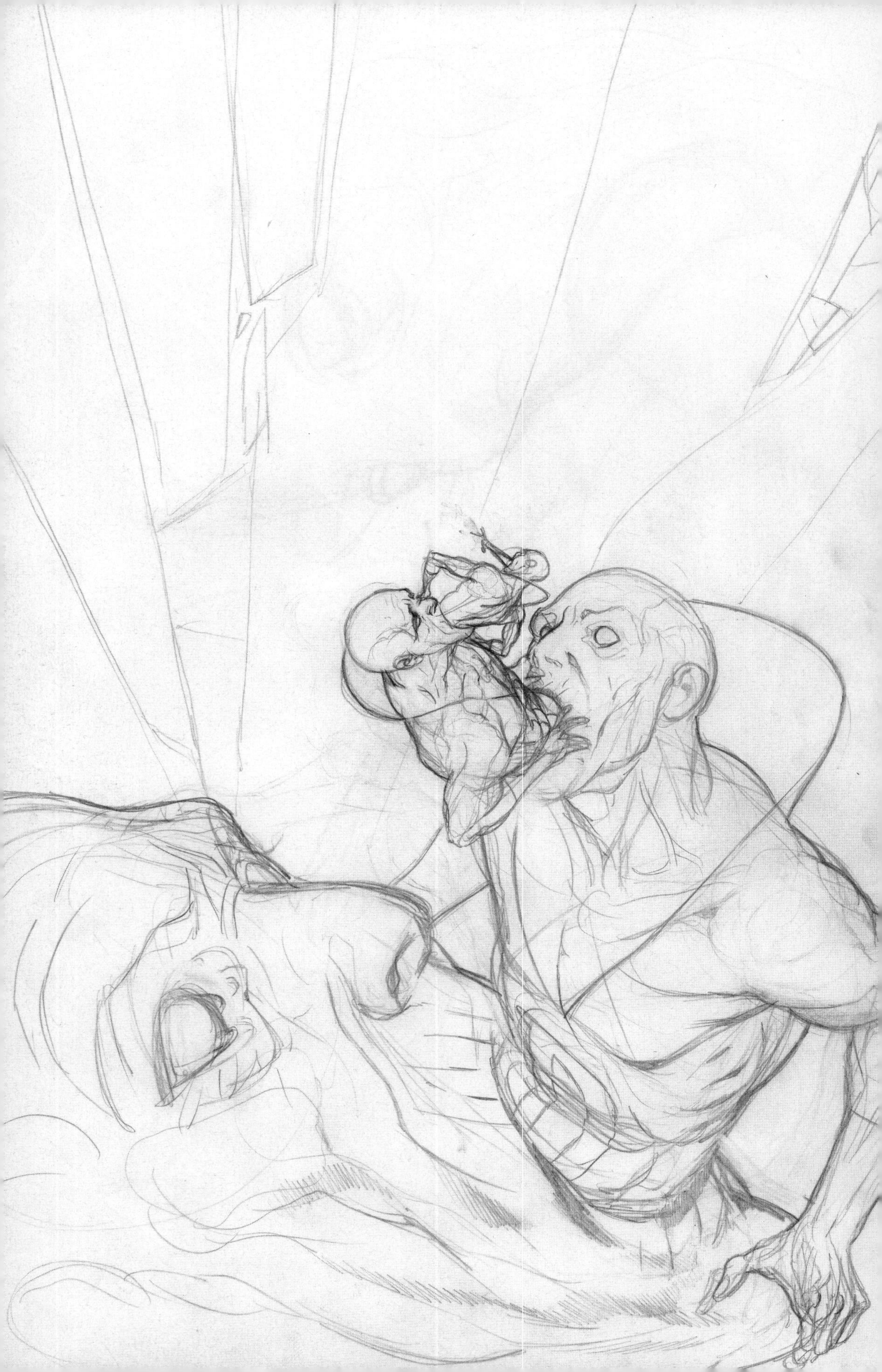

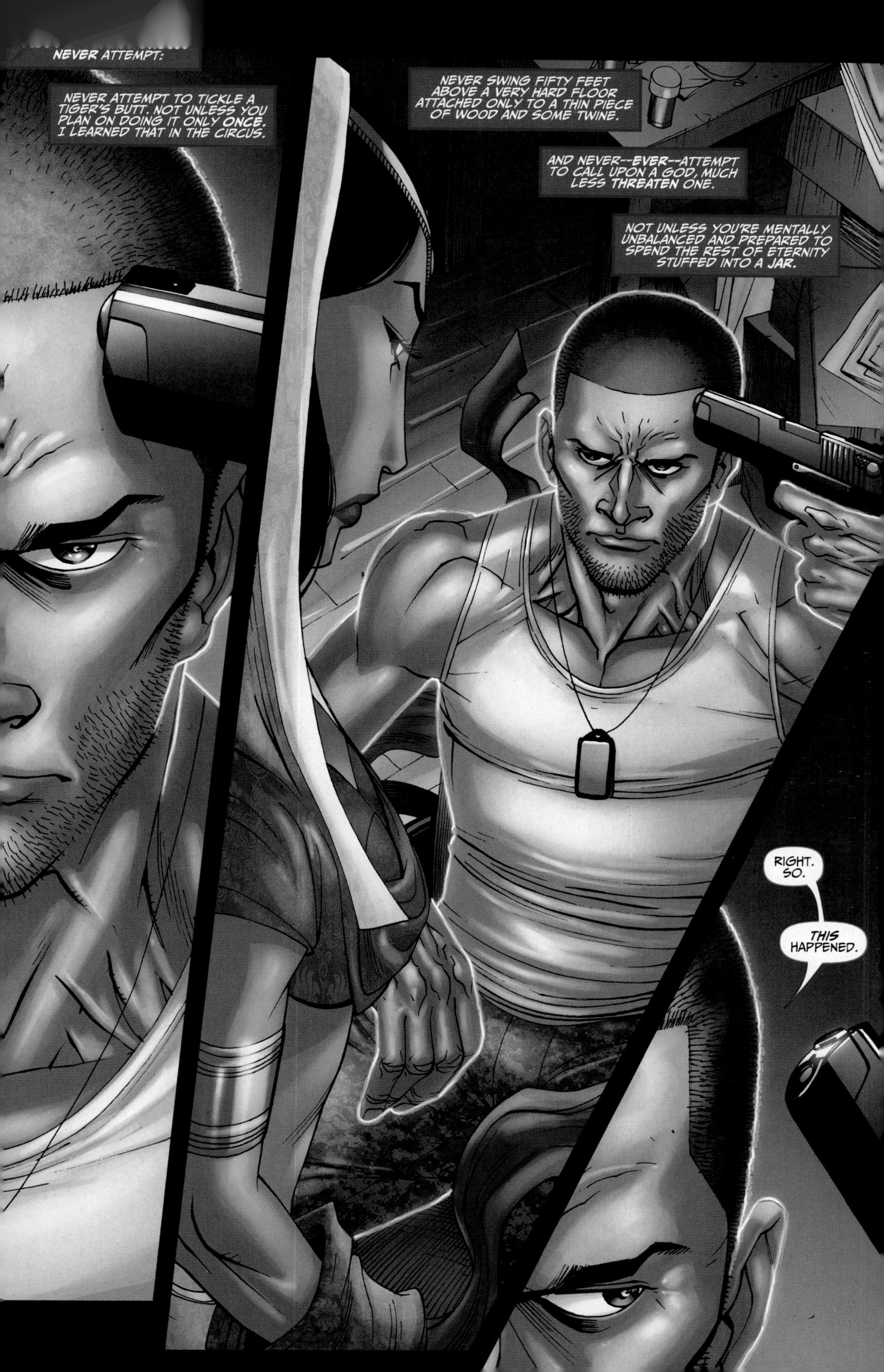
NEVER ATTEMPT:
NEVER ATTEMPT TO TICKLE A TIGER'S BUTT. NOT UNLESS YOU PLAN ON DOING IT ONLY ONCE. I LEARNED THAT IN THE CIRCUS.
NEVER SWING FIFTY FEET ABOVE A VERY HARD FLOOR ATTACHED ONLY TO A THIN PIECE OF WOOD AND SOME TWINE.
AND NEVER--EVER--ATTEMPT TO CALL UPON A GOD, MUCH LESS THREATEN ONE.
NOT UNLESS YOU'RE MENTALLY UNBALANCED AND PREPARED TO SPEND THE REST OF ETERNITY STUFFED INTO A JAR.
RIGHT. SO.
THIS HAPPENED.

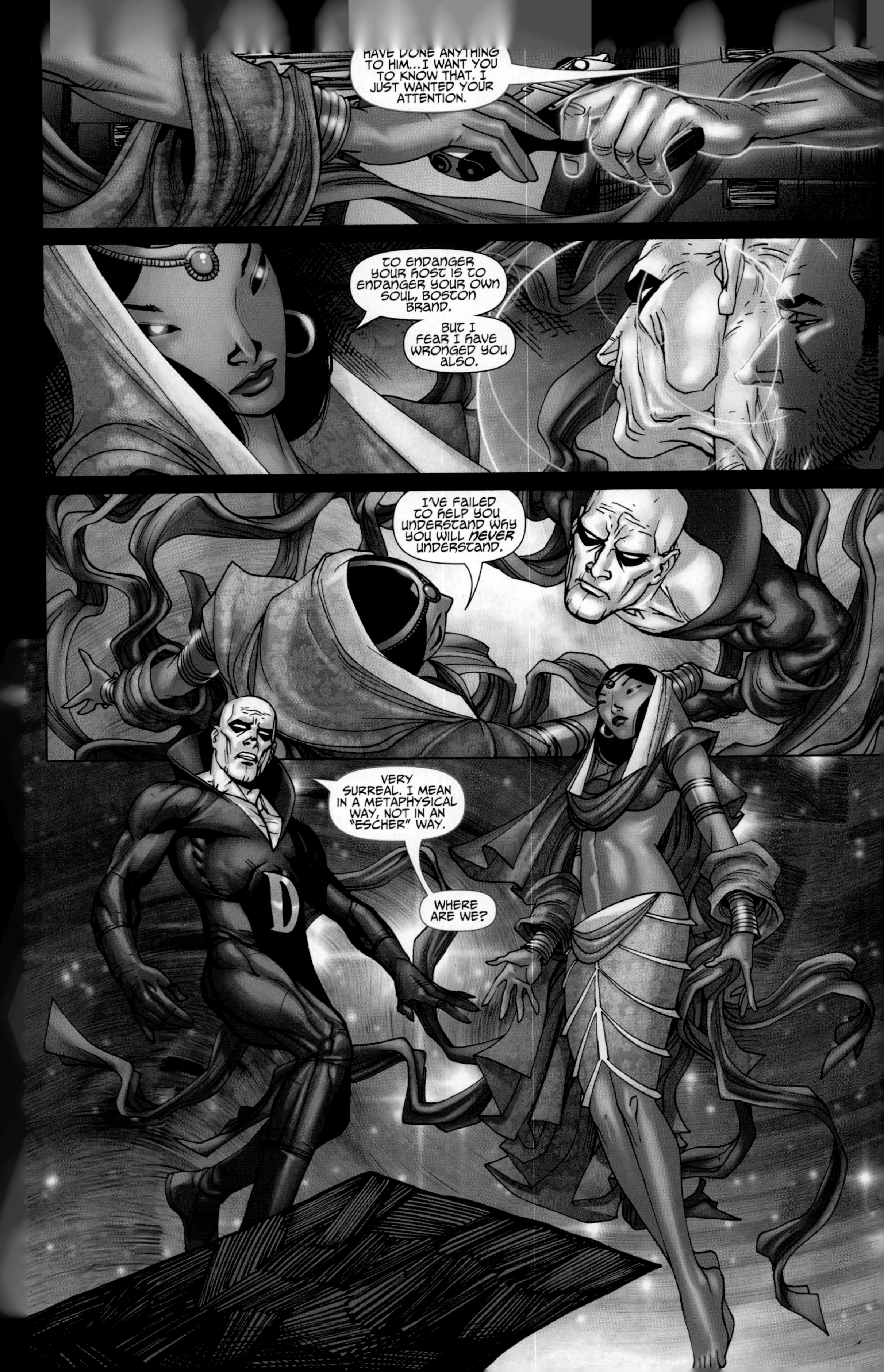
HAVE DONE ANYTHING TO HIM...I WANT YOU TO KNOW THAT. I JUST WANTED YOUR ATTENTION.
TO ENDANGER YOUR HOST IS TO ENDANGER YOUR OWN SOUL, BOSTON BRAND.
BUT I FEAR I HAVE WRONGED YOU ALSO.
I'VE FAILED TO HELP YOU UNDERSTAND WHY YOU WILL NEVER UNDERSTAND.
VERY SURREAL. I MEAN IN A METAPHYSICAL WAY, NOT IN AN "ESCHER" WAY.
WHERE ARE WE?

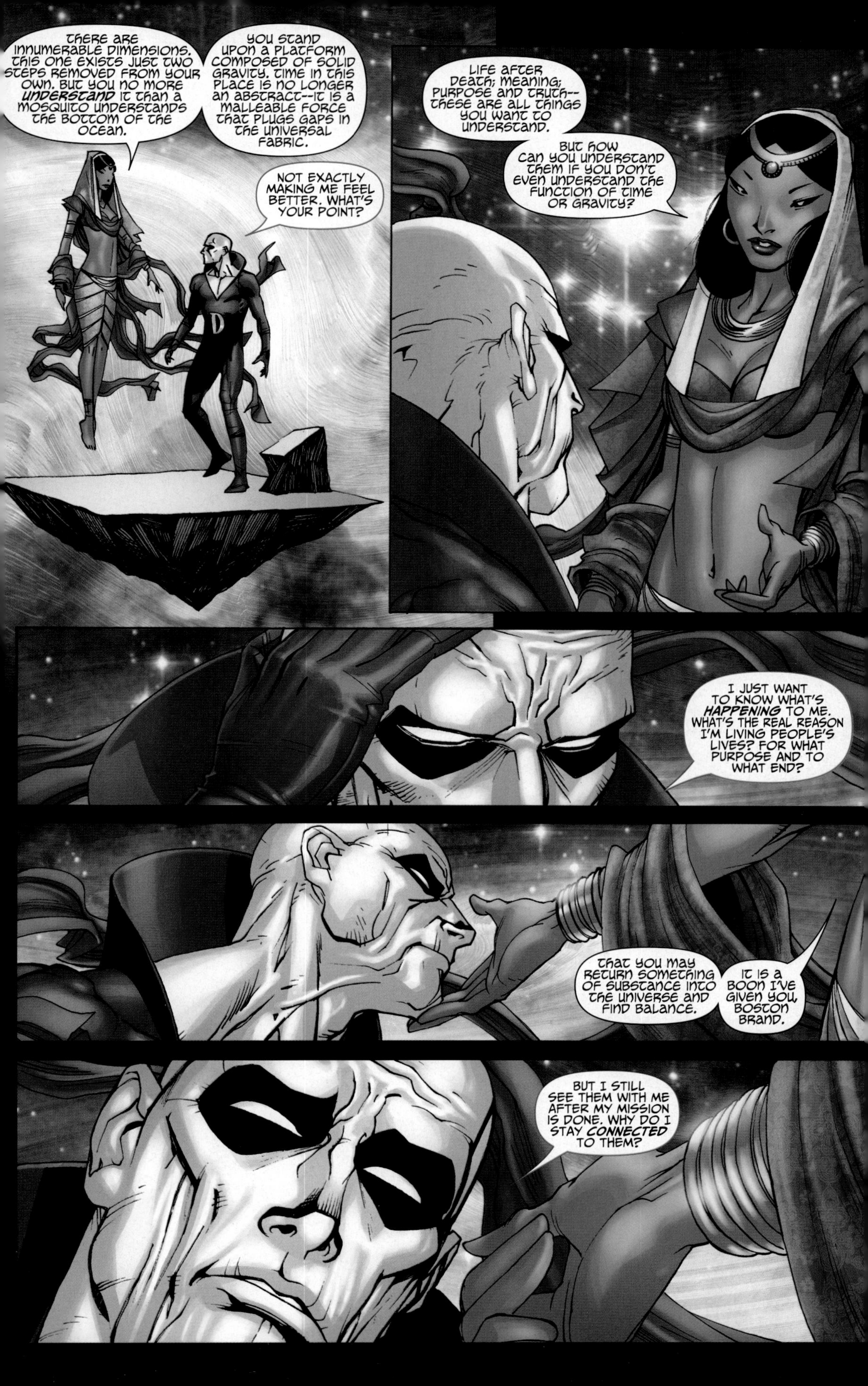
THERE ARE INNUMERABLE DIMENSIONS. THIS ONE EXISTS JUST TWO STEPS REMOVED FROM YOUR OWN. BUT YOU NO MORE UNDERSTAND IT THAN A MOSQUITO UNDERSTANDS THE BOTTOM OF THE OCEAN.
YOU STAND UPON A PLATFORM COMPOSED OF SOLID GRAVITY. TIME IN THIS PLACE IS NO LONGER AN ABSTRACT--IT IS A MALLEABLE FORCE THAT PLUGS GAPS IN THE UNIVERSAL FABRIC.
NOT EXACTLY MAKING ME FEEL BETTER. WHAT'S YOUR POINT?
LIFE AFTER DEATH; MEANING; PURPOSE AND TRUTH-- THESE ARE ALL THINGS YOU WANT TO UNDERSTAND.
BUT HOW CAN YOU UNDERSTAND THEM IF YOU DON'T EVEN UNDERSTAND THE FUNCTION OF TIME OR GRAVITY?
I JUST WANT TO KNOW WHAT'S HAPPENING TO ME. WHAT'S THE REAL REASON I'M LIVING PEOPLE'S LIVES? FOR WHAT PURPOSE AND TO WHAT END?
THAT YOU MAY RETURN SOMETHING OF SUBSTANCE INTO THE UNIVERSE AND FIND BALANCE.
IT IS A BOON I'VE GIVEN YOU, BOSTON BRAND.
BUT I STILL SEE THEM WITH ME AFTER MY MISSION IS DONE. WHY DO I STAY CONNECTED TO THEM?

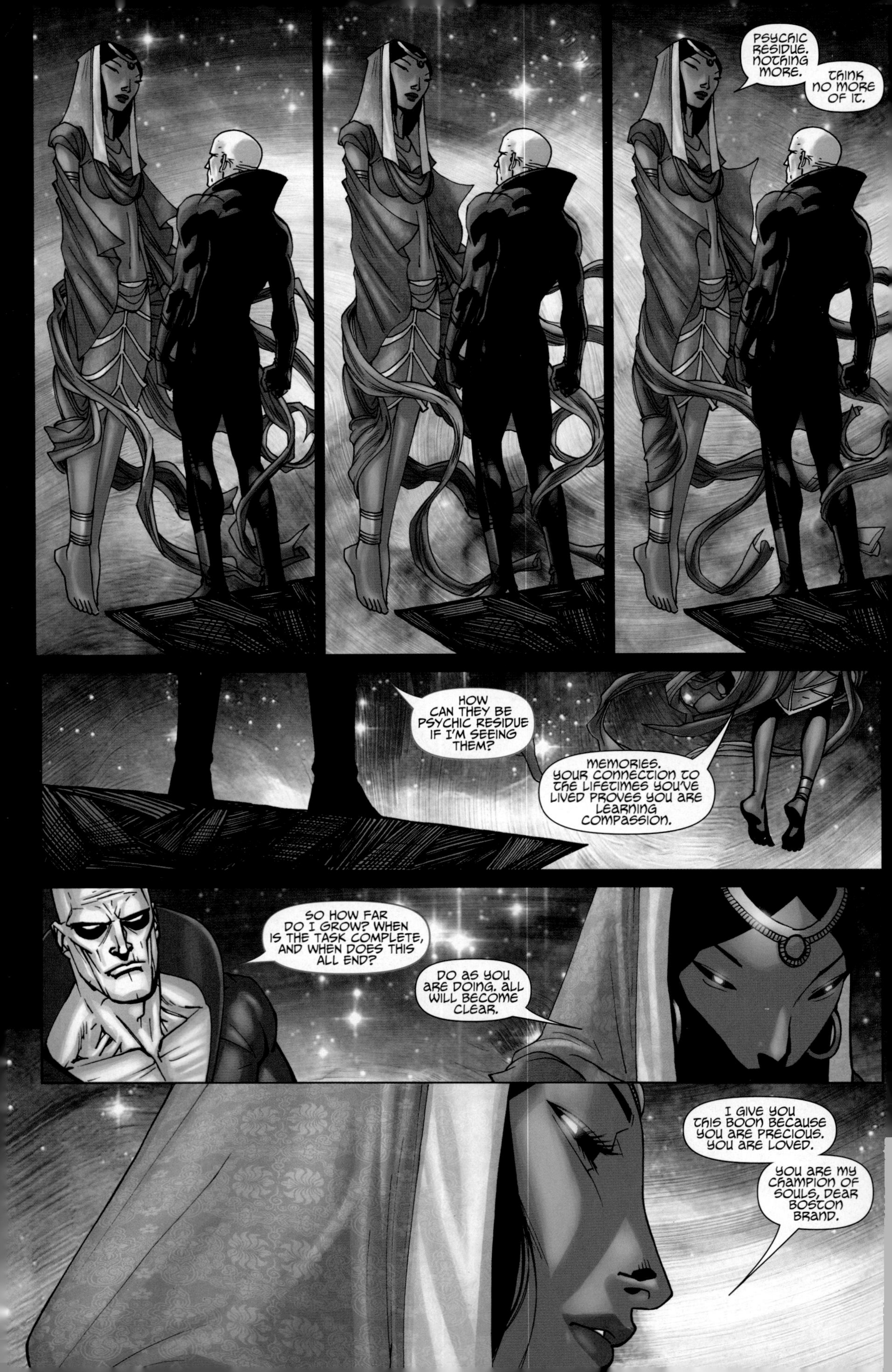
PSYCHIC RESIDUE. NOTHING MORE.
THINK NO MORE OF IT.
HOW CAN THEY BE PSYCHIC RESIDUE IF I'M SEEING THEM?
MEMORIES. YOUR CONNECTION TO THE LIFETIMES YOU'VE LIVED PROVES YOU ARE LEARNING COMPASSION.
SO HOW FAR DO I GROW? WHEN IS THE TASK COMPLETE, AND WHEN DOES THIS ALL END?
DO AS YOU ARE DOING. ALL WILL BECOME CLEAR.
I GIVE YOU THIS BOON BECAUSE YOU ARE PRECIOUS. YOU ARE LOVED.
YOU ARE MY CHAMPION OF SOULS, DEAR BOSTON BRAND.

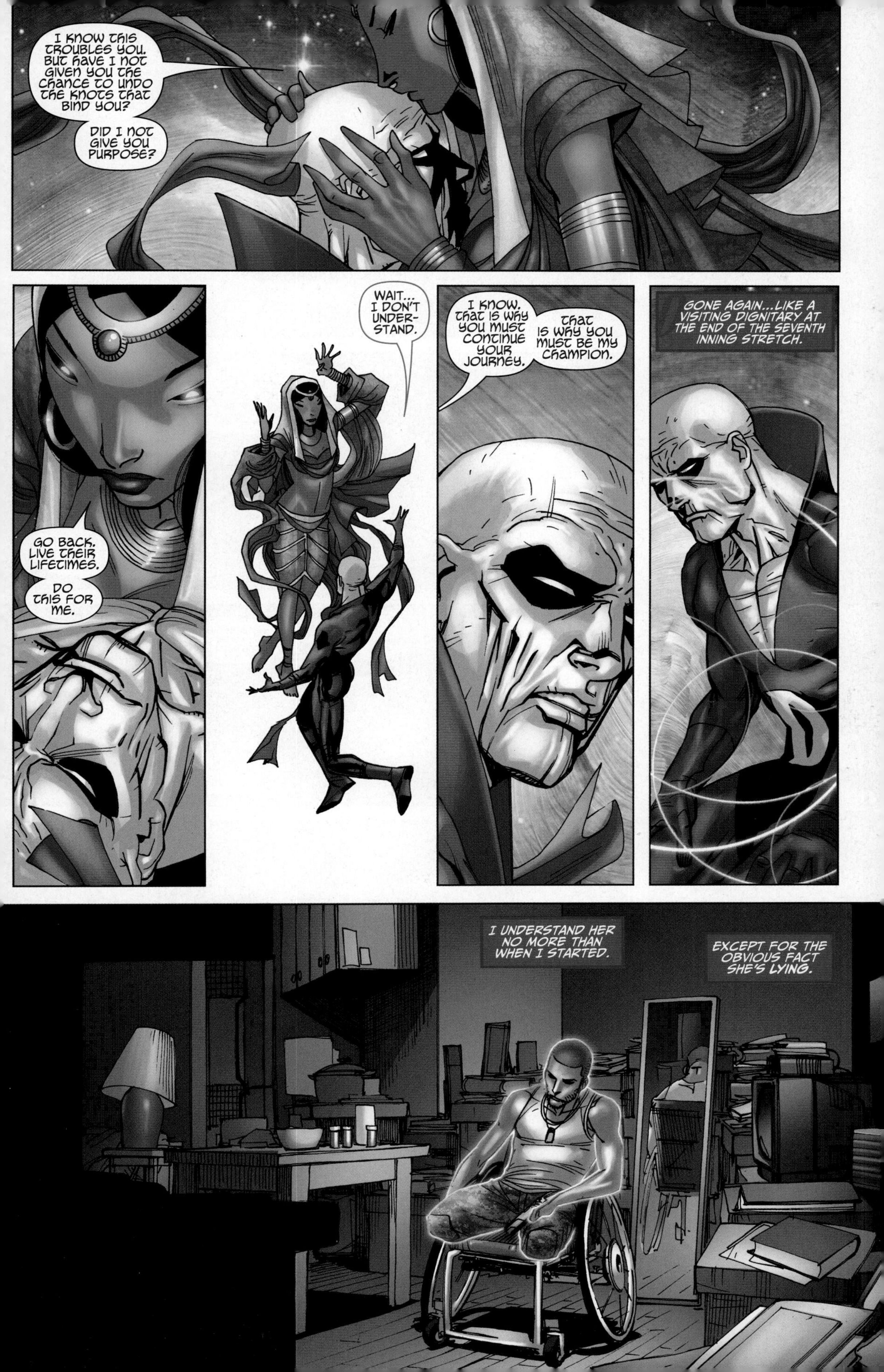
I KNOW THIS TROUBLES YOU. BUT HAVE I NOT GIVEN YOU THE CHANCE TO UNDO THE KNOTS THAT BIND YOU?
DID I NOT GIVE YOU PURPOSE?
GO BACK. LIVE THEIR LIFETIMES.
DO THIS FOR ME.
WAIT... I DON'T UNDER-STAND.
I KNOW. THAT IS WHY YOU MUST CONTINUE YOUR JOURNEY.
THAT IS WHY YOU MUST BE MY CHAMPION.
GONE AGAIN...LIKE A VISITING DIGNITARY AT THE END OF THE SEVENTH INNING STRETCH.
I UNDERSTAND HER NO MORE THAN WHEN I STARTED.
EXCEPT FOR THE OBVIOUS FACT SHE'S LYING.

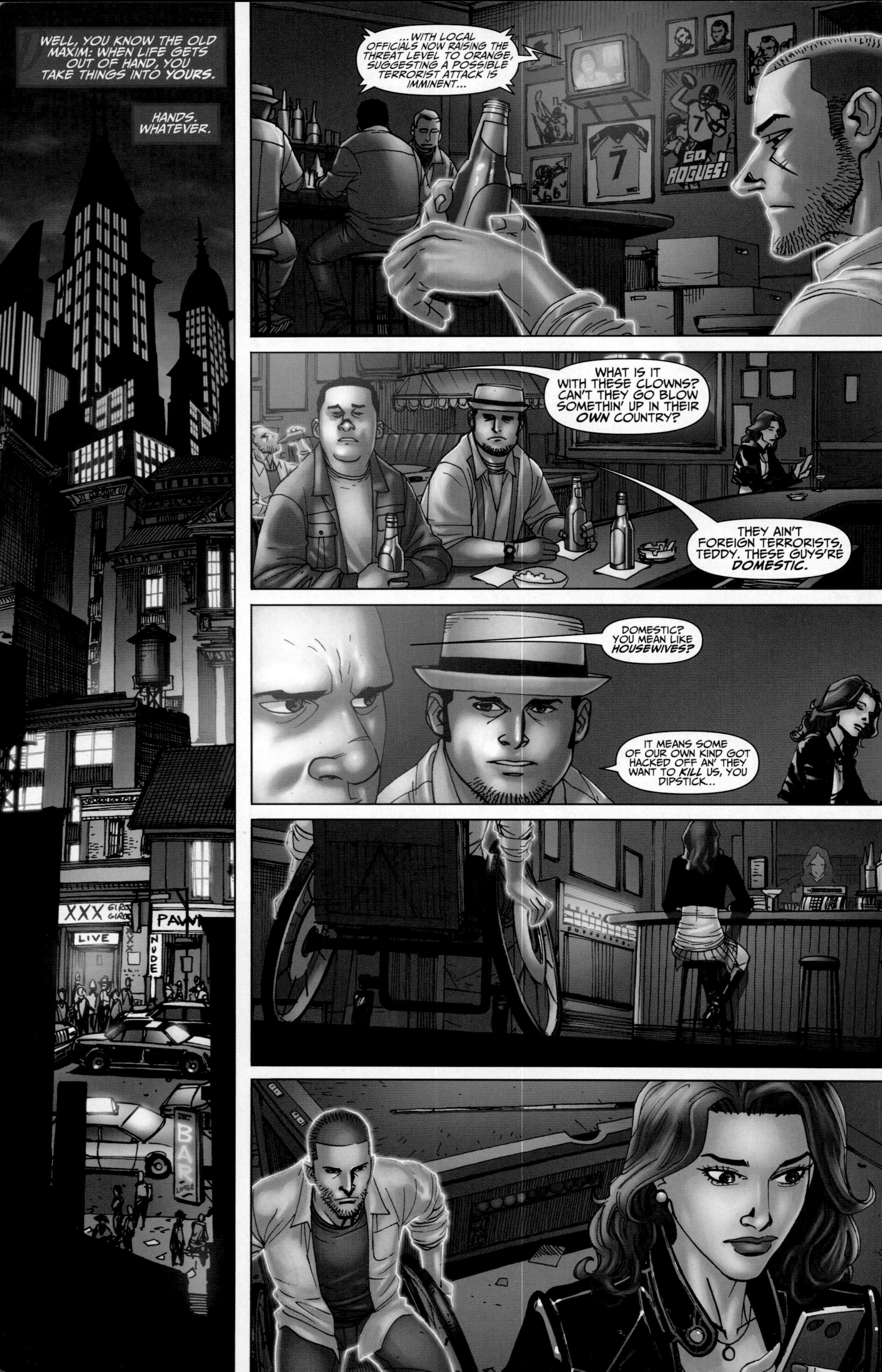

WELL, YOU KNOW THE OLD MAXIM: WHEN LIFE GETS OUT OF HAND, YOU TAKE THINGS INTO YOURS.
HANDS. WHATEVER.
...WITH LOCAL OFFICIALS NOW RAISING THE THREAT LEVEL TO ORANGE, SUGGESTING A POSSIBLE TERRORIST ATTACK IS IMMINENT...
GO ROGUES!
WHAT IS IT WITH THESE CLOWNS? CAN'T THEY GO BLOW SOMETHIN' UP IN THEIR OWN COUNTRY?
THEY AIN'T FOREIGN TERRORISTS, TEDDY. THESE GUYS'RE DOMESTIC.
DOMESTIC? YOU MEAN LIKE HOUSEWIVES?
IT MEANS SOME OF OUR OWN KIND GOT HACKED OFF AN' THEY WANT TO KILL US, YOU DIPSTICK...
XXX
LIVE
NUDE
BAR

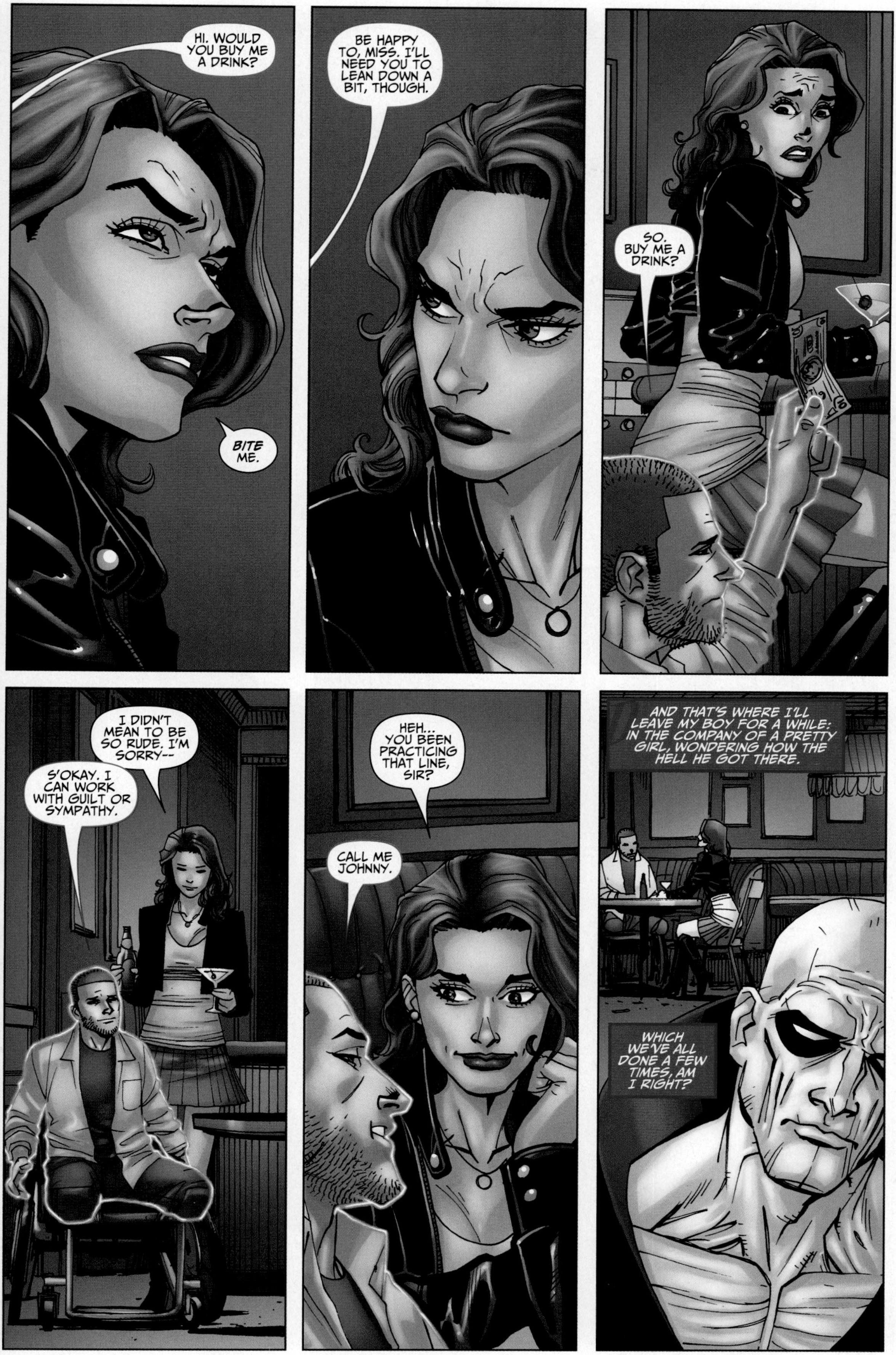
HI. WOULD YOU BUY ME A DRINK?
BITE ME.
BE HAPPY TO, MISS. I'LL NEED YOU TO LEAN DOWN A BIT, THOUGH.
SO. BUY ME A DRINK?
I DIDN'T MEAN TO BE SO RUDE. I'M SORRY--
S'OKAY. I CAN WORK WITH GUILT OR SYMPATHY.
HEH... YOU BEEN PRACTICING THAT LINE, SIR?
CALL ME JOHNNY.
AND THAT'S WHERE I'LL LEAVE MY BOY FOR A WHILE: IN THE COMPANY OF A PRETTY GIRL, WONDERING HOW THE HELL HE GOT THERE.
WHICH WE'VE ALL DONE A FEW TIMES, AM I RIGHT?

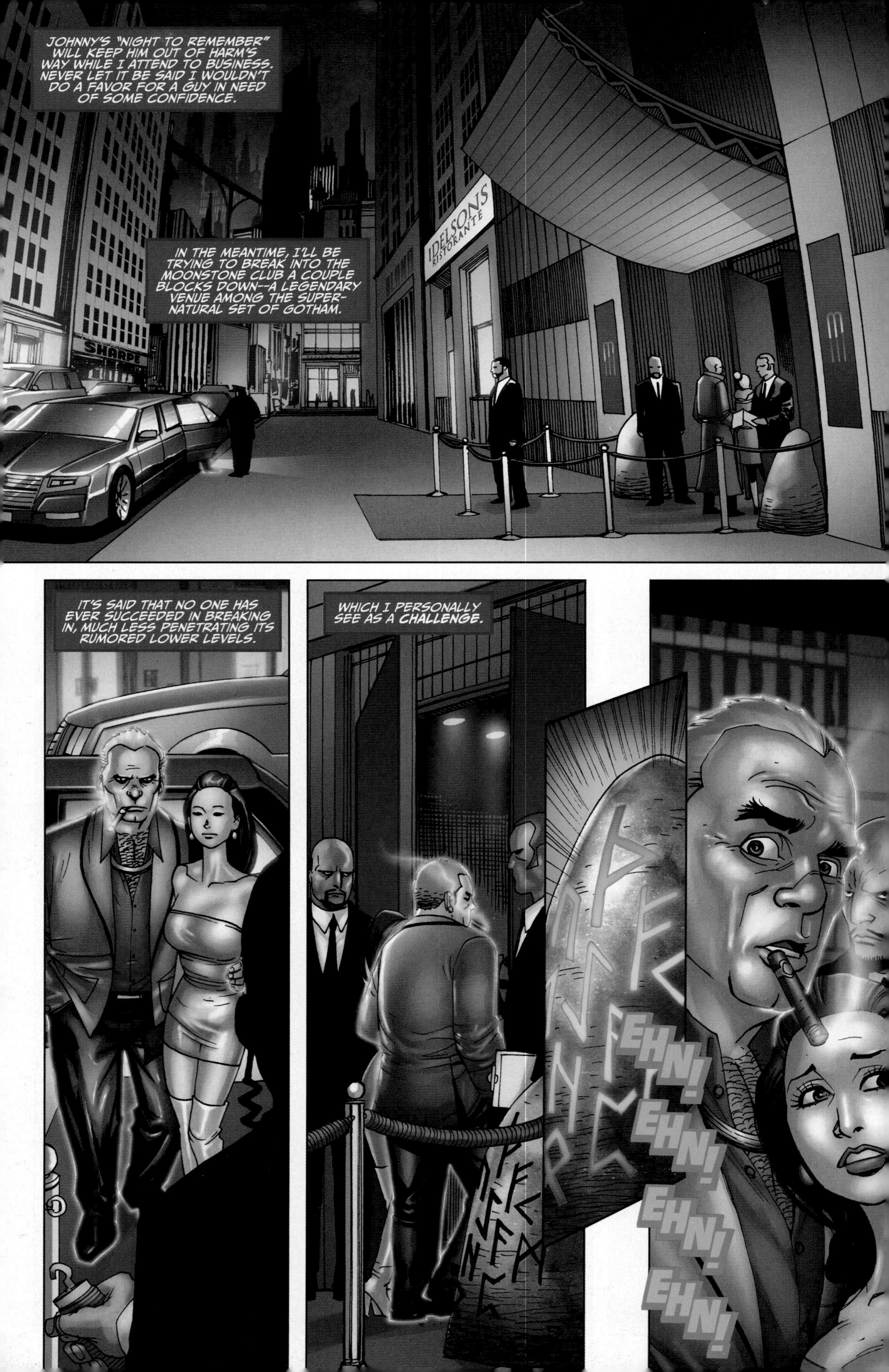
JOHNNY'S "NIGHT TO REMEMBER" WILL KEEP HIM OUT OF HARM'S WAY WHILE I ATTEND TO BUSINESS. NEVER LET IT BE SAID I WOULDN'T DO A FAVOR FOR A GUY IN NEED OF SOME CONFIDENCE.
IDELSONS RISTORANTE
IN THE MEANTIME, I'LL BE TRYING TO BREAK INTO THE MOONSTONE CLUB A COUPLE BLOCKS DOWN--A LEGENDARY VENUE AMONG THE SUPER-NATURAL SET OF GOTHAM.
SHARPE
IT'S SAID THAT NO ONE HAS EVER SUCCEEDED IN BREAKING IN, MUCH LESS PENETRATING ITS RUMORED LOWER LEVELS.
WHICH I PERSONALLY SEE AS A CHALLENGE.
EHN! EHN! EHN! EHN! EHN!

RIGHT THERE! *THAT* GUY!

WHAT IS THIS, FRICKIN' AIRPORT SECURITY?

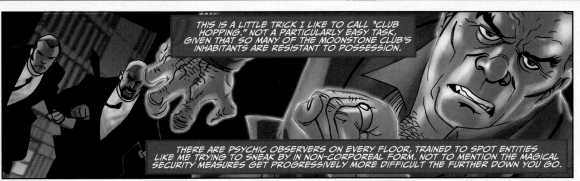

THIS IS A LITTLE TRICK I LIKE TO CALL "CLUB HOPPING." NOT A PARTICULARLY EASY TASK, GIVEN THAT SO MANY OF THE MOONSTONE CLUB'S INHABITANTS ARE RESISTANT TO POSSESSION.

THERE ARE PSYCHIC OBSERVERS ON EVERY FLOOR, TRAINED TO SPOT ENTITIES LIKE ME TRYING TO SNEAK BY IN NON-CORPOREAL FORM. NOT TO MENTION THE MAGICAL SECURITY MEASURES GET PROGRESSIVELY MORE DIFFICULT THE FURTHER DOWN YOU GO.

THE FIRST PART OF THIS TRICK IS TO GET ON THE FAR SIDE OF THE DEFENSIVE RUNIC BARRIERS THAT ARE SO POPULAR IN PLACES LIKE THIS.

NEXT, YOU RUN LIKE A FRIGHTENED DODO SMACK INTO A ROOM FULL OF PEOPLE.

AND FINALLY, YOU GET YOURSELF TRAPPED BY SOME EXTREMELY ANGRY BOUNCERS.

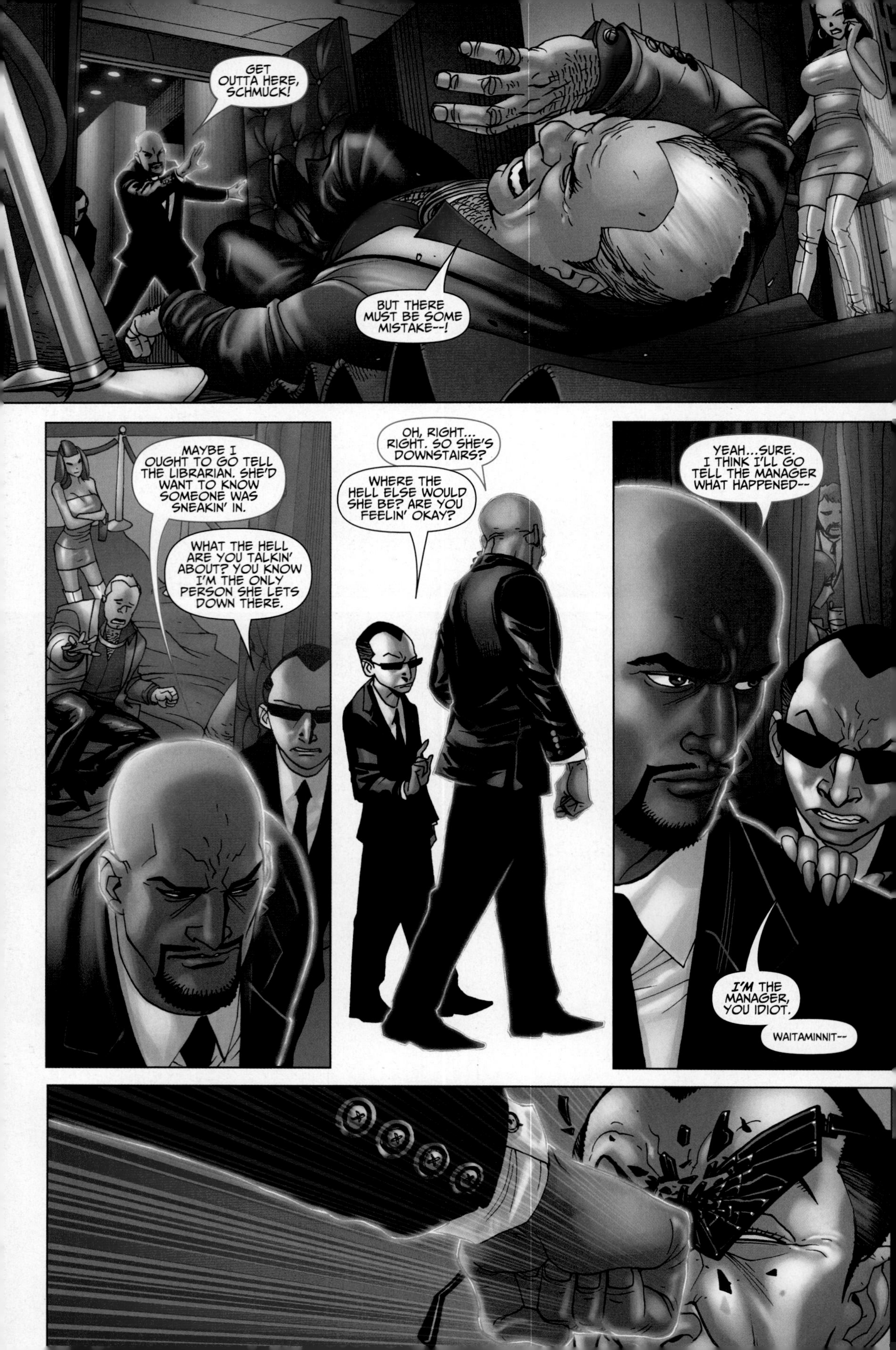
GET OUTTA HERE, SCHMUCK!
BUT THERE MUST BE SOME MISTAKE--!
MAYBE I OUGHT TO GO TELL THE LIBRARIAN. SHE'D WANT TO KNOW SOMEONE WAS SNEAKIN' IN.
WHAT THE HELL ARE YOU TALKIN' ABOUT? YOU KNOW I'M THE ONLY PERSON SHE LETS DOWN THERE.
OH, RIGHT... RIGHT. SO SHE'S DOWNSTAIRS?
WHERE THE HELL ELSE WOULD SHE BE? ARE YOU FEELIN' OKAY?
YEAH...SURE. I THINK I'LL GO TELL THE MANAGER WHAT HAPPENED--
I'M THE MANAGER, YOU IDIOT.
WAITAMINNIT--

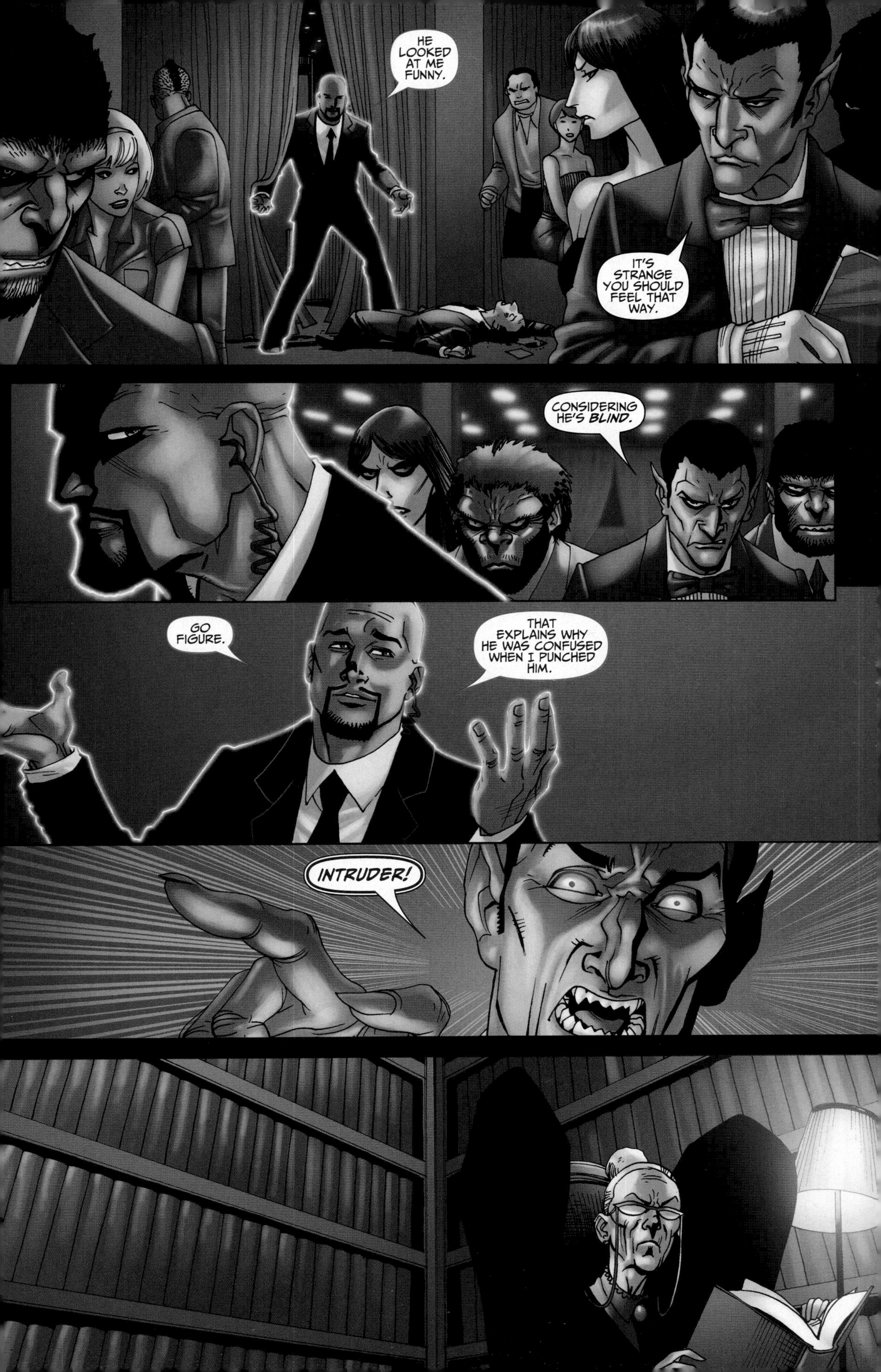

HE LOOKED AT ME FUNNY.
IT'S STRANGE YOU SHOULD FEEL THAT WAY.
CONSIDERING HE'S *BLIND.*
GO FIGURE.
THAT EXPLAINS WHY HE WAS CONFUSED WHEN I PUNCHED HIM.
INTRUDER!

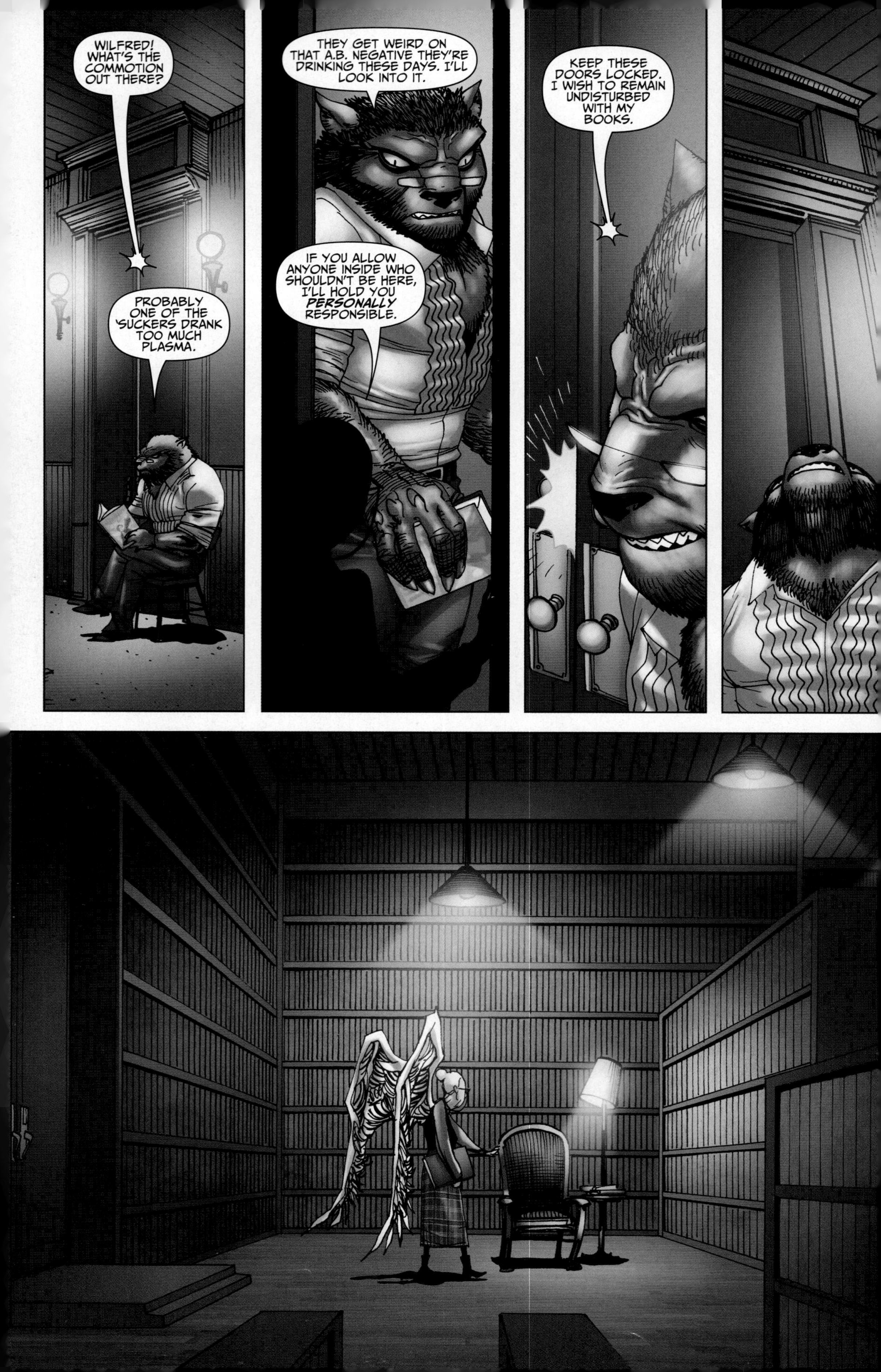
WILFRED! WHAT'S THE COMMOTION OUT THERE?
PROBABLY ONE OF THE 'SUCKERS DRANK TOO MUCH PLASMA.
THEY GET WEIRD ON THAT A.B. NEGATIVE THEY'RE DRINKING THESE DAYS. I'LL LOOK INTO IT.
IF YOU ALLOW ANYONE INSIDE WHO SHOULDN'T BE HERE, I'LL HOLD YOU *PERSONALLY* RESPONSIBLE.
KEEP THESE DOORS LOCKED. I WISH TO REMAIN UNDISTURBED WITH MY BOOKS.

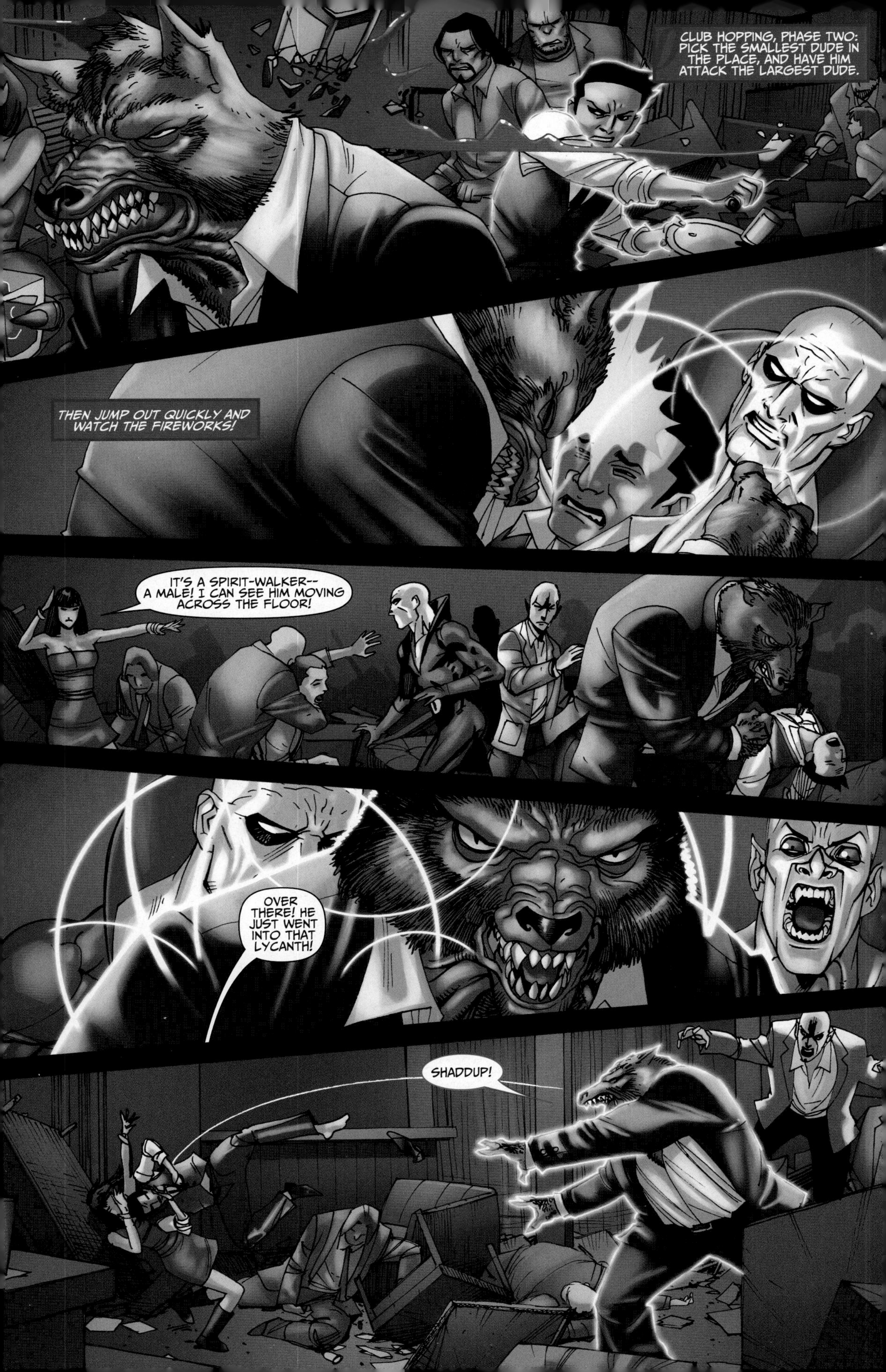
CLUB HOPPING, PHASE TWO: PICK THE SMALLEST DUDE IN THE PLACE, AND HAVE HIM ATTACK THE LARGEST DUDE.
THEN JUMP OUT QUICKLY AND WATCH THE FIREWORKS!
IT'S A SPIRIT-WALKER-- A MALE! I CAN SEE HIM MOVING ACROSS THE FLOOR!
OVER THERE! HE JUST WENT INTO THAT LYCANTH!
SHADDUP!

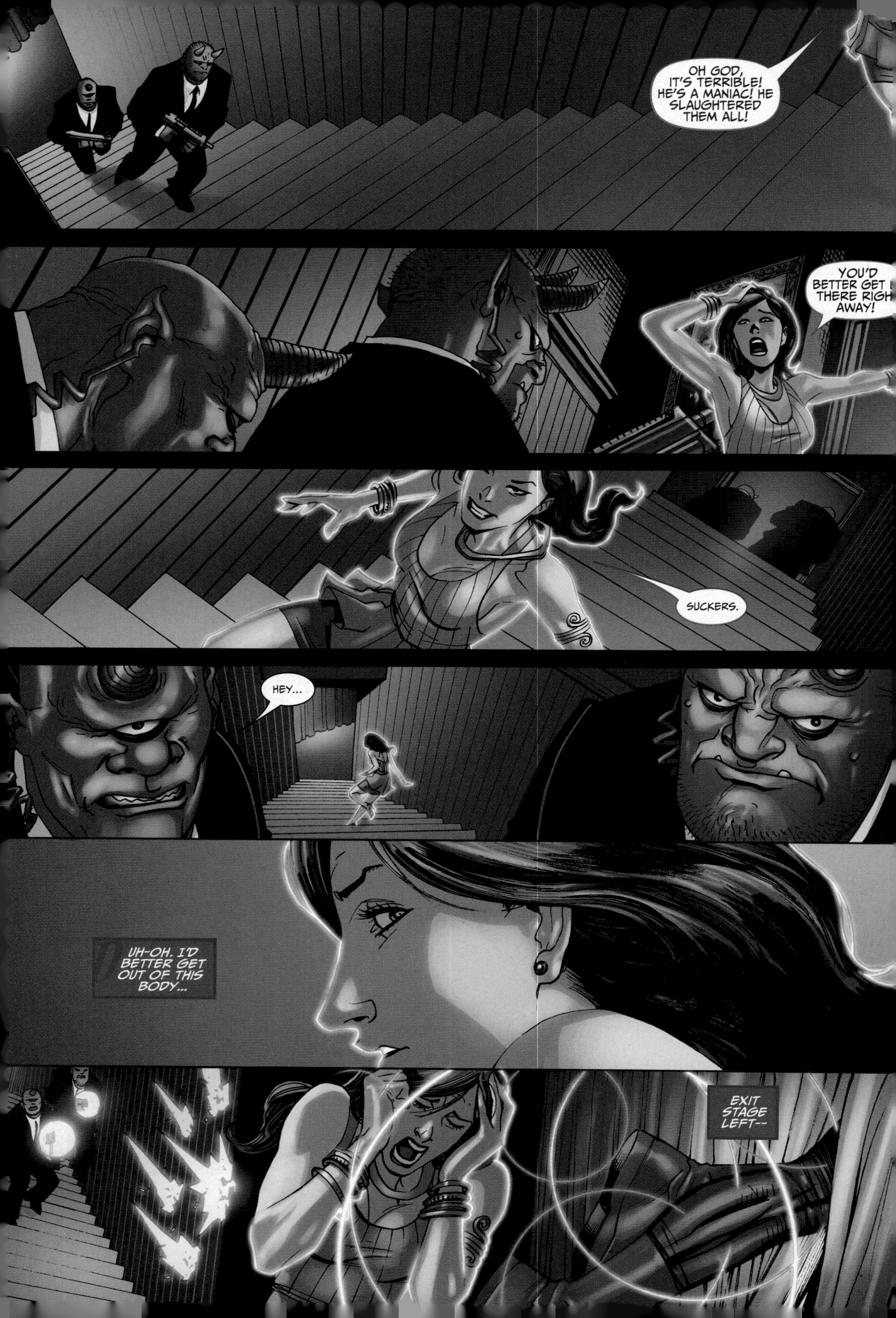
OH GOD, IT'S TERRIBLE! HE'S A MANIAC! HE SLAUGHTERED THEM ALL!
YOU'D BETTER GET THERE RIGH AWAY!
SUCKERS.
HEY...
UH-OH. I'D BETTER GET OUT OF THIS BODY...
EXIT STAGE LEFT--

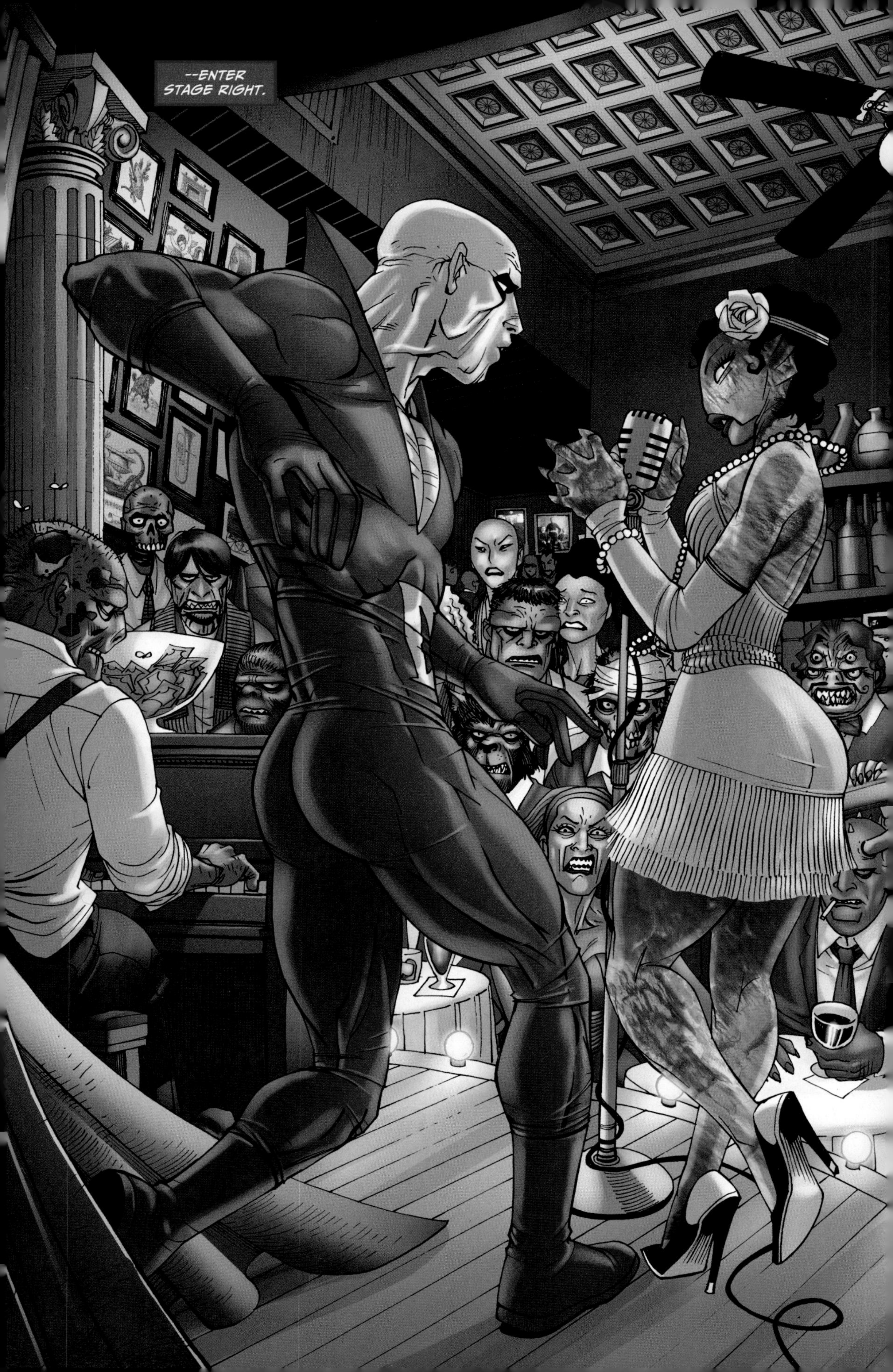
--ENTER
STAGE RIGHT.

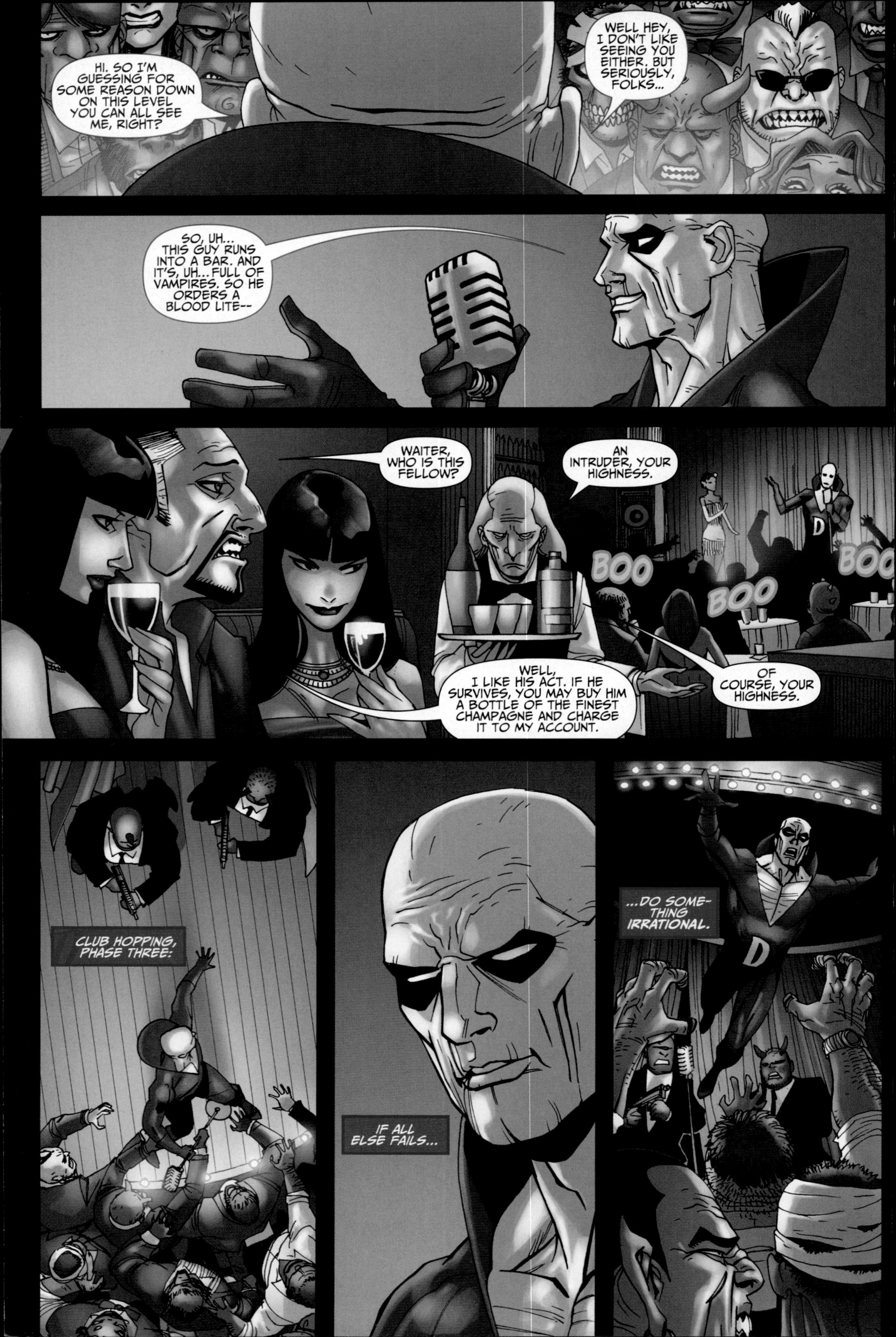
HI. SO I'M GUESSING FOR SOME REASON DOWN ON THIS LEVEL YOU CAN ALL SEE ME, RIGHT?
WELL HEY, I DON'T LIKE SEEING YOU EITHER. BUT SERIOUSLY, FOLKS...
SO, UH... THIS GUY RUNS INTO A BAR. AND IT'S, UH... FULL OF VAMPIRES. SO HE ORDERS A BLOOD LITE--
WAITER, WHO IS THIS FELLOW?
AN INTRUDER, YOUR HIGHNESS.
BOO
BOO
BOO
WELL, I LIKE HIS ACT. IF HE SURVIVES, YOU MAY BUY HIM A BOTTLE OF THE FINEST CHAMPAGNE AND CHARGE IT TO MY ACCOUNT.
OF COURSE, YOUR HIGHNESS.
CLUB HOPPING, PHASE THREE:
IF ALL ELSE FAILS...
...DO SOME-THING IRRATIONAL.

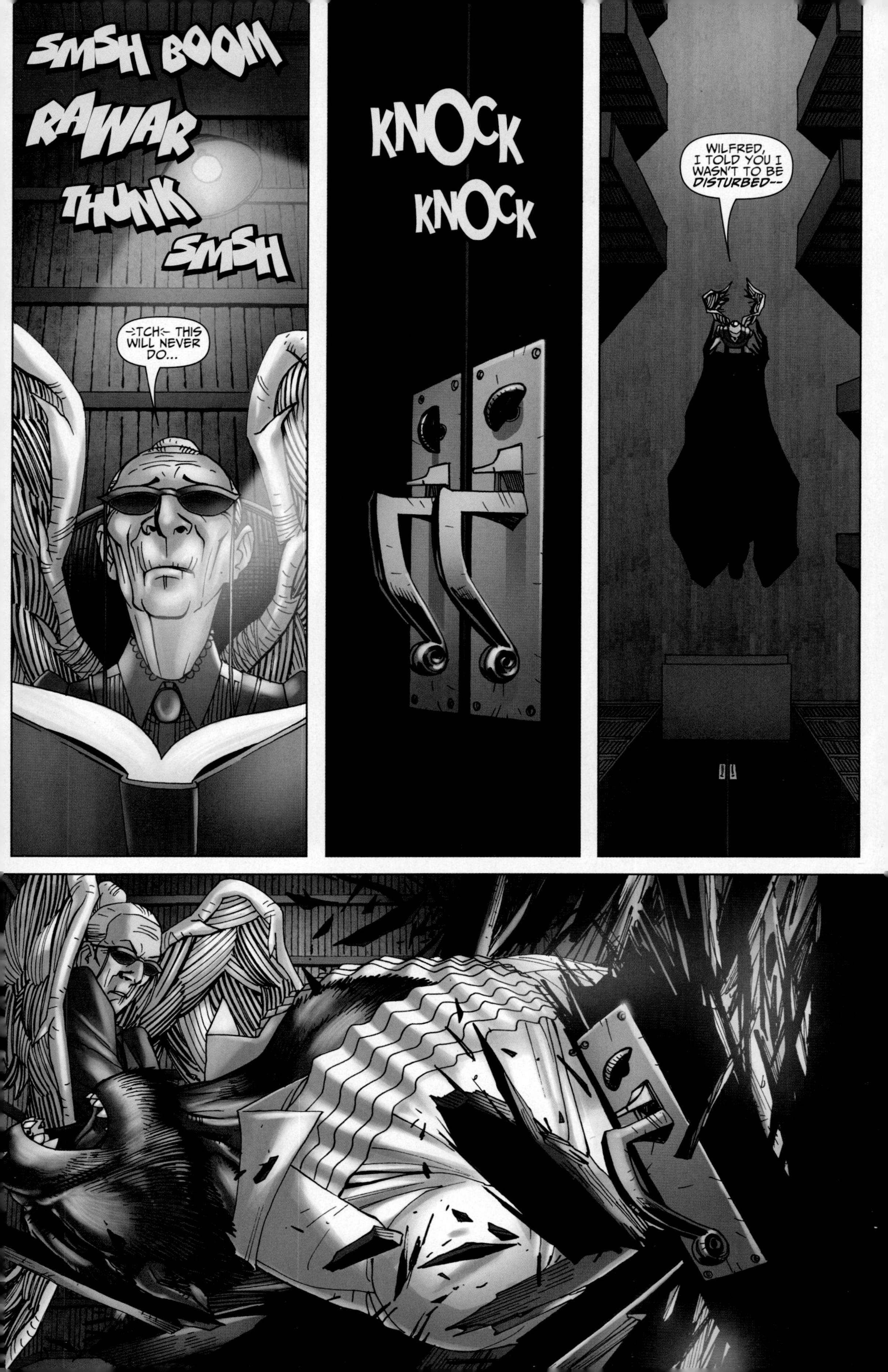
SMSH BOOM
RAWAR
THUNK
SMSH
-TCH- THIS WILL NEVER DO...
KNOCK
KNOCK
WILFRED, I TOLD YOU I WASN'T TO BE DISTURBED--

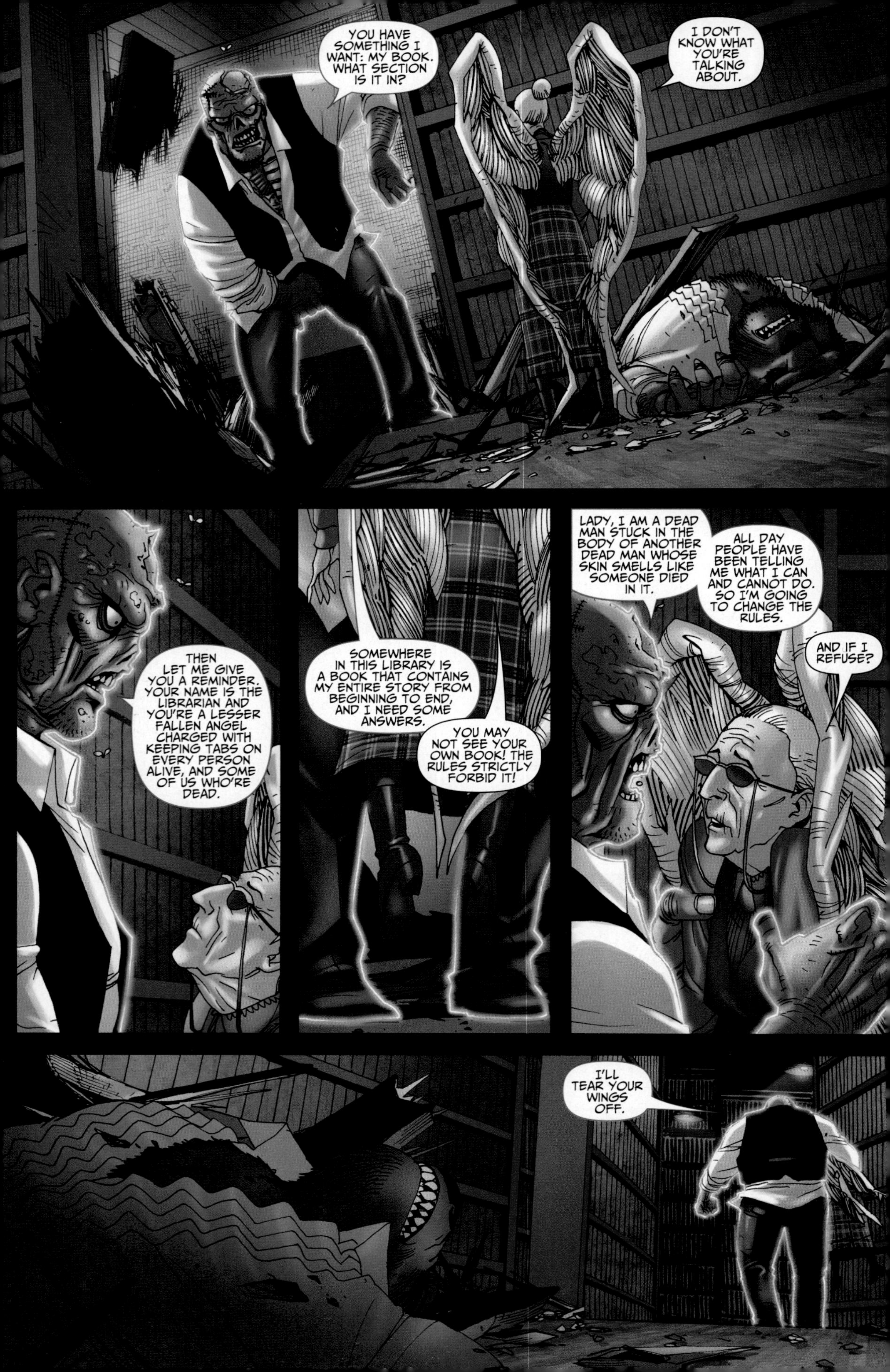
YOU HAVE SOMETHING I WANT: MY BOOK. WHAT SECTION IS IT IN?
I DON'T KNOW WHAT YOU'RE TALKING ABOUT.
THEN LET ME GIVE YOU A REMINDER. YOUR NAME IS THE LIBRARIAN AND YOU'RE A LESSER FALLEN ANGEL CHARGED WITH KEEPING TABS ON EVERY PERSON ALIVE, AND SOME OF US WHO'RE DEAD.
SOMEWHERE IN THIS LIBRARY IS A BOOK THAT CONTAINS MY ENTIRE STORY FROM BEGINNING TO END, AND I NEED SOME ANSWERS.
YOU MAY NOT SEE YOUR OWN BOOK! THE RULES STRICTLY FORBID IT!
LADY, I AM A DEAD MAN STUCK IN THE BODY OF ANOTHER DEAD MAN WHOSE SKIN SMELLS LIKE SOMEONE DIED IN IT.
ALL DAY PEOPLE HAVE BEEN TELLING ME WHAT I CAN AND CANNOT DO. SO I'M GOING TO CHANGE THE RULES.
AND IF I REFUSE?
I'LL TEAR YOUR WINGS OFF.

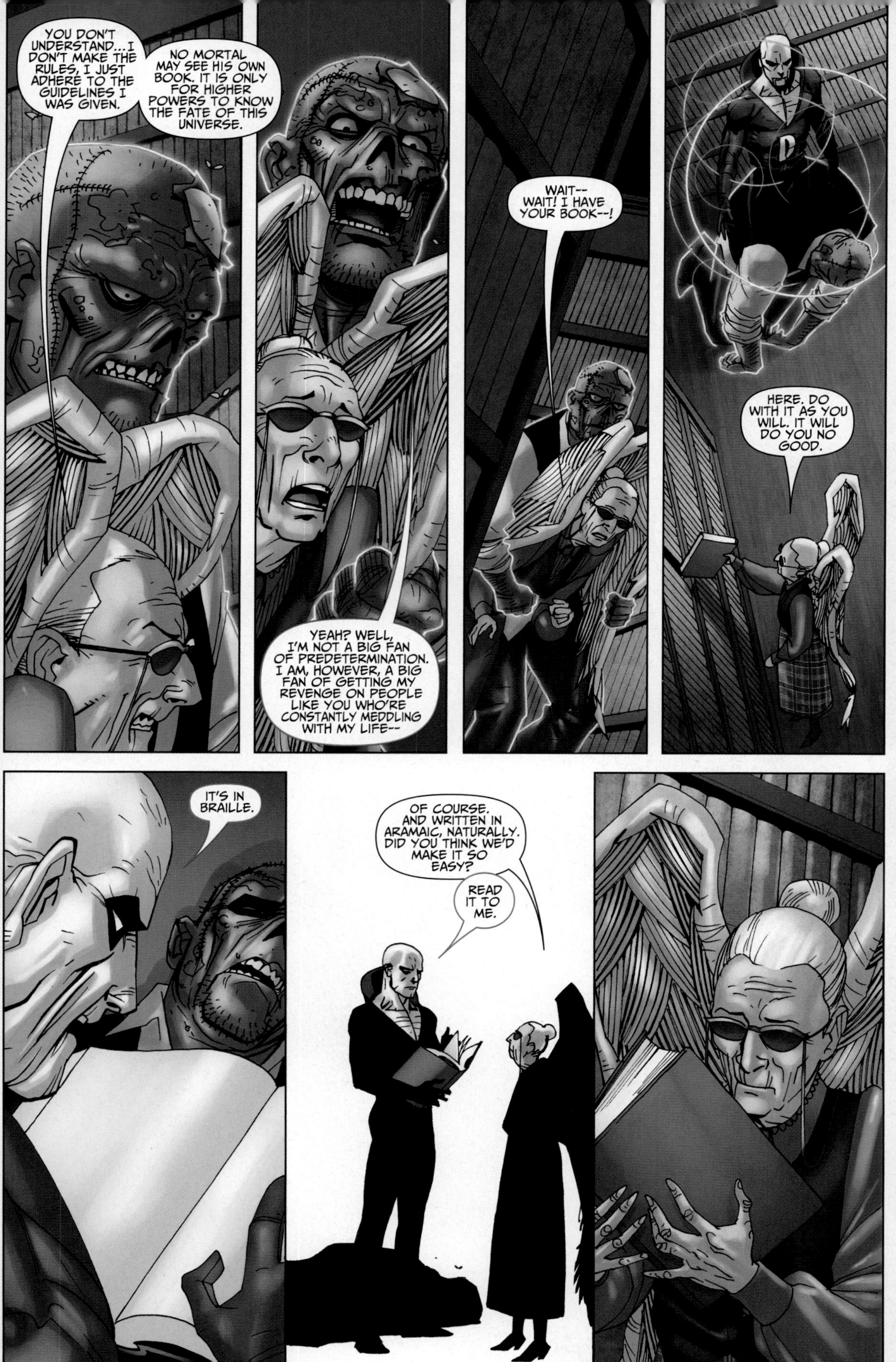
YOU DON'T UNDERSTAND... I DON'T MAKE THE RULES, I JUST ADHERE TO THE GUIDELINES I WAS GIVEN.
NO MORTAL MAY SEE HIS OWN BOOK. IT IS ONLY FOR HIGHER POWERS TO KNOW THE FATE OF THIS UNIVERSE.
YEAH? WELL, I'M NOT A BIG FAN OF PREDETERMINATION. I AM, HOWEVER, A BIG FAN OF GETTING MY REVENGE ON PEOPLE LIKE YOU WHO'RE CONSTANTLY MEDDLING WITH MY LIFE--
WAIT-- WAIT! I HAVE YOUR BOOK--!
HERE. DO WITH IT AS YOU WILL. IT WILL DO YOU NO GOOD.
IT'S IN BRAILLE.
OF COURSE. AND WRITTEN IN ARAMAIC, NATURALLY. DID YOU THINK WE'D MAKE IT SO EASY?
READ IT TO ME.

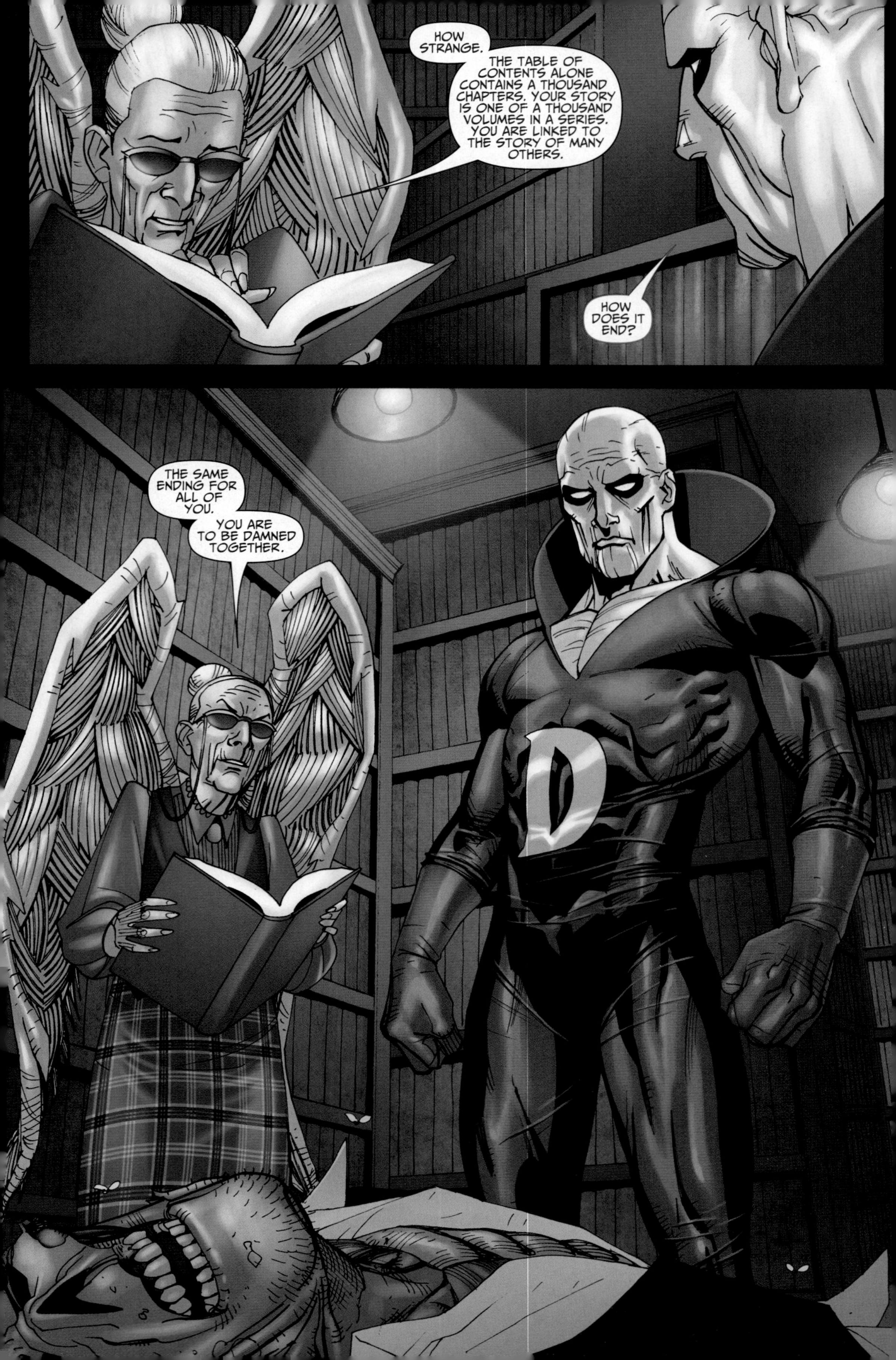
HOW STRANGE.
THE TABLE OF CONTENTS ALONE CONTAINS A THOUSAND CHAPTERS. YOUR STORY IS ONE OF A THOUSAND VOLUMES IN A SERIES. YOU ARE LINKED TO THE STORY OF MANY OTHERS.
HOW DOES IT END?
THE SAME ENDING FOR ALL OF YOU.
YOU ARE TO BE DAMNED TOGETHER.

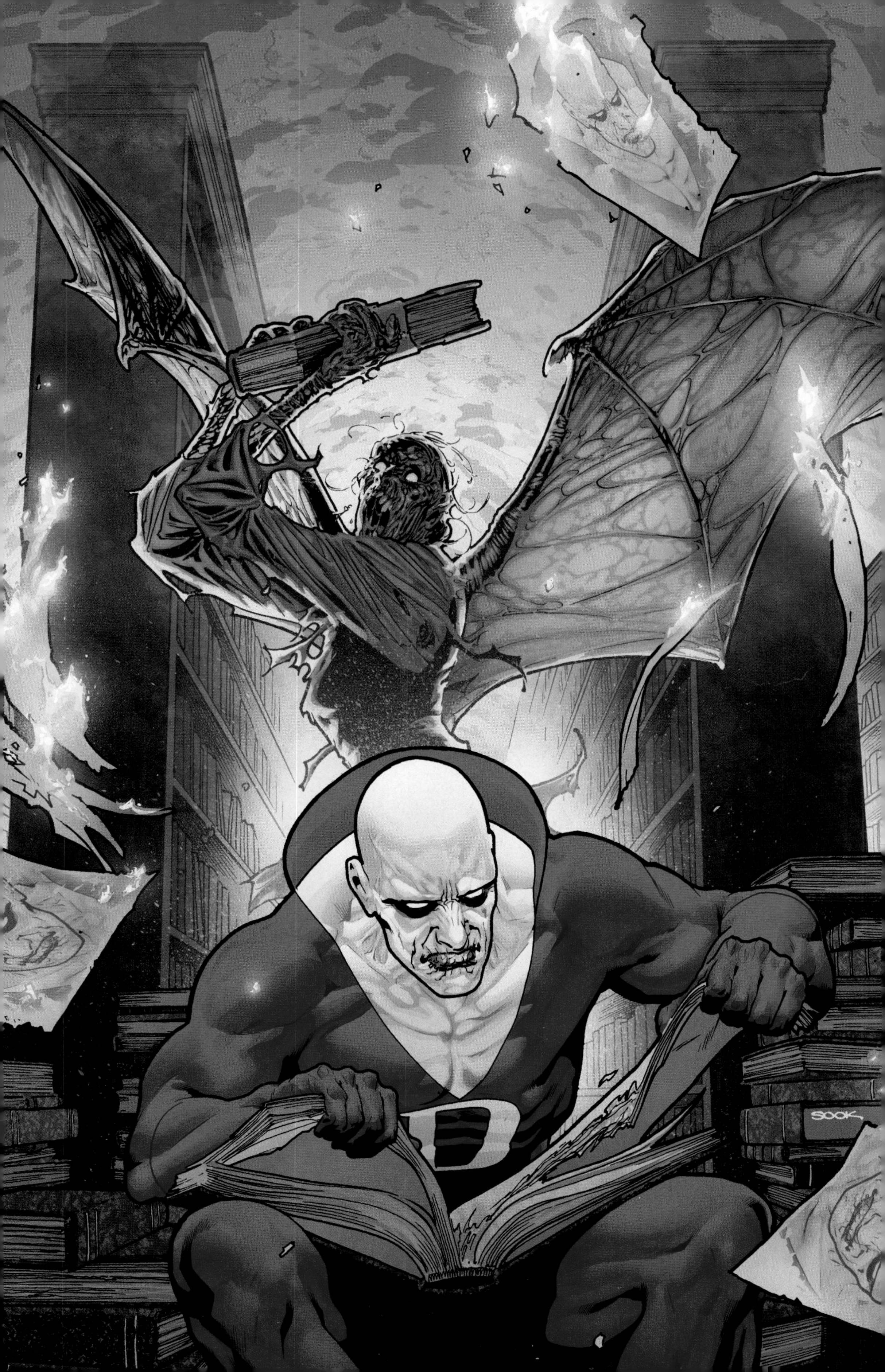
SOOK

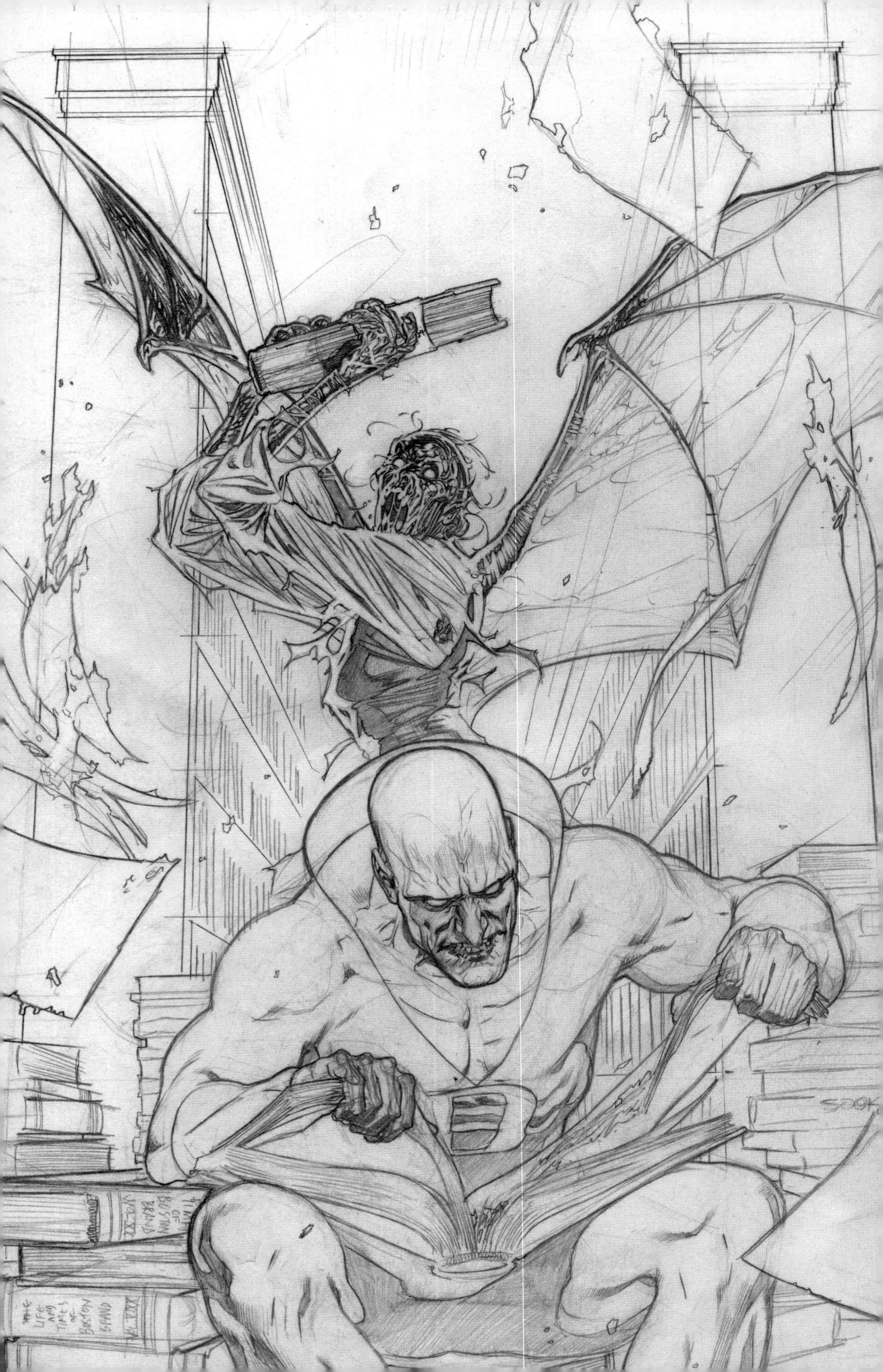
THE LIFE AND TIMES OF BOSTON BRAND
SOOK

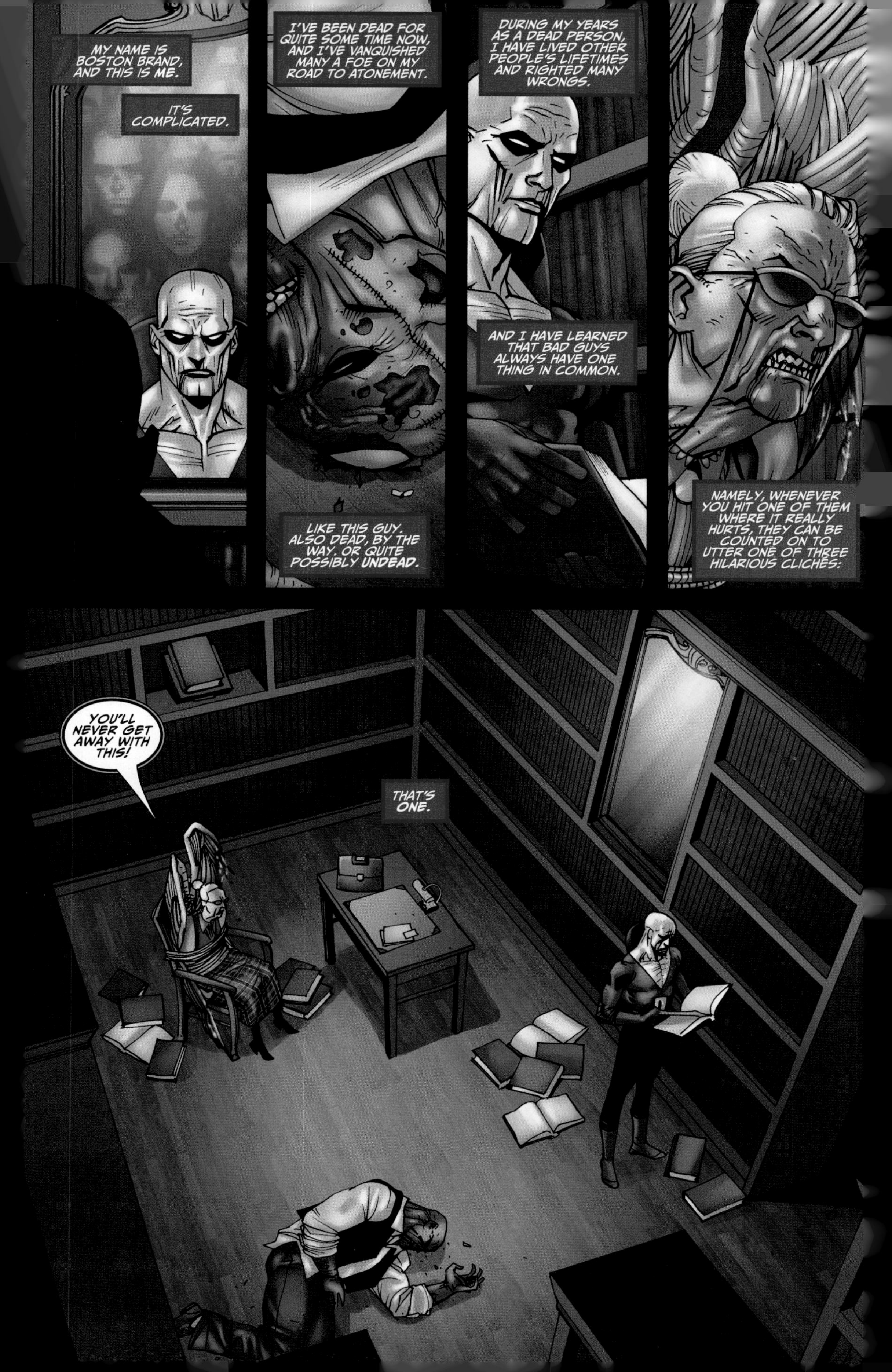
MY NAME IS BOSTON BRAND, AND THIS IS ME.
IT'S COMPLICATED.
I'VE BEEN DEAD FOR QUITE SOME TIME NOW, AND I'VE VANQUISHED MANY A FOE ON MY ROAD TO ATONEMENT.
LIKE THIS GUY. ALSO DEAD, BY THE WAY. OR QUITE POSSIBLY UNDEAD.
DURING MY YEARS AS A DEAD PERSON, I HAVE LIVED OTHER PEOPLE'S LIFETIMES AND RIGHTED MANY WRONGS.
AND I HAVE LEARNED THAT BAD GUYS ALWAYS HAVE ONE THING IN COMMON.
NAMELY, WHENEVER YOU HIT ONE OF THEM WHERE IT REALLY HURTS, THEY CAN BE COUNTED ON TO UTTER ONE OF THREE HILARIOUS CLICHÉS:
YOU'LL NEVER GET AWAY WITH THIS!
THAT'S ONE.

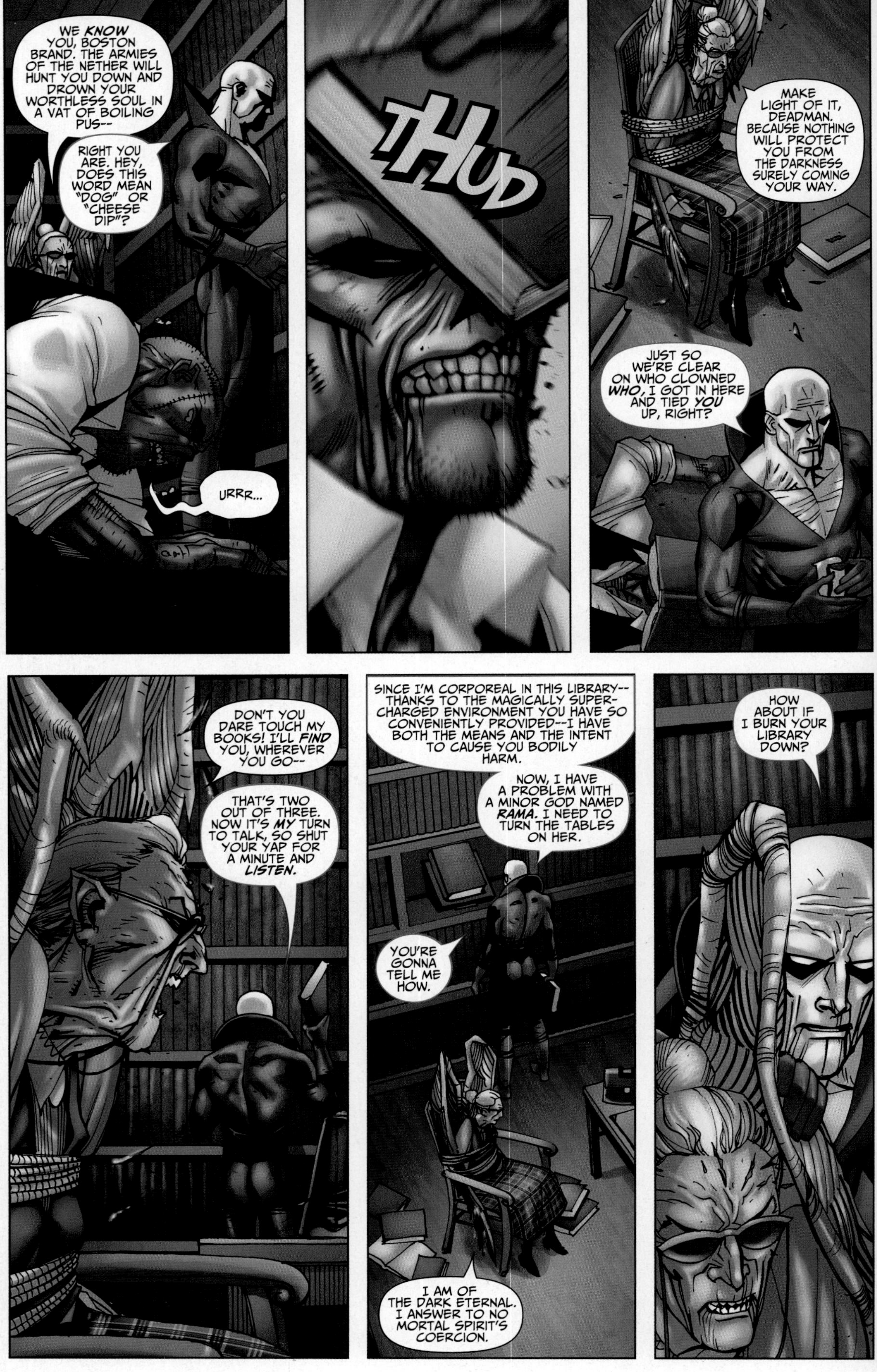
WE KNOW YOU, BOSTON BRAND. THE ARMIES OF THE NETHER WILL HUNT YOU DOWN AND DROWN YOUR WORTHLESS SOUL IN A VAT OF BOILING PUS--
RIGHT YOU ARE. HEY, DOES THIS WORD MEAN "DOG" OR "CHEESE DIP"?
URRR...
THUD
MAKE LIGHT OF IT, DEADMAN. BECAUSE NOTHING WILL PROTECT YOU FROM THE DARKNESS SURELY COMING YOUR WAY.
JUST SO WE'RE CLEAR ON WHO CLOWNED WHO, I GOT IN HERE AND TIED YOU UP, RIGHT?
DON'T YOU DARE TOUCH MY BOOKS! I'LL FIND YOU, WHEREVER YOU GO--
THAT'S TWO OUT OF THREE. NOW IT'S MY TURN TO TALK, SO SHUT YOUR YAP FOR A MINUTE AND LISTEN.
SINCE I'M CORPOREAL IN THIS LIBRARY-- THANKS TO THE MAGICALLY SUPER-CHARGED ENVIRONMENT YOU HAVE SO CONVENIENTLY PROVIDED--I HAVE BOTH THE MEANS AND THE INTENT TO CAUSE YOU BODILY HARM.
NOW, I HAVE A PROBLEM WITH A MINOR GOD NAMED RAMA. I NEED TO TURN THE TABLES ON HER.
YOU'RE GONNA TELL ME HOW.
I AM OF THE DARK ETERNAL. I ANSWER TO NO MORTAL SPIRIT'S COERCION.
HOW ABOUT IF I BURN YOUR LIBRARY DOWN?

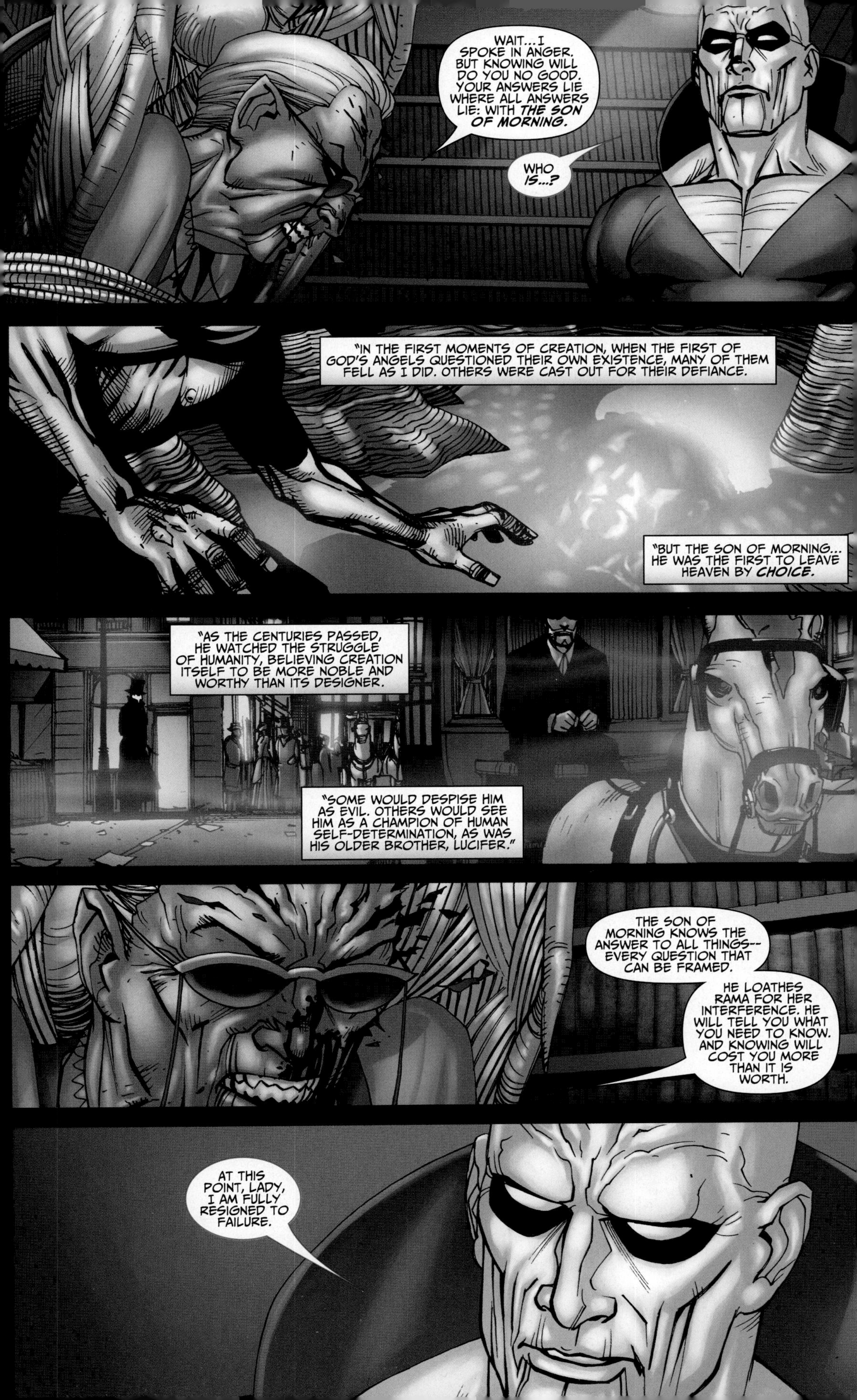
WAIT...I SPOKE IN ANGER. BUT KNOWING WILL DO YOU NO GOOD. YOUR ANSWERS LIE WHERE ALL ANSWERS LIE: WITH THE SON OF MORNING.
WHO IS...?
"IN THE FIRST MOMENTS OF CREATION, WHEN THE FIRST OF GOD'S ANGELS QUESTIONED THEIR OWN EXISTENCE, MANY OF THEM FELL AS I DID. OTHERS WERE CAST OUT FOR THEIR DEFIANCE.
"BUT THE SON OF MORNING... HE WAS THE FIRST TO LEAVE HEAVEN BY CHOICE.
"AS THE CENTURIES PASSED, HE WATCHED THE STRUGGLE OF HUMANITY, BELIEVING CREATION ITSELF TO BE MORE NOBLE AND WORTHY THAN ITS DESIGNER.
"SOME WOULD DESPISE HIM AS EVIL. OTHERS WOULD SEE HIM AS A CHAMPION OF HUMAN SELF-DETERMINATION, AS WAS HIS OLDER BROTHER, LUCIFER."
THE SON OF MORNING KNOWS THE ANSWER TO ALL THINGS-- EVERY QUESTION THAT CAN BE FRAMED.
HE LOATHES RAMA FOR HER INTERFERENCE. HE WILL TELL YOU WHAT YOU NEED TO KNOW. AND KNOWING WILL COST YOU MORE THAN IT IS WORTH.
AT THIS POINT, LADY, I AM FULLY RESIGNED TO FAILURE.

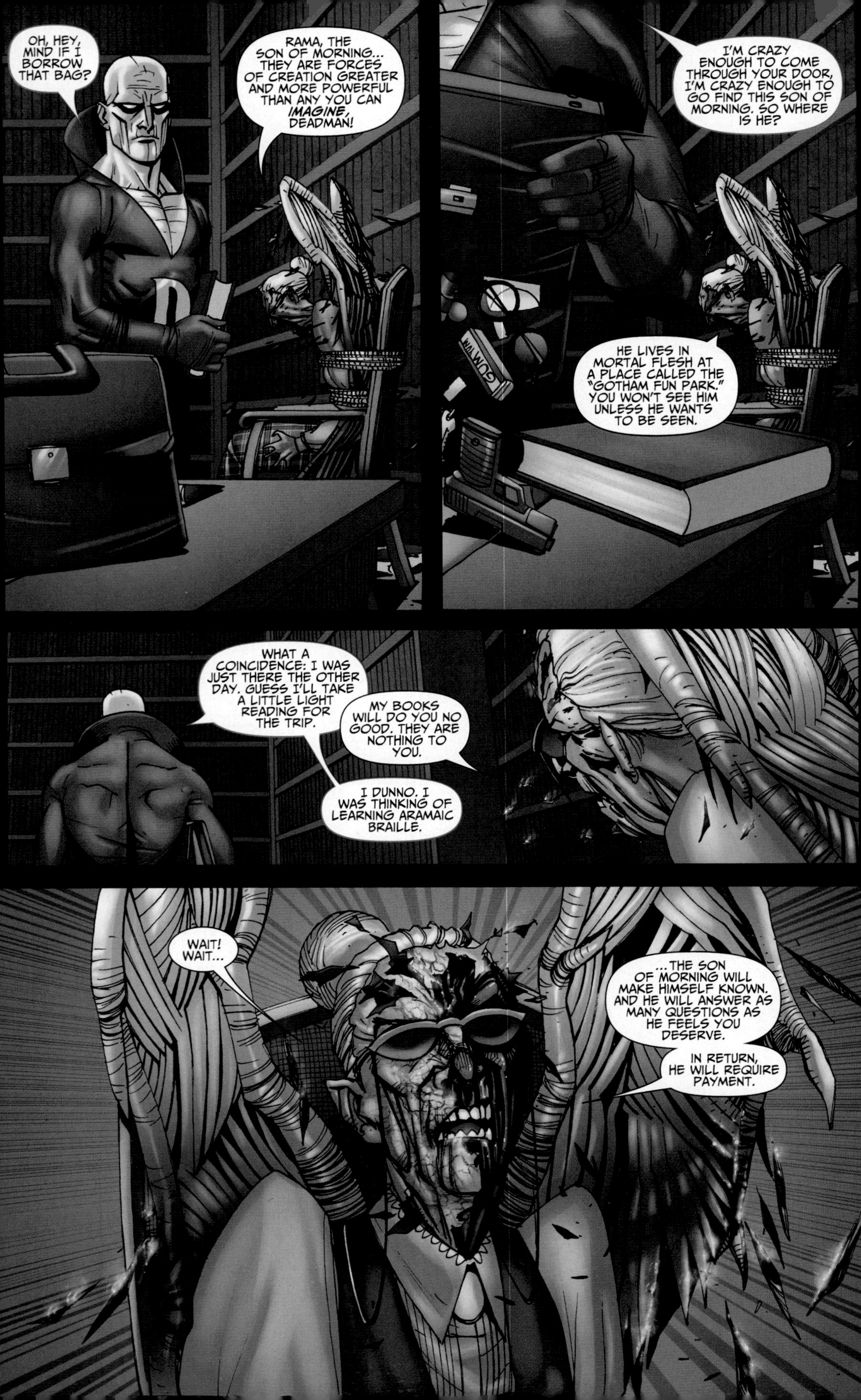
OH, HEY, MIND IF I BORROW THAT BAG?
RAMA, THE SON OF MORNING... THEY ARE FORCES OF CREATION GREATER AND MORE POWERFUL THAN ANY YOU CAN IMAGINE, DEADMAN!
I'M CRAZY ENOUGH TO COME THROUGH YOUR DOOR, I'M CRAZY ENOUGH TO GO FIND THIS SON OF MORNING. SO WHERE IS HE?
HE LIVES IN MORTAL FLESH AT A PLACE CALLED THE "GOTHAM FUN PARK." YOU WON'T SEE HIM UNLESS HE WANTS TO BE SEEN.
WHAT A COINCIDENCE: I WAS JUST THERE THE OTHER DAY. GUESS I'LL TAKE A LITTLE LIGHT READING FOR THE TRIP.
MY BOOKS WILL DO YOU NO GOOD. THEY ARE NOTHING TO YOU.
I DUNNO. I WAS THINKING OF LEARNING ARAMAIC BRAILLE.
WAIT! WAIT...
...THE SON OF MORNING WILL MAKE HIMSELF KNOWN. AND HE WILL ANSWER AS MANY QUESTIONS AS HE FEELS YOU DESERVE.
IN RETURN, HE WILL REQUIRE PAYMENT.

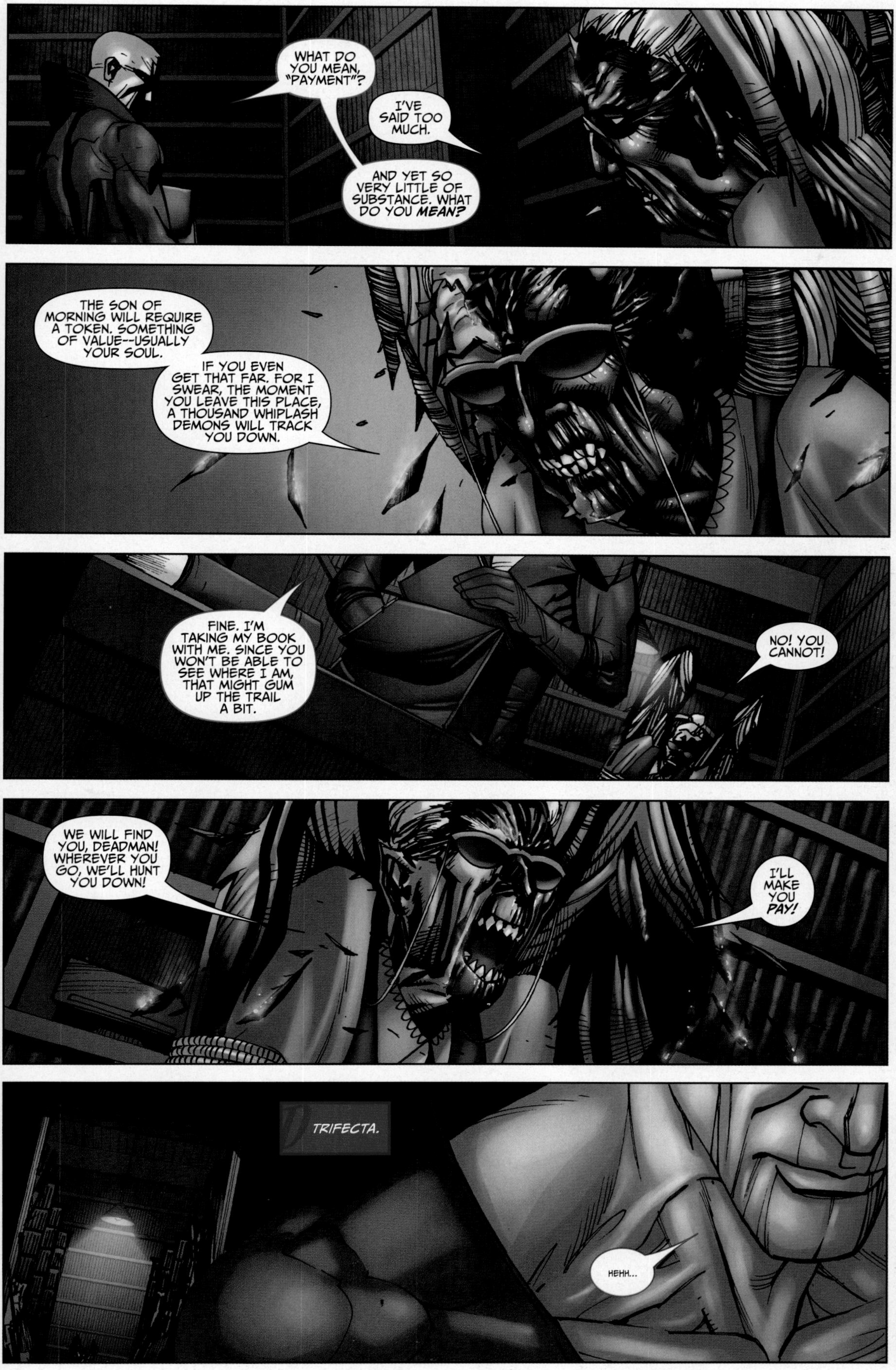
WHAT DO YOU MEAN, "PAYMENT"?
I'VE SAID TOO MUCH.
AND YET SO VERY LITTLE OF SUBSTANCE. WHAT DO YOU *MEAN?*
THE SON OF MORNING WILL REQUIRE A TOKEN. SOMETHING OF VALUE--USUALLY YOUR SOUL.
IF YOU EVEN GET THAT FAR. FOR I SWEAR, THE MOMENT YOU LEAVE THIS PLACE, A THOUSAND WHIPLASH DEMONS WILL TRACK YOU DOWN.
FINE. I'M TAKING MY BOOK WITH ME. SINCE YOU WON'T BE ABLE TO SEE WHERE I AM, THAT MIGHT GUM UP THE TRAIL A BIT.
NO! YOU CANNOT!
WE WILL FIND YOU, DEADMAN! WHEREVER YOU GO, WE'LL HUNT YOU DOWN!
I'LL MAKE YOU *PAY!*
TRIFECTA.
HEHH...

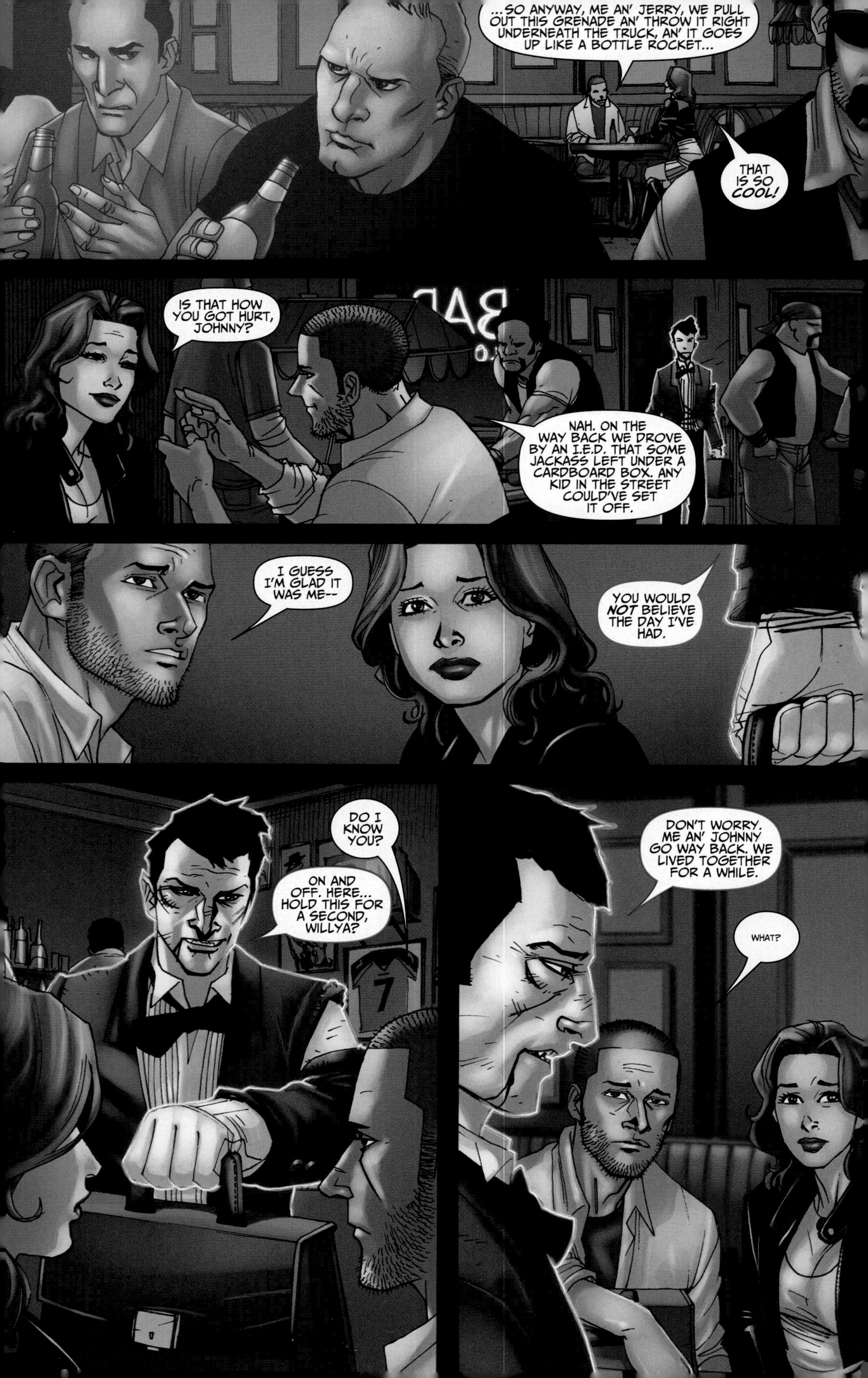
...SO ANYWAY, ME AN' JERRY, WE PULL OUT THIS GRENADE AN' THROW IT RIGHT UNDERNEATH THE TRUCK, AN' IT GOES UP LIKE A BOTTLE ROCKET...
THAT IS SO COOL!
IS THAT HOW YOU GOT HURT, JOHNNY?
NAH. ON THE WAY BACK WE DROVE BY AN I.E.D. THAT SOME JACKASS LEFT UNDER A CARDBOARD BOX. ANY KID IN THE STREET COULD'VE SET IT OFF.
I GUESS I'M GLAD IT WAS ME--
YOU WOULD NOT BELIEVE THE DAY I'VE HAD.
DO I KNOW YOU?
ON AND OFF. HERE... HOLD THIS FOR A SECOND, WILLYA?
DON'T WORRY. ME AN' JOHNNY GO WAY BACK. WE LIVED TOGETHER FOR A WHILE.
WHAT?

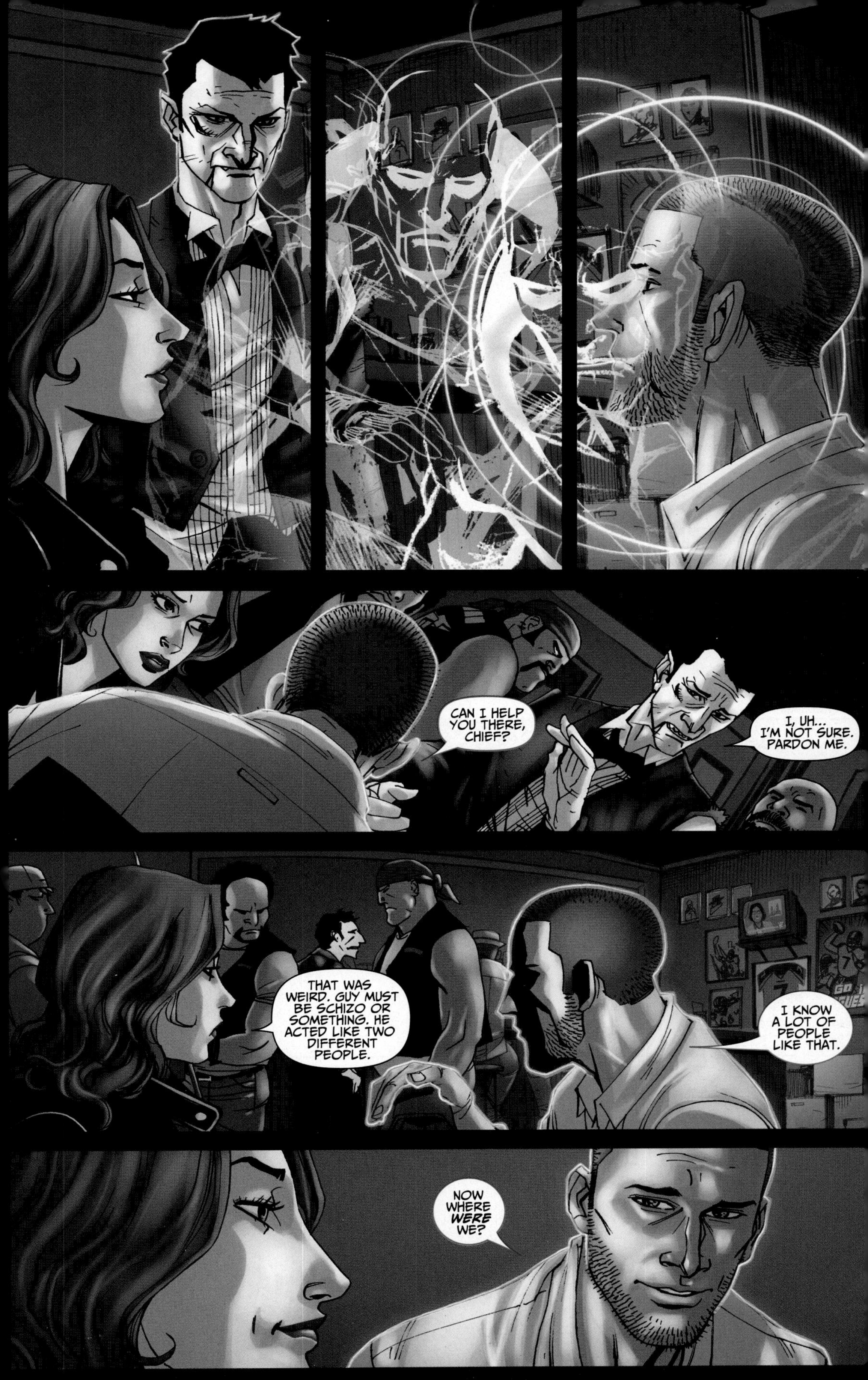
CAN I HELP YOU THERE, CHIEF?
I, UH... I'M NOT SURE. PARDON ME.
THAT WAS WEIRD. GUY MUST BE SCHIZO OR SOMETHING. HE ACTED LIKE TWO DIFFERENT PEOPLE.
I KNOW A LOT OF PEOPLE LIKE THAT.
NOW WHERE *WERE* WE?

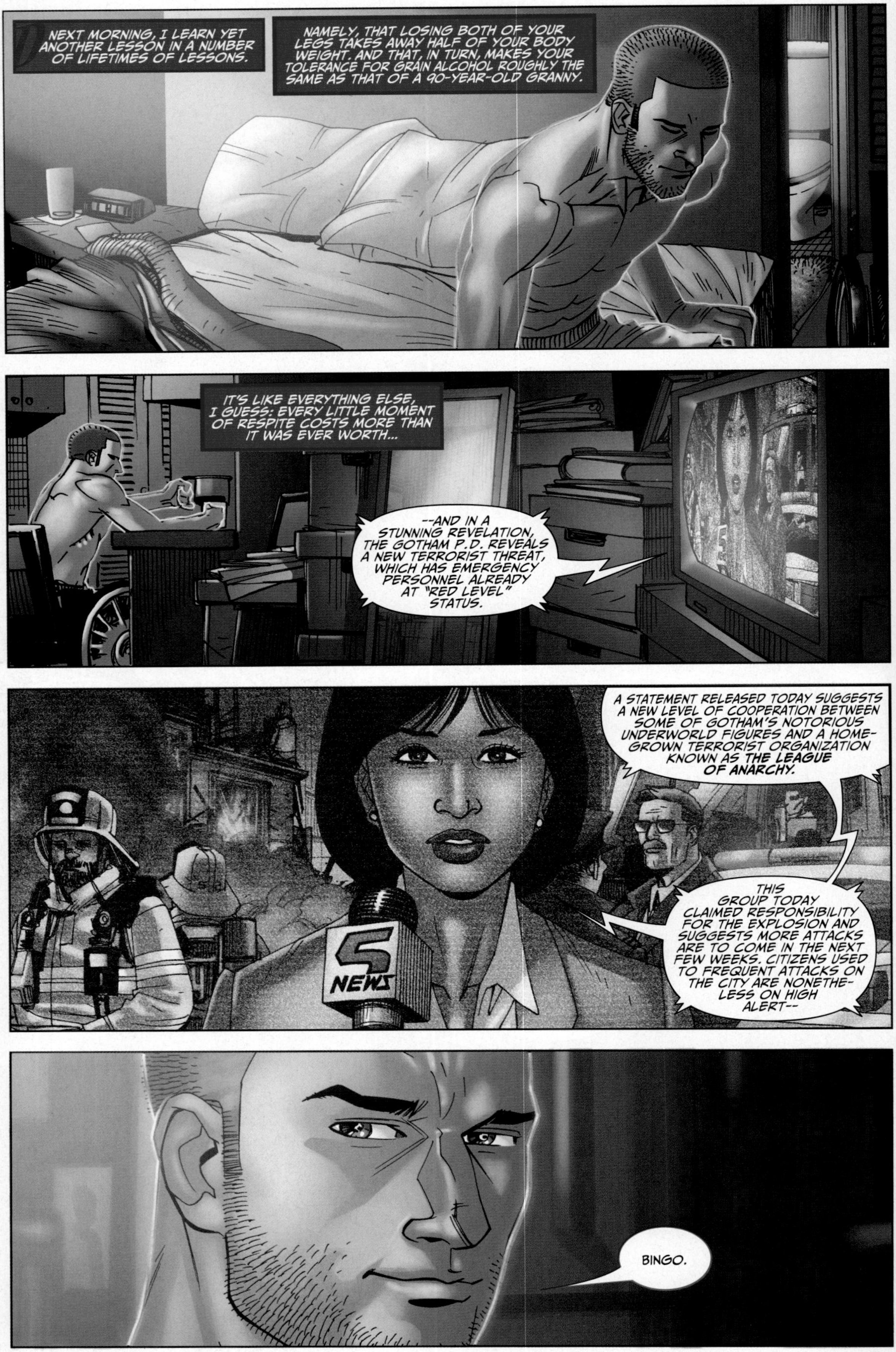
NEXT MORNING, I LEARN YET ANOTHER LESSON IN A NUMBER OF LIFETIMES OF LESSONS.
NAMELY, THAT LOSING BOTH OF YOUR LEGS TAKES AWAY HALF OF YOUR BODY WEIGHT. AND THAT, IN TURN, MAKES YOUR TOLERANCE FOR GRAIN ALCOHOL ROUGHLY THE SAME AS THAT OF A 90-YEAR-OLD GRANNY.
IT'S LIKE EVERYTHING ELSE, I GUESS: EVERY LITTLE MOMENT OF RESPITE COSTS MORE THAN IT WAS EVER WORTH...
--AND IN A STUNNING REVELATION, THE GOTHAM P.D. REVEALS A NEW TERRORIST THREAT, WHICH HAS EMERGENCY PERSONNEL ALREADY AT "RED LEVEL" STATUS.
A STATEMENT RELEASED TODAY SUGGESTS A NEW LEVEL OF COOPERATION BETWEEN SOME OF GOTHAM'S NOTORIOUS UNDERWORLD FIGURES AND A HOME-GROWN TERRORIST ORGANIZATION KNOWN AS THE LEAGUE OF ANARCHY.
THIS GROUP TODAY CLAIMED RESPONSIBILITY FOR THE EXPLOSION AND SUGGESTS MORE ATTACKS ARE TO COME IN THE NEXT FEW WEEKS. CITIZENS USED TO FREQUENT ATTACKS ON THE CITY ARE NONETHELESS ON HIGH ALERT--
5 NEWS
BINGO.

I THINK I HAVE AN IDEA-- AT LEAST WHERE MY BUDDY JOHNNY IS CONCERNED.

LEGS OR NO LEGS, IT'S WORTH A SHOT.

THE PROBLEM IS, IF I HELP HIM, HE AND I WILL STAY CONNECTED AND I WON'T HAVE HELPED HIM AT ALL. NOT REALLY.

THERE'S AN EVEN BIGGER QUESTION IN THIS SOMEWHERE. I JUST HAVE TO FIGURE IT OUT.

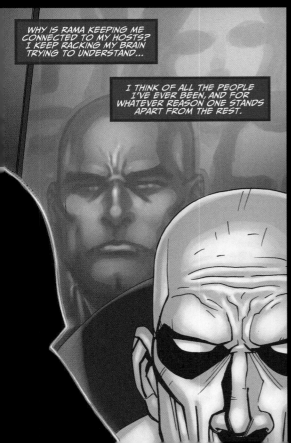

WHY IS RAMA KEEPING ME CONNECTED TO MY HOSTS? I KEEP RACKING MY BRAIN TRYING TO UNDERSTAND...

I THINK OF ALL THE PEOPLE I'VE EVER BEEN, AND FOR WHATEVER REASON ONE STANDS APART FROM THE REST.

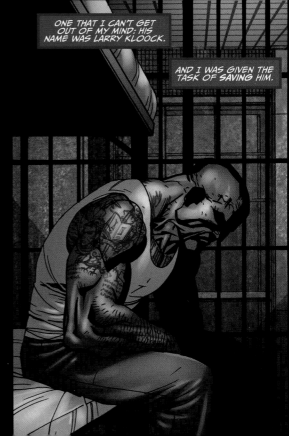

ONE THAT I CAN'T GET OUT OF MY MIND: HIS NAME WAS LARRY KLOOCK.

AND I WAS GIVEN THE TASK OF SAVING HIM.

LARRY WAS ONE OF THE PEOPLE RAMA SENT ME TO POSSESS, A FUNDAMENTALLY GOOD MAN WHO'D BEEN SENT TO DEATH ROW FOR A CRIME HE NEVER COMMITTED.

EVERYONE ON THE WALK KNEW HE DIDN'T DO IT. LARRY ALWAYS KEPT HIS FAITH IN THE SYSTEM AND HIS FAITH IN GOD INTACT. HE'D EVEN MINISTER TO A LOT OF THOSE YOUNG GUYS.

THE MOMENT I ENTERED HIS BODY, I KNEW THIS WAS DIFFERENT-- NONE OF IT MADE SENSE. LARRY WAS A BETTER MAN THAN I WAS. PROBABLY BETTER THAN ANY I'D EVER KNOWN.

I SET ABOUT HELPING HIM WIN HIS FREEDOM. BUT EVERY AVENUE PROVED TO BE A DEAD END.

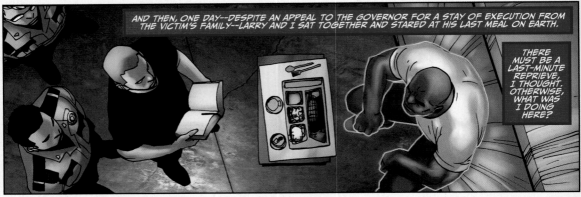

AND THEN, ONE DAY--DESPITE AN APPEAL TO THE GOVERNOR FOR A STAY OF EXECUTION FROM THE VICTIM'S FAMILY--LARRY AND I SAT TOGETHER AND STARED AT HIS LAST MEAL ON EARTH.

THERE MUST BE A LAST-MINUTE REPRIEVE, I THOUGHT. OTHERWISE, WHAT WAS I DOING HERE?

I TOOK LARRY KLOOCK'S LEGS AND WALKED HIM SLOWLY TO THE EXECUTION CHAMBER.

HE'D ALREADY ACCEPTED HIS FATE. IT WAS ME WHO WAS SCARED.

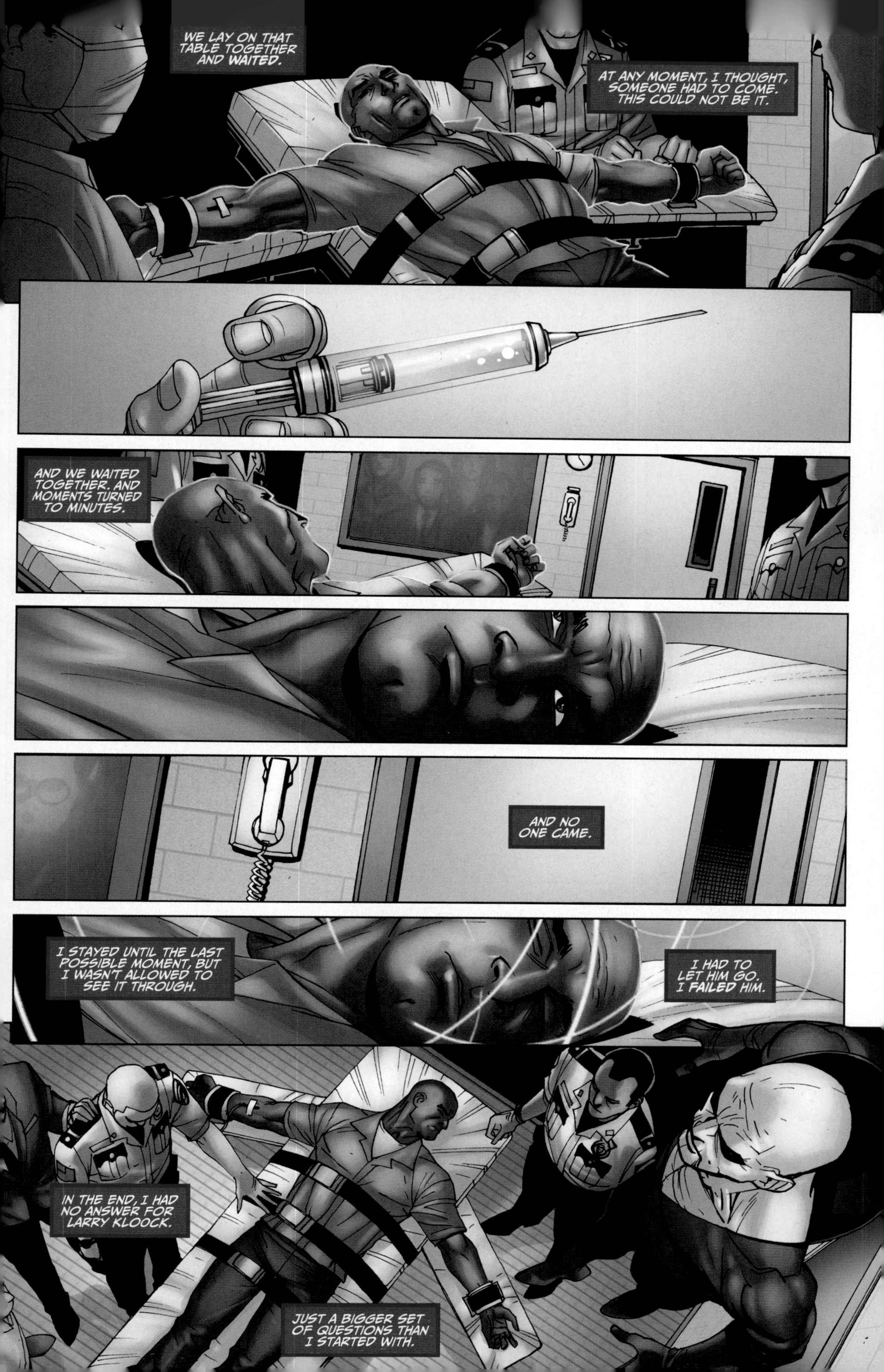
WE LAY ON THAT TABLE TOGETHER AND WAITED.
AT ANY MOMENT, I THOUGHT, SOMEONE HAD TO COME. THIS COULD NOT BE IT.
AND WE WAITED TOGETHER. AND MOMENTS TURNED TO MINUTES.
AND NO ONE CAME.
I STAYED UNTIL THE LAST POSSIBLE MOMENT, BUT I WASN'T ALLOWED TO SEE IT THROUGH.
I HAD TO LET HIM GO. I FAILED HIM.
IN THE END, I HAD NO ANSWER FOR LARRY KLOOCK.
JUST A BIGGER SET OF QUESTIONS THAN I STARTED WITH.

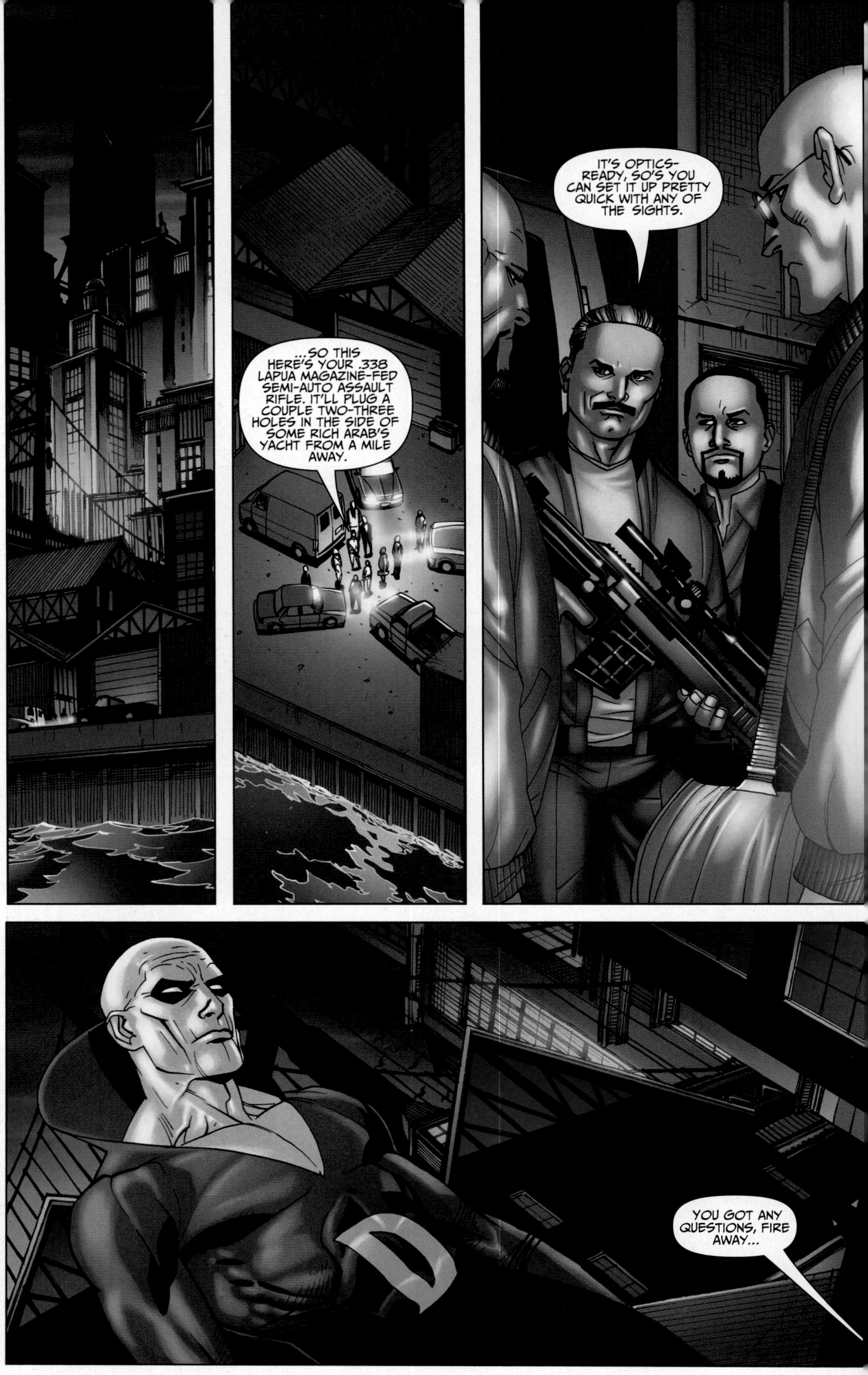
...SO THIS HERE'S YOUR .338 LAPUA MAGAZINE-FED SEMI-AUTO ASSAULT RIFLE. IT'LL PLUG A COUPLE TWO-THREE HOLES IN THE SIDE OF SOME RICH ARAB'S YACHT FROM A MILE AWAY.
IT'S OPTICS-READY, SO'S YOU CAN SET IT UP PRETTY QUICK WITH ANY OF THE SIGHTS.
YOU GOT ANY QUESTIONS, FIRE AWAY...

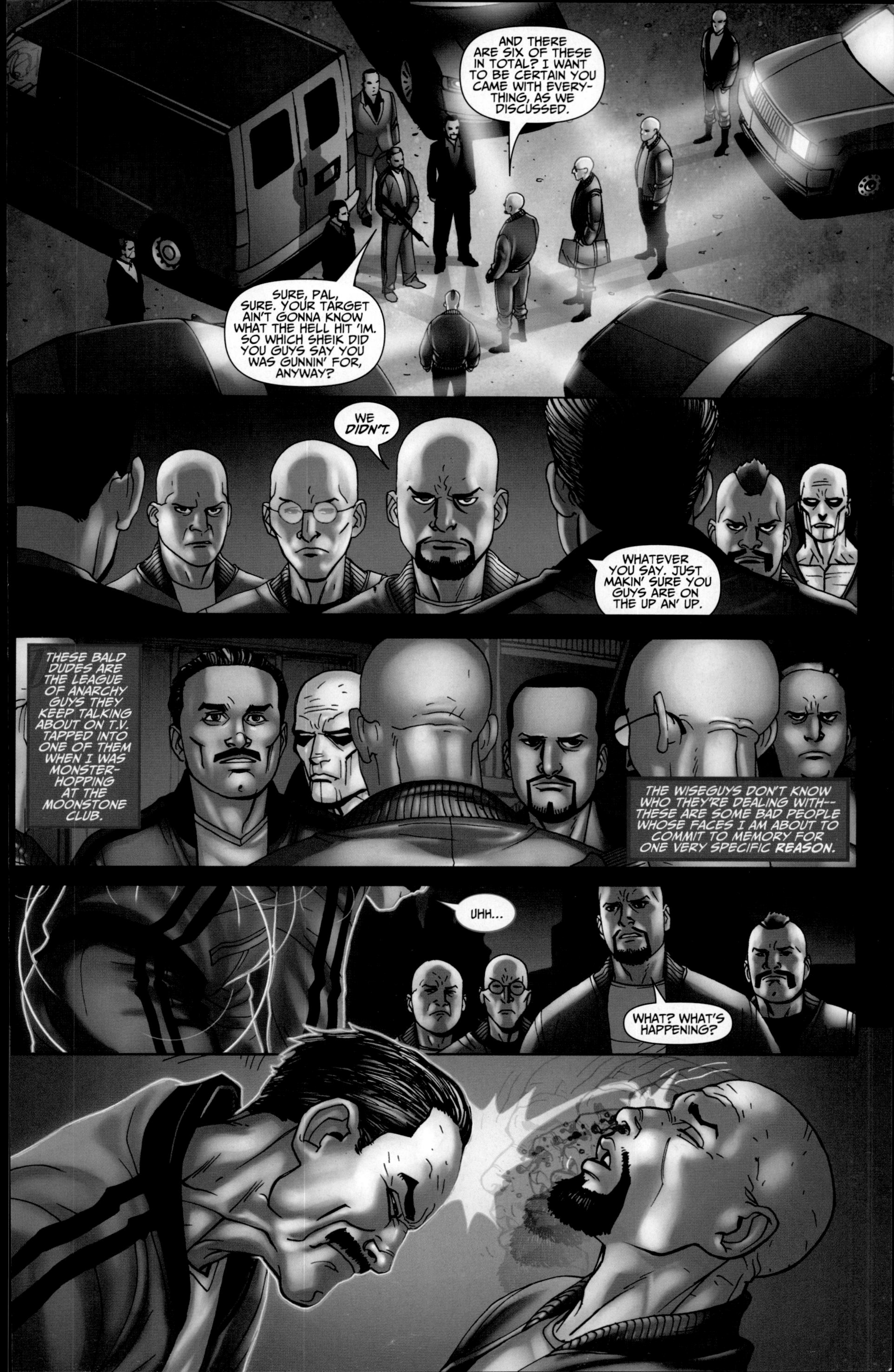
AND THERE ARE SIX OF THESE IN TOTAL? I WANT TO BE CERTAIN YOU CAME WITH EVERY-THING, AS WE DISCUSSED.
SURE, PAL, SURE. YOUR TARGET AIN'T GONNA KNOW WHAT THE HELL HIT 'IM. SO WHICH SHEIK DID YOU GUYS SAY YOU WAS GUNNIN' FOR, ANYWAY?
WE *DIDN'T.*
WHATEVER YOU SAY. JUST MAKIN' SURE YOU GUYS ARE ON THE UP AN' UP.
THESE BALD DUDES ARE THE LEAGUE OF ANARCHY GUYS THEY KEEP TALKING ABOUT ON T.V. TAPPED INTO ONE OF THEM WHEN I WAS MONSTER-HOPPING AT THE MOONSTONE CLUB.
THE WISEGUYS DON'T KNOW WHO THEY'RE DEALING WITH-- THESE ARE SOME BAD PEOPLE WHOSE FACES I AM ABOUT TO COMMIT TO MEMORY FOR ONE VERY SPECIFIC **REASON.**
UHH...
WHAT? WHAT'S HAPPENING?

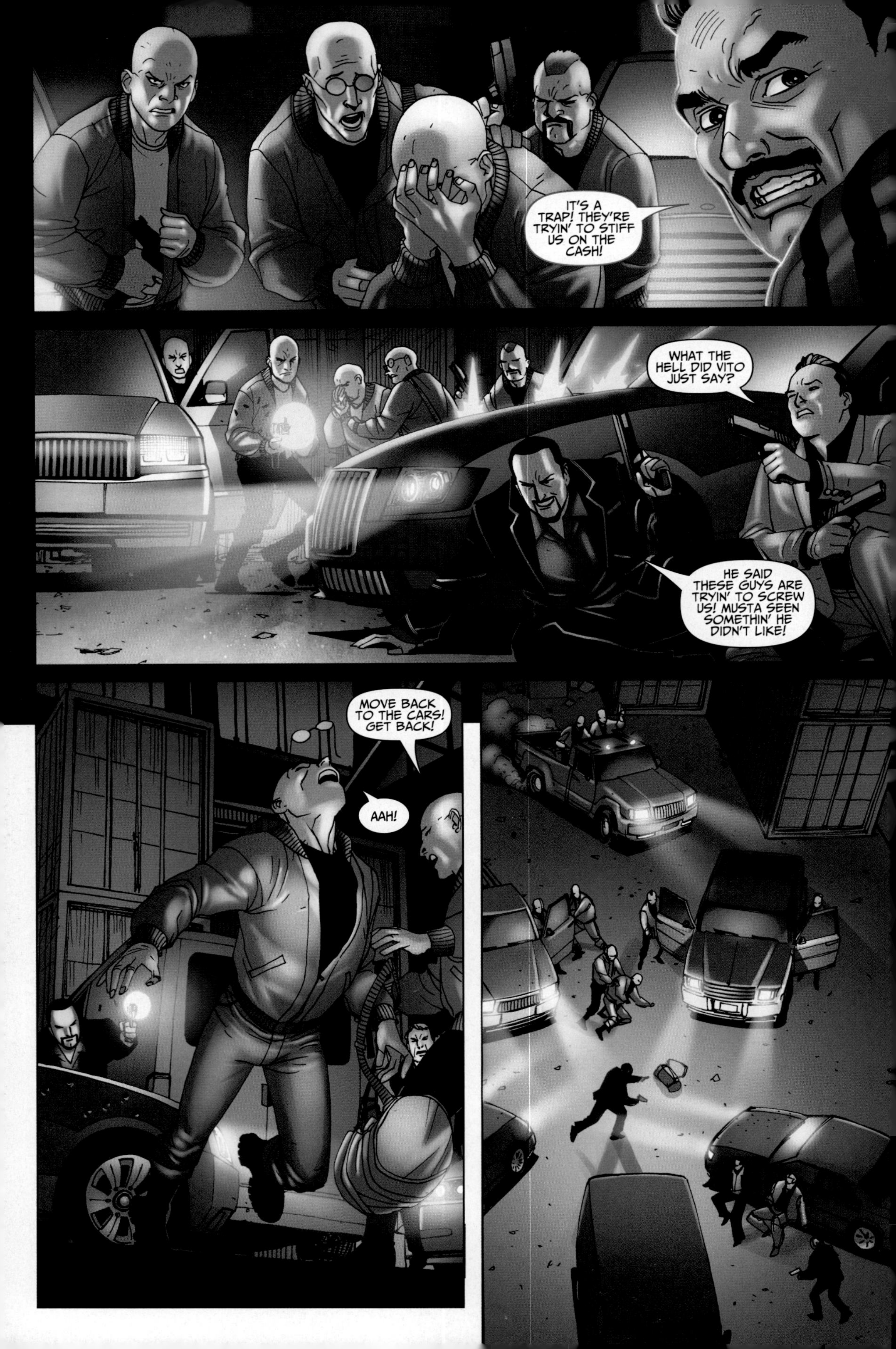
IT'S A TRAP! THEY'RE TRYIN' TO STIFF US ON THE CASH!
WHAT THE HELL DID VITO JUST SAY?
HE SAID THESE GUYS ARE TRYIN' TO SCREW US! MUSTA SEEN SOMETHIN' HE DIDN'T LIKE!
MOVE BACK TO THE CARS! GET BACK!
AAH!

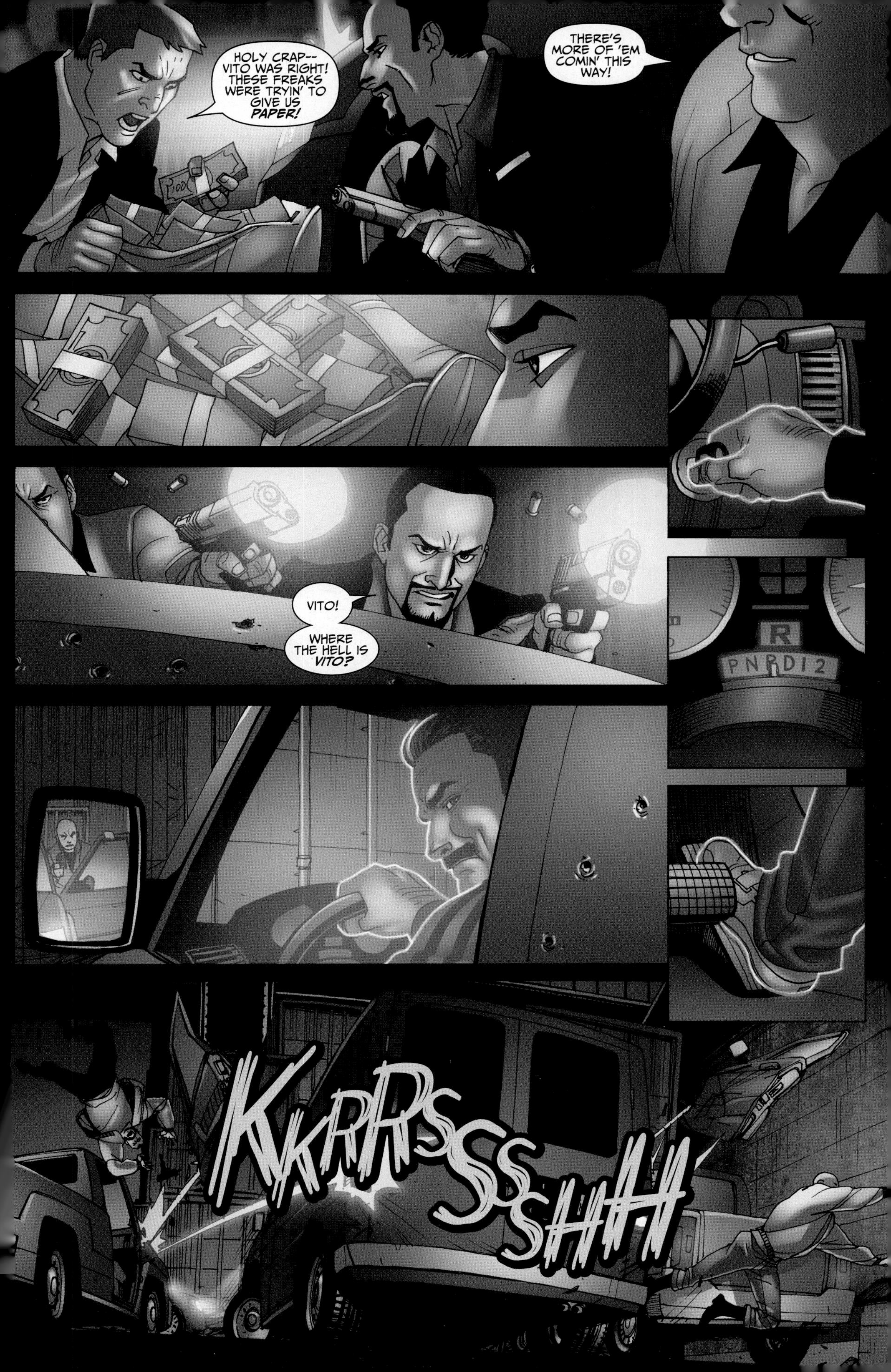
HOLY CRAP-- VITO WAS RIGHT! THESE FREAKS WERE TRYIN' TO GIVE US PAPER!
THERE'S MORE OF 'EM COMIN' THIS WAY!
VITO!
WHERE THE HELL IS VITO?
KRRSSSHH

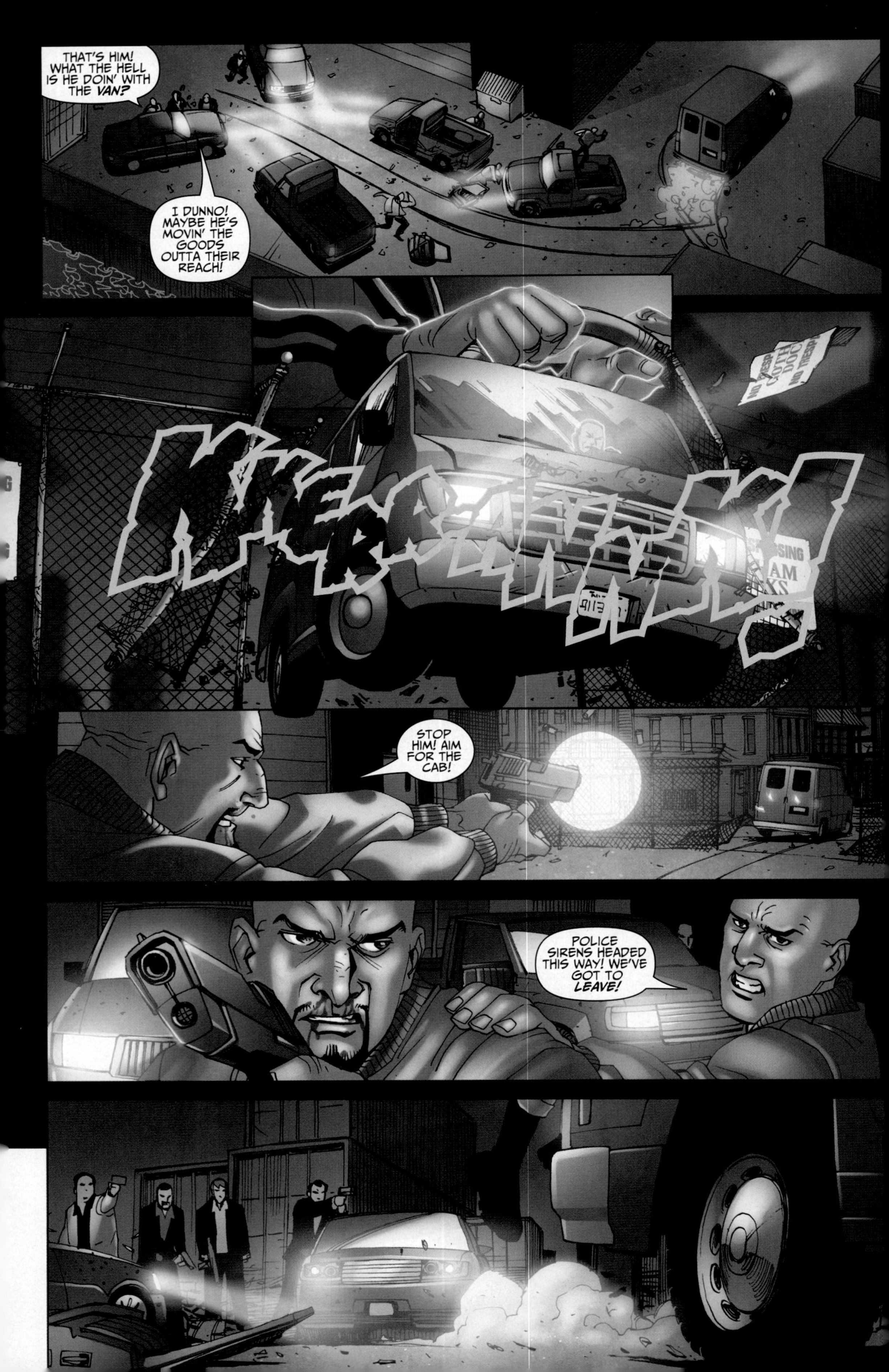
THAT'S HIM! WHAT THE HELL IS HE DOIN' WITH THE VAN?
I DUNNO! MAYBE HE'S MOVIN' THE GOODS OUTTA THEIR REACH!
STOP HIM! AIM FOR THE CAB!
POLICE SIRENS HEADED THIS WAY! WE'VE GOT TO LEAVE!

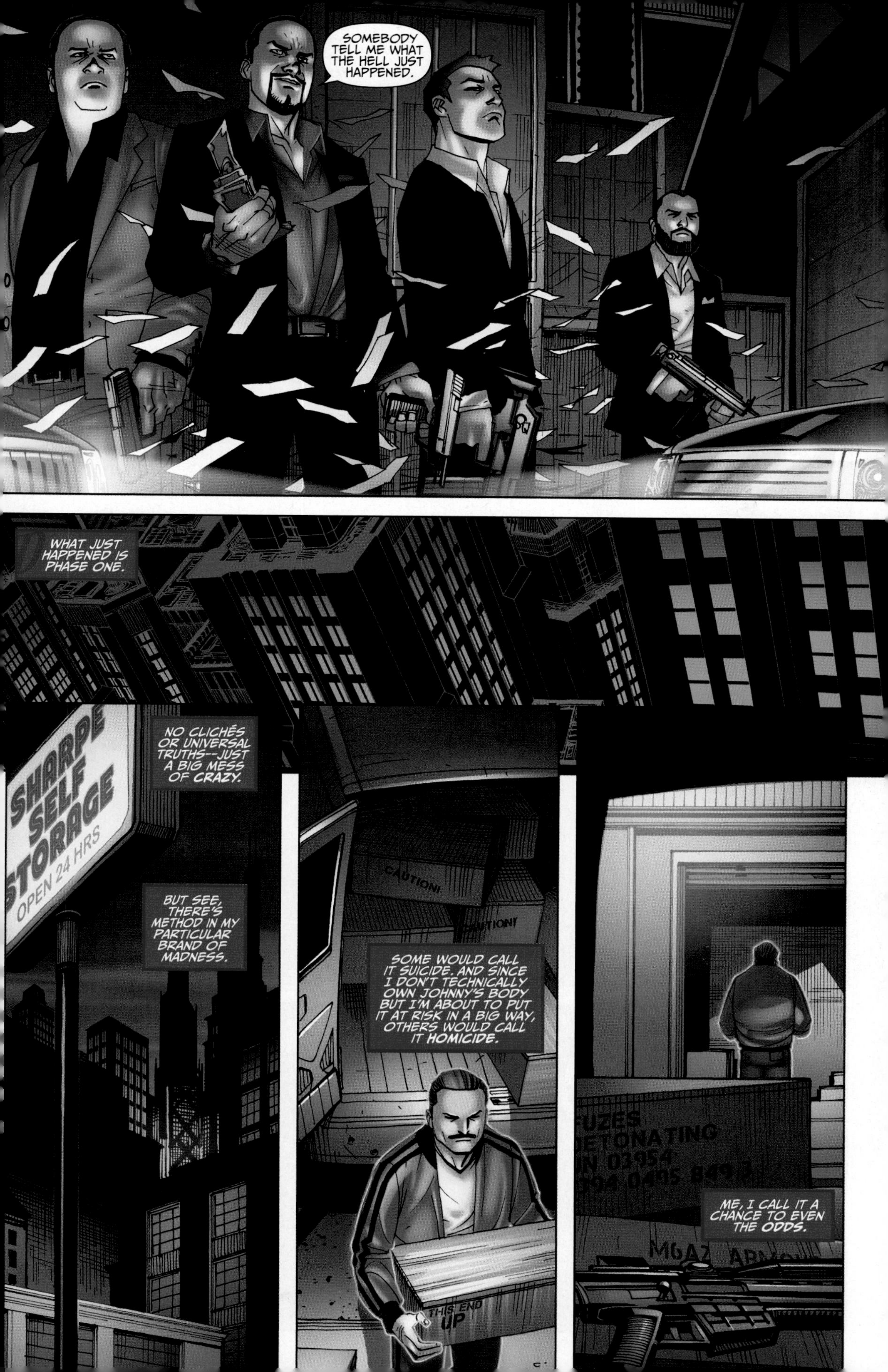
SOMEBODY TELL ME WHAT THE HELL JUST HAPPENED.
WHAT JUST HAPPENED IS PHASE ONE.
SHARPE SELF STORAGE
OPEN 24 HRS
NO CLICHÉS OR UNIVERSAL TRUTHS--JUST A BIG MESS OF CRAZY.
BUT SEE, THERE'S METHOD IN MY PARTICULAR BRAND OF MADNESS.
CAUTION!
CAUTION!
SOME WOULD CALL IT SUICIDE. AND SINCE I DON'T TECHNICALLY OWN JOHNNY'S BODY BUT I'M ABOUT TO PUT IT AT RISK IN A BIG WAY, OTHERS WOULD CALL IT HOMICIDE.
THIS END UP
ME, I CALL IT A CHANCE TO EVEN THE ODDS.

IF I'M GOING TO SOLVE JOHNNY'S PROBLEM, I'LL HAVE TO SOLVE THE BIGGER PROBLEM AS WELL.

GOTHAM FUN PARK

FUNNEST PLACE ON EARTH

LOVERS LANE

TICKETS

I HAVE BUSINESS TO CONCLUDE INVOLVING RAMA, MYSELF, AND A LARGE NUMBER OF PEOPLE TO WHOM I HAVE BECOME PSYCHICALLY CONNECTED-- JOHNNY INCLUDED.

I NEED TO OUTWIT A GOD. AND THE ONE PERSON WHO CAN HELP ME WILL PROBABLY ASK FOR MY MORTAL SOUL AS PAYMENT.

THE SON OF MORNING. I HEAR HE'S EXPECTING ME.

I DON'T THINK IT'S A COINCIDENCE THAT I WAS HERE JUST A COUPLE OF DAYS AGO.

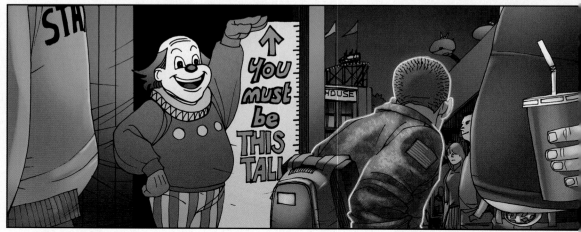

YOU must be THIS TALL

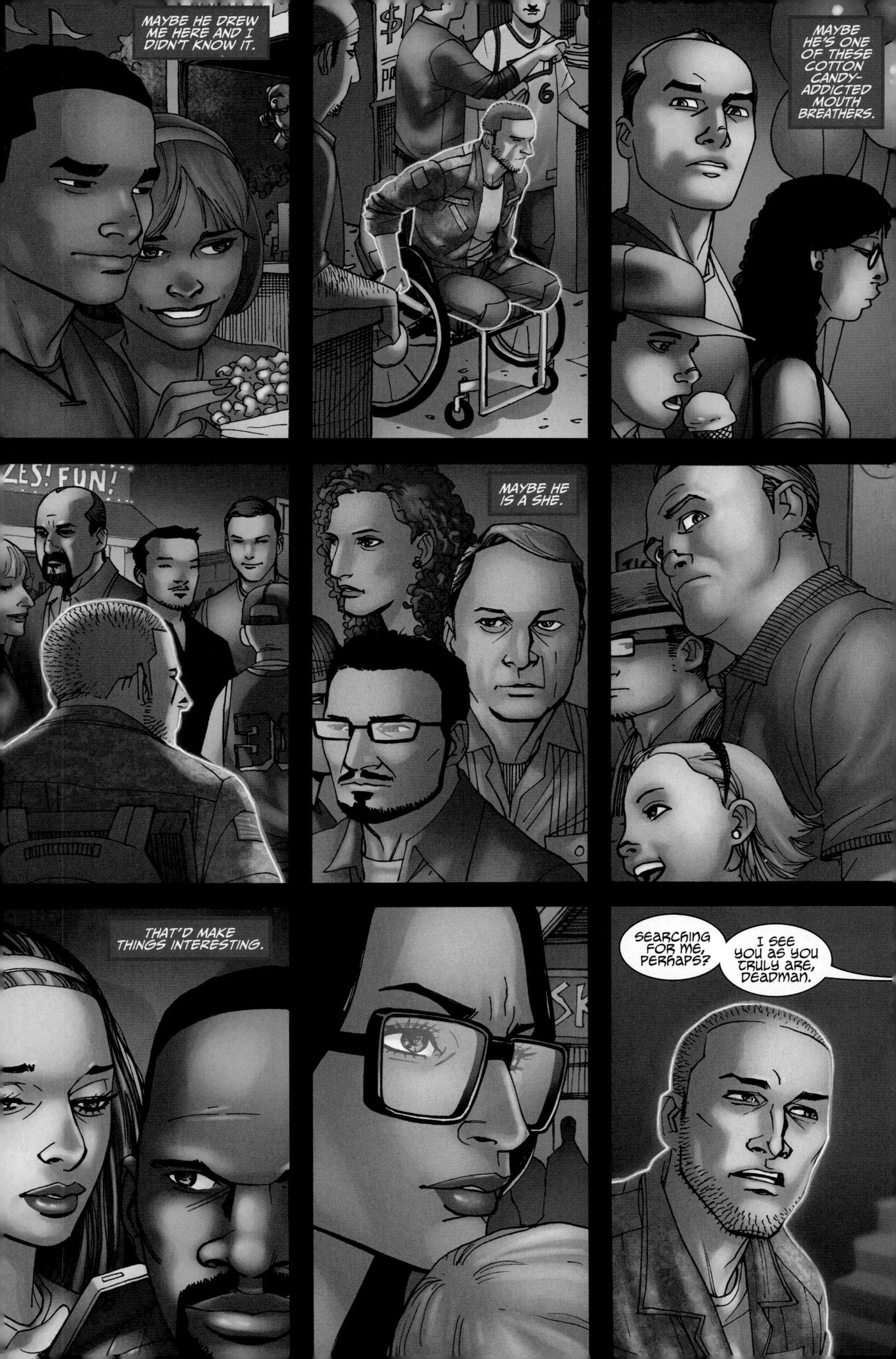
MAYBE HE DREW ME HERE AND I DIDN'T KNOW IT.
MAYBE HE'S ONE OF THESE COTTON CANDY-ADDICTED MOUTH BREATHERS.
ZES! FUN!
MAYBE HE IS A SHE.
THAT'D MAKE THINGS INTERESTING.
SEARCHING FOR ME, PERHAPS?
I SEE YOU AS YOU TRULY ARE, DEADMAN.

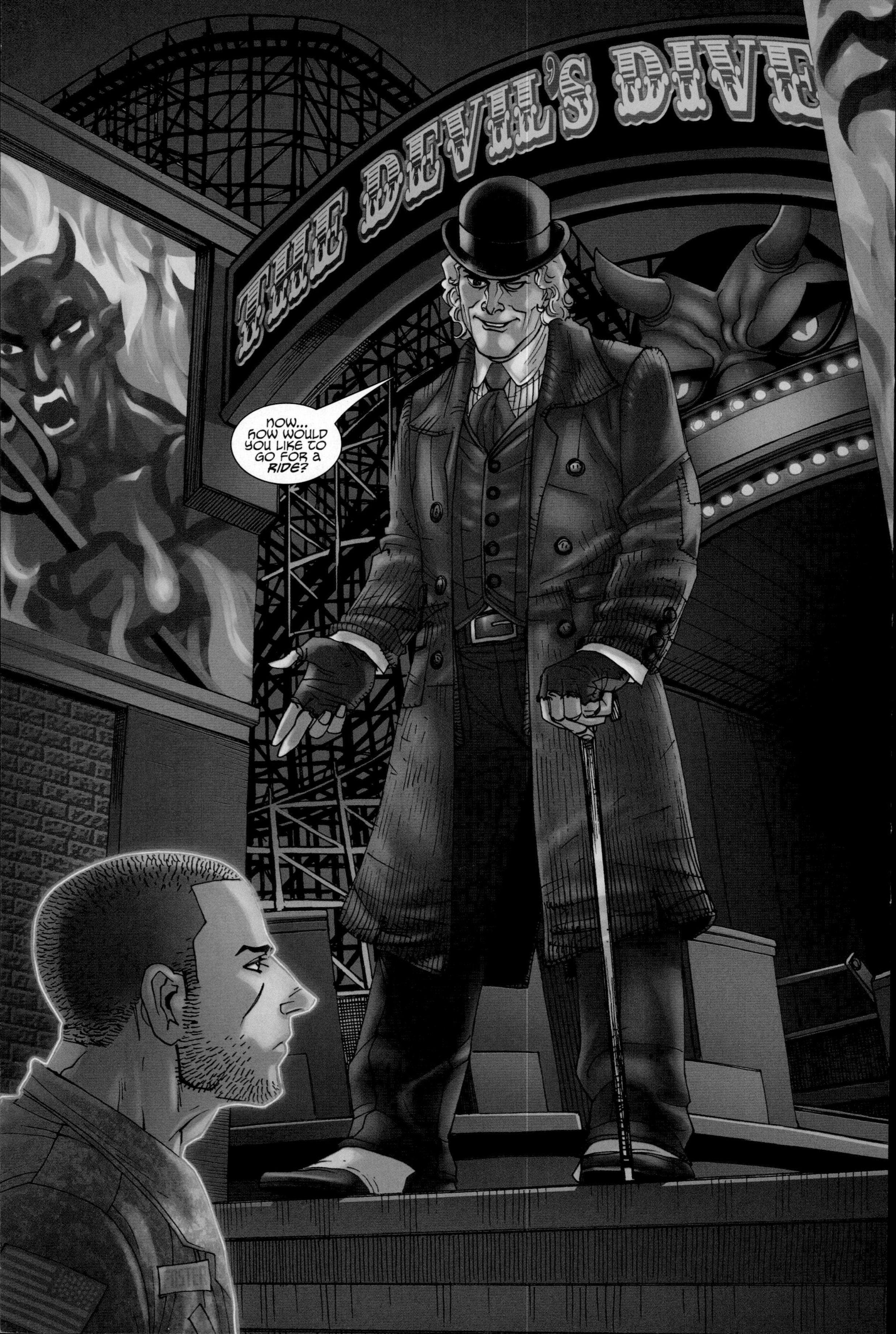
THE DEVIL'S DIVE
NOW... HOW WOULD YOU LIKE TO GO FOR A *RIDE?*

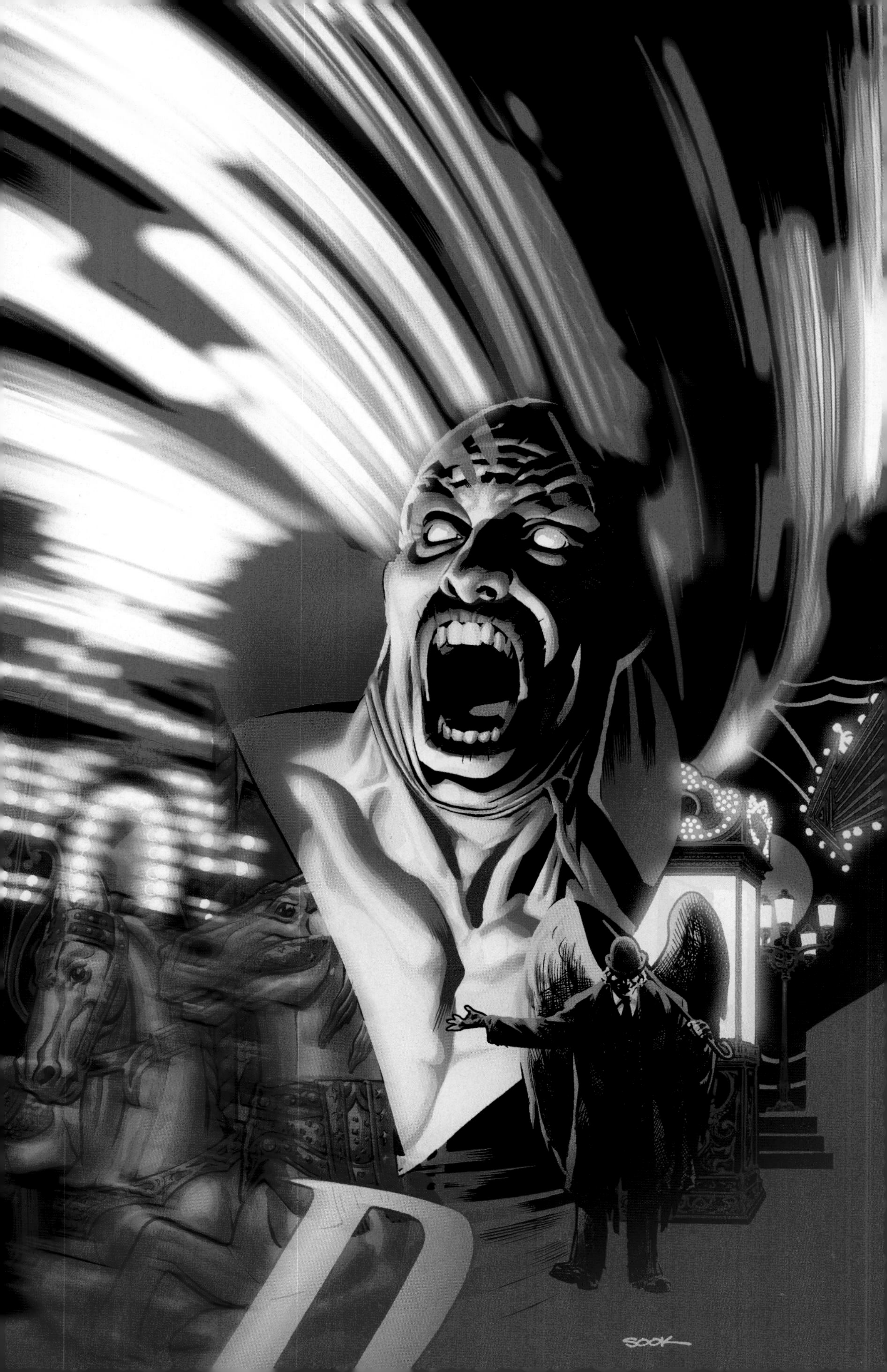
SOOK

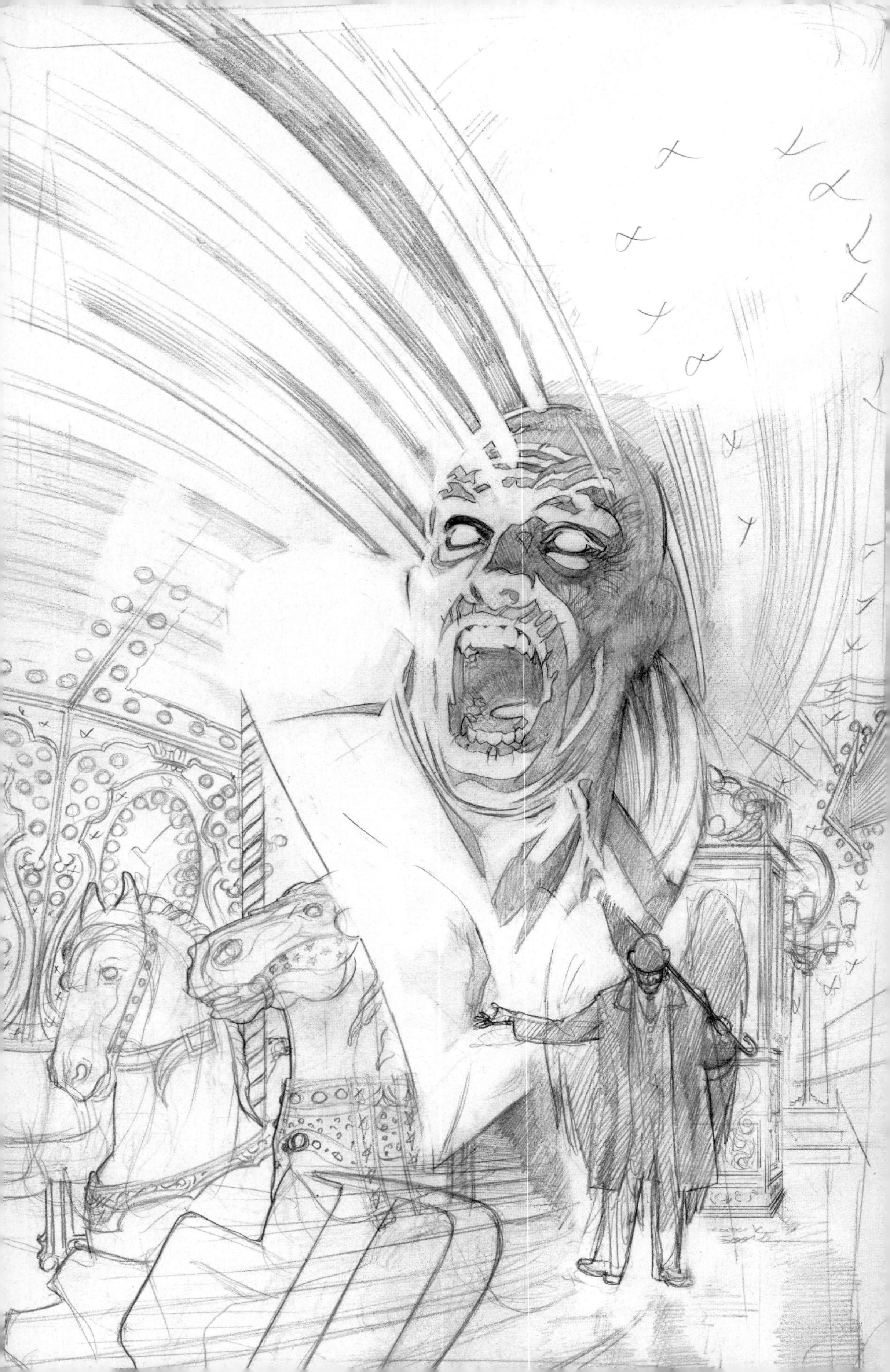

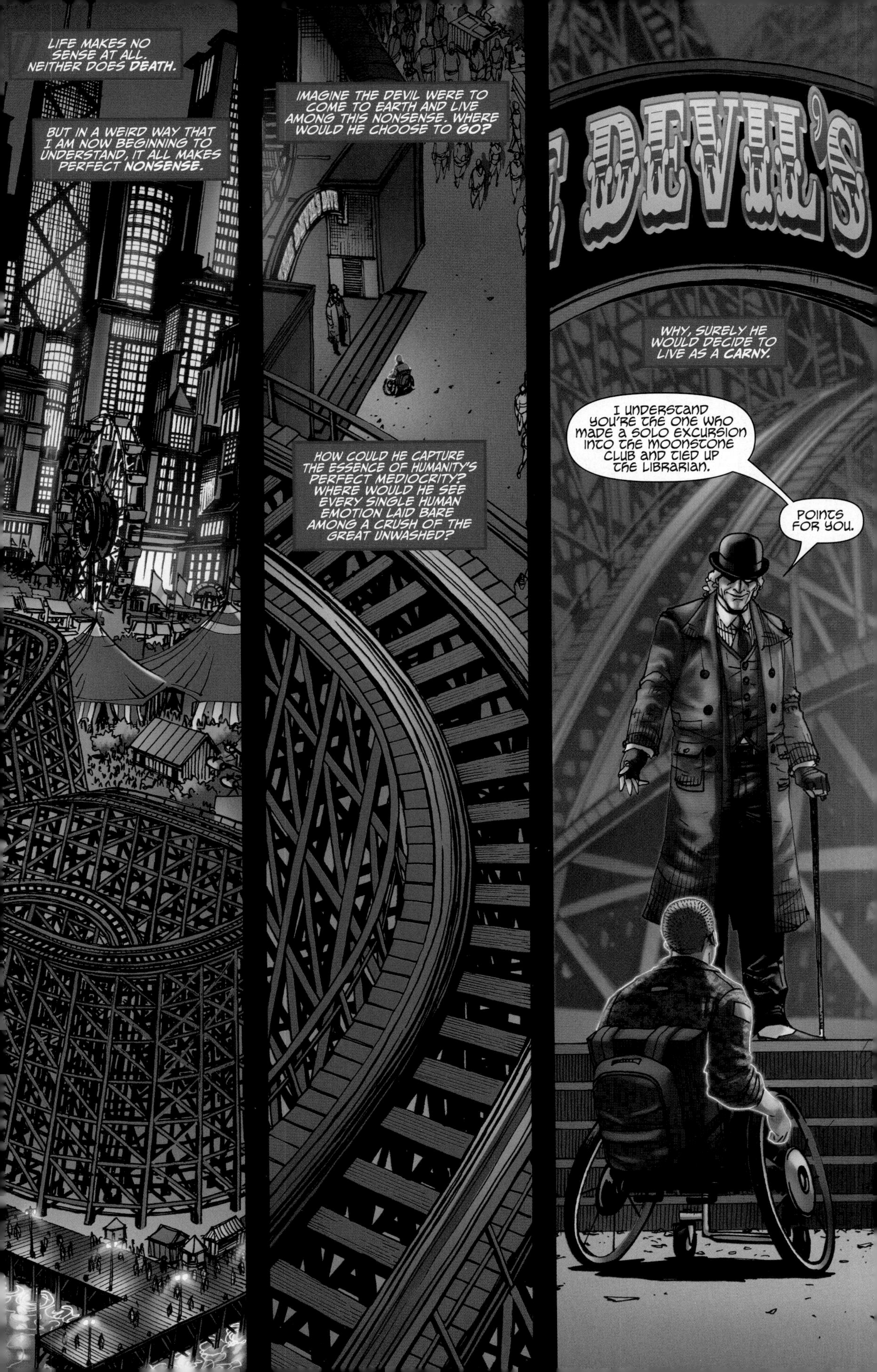
LIFE MAKES NO SENSE AT ALL. NEITHER DOES DEATH.
BUT IN A WEIRD WAY THAT I AM NOW BEGINNING TO UNDERSTAND, IT ALL MAKES PERFECT NONSENSE.
IMAGINE THE DEVIL WERE TO COME TO EARTH AND LIVE AMONG THIS NONSENSE. WHERE WOULD HE CHOOSE TO GO?
HOW COULD HE CAPTURE THE ESSENCE OF HUMANITY'S PERFECT MEDIOCRITY? WHERE WOULD HE SEE EVERY SINGLE HUMAN EMOTION LAID BARE AMONG A CRUSH OF THE GREAT UNWASHED?
DEVIL'S
WHY, SURELY HE WOULD DECIDE TO LIVE AS A CARNY.
I UNDERSTAND YOU'RE THE ONE WHO MADE A SOLO EXCURSION INTO THE MOONSTONE CLUB AND TIED UP THE LIBRARIAN.
POINTS FOR YOU.

YEAH, WELL... I MIGHT PAY FOR THAT. SPEAKING OF WHICH, HOW MUCH IS THIS GOING TO COST ME, ASSUMING YOU'RE WHO I THINK YOU ARE?

THE SON OF MORNING, YES.

WHY DON'T YOU LET THE BOY GO FOR A WHILE AND WE'LL DISCUSS?

WHAT THE HELL--?

YOU WERE JUST TELLING ME HOW FORGETFUL YOU ARE SINCE YOUR HEAD INJURY, JOHNNY. HOWEVER, YOU ENJOYED YOUR RIDE ON OUR ROLLER COASTER.

THIS IS YOUR CHANGE. YOU MAY SPEND IT IN THE FAIRGROUND AND BE BACK IN TWENTY MINUTES, THERE'S A GOOD BOY.

SURE... THANKS AGAIN, MISTER.

MY PLEASURE. DON'T FORGET TO TELL YOUR FRIENDS.

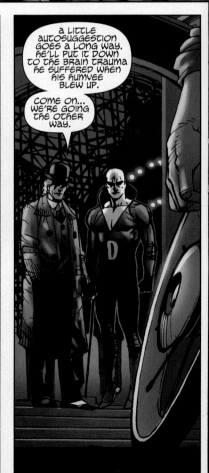

A LITTLE AUTOSUGGESTION GOES A LONG WAY. HE'LL PUT IT DOWN TO THE BRAIN TRAUMA HE SUFFERED WHEN HIS HUMVEE BLEW UP.

COME ON... WE'RE GOING THE OTHER WAY.

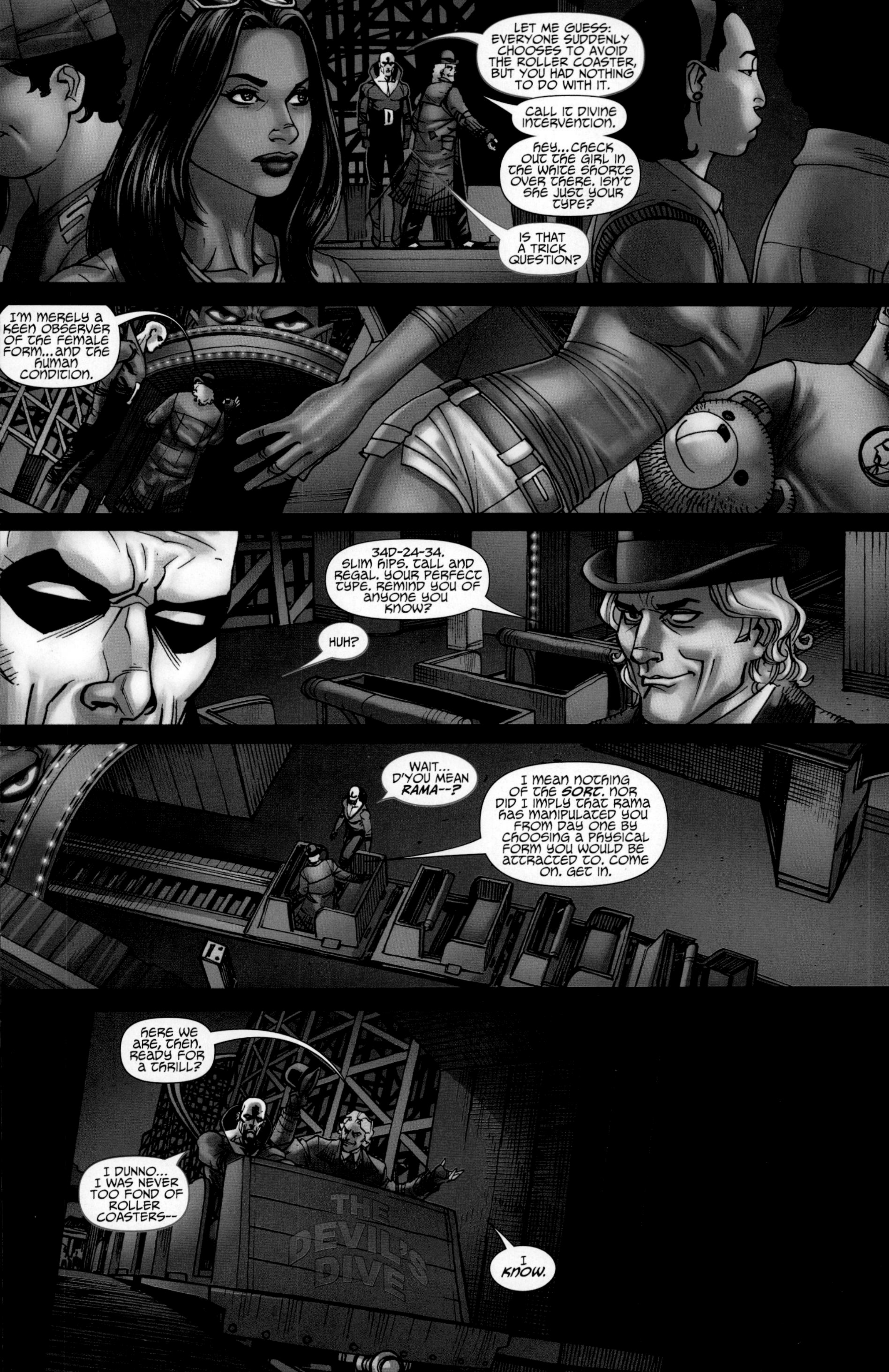
LET ME GUESS: EVERYONE SUDDENLY CHOOSES TO AVOID THE ROLLER COASTER, BUT YOU HAD NOTHING TO DO WITH IT.
CALL IT DIVINE INTERVENTION.
HEY...CHECK OUT THE GIRL IN THE WHITE SHORTS OVER THERE. ISN'T SHE JUST YOUR TYPE?
IS THAT A TRICK QUESTION?
I'M MERELY A KEEN OBSERVER OF THE FEMALE FORM...AND THE HUMAN CONDITION.
34D-24-34. SLIM HIPS. TALL AND REGAL. YOUR PERFECT TYPE. REMIND YOU OF ANYONE YOU KNOW?
HUH?
WAIT... D'YOU MEAN *RAMA--?*
I MEAN NOTHING OF THE *SORT*. NOR DID I IMPLY THAT RAMA HAS MANIPULATED YOU FROM DAY ONE BY CHOOSING A PHYSICAL FORM YOU WOULD BE ATTRACTED TO. COME ON. GET IN.
HERE WE ARE, THEN. READY FOR A THRILL?
I DUNNO... I WAS NEVER TOO FOND OF ROLLER COASTERS--
THE DEVIL'S DIVE
I *KNOW.*

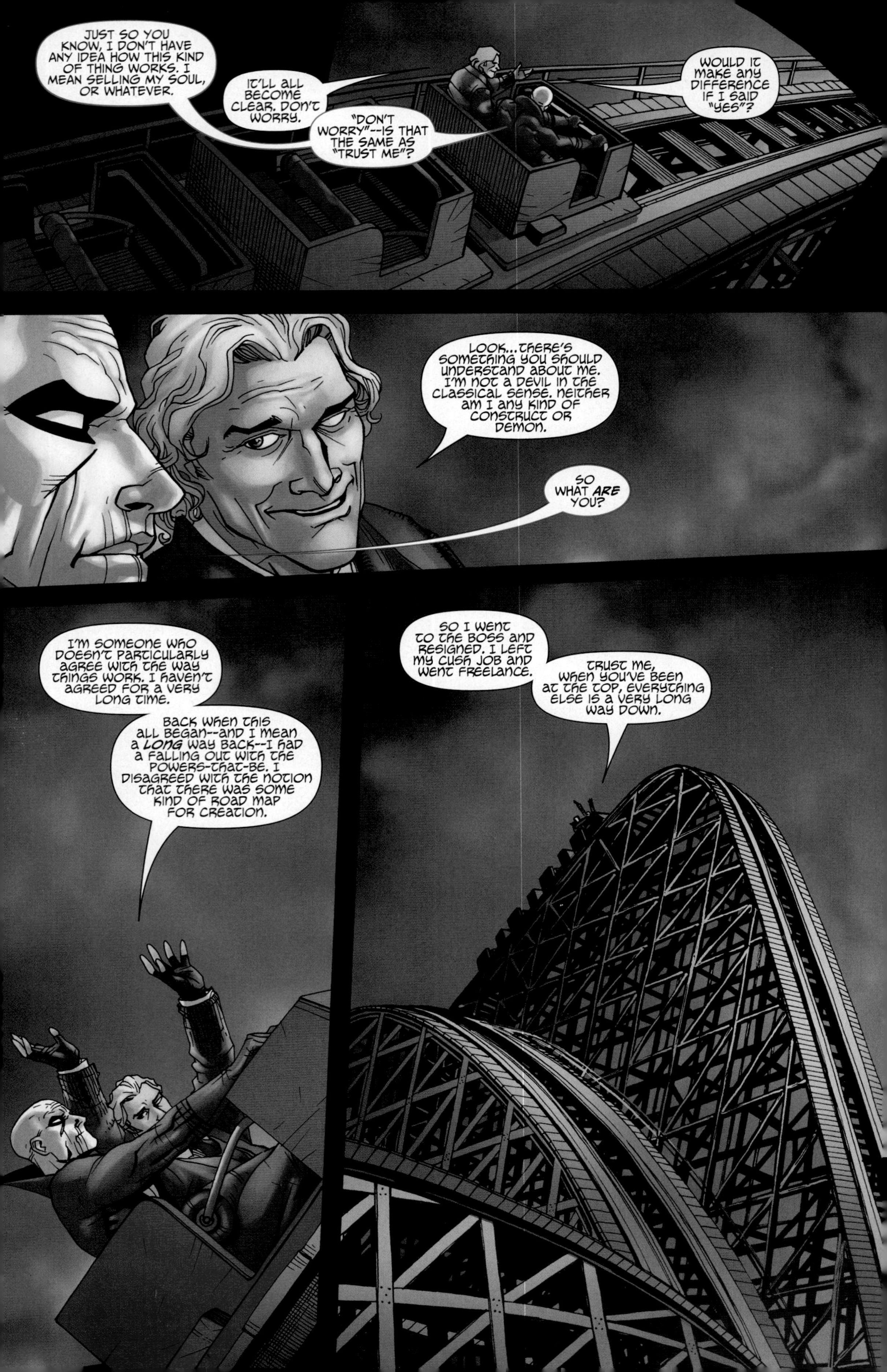
JUST SO YOU KNOW, I DON'T HAVE ANY IDEA HOW THIS KIND OF THING WORKS. I MEAN SELLING MY SOUL, OR WHATEVER.
IT'LL ALL BECOME CLEAR. DON'T WORRY.
"DON'T WORRY"--IS THAT THE SAME AS "TRUST ME"?
WOULD IT MAKE ANY DIFFERENCE IF I SAID "YES"?
LOOK...THERE'S SOMETHING YOU SHOULD UNDERSTAND ABOUT ME. I'M NOT A DEVIL IN THE CLASSICAL SENSE. NEITHER AM I ANY KIND OF CONSTRUCT OR DEMON.
SO WHAT ARE YOU?
I'M SOMEONE WHO DOESN'T PARTICULARLY AGREE WITH THE WAY THINGS WORK. I HAVEN'T AGREED FOR A VERY LONG TIME.
BACK WHEN THIS ALL BEGAN--AND I MEAN A LONG WAY BACK--I HAD A FALLING OUT WITH THE POWERS-THAT-BE. I DISAGREED WITH THE NOTION THAT THERE WAS SOME KIND OF ROAD MAP FOR CREATION.
SO I WENT TO THE BOSS AND RESIGNED. I LEFT MY CUSH JOB AND WENT FREELANCE.
TRUST ME, WHEN YOU'VE BEEN AT THE TOP, EVERYTHING ELSE IS A VERY LONG WAY DOWN.

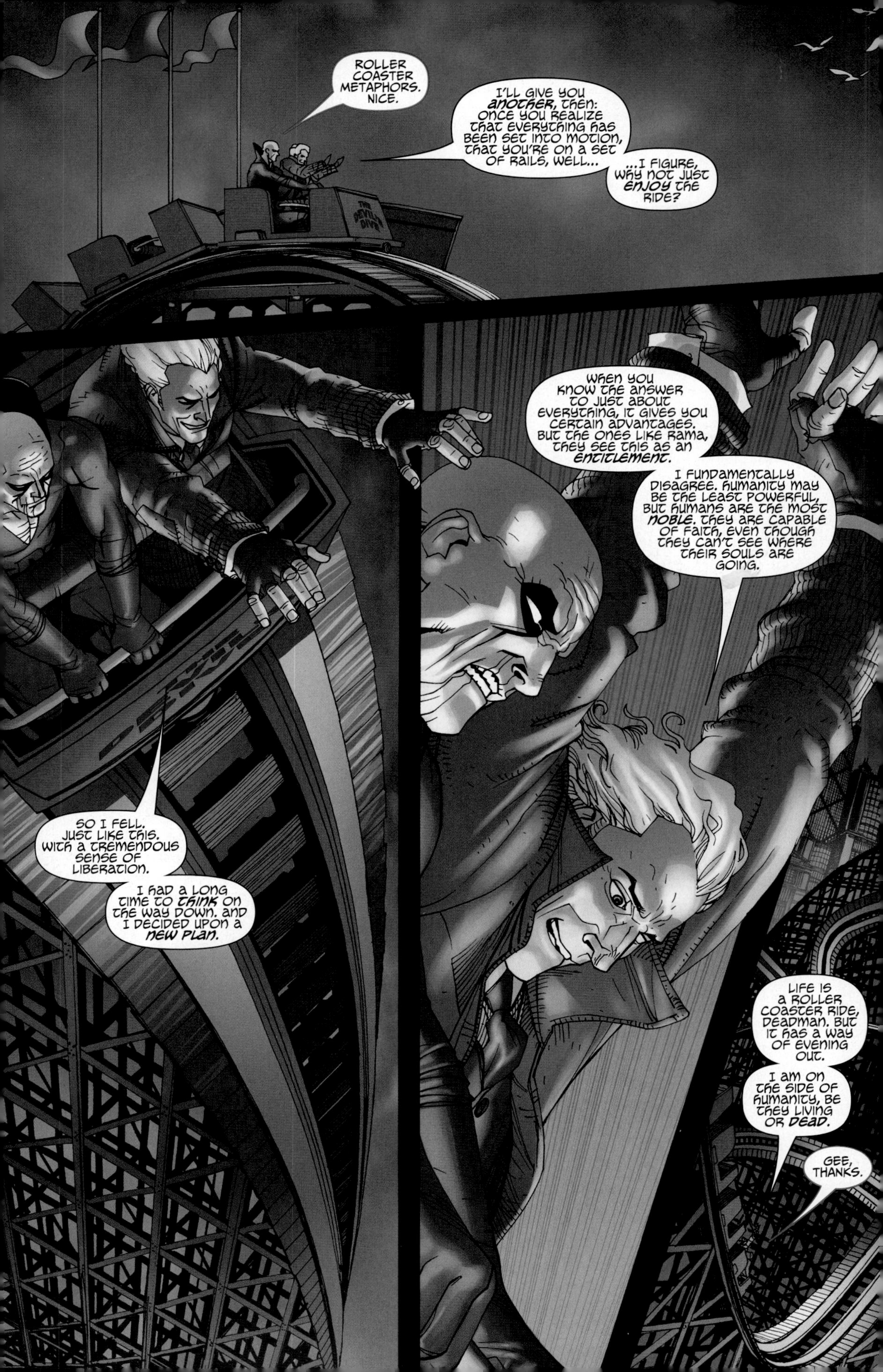
ROLLER COASTER METAPHORS. NICE.
I'LL GIVE YOU *ANOTHER*, THEN: ONCE YOU REALIZE THAT EVERYTHING HAS BEEN SET INTO MOTION, THAT YOU'RE ON A SET OF RAILS, WELL...
...I FIGURE, WHY NOT JUST *ENJOY* THE RIDE?
SO I FELL. JUST LIKE THIS. WITH A TREMENDOUS SENSE OF LIBERATION.
I HAD A LONG TIME TO *THINK* ON THE WAY DOWN, AND I DECIDED UPON A *NEW PLAN*.
WHEN YOU KNOW THE ANSWER TO JUST ABOUT EVERYTHING, IT GIVES YOU CERTAIN ADVANTAGES. BUT THE ONES LIKE RAMA, THEY SEE THIS AS AN *ENTITLEMENT*.
I FUNDAMENTALLY DISAGREE. HUMANITY MAY BE THE LEAST POWERFUL, BUT HUMANS ARE THE MOST *NOBLE*. THEY ARE CAPABLE OF FAITH, EVEN THOUGH THEY CAN'T SEE WHERE THEIR SOULS ARE GOING.
LIFE IS A ROLLER COASTER RIDE, DEADMAN. BUT IT HAS A WAY OF EVENING OUT.
I AM ON THE SIDE OF HUMANITY, BE THEY LIVING OR *DEAD*.
GEE, THANKS.

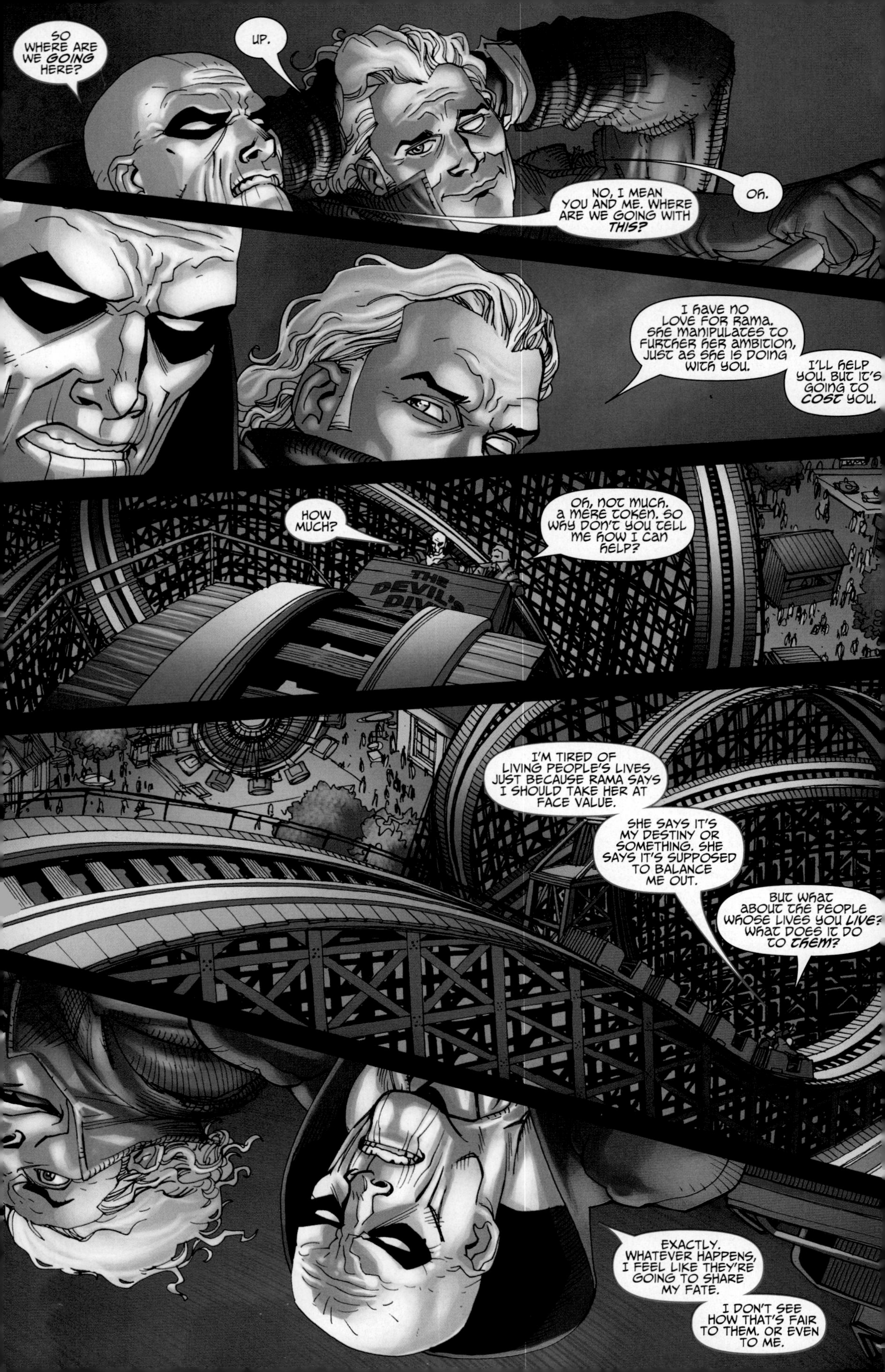
SO WHERE ARE WE GOING HERE?
UP.
NO, I MEAN YOU AND ME. WHERE ARE WE GOING WITH THIS?
OH.
I HAVE NO LOVE FOR RAMA. SHE MANIPULATES TO FURTHER HER AMBITION, JUST AS SHE IS DOING WITH YOU.
I'LL HELP YOU. BUT IT'S GOING TO COST YOU.
HOW MUCH?
OH, NOT MUCH. A MERE TOKEN. SO WHY DON'T YOU TELL ME HOW I CAN HELP?
THE DEVIL'S DIVE
I'M TIRED OF LIVING PEOPLE'S LIVES JUST BECAUSE RAMA SAYS I SHOULD TAKE HER AT FACE VALUE.
SHE SAYS IT'S MY DESTINY OR SOMETHING. SHE SAYS IT'S SUPPOSED TO BALANCE ME OUT.
BUT WHAT ABOUT THE PEOPLE WHOSE LIVES YOU LIVE? WHAT DOES IT DO TO THEM?
EXACTLY. WHATEVER HAPPENS, I FEEL LIKE THEY'RE GOING TO SHARE MY FATE.
I DON'T SEE HOW THAT'S FAIR TO THEM. OR EVEN TO ME.

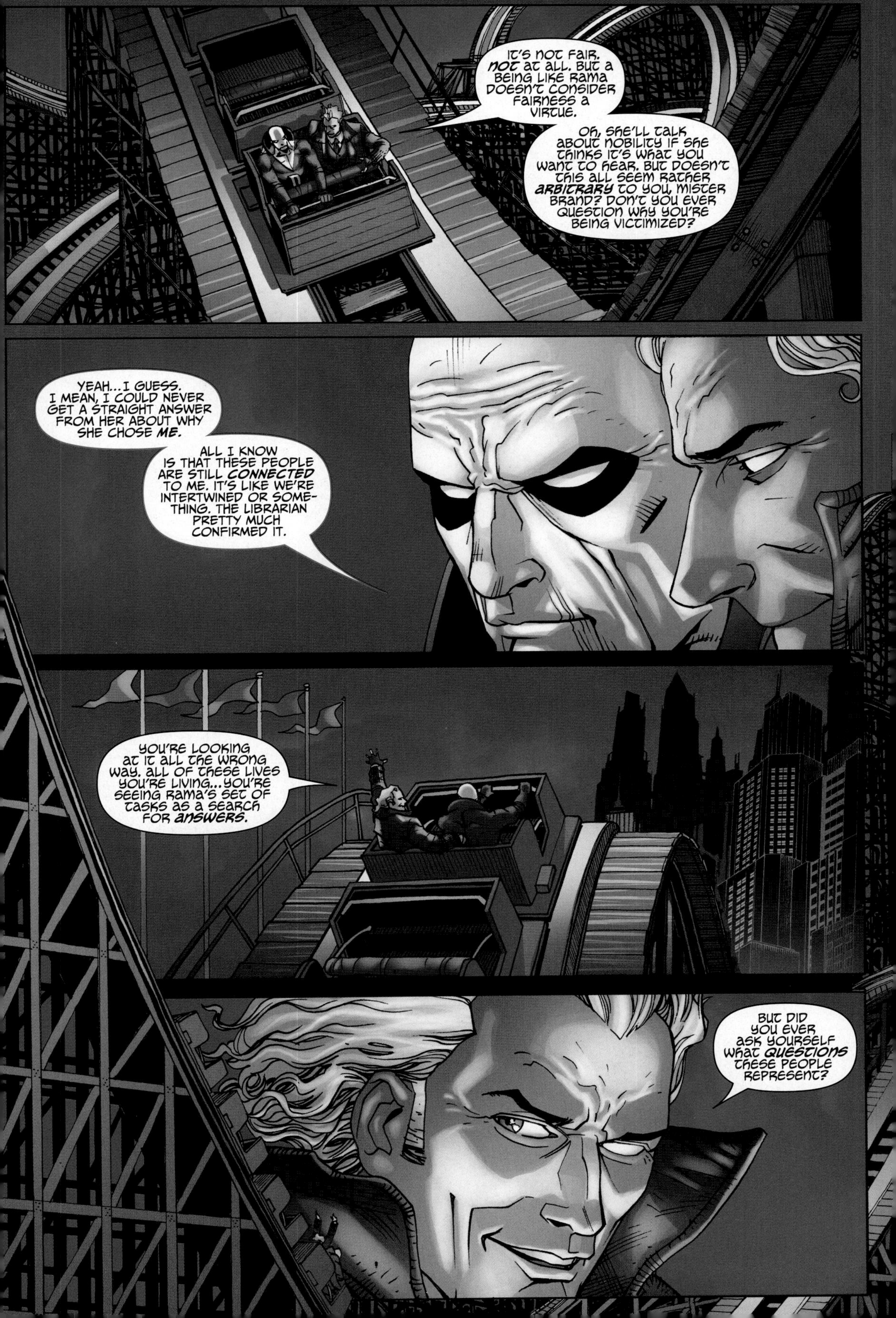
IT'S NOT FAIR. NOT AT ALL. BUT A BEING LIKE RAMA DOESN'T CONSIDER FAIRNESS A VIRTUE.
OH, SHE'LL TALK ABOUT NOBILITY IF SHE THINKS IT'S WHAT YOU WANT TO HEAR. BUT DOESN'T THIS ALL SEEM RATHER ARBITRARY TO YOU, MISTER BRAND? DON'T YOU EVER QUESTION WHY YOU'RE BEING VICTIMIZED?
YEAH...I GUESS. I MEAN, I COULD NEVER GET A STRAIGHT ANSWER FROM HER ABOUT WHY SHE CHOSE ME.
ALL I KNOW IS THAT THESE PEOPLE ARE STILL CONNECTED TO ME. IT'S LIKE WE'RE INTERTWINED OR SOME-THING. THE LIBRARIAN PRETTY MUCH CONFIRMED IT.
YOU'RE LOOKING AT IT ALL THE WRONG WAY. ALL OF THESE LIVES YOU'RE LIVING...YOU'RE SEEING RAMA'S SET OF TASKS AS A SEARCH FOR ANSWERS.
BUT DID YOU EVER ASK YOURSELF WHAT QUESTIONS THESE PEOPLE REPRESENT?

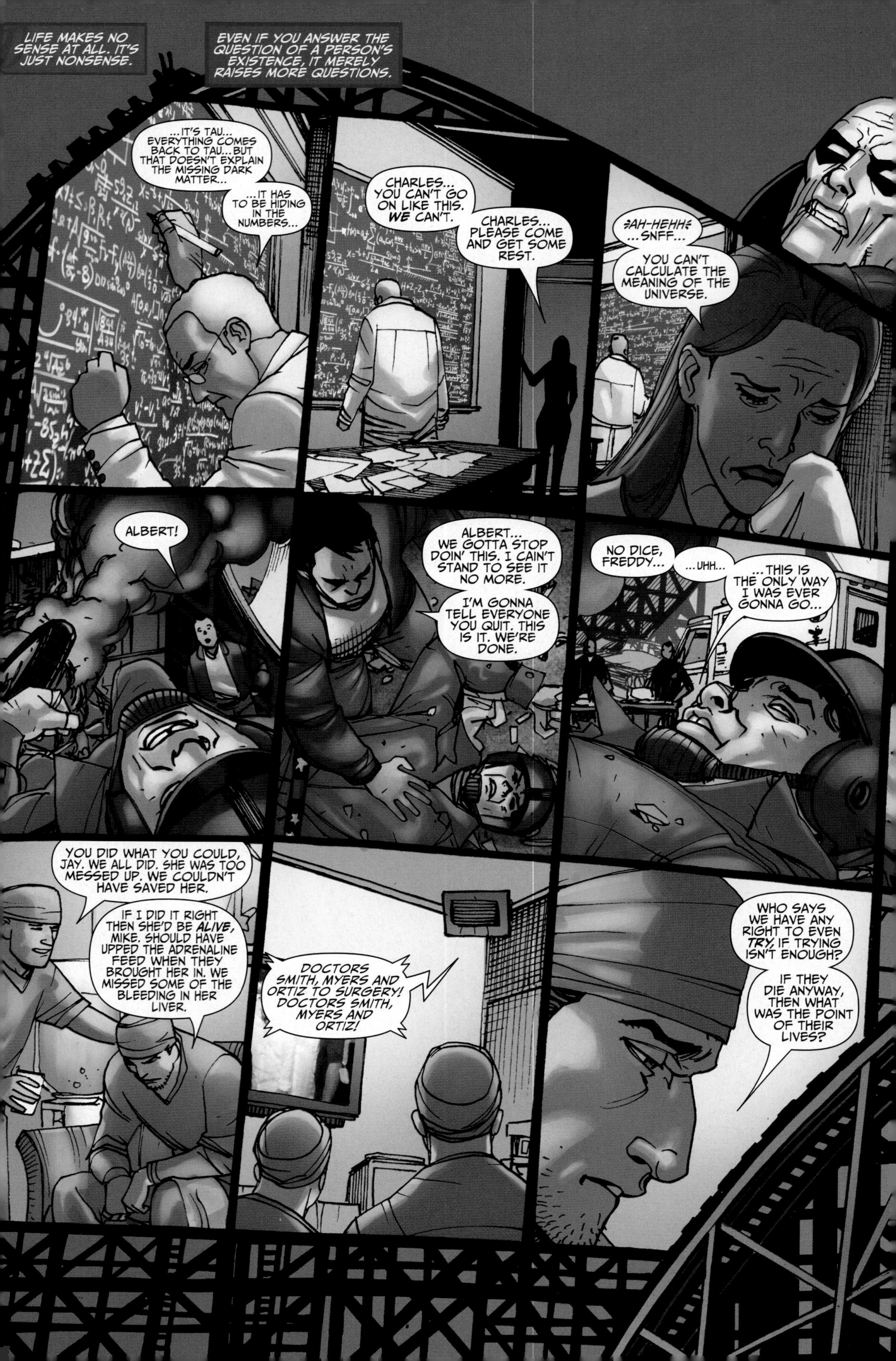
LIFE MAKES NO SENSE AT ALL. IT'S JUST NONSENSE.
EVEN IF YOU ANSWER THE QUESTION OF A PERSON'S EXISTENCE, IT MERELY RAISES MORE QUESTIONS.
...IT'S TAU... EVERYTHING COMES BACK TO TAU...BUT THAT DOESN'T EXPLAIN THE MISSING DARK MATTER...
...IT HAS TO BE HIDING IN THE NUMBERS...
CHARLES... YOU CAN'T GO ON LIKE THIS. WE CAN'T.
CHARLES... PLEASE COME AND GET SOME REST.
AH-HEHH ...SNFF...
YOU CAN'T CALCULATE THE MEANING OF THE UNIVERSE.
ALBERT!
ALBERT... WE GOTTA STOP DOIN' THIS. I CAIN'T STAND TO SEE IT NO MORE.
I'M GONNA TELL EVERYONE YOU QUIT. THIS IS IT. WE'RE DONE.
NO DICE, FREDDY...
...UHH...
...THIS IS THE ONLY WAY I WAS EVER GONNA GO...
YOU DID WHAT YOU COULD, JAY. WE ALL DID. SHE WAS TOO MESSED UP. WE COULDN'T HAVE SAVED HER.
IF I DID IT RIGHT THEN SHE'D BE ALIVE, MIKE. SHOULD HAVE UPPED THE ADRENALINE FEED WHEN THEY BROUGHT HER IN. WE MISSED SOME OF THE BLEEDING IN HER LIVER.
DOCTORS SMITH, MYERS AND ORTIZ TO SURGERY! DOCTORS SMITH, MYERS AND ORTIZ!
WHO SAYS WE HAVE ANY RIGHT TO EVEN TRY, IF TRYING ISN'T ENOUGH?
IF THEY DIE ANYWAY, THEN WHAT WAS THE POINT OF THEIR LIVES?

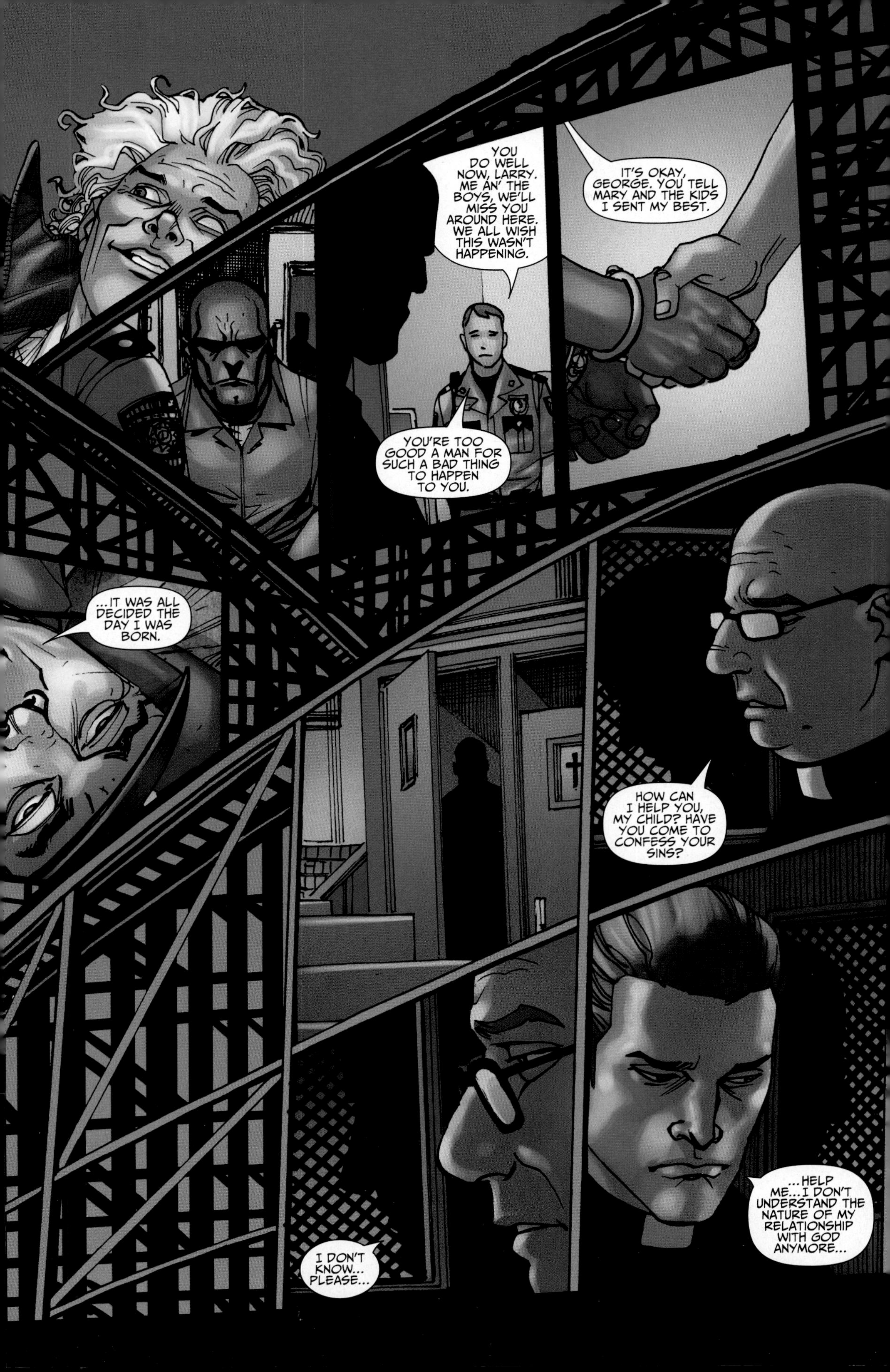
YOU DO WELL NOW, LARRY. ME AN' THE BOYS, WE'LL MISS YOU AROUND HERE. WE ALL WISH THIS WASN'T HAPPENING.
IT'S OKAY, GEORGE. YOU TELL MARY AND THE KIDS I SENT MY BEST.
YOU'RE TOO GOOD A MAN FOR SUCH A BAD THING TO HAPPEN TO YOU.
...IT WAS ALL DECIDED THE DAY I WAS BORN.
HOW CAN I HELP YOU, MY CHILD? HAVE YOU COME TO CONFESS YOUR SINS?
I DON'T KNOW... PLEASE...
...HELP ME...I DON'T UNDERSTAND THE NATURE OF MY RELATIONSHIP WITH GOD ANYMORE...

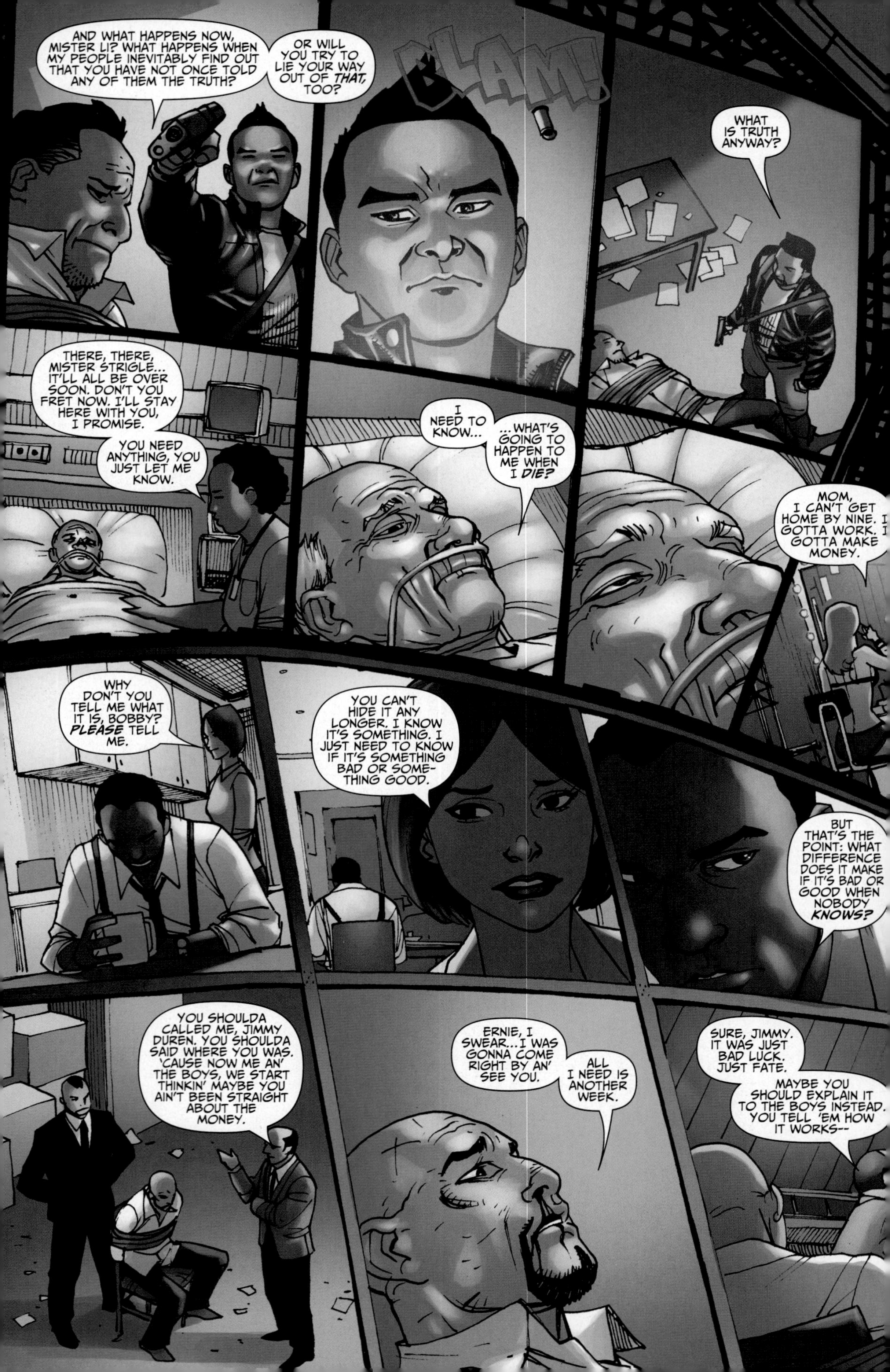

AND WHAT HAPPENS NOW, MISTER LI? WHAT HAPPENS WHEN MY PEOPLE INEVITABLY FIND OUT THAT YOU HAVE NOT ONCE TOLD ANY OF THEM THE TRUTH?
OR WILL YOU TRY TO LIE YOUR WAY OUT OF *THAT*, TOO?
BLAM!
WHAT IS TRUTH ANYWAY?
THERE, THERE, MISTER STRIGLE... IT'LL ALL BE OVER SOON. DON'T YOU FRET NOW. I'LL STAY HERE WITH YOU, I PROMISE.
YOU NEED ANYTHING, YOU JUST LET ME KNOW.
I NEED TO KNOW...
...WHAT'S GOING TO HAPPEN TO ME WHEN I *DIE?*
MOM, I CAN'T GET HOME BY NINE. I GOTTA WORK. I GOTTA MAKE MONEY.
WHY DON'T YOU TELL ME WHAT IT IS, BOBBY? ***PLEASE*** TELL ME.
YOU CAN'T HIDE IT ANY LONGER. I KNOW IT'S SOMETHING. I JUST NEED TO KNOW IF IT'S SOMETHING BAD OR SOMETHING GOOD.
BUT THAT'S THE POINT: WHAT DIFFERENCE DOES IT MAKE IF IT'S BAD OR GOOD WHEN NOBODY ***KNOWS?***
YOU SHOULDA CALLED ME, JIMMY DUREN. YOU SHOULDA SAID WHERE YOU WAS. 'CAUSE NOW ME AN' THE BOYS, WE START THINKIN' MAYBE YOU AIN'T BEEN STRAIGHT ABOUT THE MONEY.
ERNIE, I SWEAR...I WAS GONNA COME RIGHT BY AN' SEE YOU.
ALL I NEED IS ANOTHER WEEK.
SURE, JIMMY. IT WAS JUST BAD LUCK. JUST FATE.
MAYBE YOU SHOULD EXPLAIN IT TO THE BOYS INSTEAD. YOU TELL 'EM HOW IT WORKS--

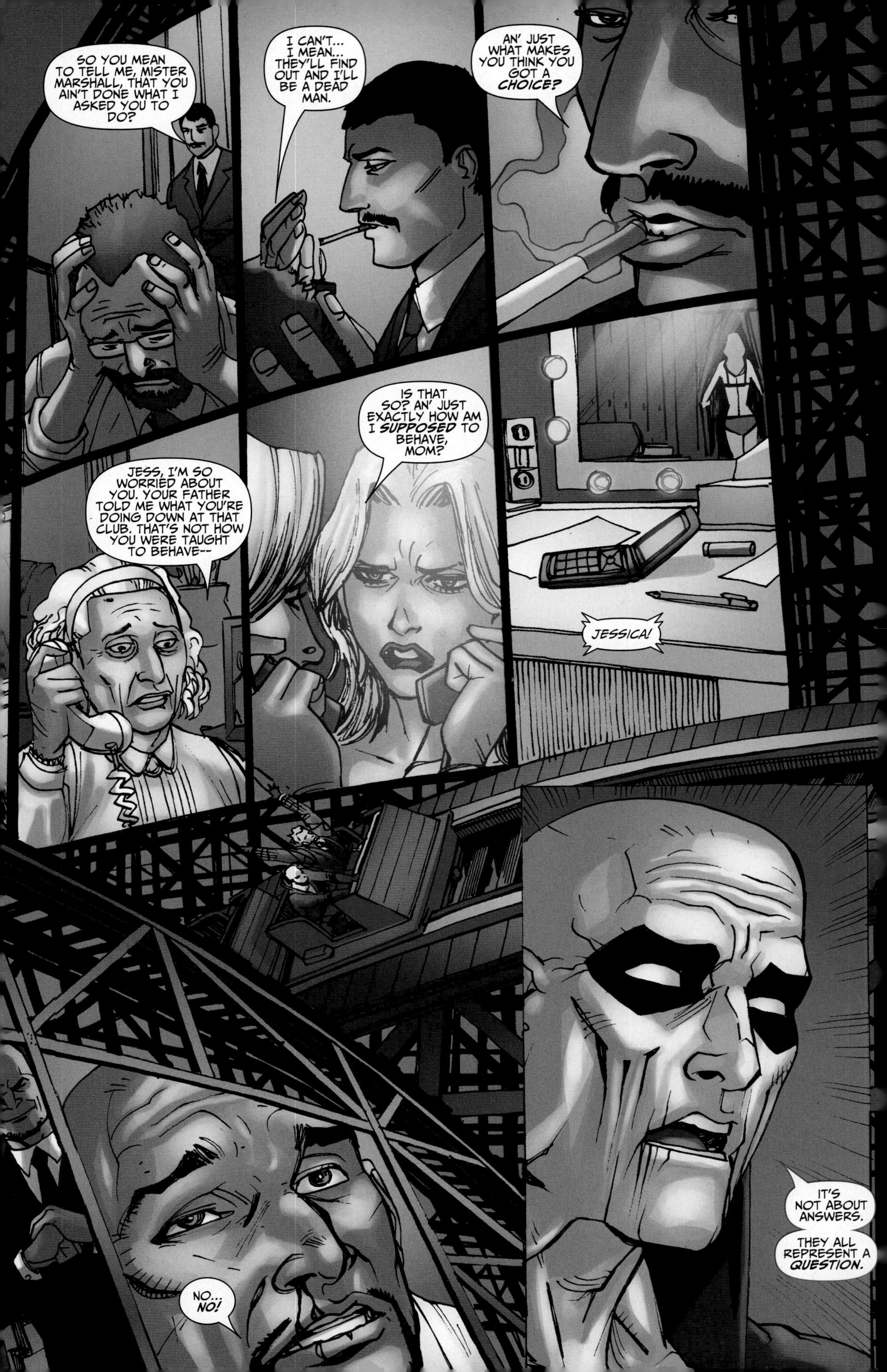
SO YOU MEAN TO TELL ME, MISTER MARSHALL, THAT YOU AIN'T DONE WHAT I ASKED YOU TO DO?
I CAN'T... I MEAN... THEY'LL FIND OUT AND I'LL BE A DEAD MAN.
AN' JUST WHAT MAKES YOU THINK YOU GOT A CHOICE?
JESS, I'M SO WORRIED ABOUT YOU. YOUR FATHER TOLD ME WHAT YOU'RE DOING DOWN AT THAT CLUB. THAT'S NOT HOW YOU WERE TAUGHT TO BEHAVE--
IS THAT SO? AN' JUST EXACTLY HOW AM I SUPPOSED TO BEHAVE, MOM?
JESSICA!
NO... NO!
IT'S NOT ABOUT ANSWERS.
THEY ALL REPRESENT A QUESTION.

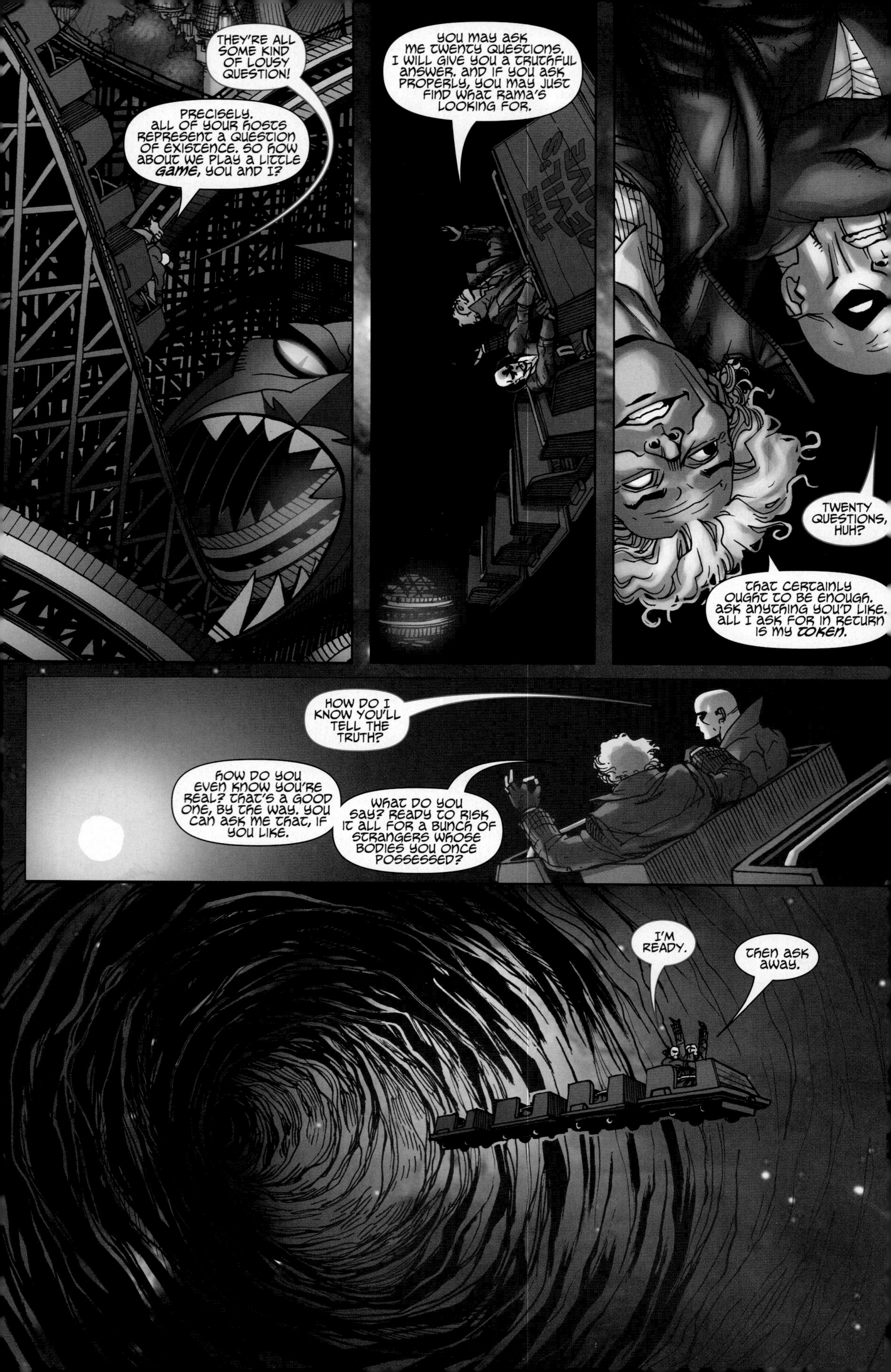

THEY'RE ALL SOME KIND OF LOUSY QUESTION!
PRECISELY. ALL OF YOUR HOSTS REPRESENT A QUESTION OF EXISTENCE. SO HOW ABOUT WE PLAY A LITTLE *GAME*, YOU AND I?
YOU MAY ASK ME TWENTY QUESTIONS. I WILL GIVE YOU A TRUTHFUL ANSWER. AND IF YOU ASK PROPERLY, YOU MAY JUST FIND WHAT RAMA'S LOOKING FOR.
TWENTY QUESTIONS, HUH?
THAT CERTAINLY OUGHT TO BE ENOUGH. ASK ANYTHING YOU'D LIKE. ALL I ASK FOR IN RETURN IS MY *TOKEN*.
HOW DO I KNOW YOU'LL TELL THE TRUTH?
HOW DO YOU EVEN KNOW YOU'RE REAL? THAT'S A GOOD ONE, BY THE WAY. YOU CAN ASK ME THAT, IF YOU LIKE.
WHAT DO YOU SAY? READY TO RISK IT ALL FOR A BUNCH OF STRANGERS WHOSE BODIES YOU ONCE POSSESSED?
I'M READY.
THEN ASK AWAY.

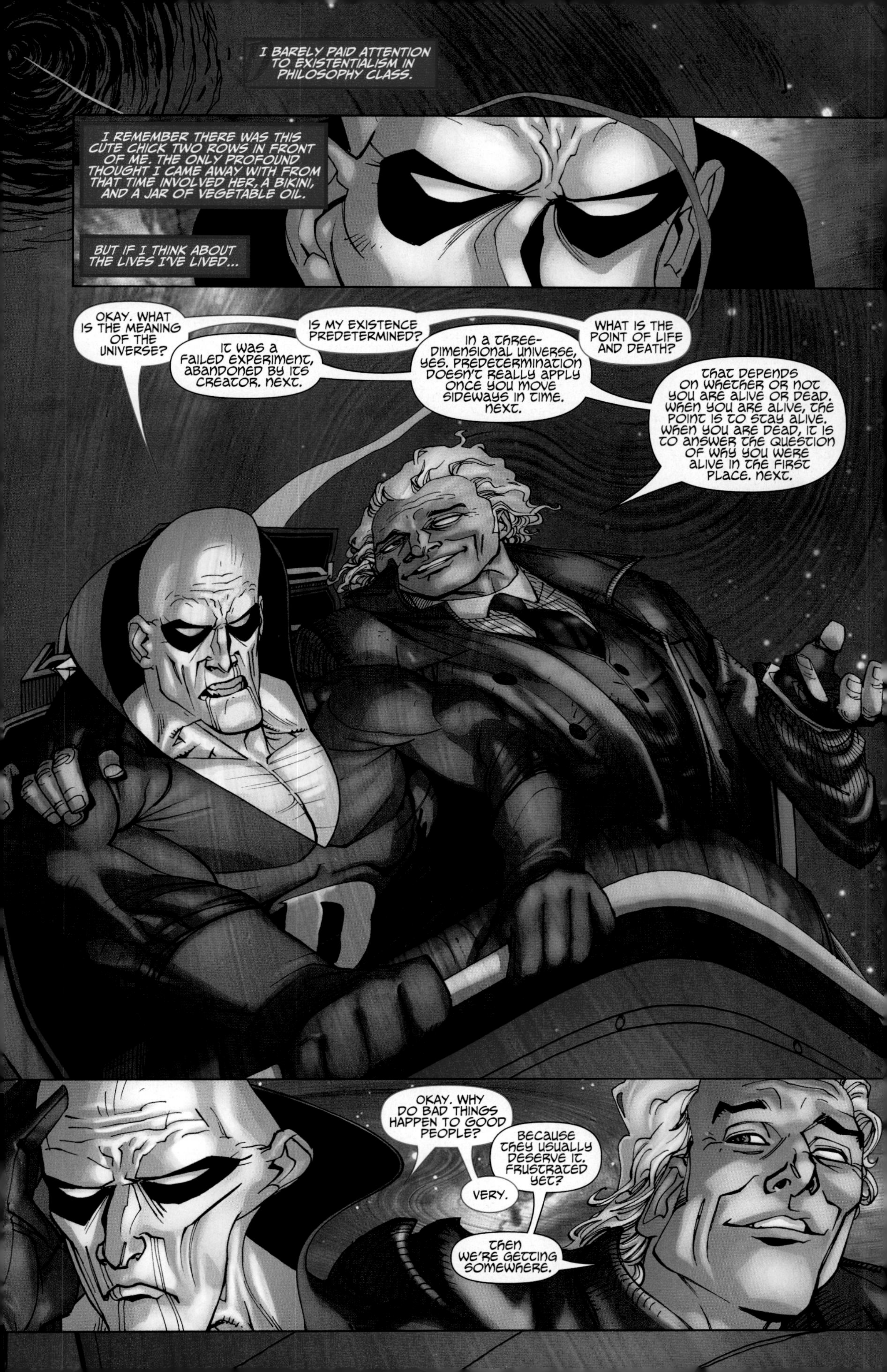

I BARELY PAID ATTENTION TO EXISTENTIALISM IN PHILOSOPHY CLASS.
I REMEMBER THERE WAS THIS CUTE CHICK TWO ROWS IN FRONT OF ME. THE ONLY PROFOUND THOUGHT I CAME AWAY WITH FROM THAT TIME INVOLVED HER, A BIKINI, AND A JAR OF VEGETABLE OIL.
BUT IF I THINK ABOUT THE LIVES I'VE LIVED...
OKAY. WHAT IS THE MEANING OF THE UNIVERSE?
IT WAS A FAILED EXPERIMENT, ABANDONED BY ITS CREATOR. NEXT.
IS MY EXISTENCE PREDETERMINED?
IN A THREE-DIMENSIONAL UNIVERSE, YES. PREDETERMINATION DOESN'T REALLY APPLY ONCE YOU MOVE SIDEWAYS IN TIME. NEXT.
WHAT IS THE POINT OF LIFE AND DEATH?
THAT DEPENDS ON WHETHER OR NOT YOU ARE ALIVE OR DEAD. WHEN YOU ARE ALIVE, THE POINT IS TO STAY ALIVE. WHEN YOU ARE DEAD, IT IS TO ANSWER THE QUESTION OF WHY YOU WERE ALIVE IN THE FIRST PLACE. NEXT.
OKAY. WHY DO BAD THINGS HAPPEN TO GOOD PEOPLE?
BECAUSE THEY USUALLY DESERVE IT. FRUSTRATED YET?
VERY.
THEN WE'RE GETTING SOMEWHERE.

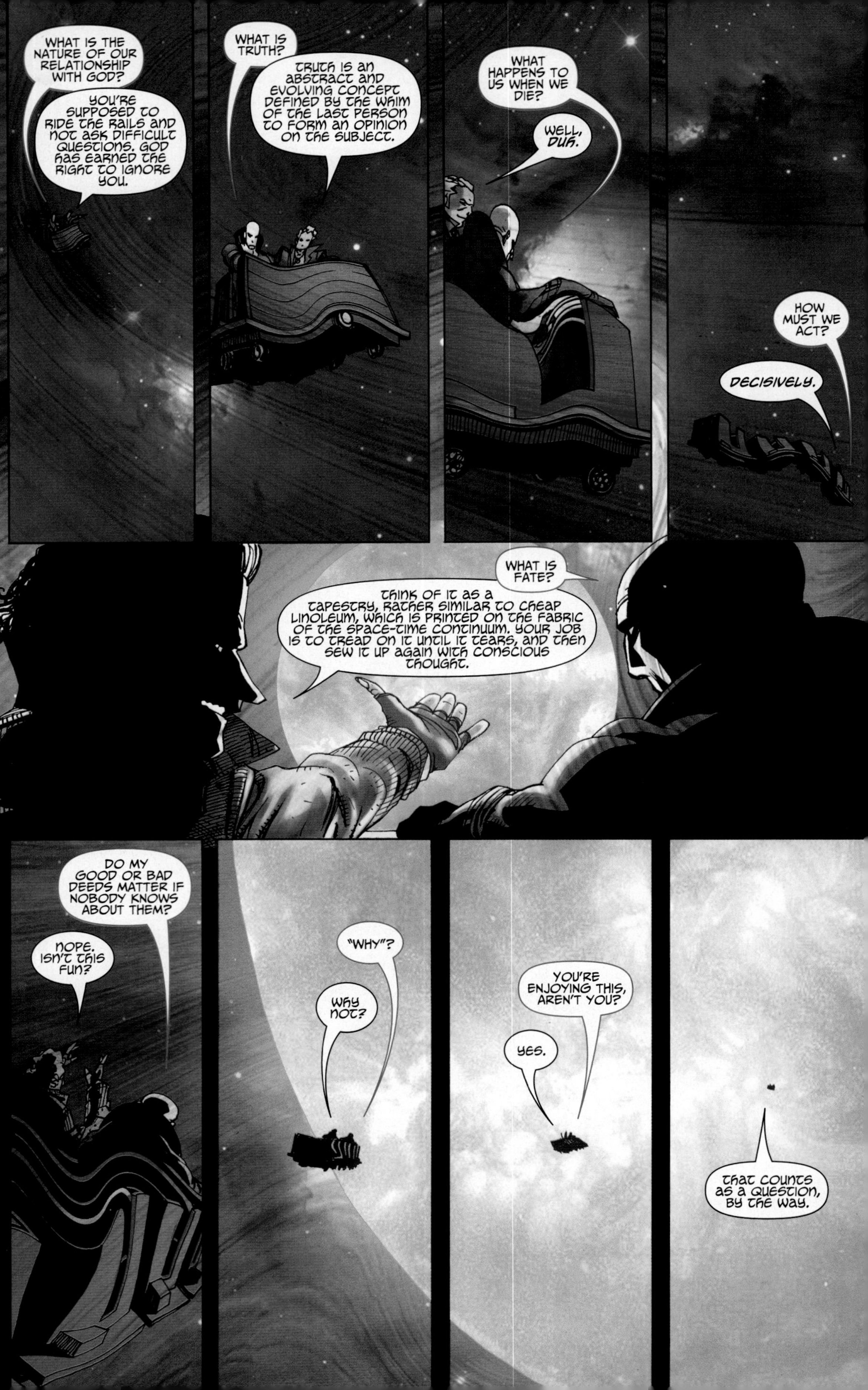
WHAT IS THE NATURE OF OUR RELATIONSHIP WITH GOD?
YOU'RE SUPPOSED TO RIDE THE RAILS AND NOT ASK DIFFICULT QUESTIONS. GOD HAS EARNED THE RIGHT TO IGNORE YOU.
WHAT IS TRUTH?
TRUTH IS AN ABSTRACT AND EVOLVING CONCEPT DEFINED BY THE WHIM OF THE LAST PERSON TO FORM AN OPINION ON THE SUBJECT.
WHAT HAPPENS TO US WHEN WE DIE?
WELL, DUH.
HOW MUST WE ACT?
DECISIVELY.
WHAT IS FATE?
THINK OF IT AS A TAPESTRY, RATHER SIMILAR TO CHEAP LINOLEUM, WHICH IS PRINTED ON THE FABRIC OF THE SPACE-TIME CONTINUUM. YOUR JOB IS TO TREAD ON IT UNTIL IT TEARS, AND THEN SEW IT UP AGAIN WITH CONSCIOUS THOUGHT.
DO MY GOOD OR BAD DEEDS MATTER IF NOBODY KNOWS ABOUT THEM?
NOPE. ISN'T THIS FUN?
"WHY"?
WHY NOT?
YOU'RE ENJOYING THIS, AREN'T YOU?
YES.
THAT COUNTS AS A QUESTION, BY THE WAY.

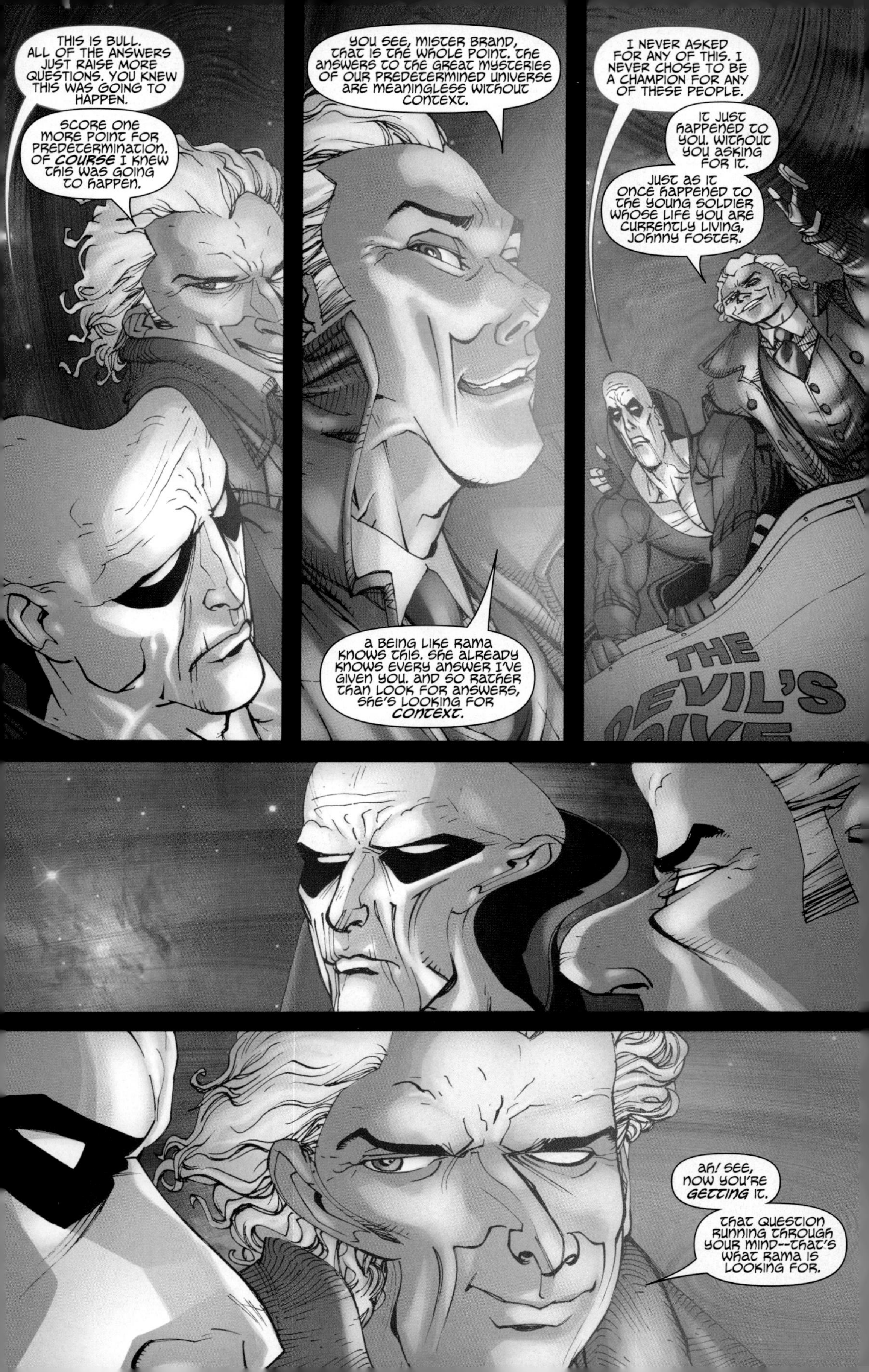
THIS IS BULL. ALL OF THE ANSWERS JUST RAISE MORE QUESTIONS. YOU KNEW THIS WAS GOING TO HAPPEN.
SCORE ONE MORE POINT FOR PREDETERMINATION. OF *COURSE* I KNEW THIS WAS GOING TO HAPPEN.
YOU SEE, MISTER BRAND, THAT IS THE WHOLE POINT. THE ANSWERS TO THE GREAT MYSTERIES OF OUR PREDETERMINED UNIVERSE ARE MEANINGLESS WITHOUT CONTEXT.
A BEING LIKE RAMA KNOWS THIS. SHE ALREADY KNOWS EVERY ANSWER I'VE GIVEN YOU. AND SO RATHER THAN LOOK FOR ANSWERS, SHE'S LOOKING FOR *CONTEXT*.
I NEVER ASKED FOR ANY OF THIS. I NEVER CHOSE TO BE A CHAMPION FOR ANY OF THESE PEOPLE.
IT JUST HAPPENED TO YOU. WITHOUT YOU ASKING FOR IT.
JUST AS IT ONCE HAPPENED TO THE YOUNG SOLDIER WHOSE LIFE YOU ARE CURRENTLY LIVING, JOHNNY FOSTER.
THE DEVIL'S
AH! SEE, NOW YOU'RE *GETTING* IT.
THAT QUESTION RUNNING THROUGH YOUR MIND--THAT'S WHAT RAMA IS LOOKING FOR.

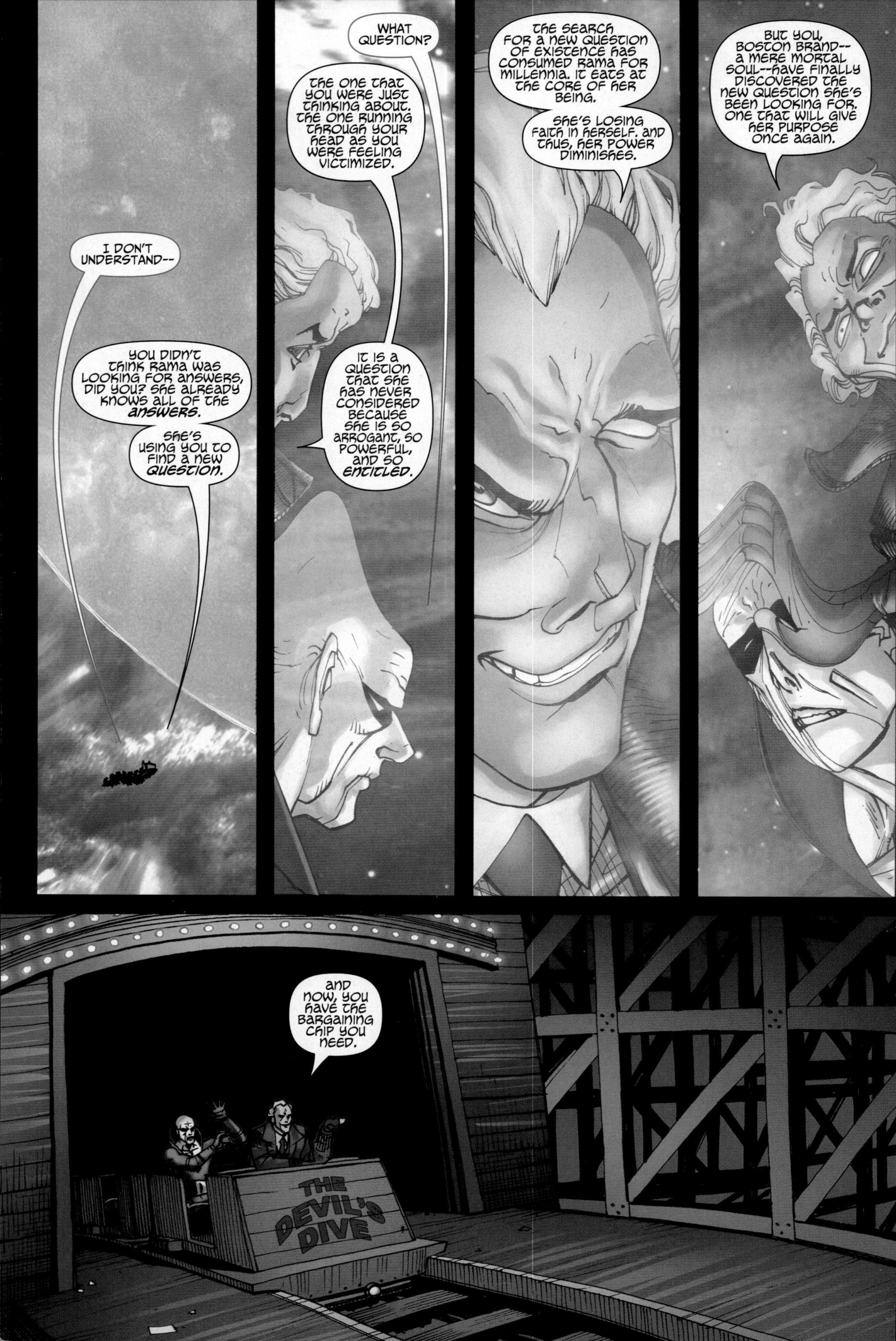
I DON'T UNDERSTAND--
WHAT QUESTION?
THE ONE THAT YOU WERE JUST THINKING ABOUT. THE ONE RUNNING THROUGH YOUR HEAD AS YOU WERE FEELING VICTIMIZED.
YOU DIDN'T THINK RAMA WAS LOOKING FOR ANSWERS, DID YOU? SHE ALREADY KNOWS ALL OF THE ANSWERS.
SHE'S USING YOU TO FIND A NEW QUESTION.
IT IS A QUESTION THAT SHE HAS NEVER CONSIDERED BECAUSE SHE IS SO ARROGANT, SO POWERFUL, AND SO ENTITLED.
THE SEARCH FOR A NEW QUESTION OF EXISTENCE HAS CONSUMED RAMA FOR MILLENNIA. IT EATS AT THE CORE OF HER BEING.
SHE'S LOSING FAITH IN HERSELF, AND THUS, HER POWER DIMINISHES.
BUT YOU, BOSTON BRAND--A MERE MORTAL SOUL--HAVE FINALLY DISCOVERED THE NEW QUESTION SHE'S BEEN LOOKING FOR. ONE THAT WILL GIVE HER PURPOSE ONCE AGAIN.
AND NOW, YOU HAVE THE BARGAINING CHIP YOU NEED.
THE DEVIL'S DIVE

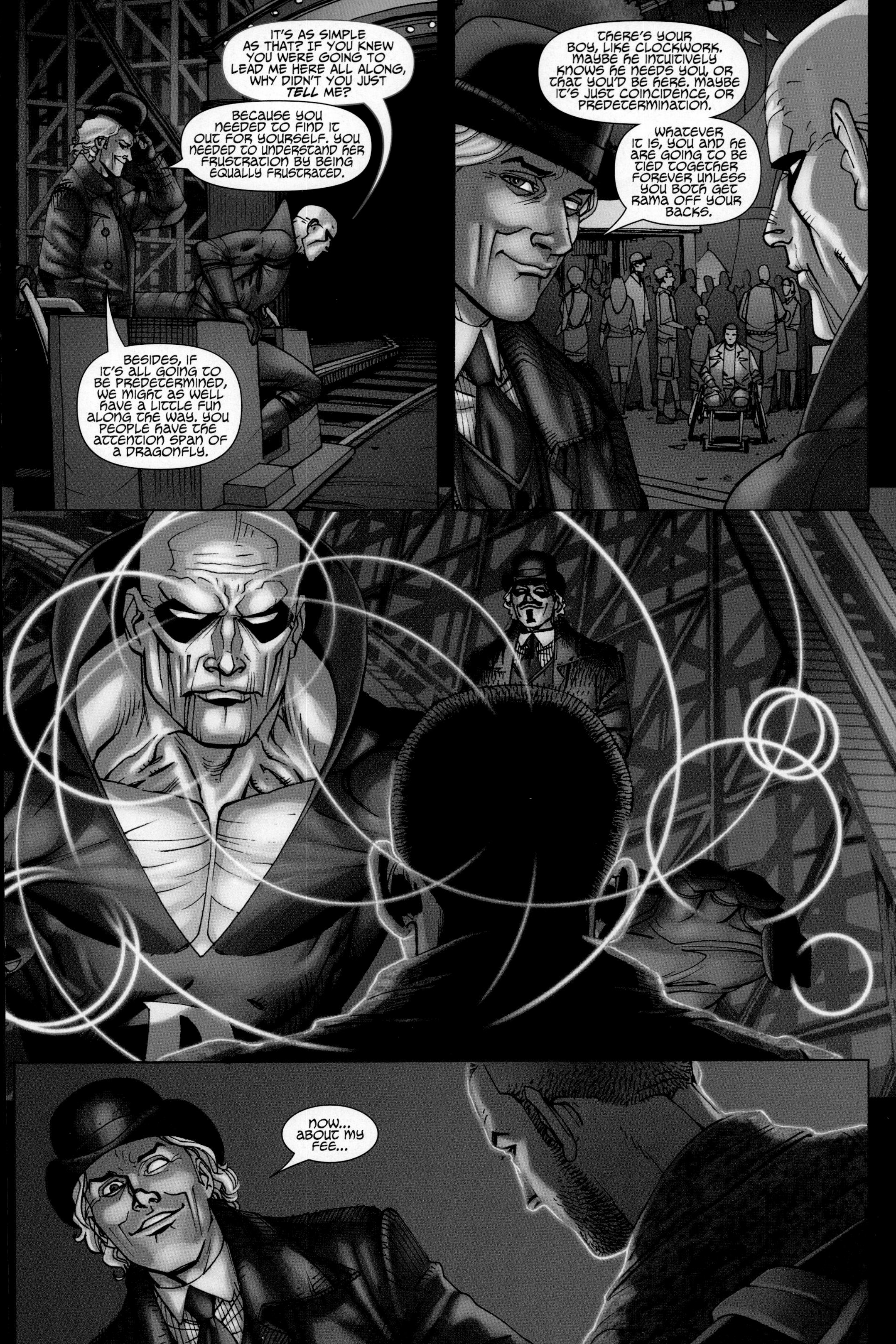
IT'S AS SIMPLE AS THAT? IF YOU KNEW YOU WERE GOING TO LEAD ME HERE ALL ALONG, WHY DIDN'T YOU JUST *TELL* ME?
BECAUSE YOU NEEDED TO FIND IT OUT FOR YOURSELF. YOU NEEDED TO UNDERSTAND HER FRUSTRATION BY BEING EQUALLY FRUSTRATED.
BESIDES, IF IT'S ALL GOING TO BE PREDETERMINED, WE MIGHT AS WELL HAVE A LITTLE FUN ALONG THE WAY. YOU PEOPLE HAVE THE ATTENTION SPAN OF A DRAGONFLY.
THERE'S YOUR BOY, LIKE CLOCKWORK. MAYBE HE INTUITIVELY KNOWS HE NEEDS YOU, OR THAT YOU'D BE HERE. MAYBE IT'S JUST COINCIDENCE, OR PREDETERMINATION.
WHATEVER IT IS, YOU AND HE ARE GOING TO BE TIED TOGETHER FOREVER UNLESS YOU BOTH GET RAMA OFF YOUR BACKS.
NOW... ABOUT MY FEE...

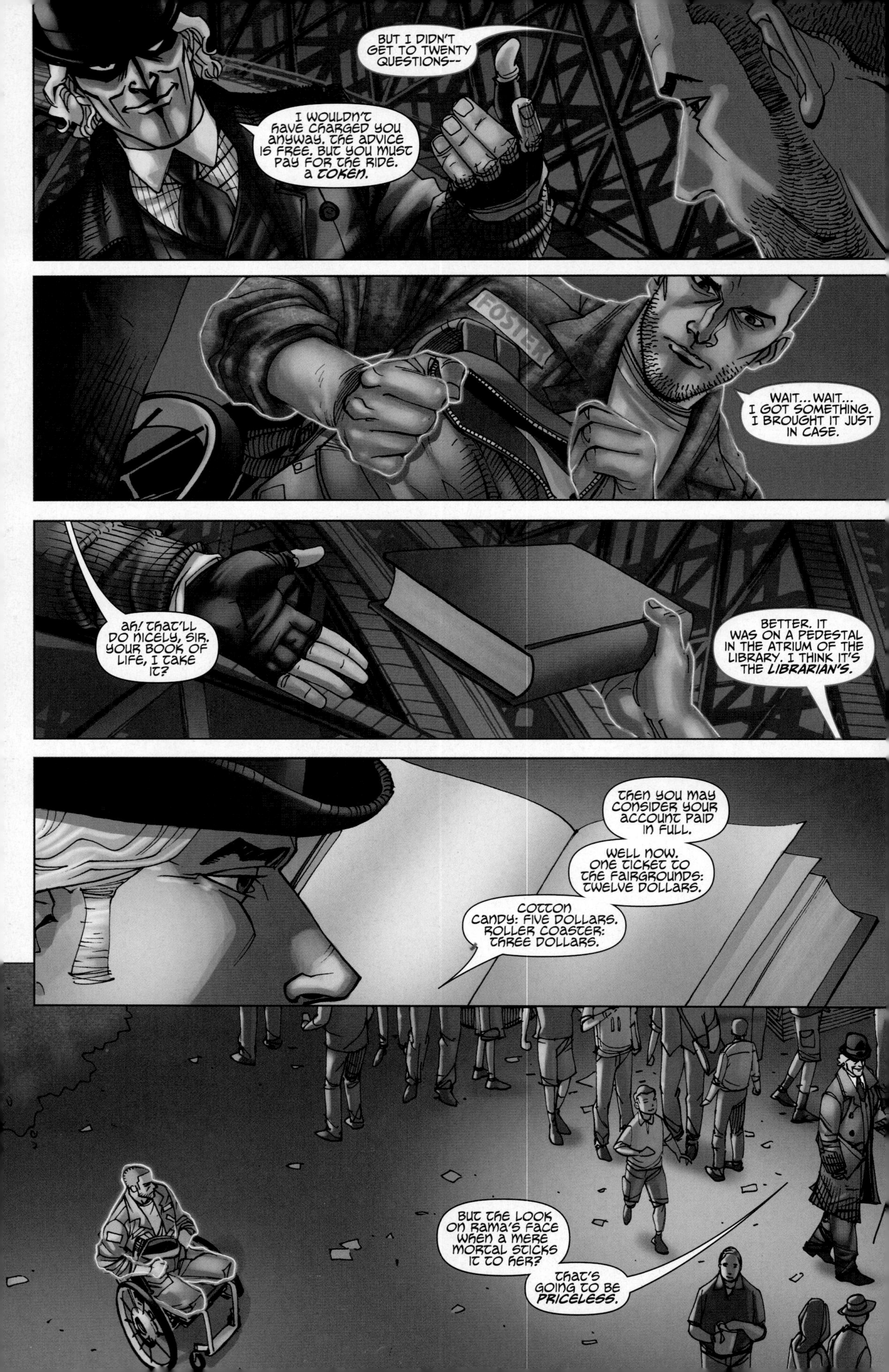
BUT I DIDN'T GET TO TWENTY QUESTIONS--
I WOULDN'T HAVE CHARGED YOU ANYWAY. THE ADVICE IS FREE. BUT YOU MUST PAY FOR THE RIDE. A TOKEN.
FOSTER
WAIT...WAIT... I GOT SOMETHING. I BROUGHT IT JUST IN CASE.
AH! THAT'LL DO NICELY, SIR. YOUR BOOK OF LIFE, I TAKE IT?
BETTER. IT WAS ON A PEDESTAL IN THE ATRIUM OF THE LIBRARY. I THINK IT'S THE LIBRARIAN'S.
THEN YOU MAY CONSIDER YOUR ACCOUNT PAID IN FULL.
WELL NOW. ONE TICKET TO THE FAIRGROUNDS: TWELVE DOLLARS.
COTTON CANDY: FIVE DOLLARS. ROLLER COASTER: THREE DOLLARS.
BUT THE LOOK ON RAMA'S FACE WHEN A MERE MORTAL STICKS IT TO HER?
THAT'S GOING TO BE PRICELESS.

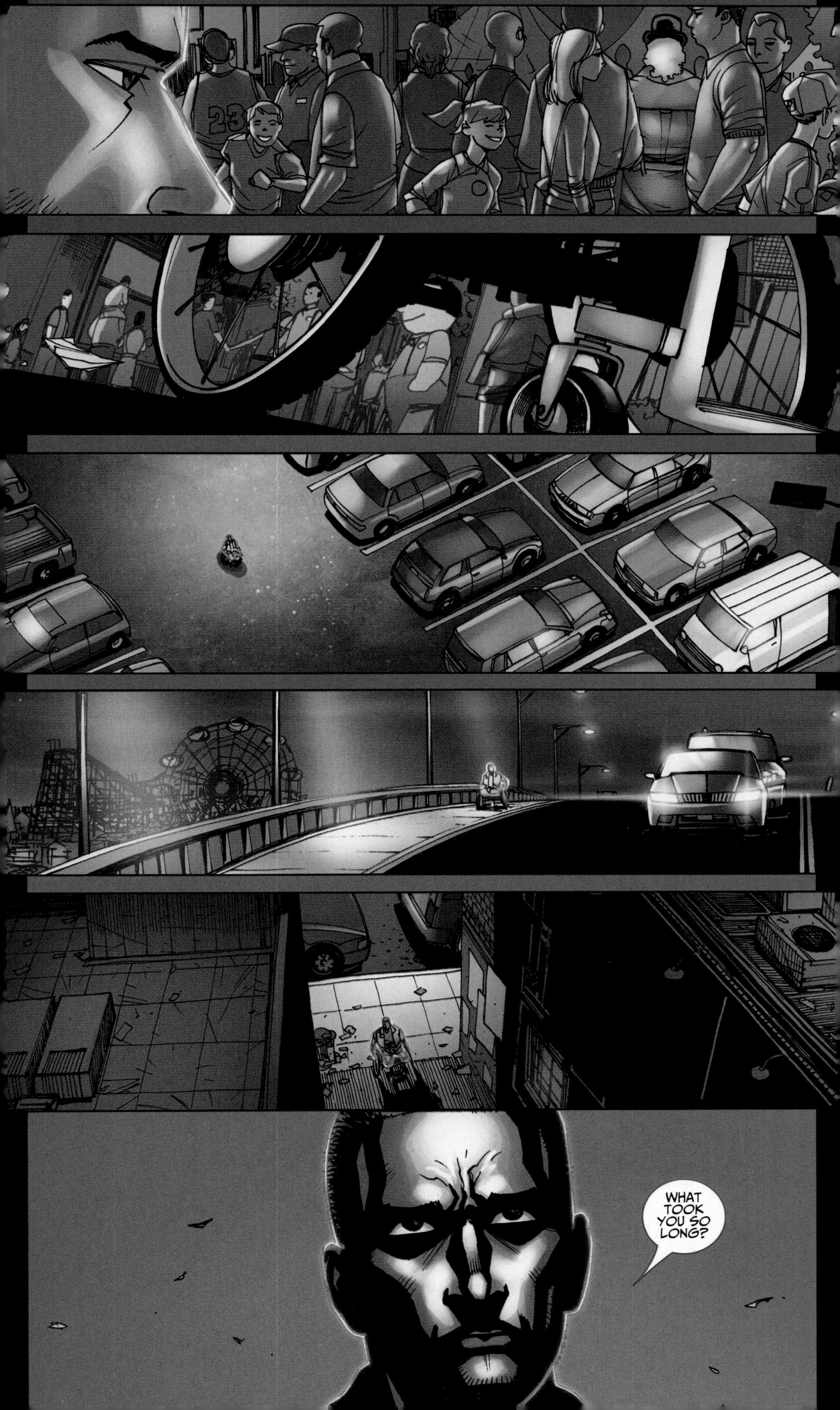

WHAT TOOK YOU SO LONG?

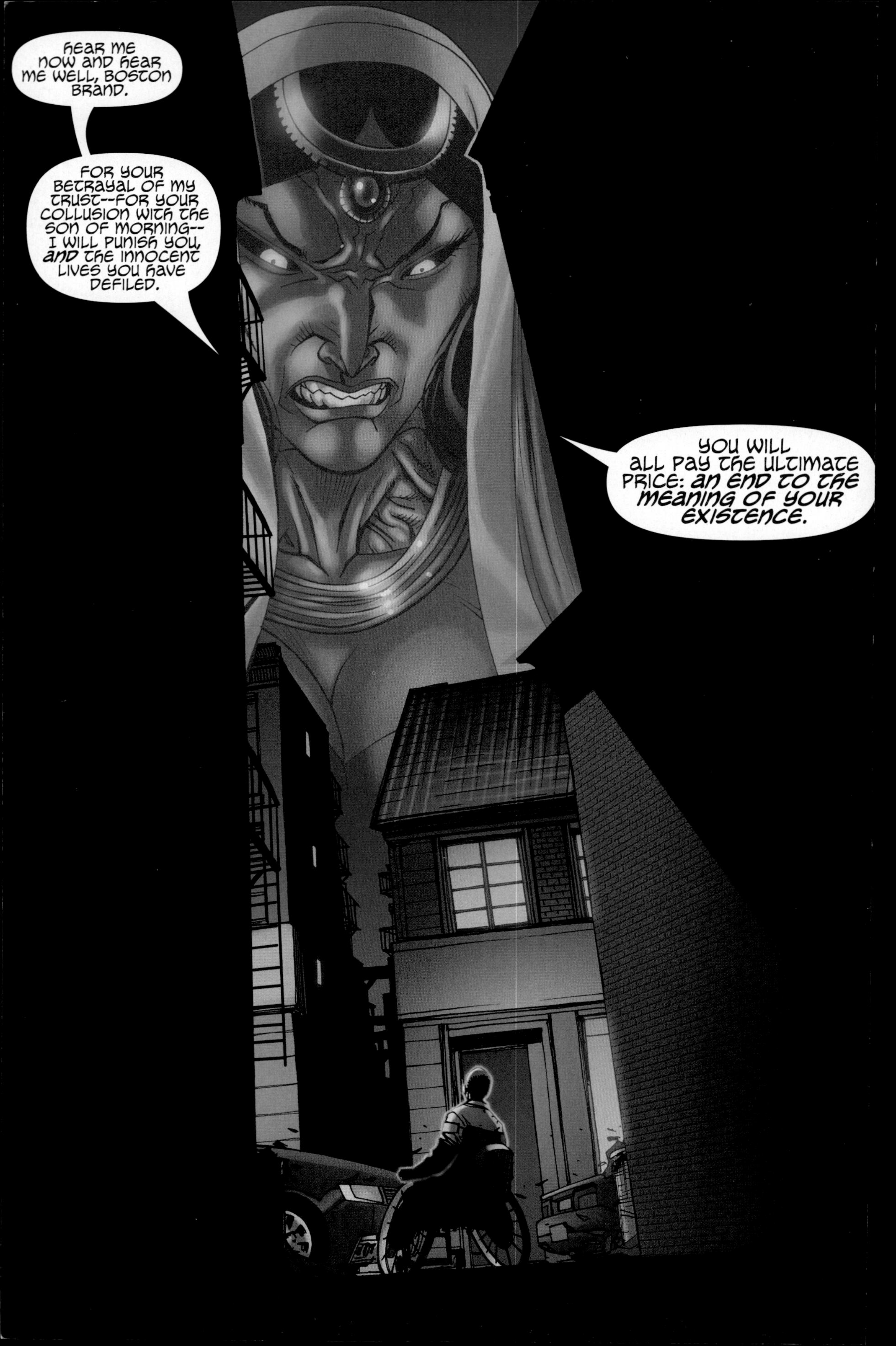
HEAR ME NOW AND HEAR ME WELL, BOSTON BRAND.
FOR YOUR BETRAYAL OF MY TRUST--FOR YOUR COLLUSION WITH THE SON OF MORNING-- I WILL PUNISH YOU, AND THE INNOCENT LIVES YOU HAVE DEFILED.
YOU WILL ALL PAY THE ULTIMATE PRICE: AN END TO THE MEANING OF YOUR EXISTENCE.

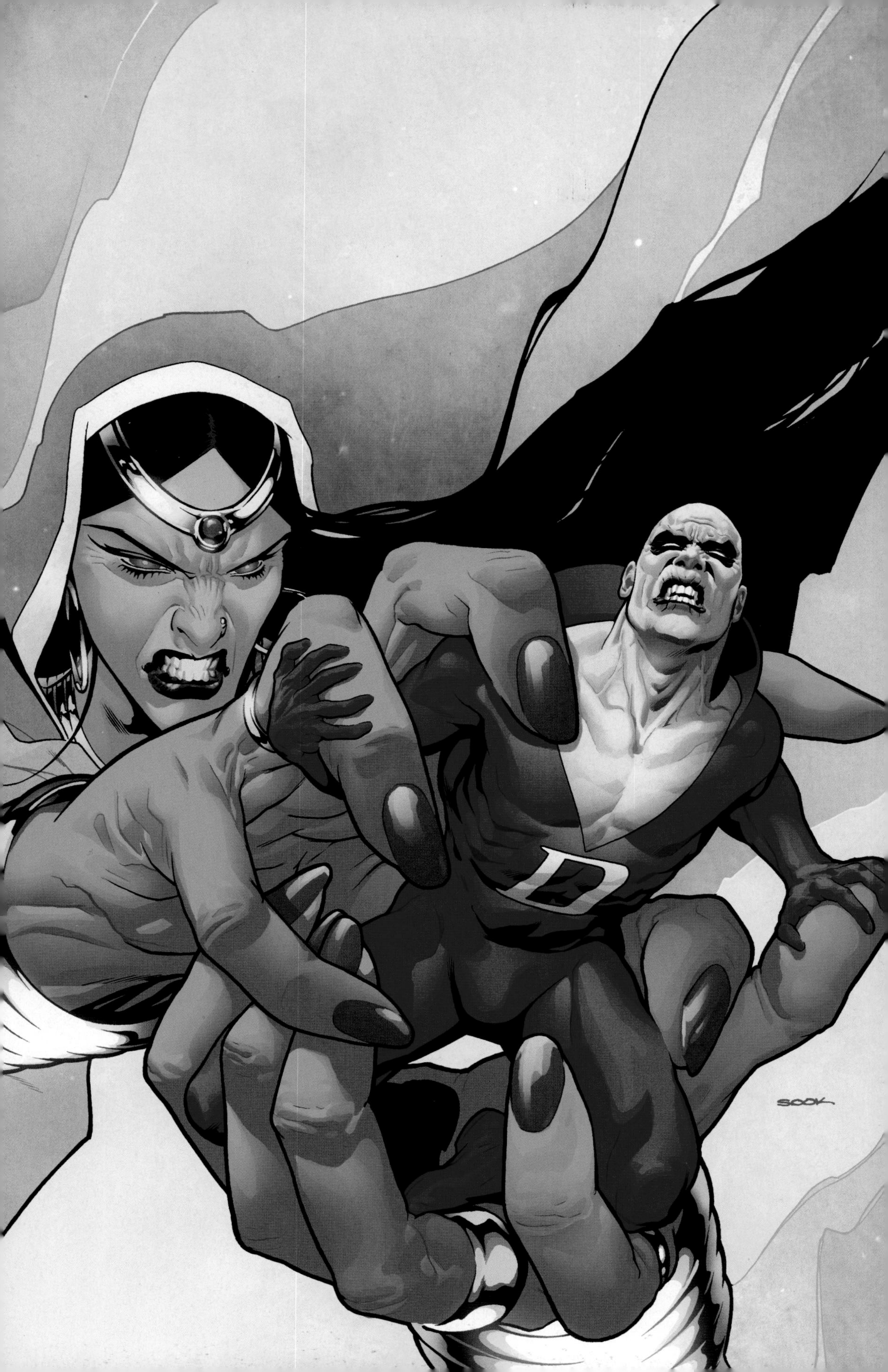
SOOK

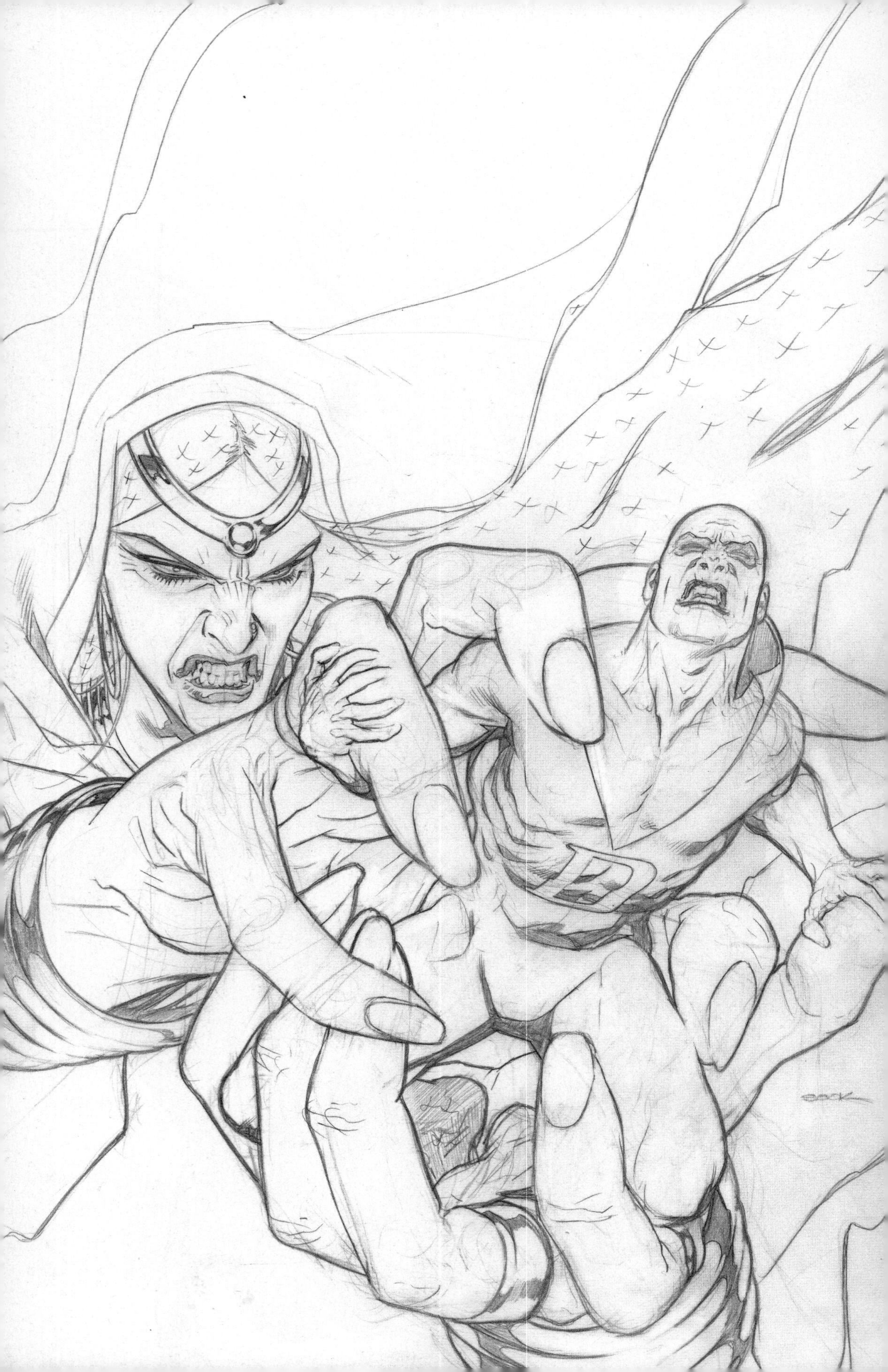

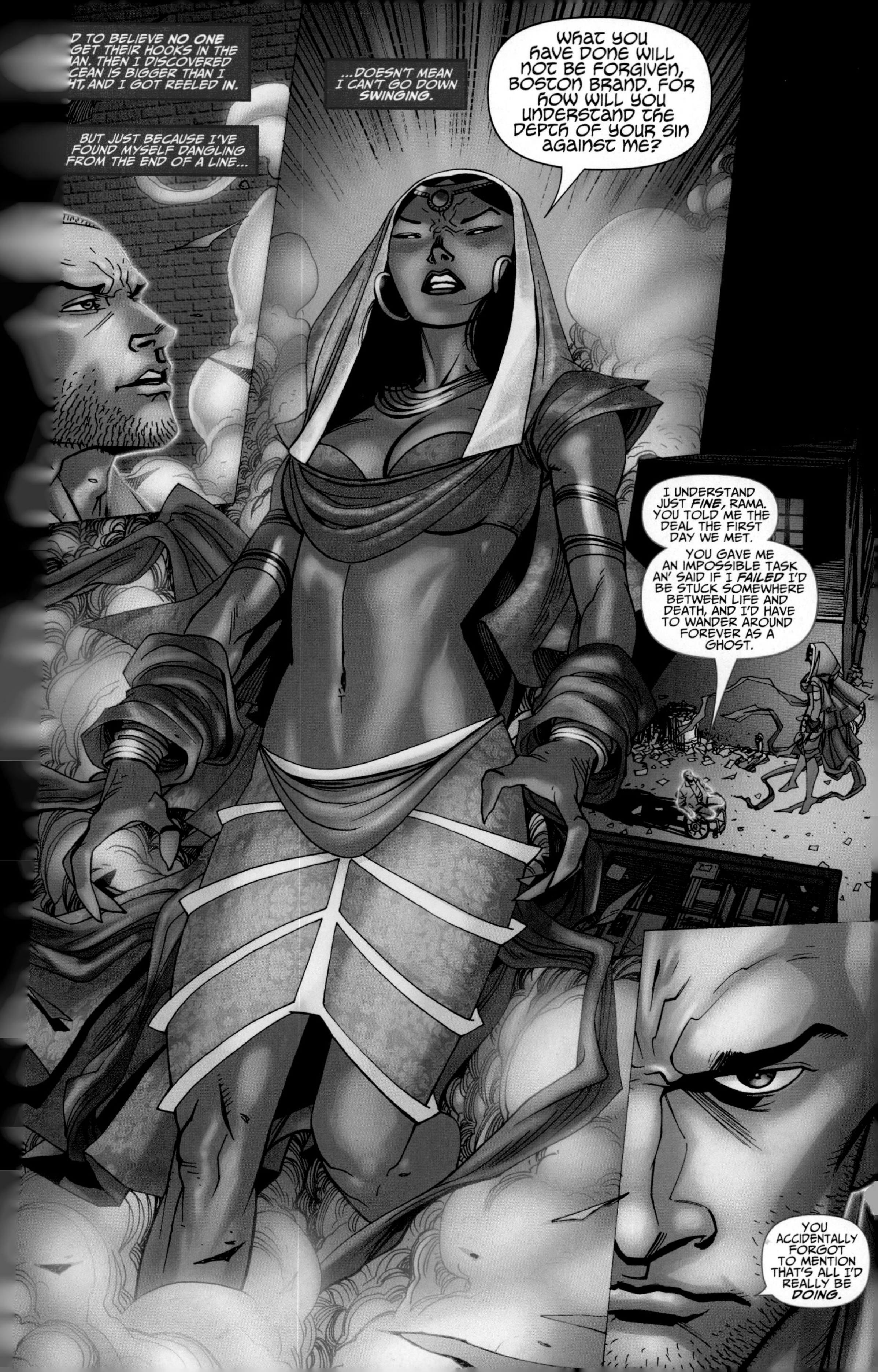

D TO BELIEVE NO ONE GET THEIR HOOKS IN THE AN. THEN I DISCOVERED CEAN IS BIGGER THAN I HT, AND I GOT REELED IN.
BUT JUST BECAUSE I'VE FOUND MYSELF DANGLING FROM THE END OF A LINE...
...DOESN'T MEAN I CAN'T GO DOWN SWINGING.
WHAT YOU HAVE DONE WILL NOT BE FORGIVEN, BOSTON BRAND. FOR HOW WILL YOU UNDERSTAND THE DEPTH OF YOUR SIN AGAINST ME?
I UNDERSTAND JUST FINE, RAMA. YOU TOLD ME THE DEAL THE FIRST DAY WE MET.
YOU GAVE ME AN IMPOSSIBLE TASK AN' SAID IF I FAILED I'D BE STUCK SOMEWHERE BETWEEN LIFE AND DEATH, AND I'D HAVE TO WANDER AROUND FOREVER AS A GHOST.
YOU ACCIDENTALLY FORGOT TO MENTION THAT'S ALL I'D REALLY BE DOING.

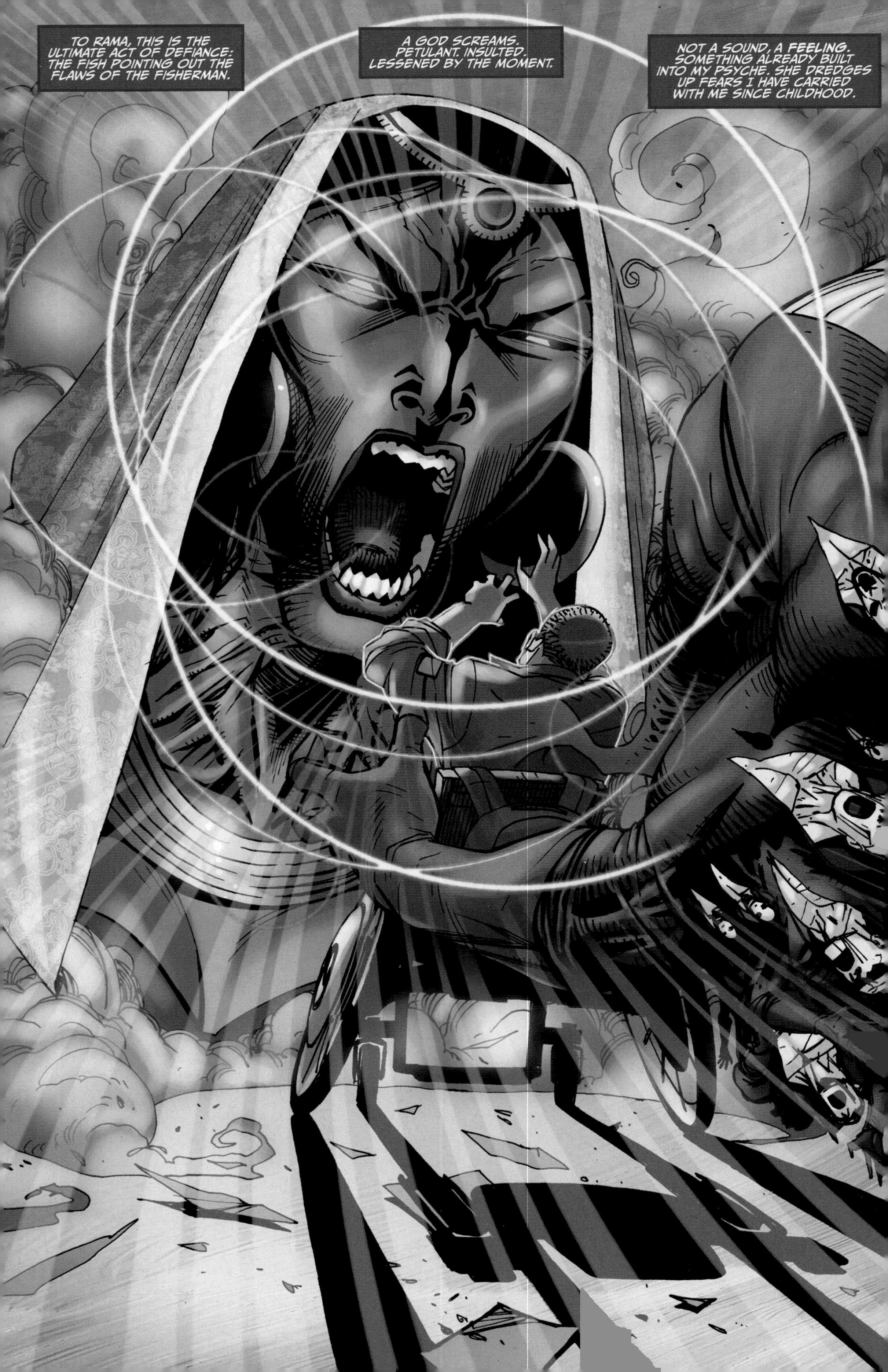
TO RAMA, THIS IS THE ULTIMATE ACT OF DEFIANCE: THE FISH POINTING OUT THE FLAWS OF THE FISHERMAN.
A GOD SCREAMS. PETULANT. INSULTED. LESSENED BY THE MOMENT.
NOT A SOUND, A FEELING. SOMETHING ALREADY BUILT INTO MY PSYCHE. SHE DREDGES UP FEARS I HAVE CARRIED WITH ME SINCE CHILDHOOD.

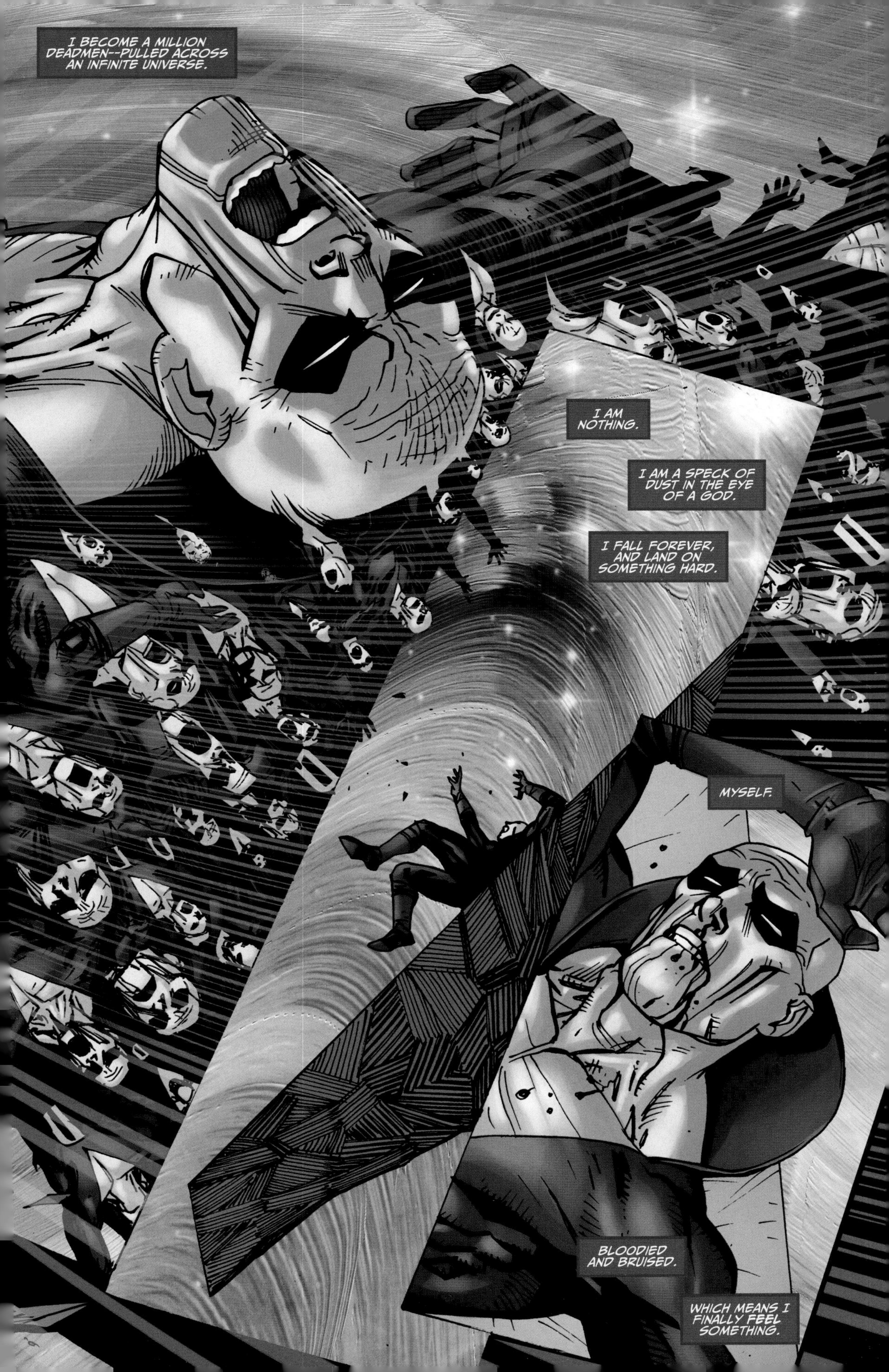
I BECOME A MILLION DEADMEN--PULLED ACROSS AN INFINITE UNIVERSE.
I AM NOTHING.
I AM A SPECK OF DUST IN THE EYE OF A GOD.
I FALL FOREVER, AND LAND ON SOMETHING HARD.
MYSELF.
BLOODIED AND BRUISED.
WHICH MEANS I FINALLY FEEL SOMETHING.

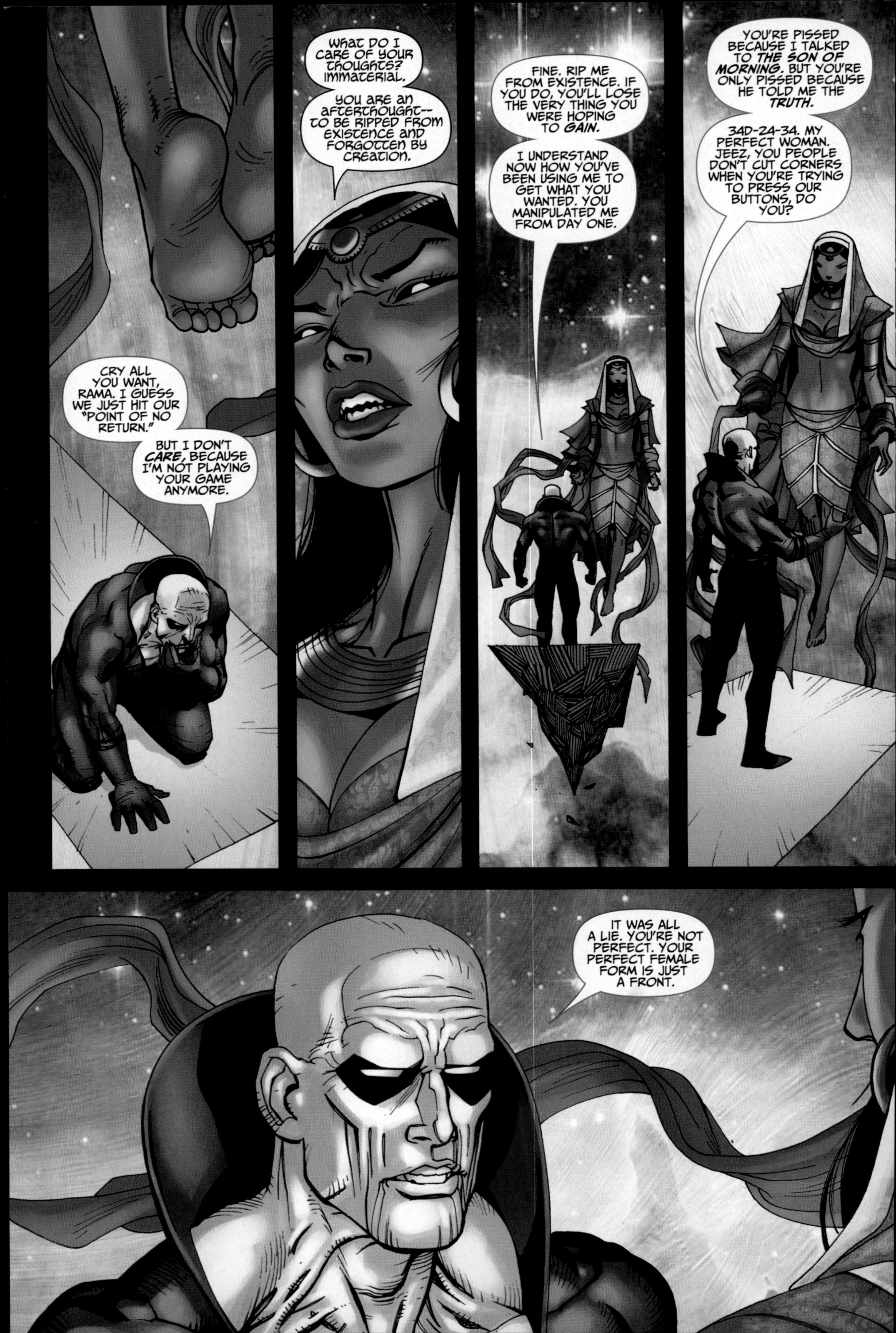
CRY ALL YOU WANT, RAMA. I GUESS WE JUST HIT OUR "POINT OF NO RETURN."
BUT I DON'T CARE, BECAUSE I'M NOT PLAYING YOUR GAME ANYMORE.
WHAT DO I CARE OF YOUR THOUGHTS? IMMATERIAL.
YOU ARE AN AFTERTHOUGHT-- TO BE RIPPED FROM EXISTENCE AND FORGOTTEN BY CREATION.
FINE. RIP ME FROM EXISTENCE. IF YOU DO, YOU'LL LOSE THE VERY THING YOU WERE HOPING TO GAIN.
I UNDERSTAND NOW HOW YOU'VE BEEN USING ME TO GET WHAT YOU WANTED. YOU MANIPULATED ME FROM DAY ONE.
YOU'RE PISSED BECAUSE I TALKED TO THE SON OF MORNING. BUT YOU'RE ONLY PISSED BECAUSE HE TOLD ME THE TRUTH.
34D-24-34. MY PERFECT WOMAN. JEEZ, YOU PEOPLE DON'T CUT CORNERS WHEN YOU'RE TRYING TO PRESS OUR BUTTONS, DO YOU?
IT WAS ALL A LIE. YOU'RE NOT PERFECT. YOUR PERFECT FEMALE FORM IS JUST A FRONT.

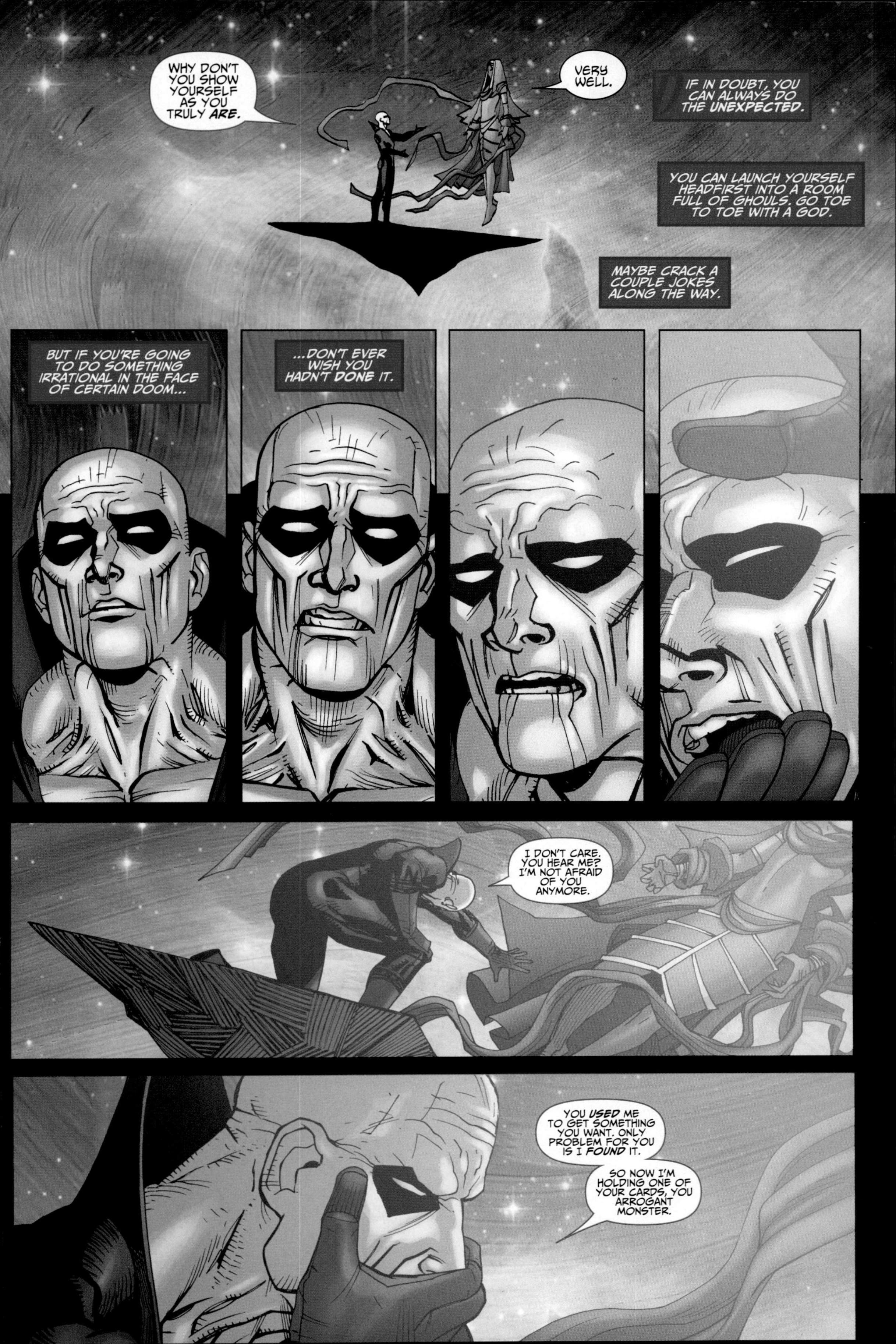
WHY DON'T YOU SHOW YOURSELF AS YOU TRULY ARE.
VERY WELL.
IF IN DOUBT, YOU CAN ALWAYS DO THE UNEXPECTED.
YOU CAN LAUNCH YOURSELF HEADFIRST INTO A ROOM FULL OF GHOULS. GO TOE TO TOE WITH A GOD.
MAYBE CRACK A COUPLE JOKES ALONG THE WAY.
BUT IF YOU'RE GOING TO DO SOMETHING IRRATIONAL IN THE FACE OF CERTAIN DOOM...
...DON'T EVER WISH YOU HADN'T DONE IT.
I DON'T CARE. YOU HEAR ME? I'M NOT AFRAID OF YOU ANYMORE.
YOU USED ME TO GET SOMETHING YOU WANT. ONLY PROBLEM FOR YOU IS I FOUND IT.
SO NOW I'M HOLDING ONE OF YOUR CARDS, YOU ARROGANT MONSTER.

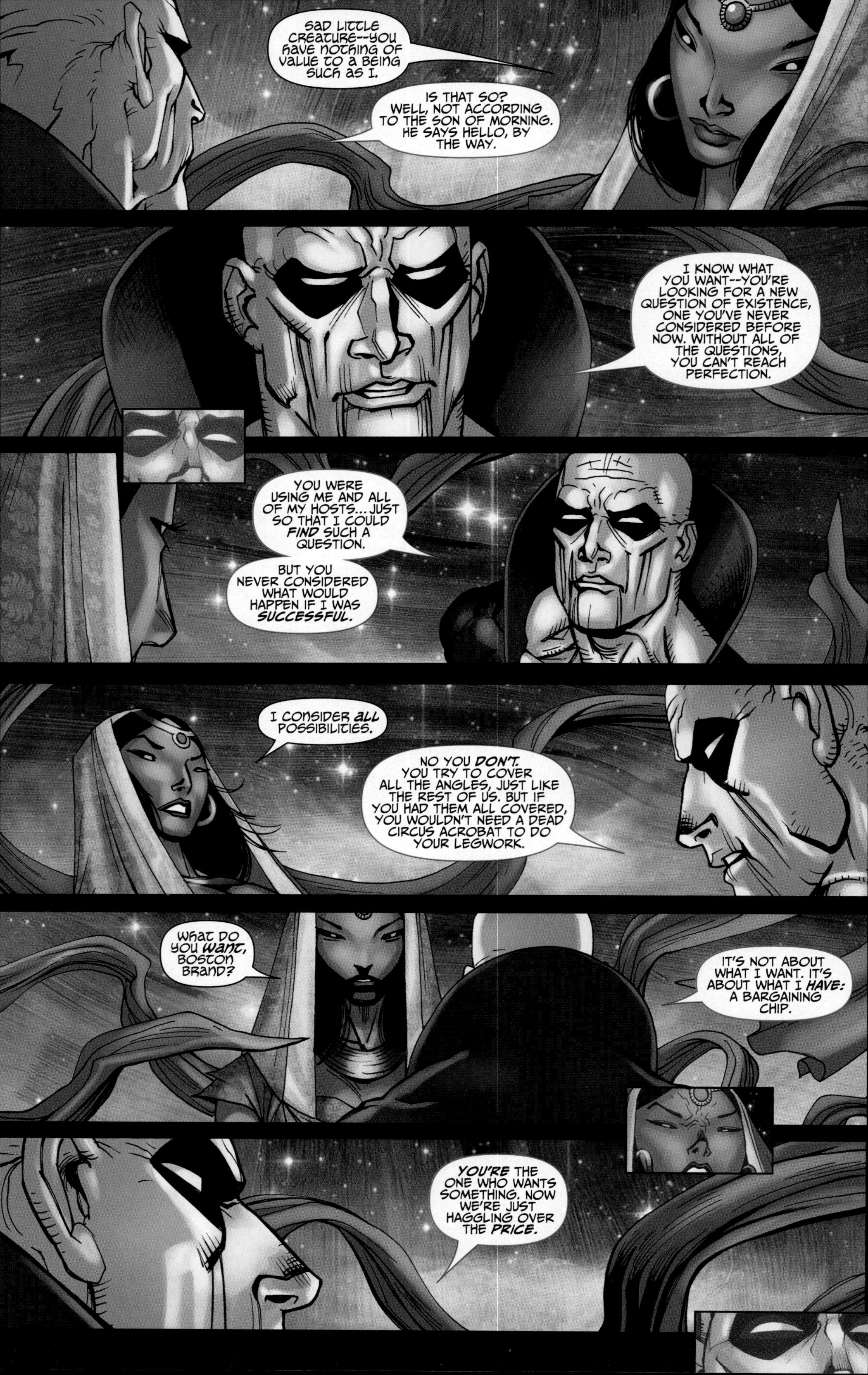

SAD LITTLE CREATURE--YOU HAVE NOTHING OF VALUE TO A BEING SUCH AS I.
IS THAT SO? WELL, NOT ACCORDING TO THE SON OF MORNING. HE SAYS HELLO, BY THE WAY.
I KNOW WHAT YOU WANT--YOU'RE LOOKING FOR A NEW QUESTION OF EXISTENCE, ONE YOU'VE NEVER CONSIDERED BEFORE NOW. WITHOUT ALL OF THE QUESTIONS, YOU CAN'T REACH PERFECTION.
YOU WERE USING ME AND ALL OF MY HOSTS... JUST SO THAT I COULD *FIND* SUCH A QUESTION.
BUT YOU NEVER CONSIDERED WHAT WOULD HAPPEN IF I WAS *SUCCESSFUL.*
I CONSIDER *ALL* POSSIBILITIES.
NO YOU *DON'T.* YOU TRY TO COVER ALL THE ANGLES, JUST LIKE THE REST OF US. BUT IF YOU HAD THEM ALL COVERED, YOU WOULDN'T NEED A DEAD CIRCUS ACROBAT TO DO YOUR LEGWORK.
WHAT DO YOU *WANT,* BOSTON BRAND?
IT'S NOT ABOUT WHAT I WANT. IT'S ABOUT WHAT I *HAVE:* A BARGAINING CHIP.
YOU'RE THE ONE WHO WANTS SOMETHING. NOW WE'RE JUST HAGGLING OVER THE *PRICE.*

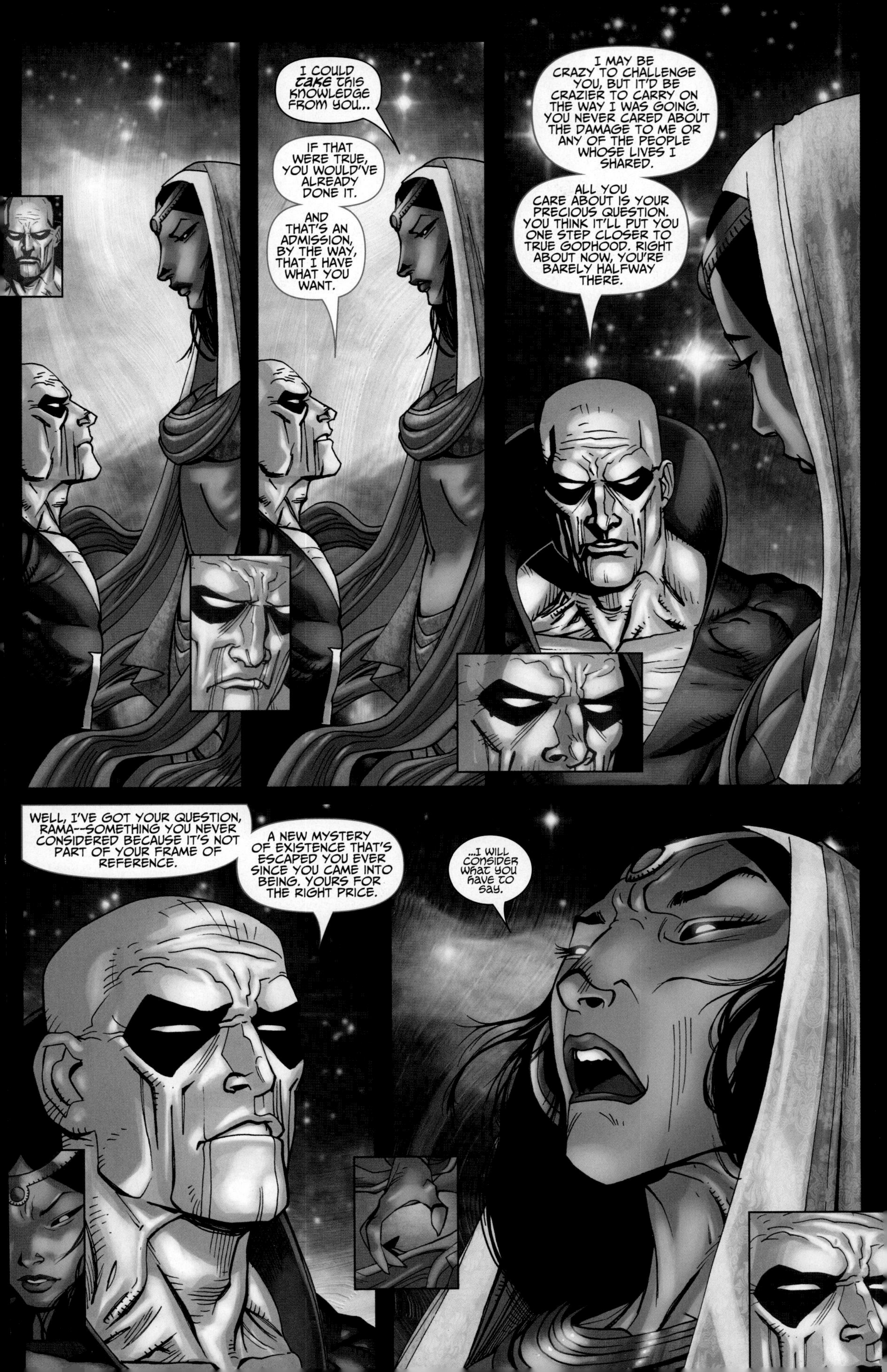
I COULD TAKE THIS KNOWLEDGE FROM YOU...
IF THAT WERE TRUE, YOU WOULD'VE ALREADY DONE IT.
AND THAT'S AN ADMISSION, BY THE WAY, THAT I HAVE WHAT YOU WANT.
I MAY BE CRAZY TO CHALLENGE YOU, BUT IT'D BE CRAZIER TO CARRY ON THE WAY I WAS GOING. YOU NEVER CARED ABOUT THE DAMAGE TO ME OR ANY OF THE PEOPLE WHOSE LIVES I SHARED.
ALL YOU CARE ABOUT IS YOUR PRECIOUS QUESTION. YOU THINK IT'LL PUT YOU ONE STEP CLOSER TO TRUE GODHOOD. RIGHT ABOUT NOW, YOU'RE BARELY HALFWAY THERE.
WELL, I'VE GOT YOUR QUESTION, RAMA--SOMETHING YOU NEVER CONSIDERED BECAUSE IT'S NOT PART OF YOUR FRAME OF REFERENCE.
A NEW MYSTERY OF EXISTENCE THAT'S ESCAPED YOU EVER SINCE YOU CAME INTO BEING. YOURS FOR THE RIGHT PRICE.
...I WILL CONSIDER WHAT YOU HAVE TO SAY.

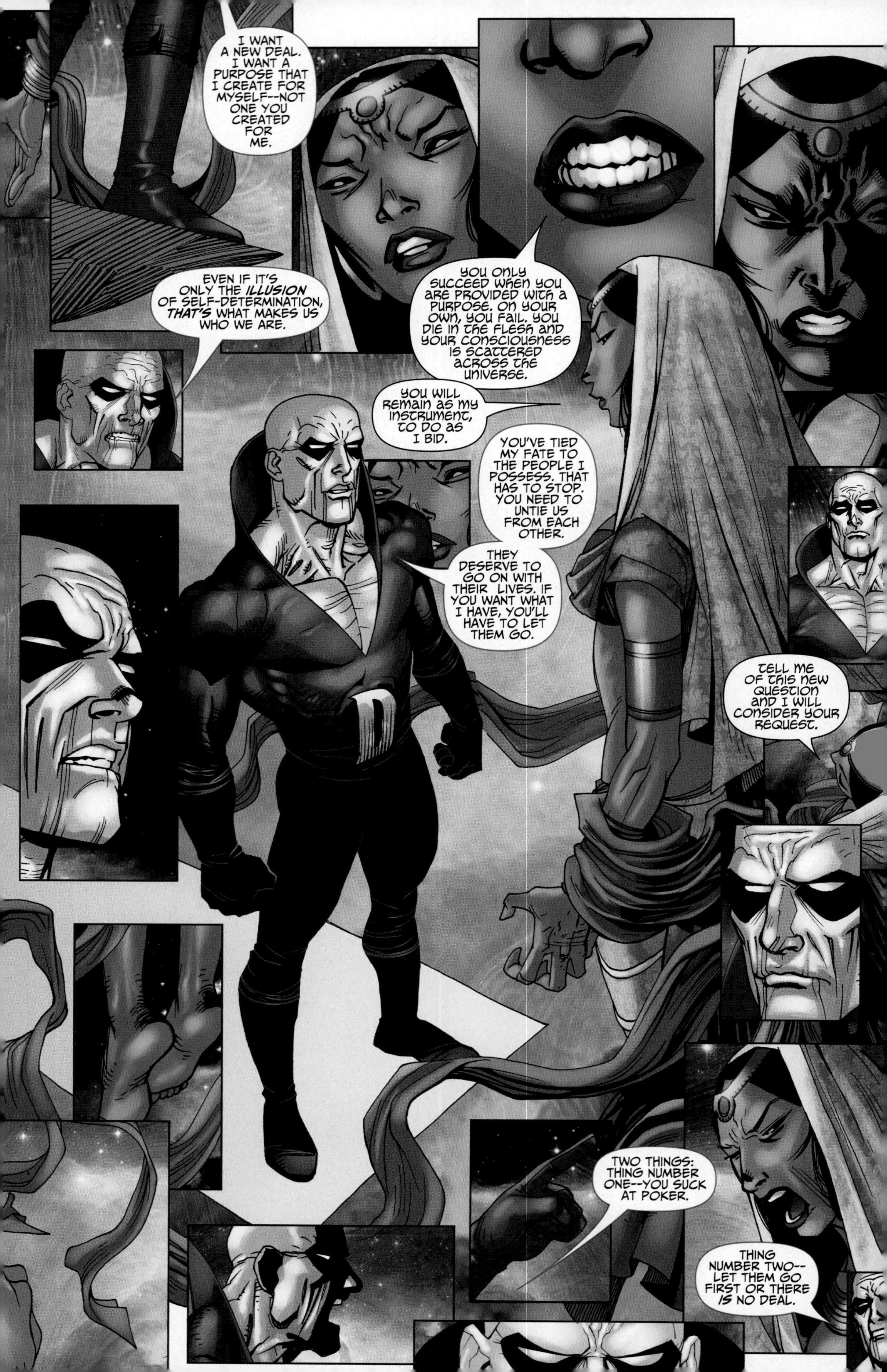
I WANT A NEW DEAL. I WANT A PURPOSE THAT I CREATE FOR MYSELF--NOT ONE YOU CREATED FOR ME.
EVEN IF IT'S ONLY THE *ILLUSION* OF SELF-DETERMINATION, *THAT'S* WHAT MAKES US WHO WE ARE.
YOU ONLY SUCCEED WHEN YOU ARE PROVIDED WITH A PURPOSE. ON YOUR OWN, YOU FAIL. YOU DIE IN THE FLESH AND YOUR CONSCIOUSNESS IS SCATTERED ACROSS THE UNIVERSE.
YOU WILL REMAIN AS MY INSTRUMENT, TO DO AS I BID.
YOU'VE TIED MY FATE TO THE PEOPLE I POSSESS. THAT HAS TO STOP. YOU NEED TO UNTIE US FROM EACH OTHER.
THEY DESERVE TO GO ON WITH THEIR LIVES. IF YOU WANT WHAT I HAVE, YOU'LL HAVE TO LET THEM GO.
TELL ME OF THIS NEW QUESTION AND I WILL CONSIDER YOUR REQUEST.
TWO THINGS: THING NUMBER ONE--YOU SUCK AT POKER.
THING NUMBER TWO--LET THEM GO FIRST OR THERE *IS* NO DEAL.

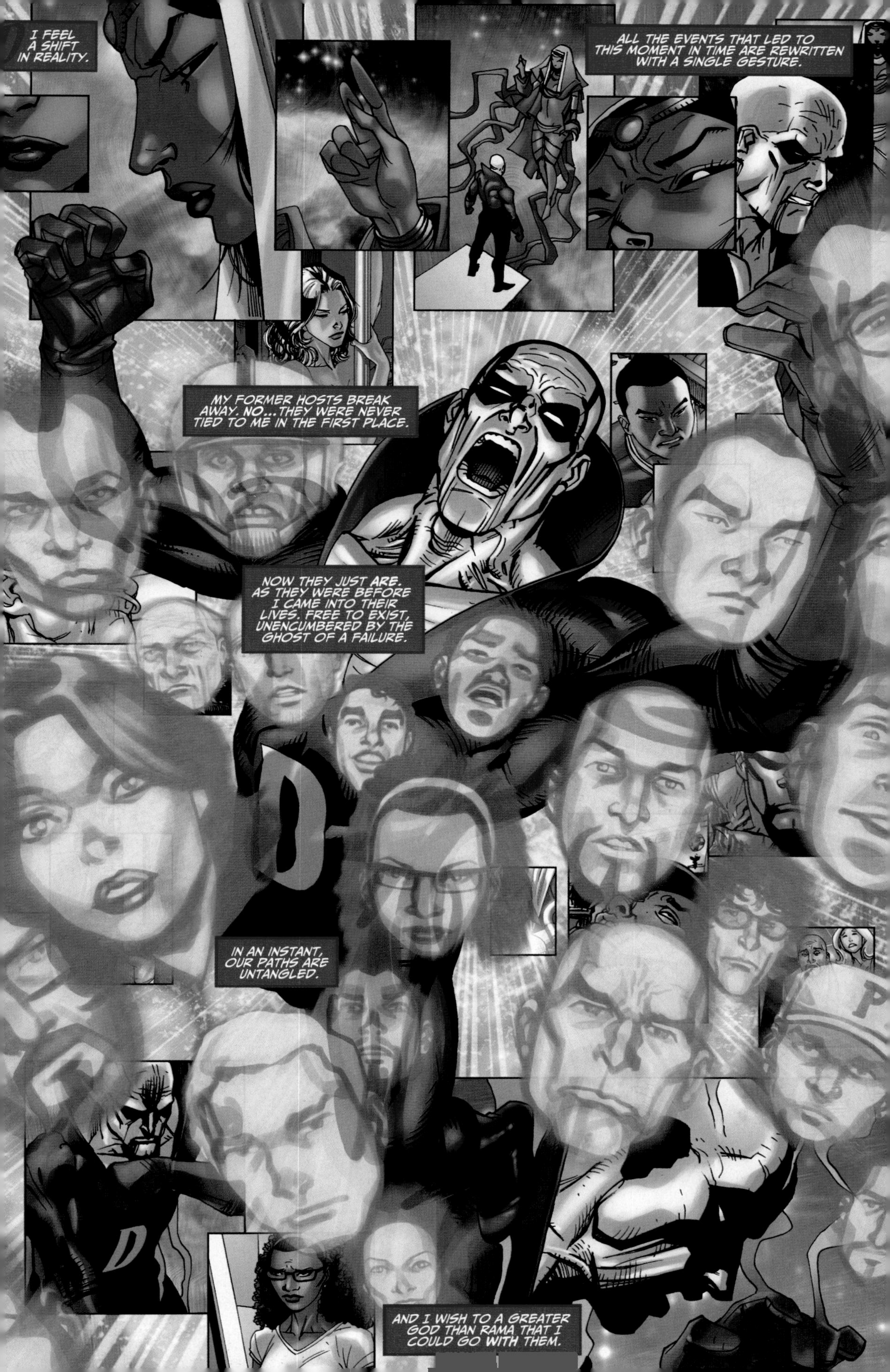
I FEEL A SHIFT IN REALITY.
ALL THE EVENTS THAT LED TO THIS MOMENT IN TIME ARE REWRITTEN WITH A SINGLE GESTURE.
MY FORMER HOSTS BREAK AWAY. NO... THEY WERE NEVER TIED TO ME IN THE FIRST PLACE.
NOW THEY JUST ARE. AS THEY WERE BEFORE I CAME INTO THEIR LIVES. FREE TO EXIST, UNENCUMBERED BY THE GHOST OF A FAILURE.
IN AN INSTANT, OUR PATHS ARE UNTANGLED.
AND I WISH TO A GREATER GOD THAN RAMA THAT I COULD GO WITH THEM.

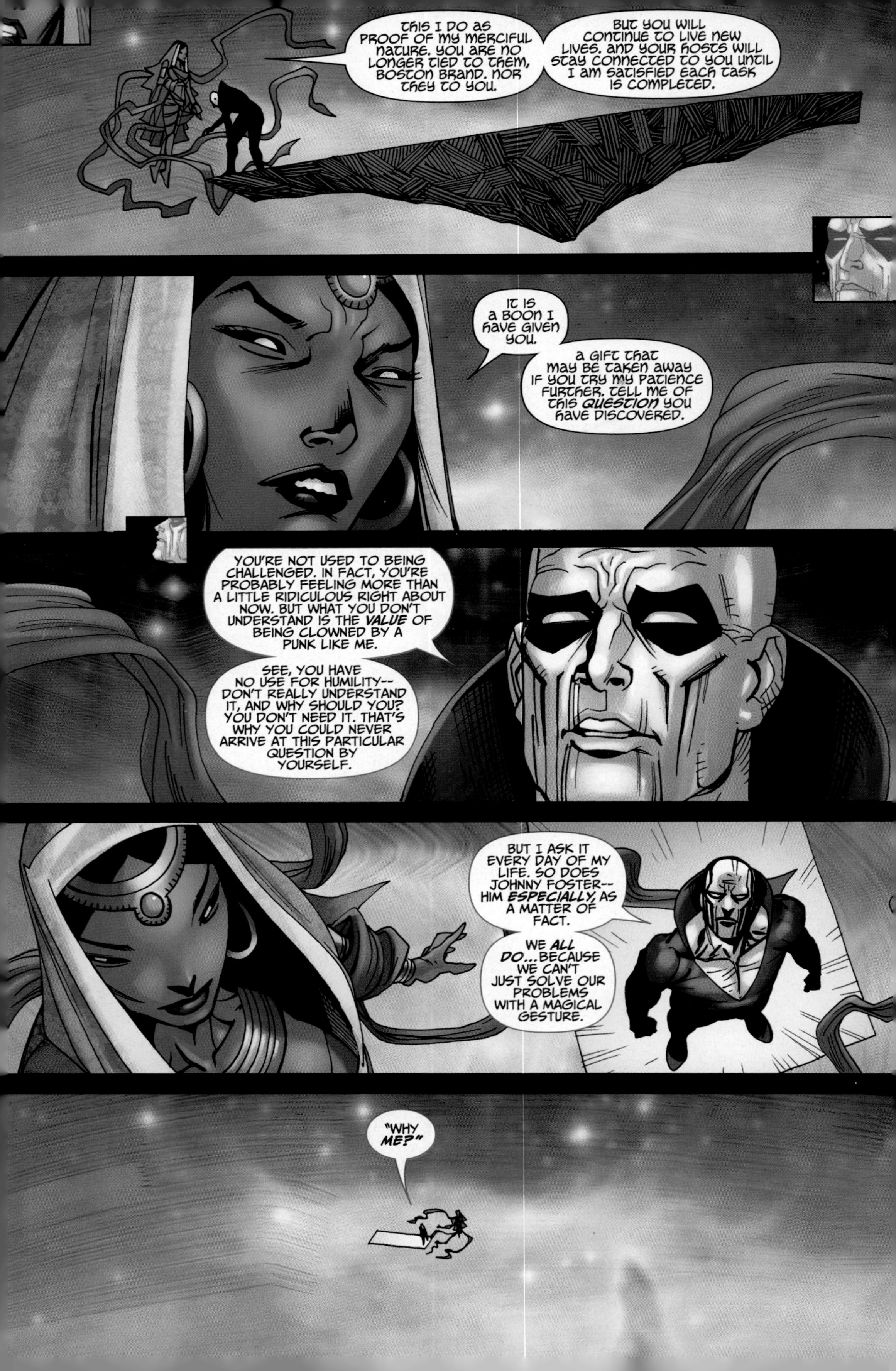
THIS I DO AS PROOF OF MY MERCIFUL NATURE. YOU ARE NO LONGER TIED TO THEM, BOSTON BRAND. NOR THEY TO YOU.
BUT YOU WILL CONTINUE TO LIVE NEW LIVES. AND YOUR HOSTS WILL STAY CONNECTED TO YOU UNTIL I AM SATISFIED EACH TASK IS COMPLETED.
IT IS A BOON I HAVE GIVEN YOU.
A GIFT THAT MAY BE TAKEN AWAY IF YOU TRY MY PATIENCE FURTHER. TELL ME OF THIS QUESTION YOU HAVE DISCOVERED.
YOU'RE NOT USED TO BEING CHALLENGED. IN FACT, YOU'RE PROBABLY FEELING MORE THAN A LITTLE RIDICULOUS RIGHT ABOUT NOW. BUT WHAT YOU DON'T UNDERSTAND IS THE VALUE OF BEING CLOWNED BY A PUNK LIKE ME.
SEE, YOU HAVE NO USE FOR HUMILITY-- DON'T REALLY UNDERSTAND IT, AND WHY SHOULD YOU? YOU DON'T NEED IT. THAT'S WHY YOU COULD NEVER ARRIVE AT THIS PARTICULAR QUESTION BY YOURSELF.
BUT I ASK IT EVERY DAY OF MY LIFE. SO DOES JOHNNY FOSTER-- HIM ESPECIALLY, AS A MATTER OF FACT.
WE ALL DO... BECAUSE WE CAN'T JUST SOLVE OUR PROBLEMS WITH A MAGICAL GESTURE.
"WHY ME?"

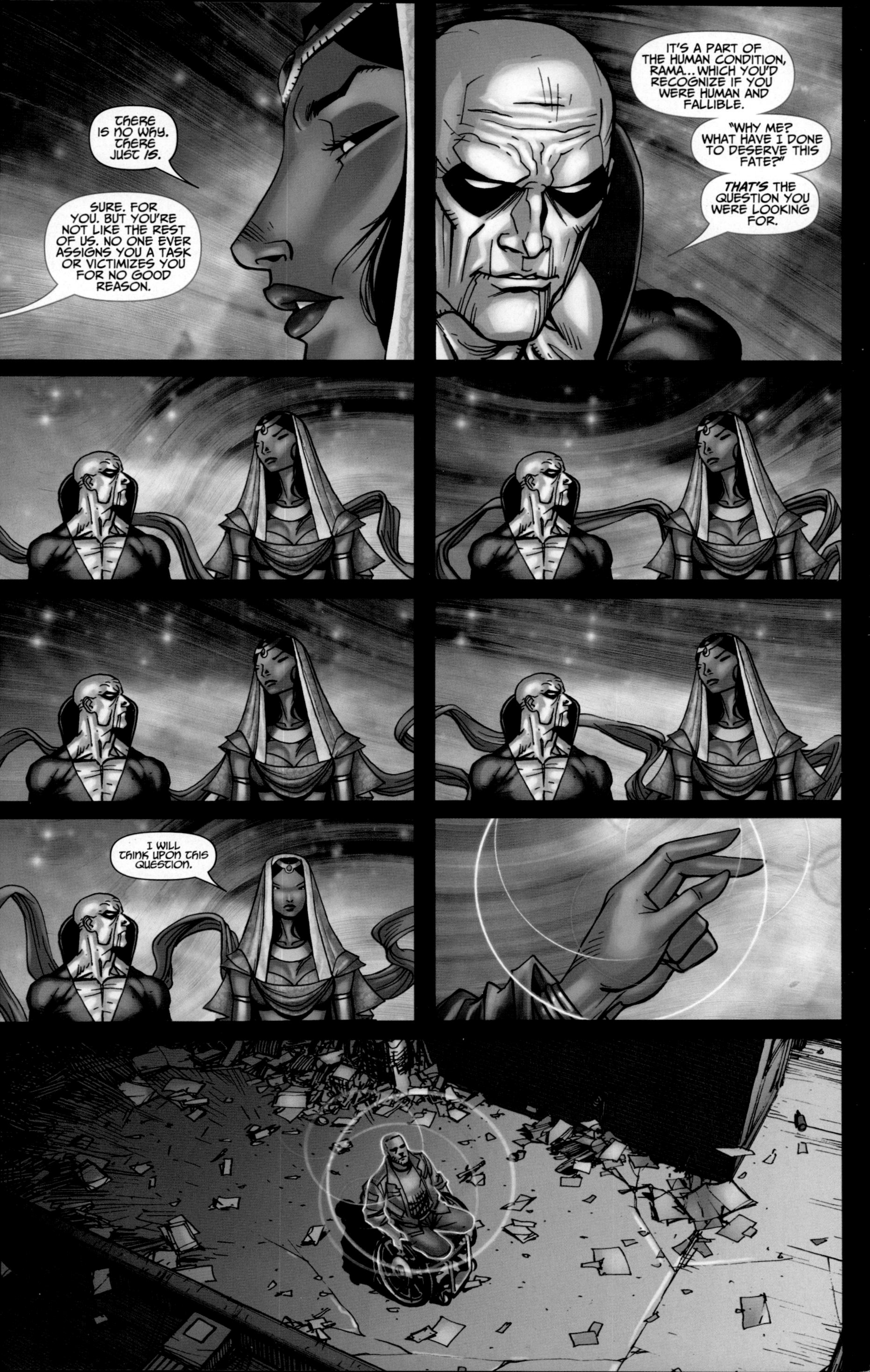
THERE IS NO WHY. THERE JUST *IS.*
SURE. FOR YOU. BUT YOU'RE NOT LIKE THE REST OF US. NO ONE EVER ASSIGNS YOU A TASK OR VICTIMIZES YOU FOR NO GOOD REASON.
IT'S A PART OF THE HUMAN CONDITION, RAMA... WHICH YOU'D RECOGNIZE IF YOU WERE HUMAN AND FALLIBLE.
"WHY ME? WHAT HAVE I DONE TO DESERVE THIS FATE?"
THAT'S THE QUESTION YOU WERE LOOKING FOR.
I WILL THINK UPON THIS QUESTION.

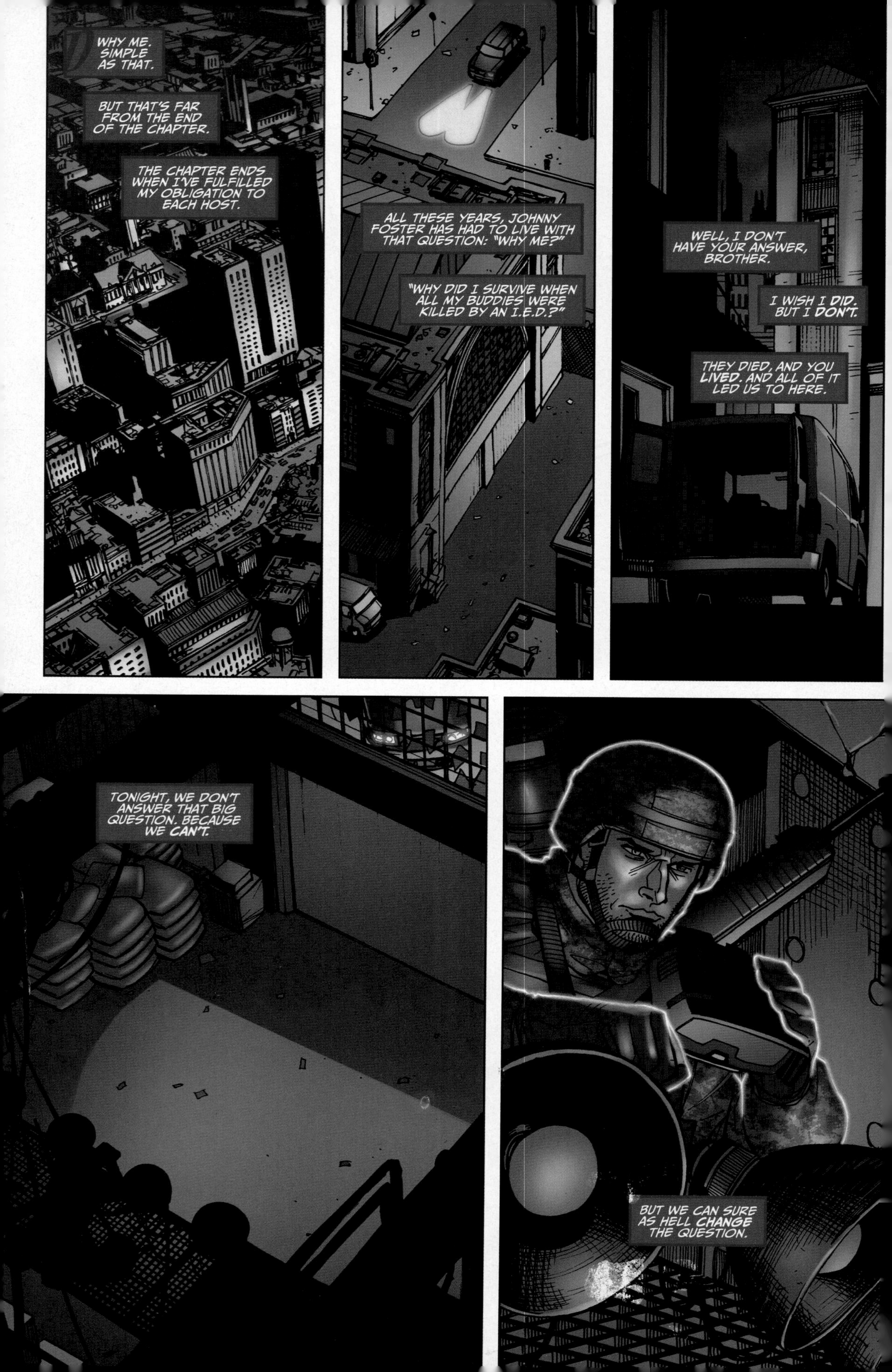
WHY ME. SIMPLE AS THAT.
BUT THAT'S FAR FROM THE END OF THE CHAPTER.
THE CHAPTER ENDS WHEN I'VE FULFILLED MY OBLIGATION TO EACH HOST.
ALL THESE YEARS, JOHNNY FOSTER HAS HAD TO LIVE WITH THAT QUESTION: "WHY ME?"
"WHY DID I SURVIVE WHEN ALL MY BUDDIES WERE KILLED BY AN I.E.D.?"
WELL, I DON'T HAVE YOUR ANSWER, BROTHER.
I WISH I DID. BUT I DON'T.
THEY DIED, AND YOU LIVED. AND ALL OF IT LED US TO HERE.
TONIGHT, WE DON'T ANSWER THAT BIG QUESTION. BECAUSE WE CAN'T.
BUT WE CAN SURE AS HELL CHANGE THE QUESTION.

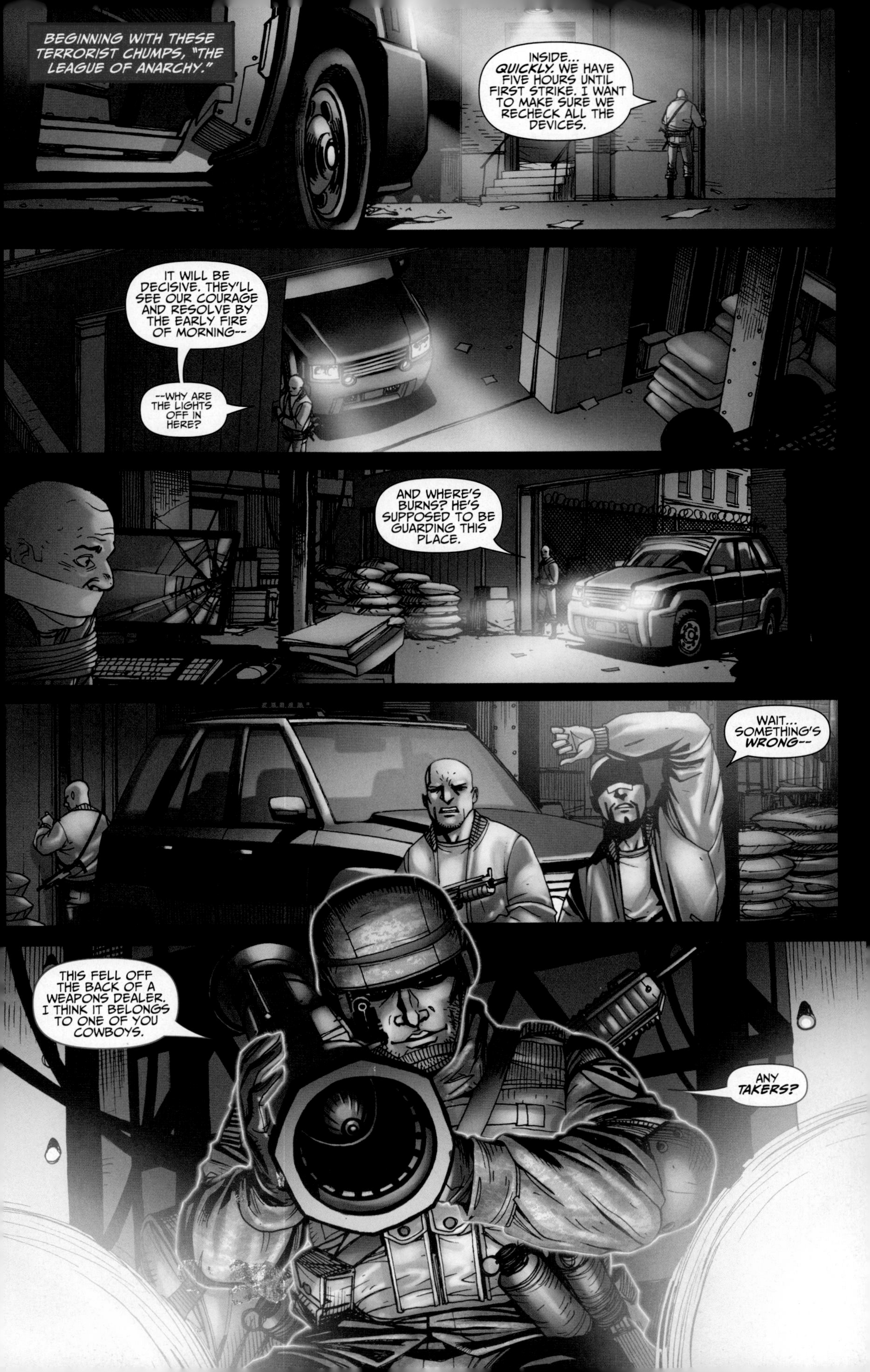
BEGINNING WITH THESE TERRORIST CHUMPS, "THE LEAGUE OF ANARCHY."
INSIDE... QUICKLY. WE HAVE FIVE HOURS UNTIL FIRST STRIKE. I WANT TO MAKE SURE WE RECHECK ALL THE DEVICES.
IT WILL BE DECISIVE. THEY'LL SEE OUR COURAGE AND RESOLVE BY THE EARLY FIRE OF MORNING--
--WHY ARE THE LIGHTS OFF IN HERE?
AND WHERE'S BURNS? HE'S SUPPOSED TO BE GUARDING THIS PLACE.
WAIT... SOMETHING'S WRONG--
THIS FELL OFF THE BACK OF A WEAPONS DEALER. I THINK IT BELONGS TO ONE OF YOU COWBOYS.
ANY TAKERS?

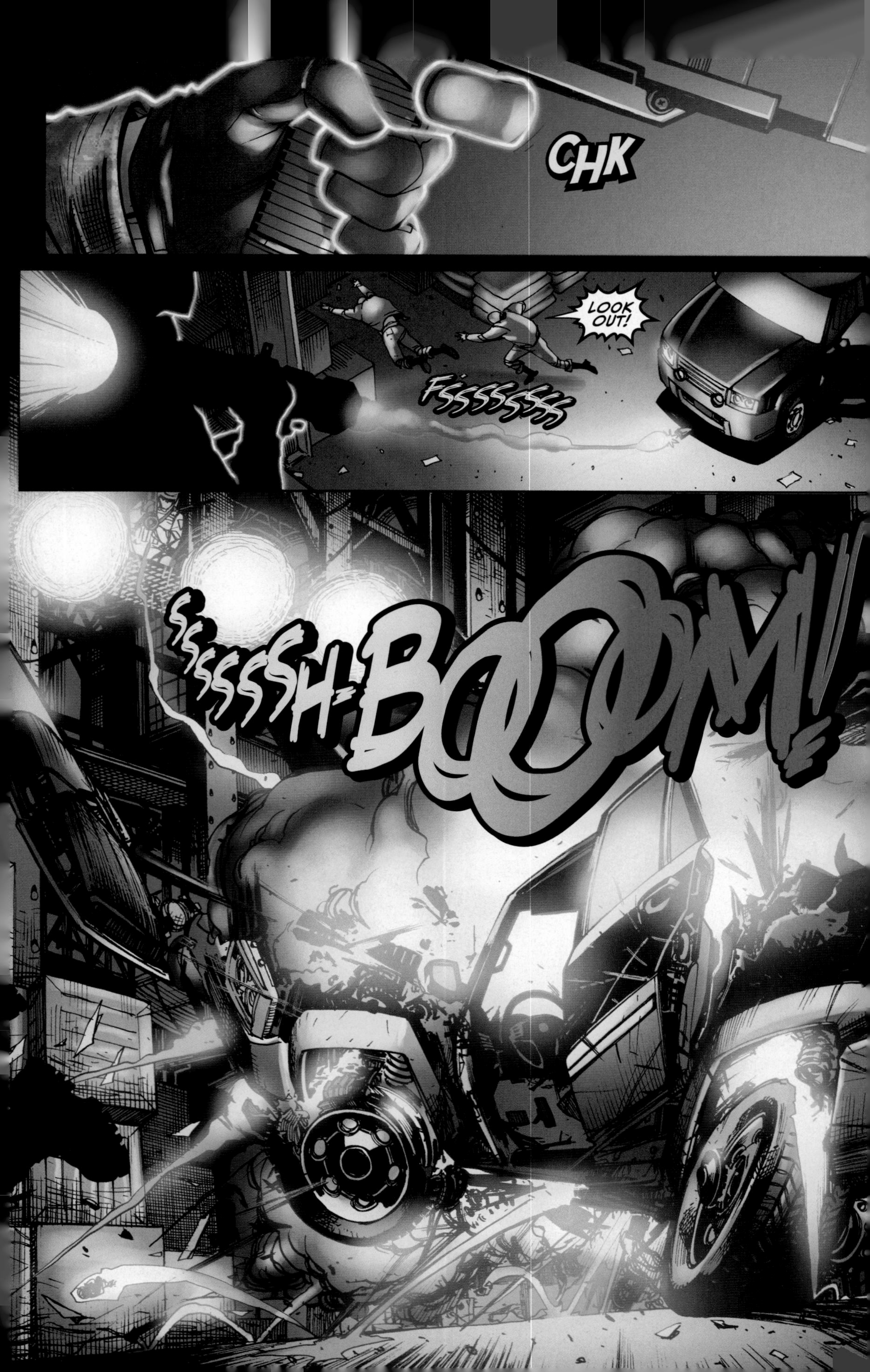

CHK
LOOK OUT!
FSSSSSSS
SSSSSSH-BOOM!

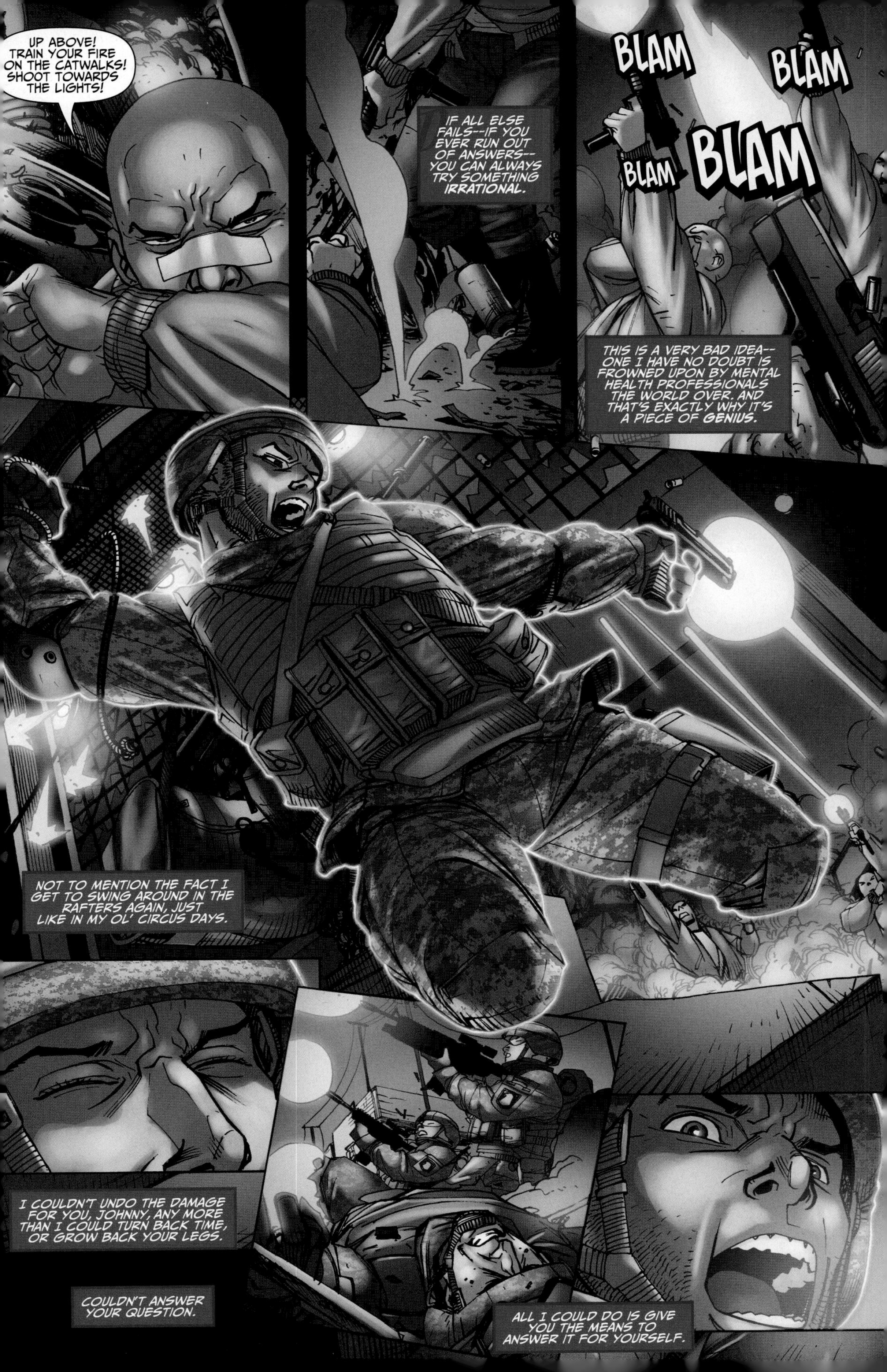
UP ABOVE! TRAIN YOUR FIRE ON THE CATWALKS! SHOOT TOWARDS THE LIGHTS!
IF ALL ELSE FAILS--IF YOU EVER RUN OUT OF ANSWERS-- YOU CAN ALWAYS TRY SOMETHING IRRATIONAL.
BLAM
BLAM
BLAM
BLAM
THIS IS A VERY BAD IDEA-- ONE I HAVE NO DOUBT IS FROWNED UPON BY MENTAL HEALTH PROFESSIONALS THE WORLD OVER. AND THAT'S EXACTLY WHY IT'S A PIECE OF GENIUS.
NOT TO MENTION THE FACT I GET TO SWING AROUND IN THE RAFTERS AGAIN, JUST LIKE IN MY OL' CIRCUS DAYS.
I COULDN'T UNDO THE DAMAGE FOR YOU, JOHNNY, ANY MORE THAN I COULD TURN BACK TIME, OR GROW BACK YOUR LEGS.
COULDN'T ANSWER YOUR QUESTION.
ALL I COULD DO IS GIVE YOU THE MEANS TO ANSWER IT FOR YOURSELF.

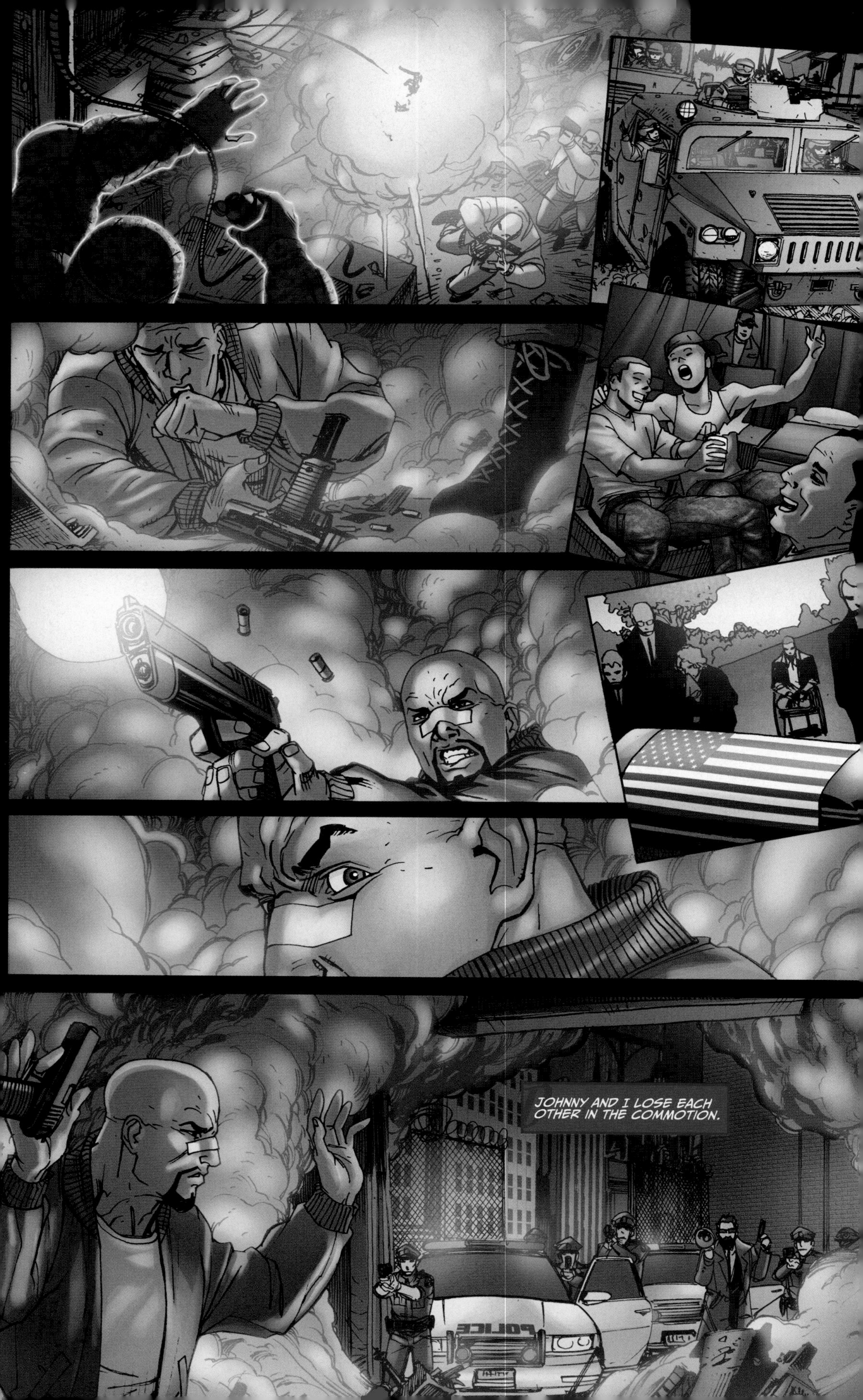
JOHNNY AND I LOSE EACH OTHER IN THE COMMOTION.

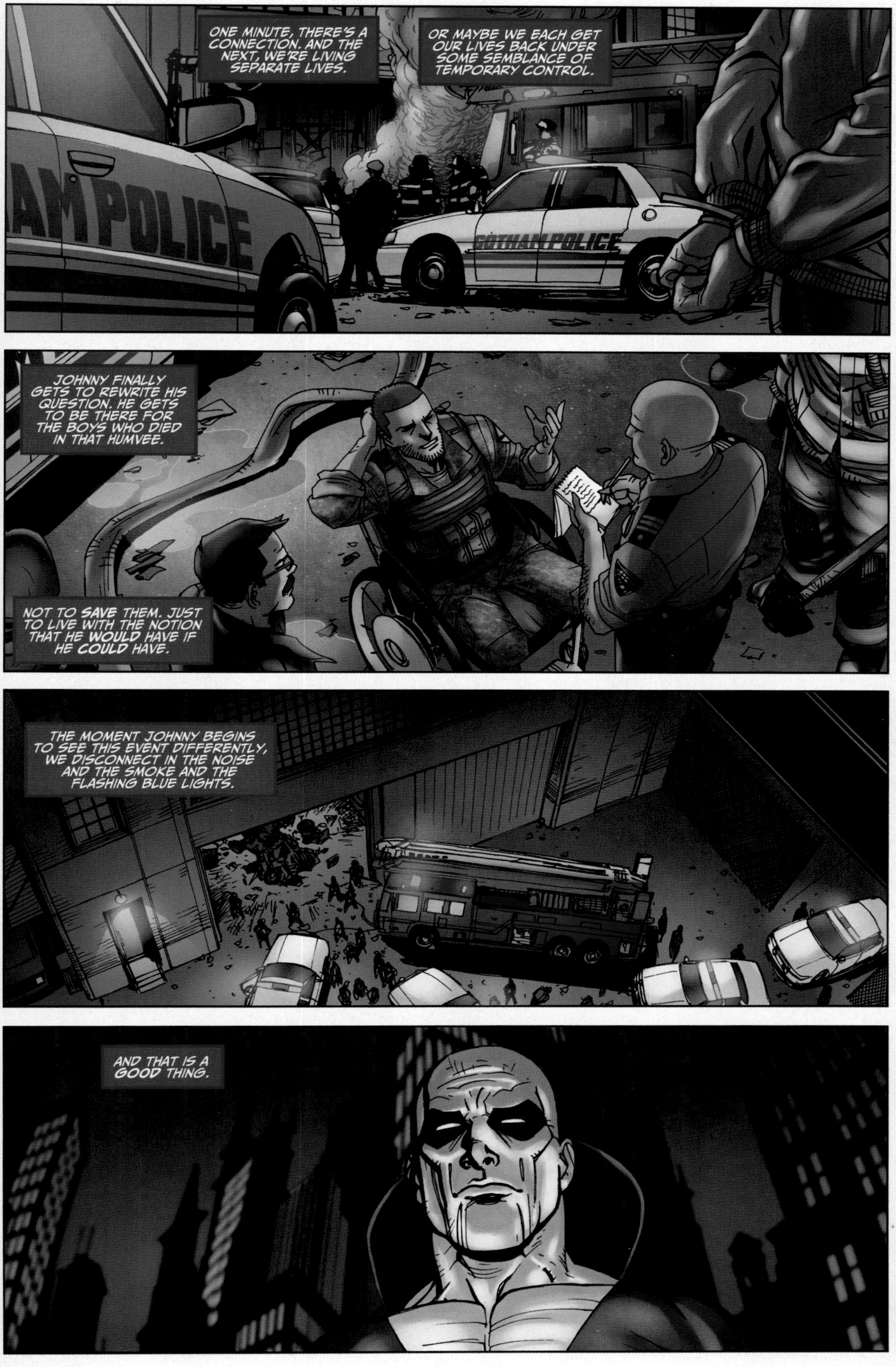

ONE MINUTE, THERE'S A CONNECTION. AND THE NEXT, WE'RE LIVING SEPARATE LIVES.
OR MAYBE WE EACH GET OUR LIVES BACK UNDER SOME SEMBLANCE OF TEMPORARY CONTROL.
GOTHAM POLICE
JOHNNY FINALLY GETS TO REWRITE HIS QUESTION. HE GETS TO BE THERE FOR THE BOYS WHO DIED IN THAT HUMVEE.
NOT TO SAVE THEM. JUST TO LIVE WITH THE NOTION THAT HE WOULD HAVE IF HE COULD HAVE.
THE MOMENT JOHNNY BEGINS TO SEE THIS EVENT DIFFERENTLY, WE DISCONNECT IN THE NOISE AND THE SMOKE AND THE FLASHING BLUE LIGHTS.
AND THAT IS A GOOD THING.

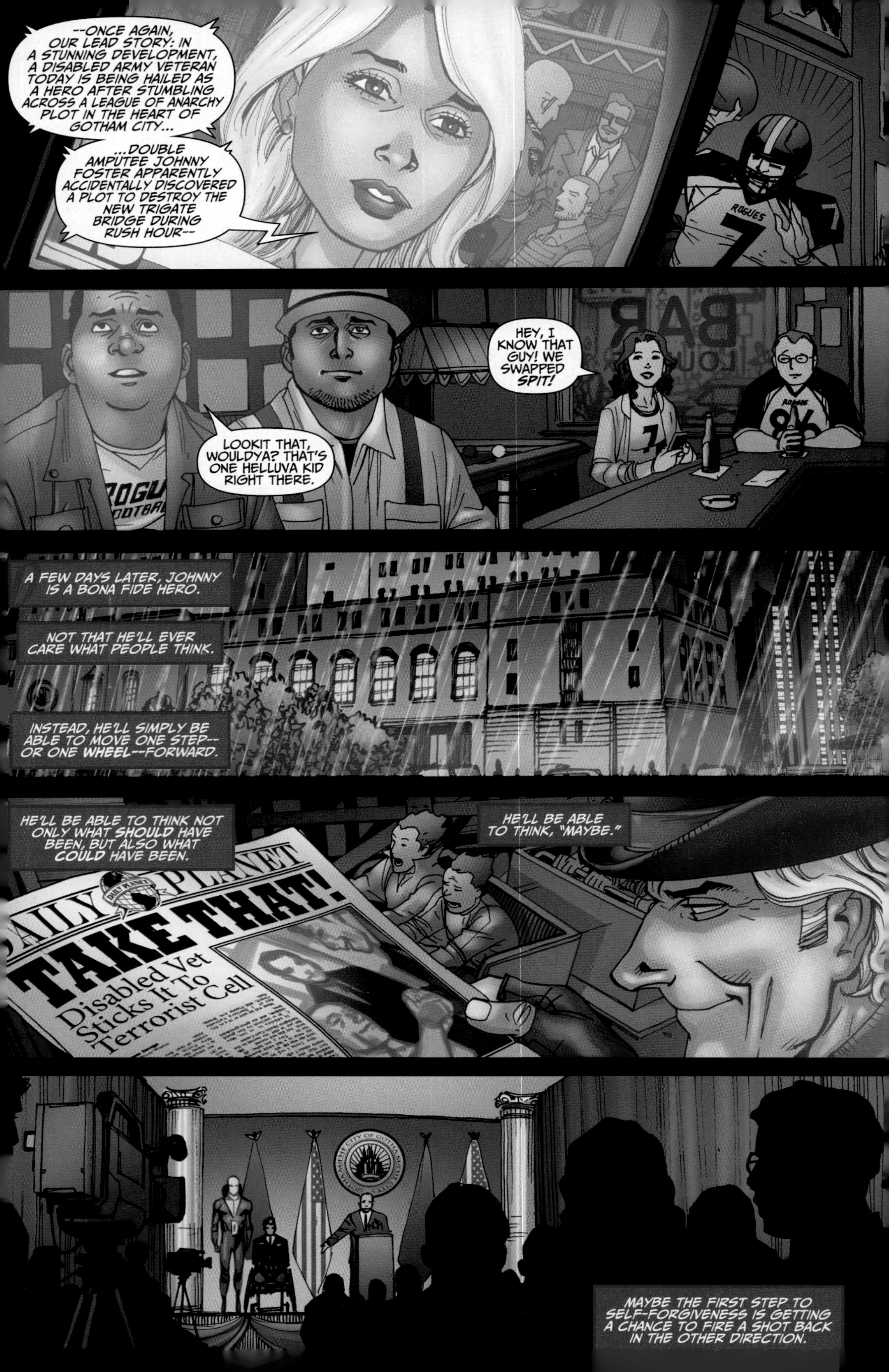
--ONCE AGAIN, OUR LEAD STORY: IN A STUNNING DEVELOPMENT, A DISABLED ARMY VETERAN TODAY IS BEING HAILED AS A HERO AFTER STUMBLING ACROSS A LEAGUE OF ANARCHY PLOT IN THE HEART OF GOTHAM CITY...
...DOUBLE AMPUTEE JOHNNY FOSTER APPARENTLY ACCIDENTALLY DISCOVERED A PLOT TO DESTROY THE NEW TRIGATE BRIDGE DURING RUSH HOUR--
ROGUES
7
HEY, I KNOW THAT GUY! WE SWAPPED SPIT!
LOOKIT THAT, WOULDYA? THAT'S ONE HELLUVA KID RIGHT THERE.
BAR
A FEW DAYS LATER, JOHNNY IS A BONA FIDE HERO.
NOT THAT HE'LL EVER CARE WHAT PEOPLE THINK.
INSTEAD, HE'LL SIMPLY BE ABLE TO MOVE ONE STEP--OR ONE WHEEL--FORWARD.
HE'LL BE ABLE TO THINK NOT ONLY WHAT SHOULD HAVE BEEN, BUT ALSO WHAT COULD HAVE BEEN.
HE'LL BE ABLE TO THINK, "MAYBE."
DAILY PLANET
TAKE THAT!
Disabled Vet Sticks It To Terrorist Cell
MAYBE THE FIRST STEP TO SELF-FORGIVENESS IS GETTING A CHANCE TO FIRE A SHOT BACK IN THE OTHER DIRECTION.

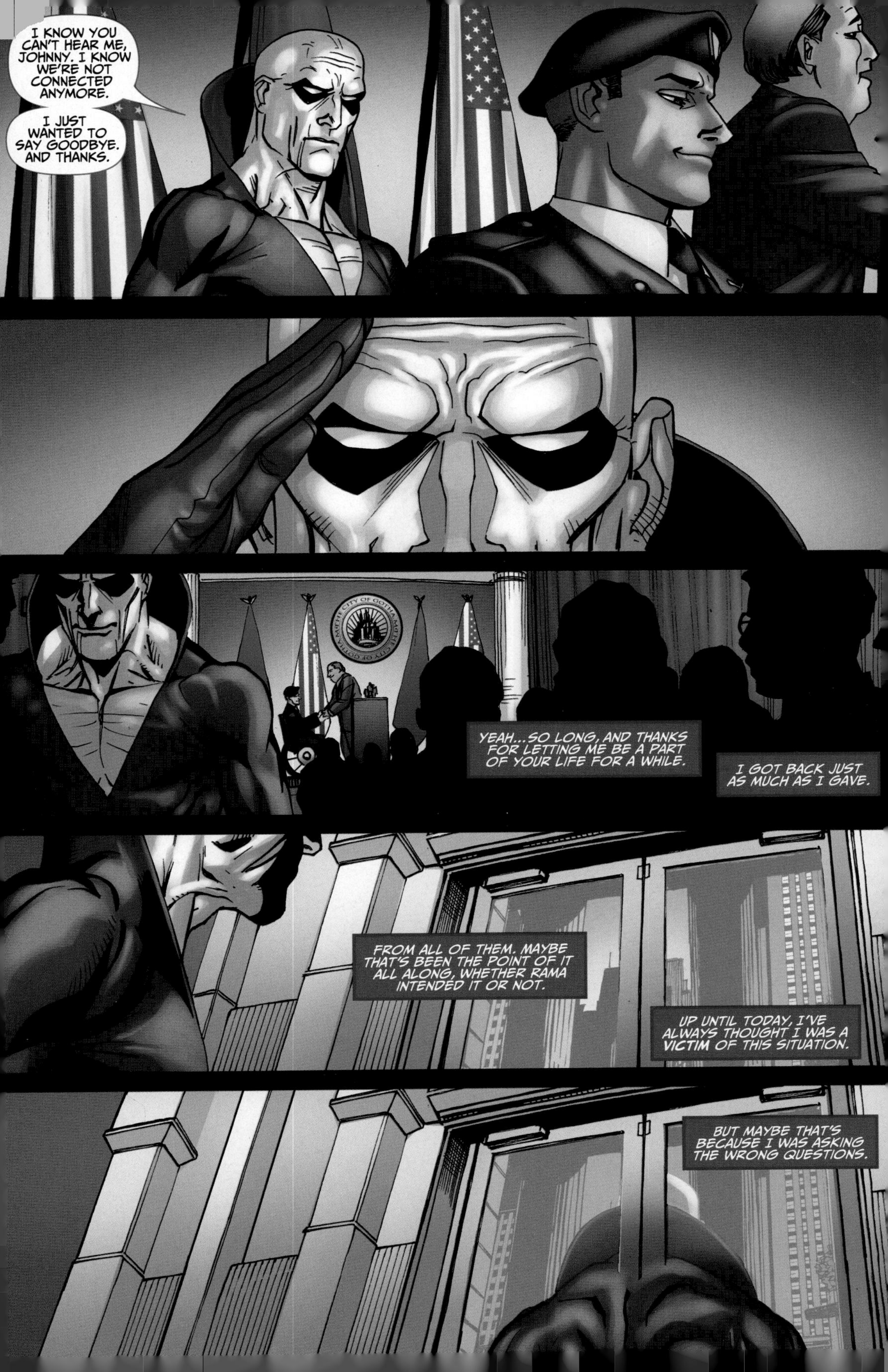
I KNOW YOU CAN'T HEAR ME, JOHNNY. I KNOW WE'RE NOT CONNECTED ANYMORE.
I JUST WANTED TO SAY GOODBYE. AND THANKS.
THE CITY OF GOTHAM
YEAH...SO LONG, AND THANKS FOR LETTING ME BE A PART OF YOUR LIFE FOR A WHILE.
I GOT BACK JUST AS MUCH AS I GAVE.
FROM ALL OF THEM. MAYBE THAT'S BEEN THE POINT OF IT ALL ALONG, WHETHER RAMA INTENDED IT OR NOT.
UP UNTIL TODAY, I'VE ALWAYS THOUGHT I WAS A **VICTIM** OF THIS SITUATION.
BUT MAYBE THAT'S BECAUSE I WAS ASKING THE WRONG QUESTIONS.

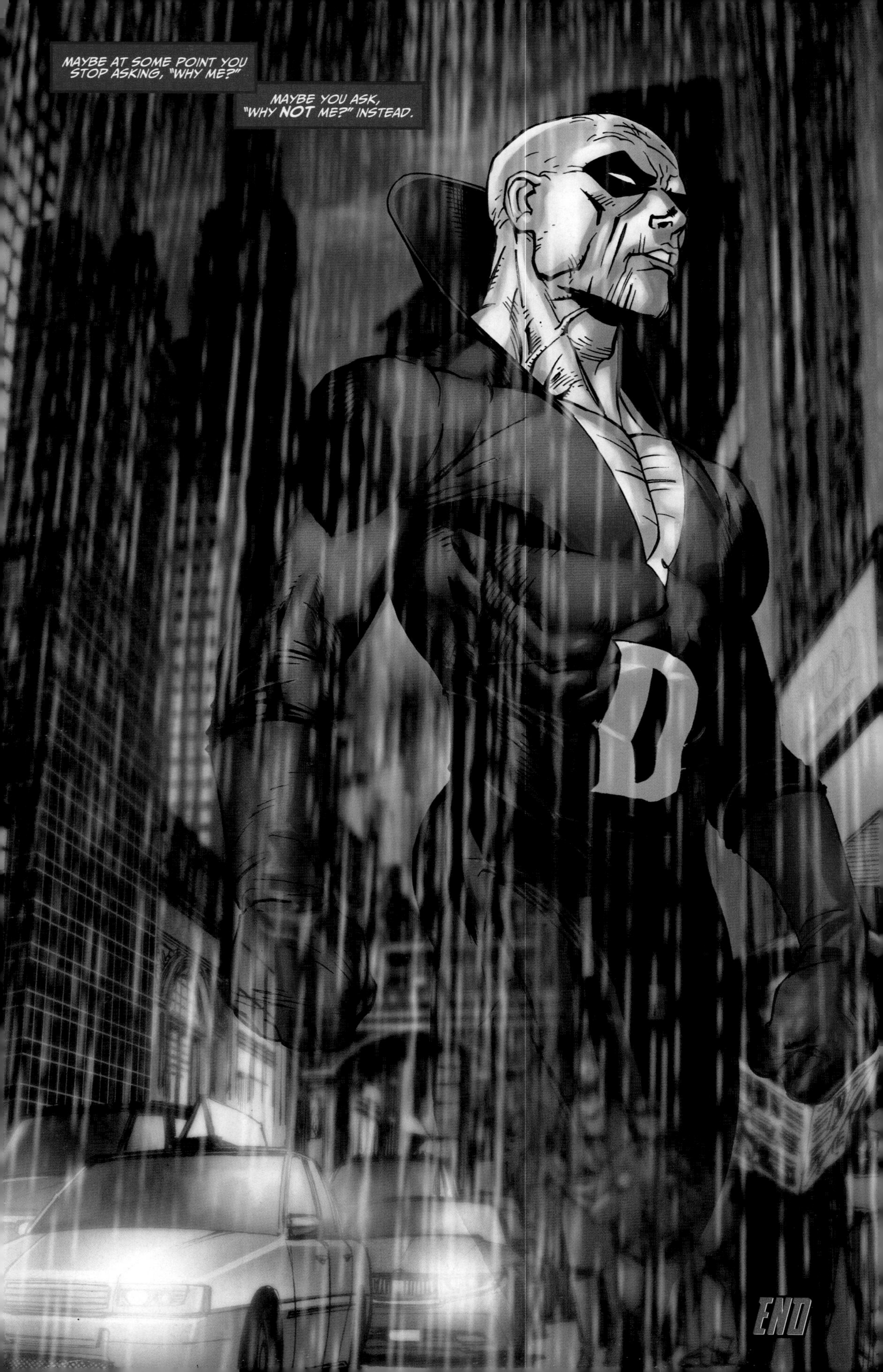
MAYBE AT SOME POINT YOU STOP ASKING, "WHY ME?"
MAYBE YOU ASK, "WHY NOT ME?" INSTEAD.
END

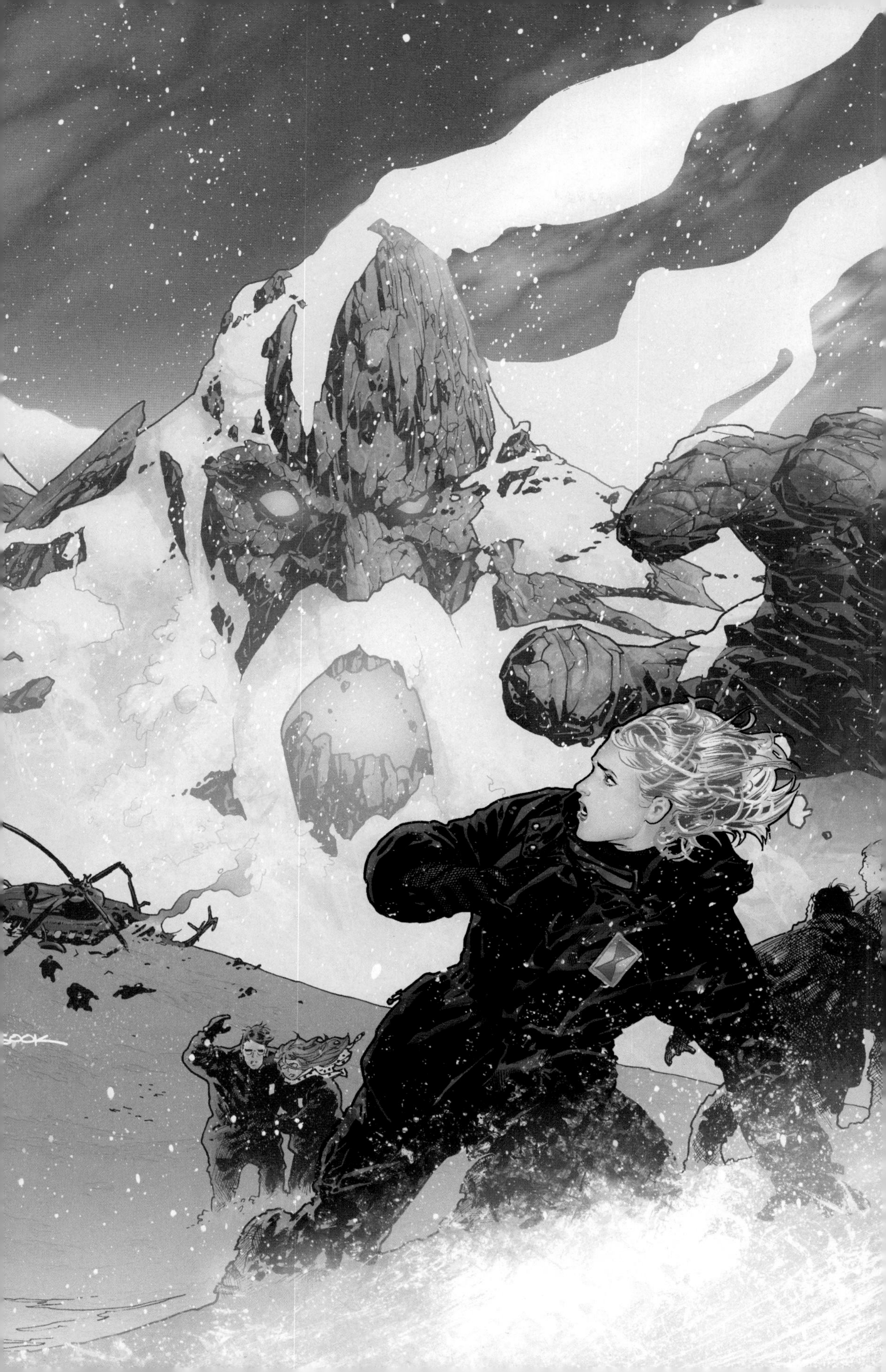

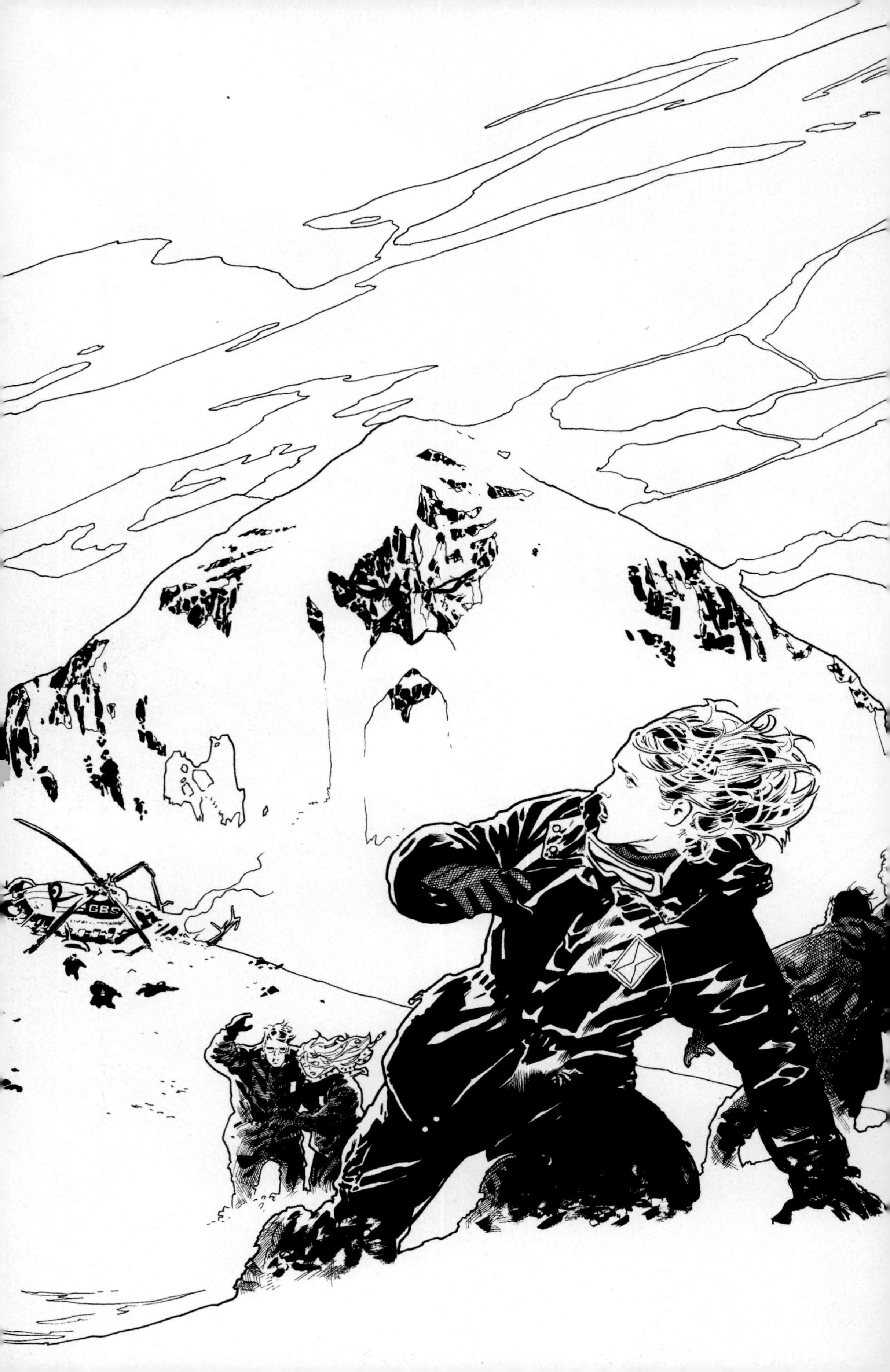
GBS

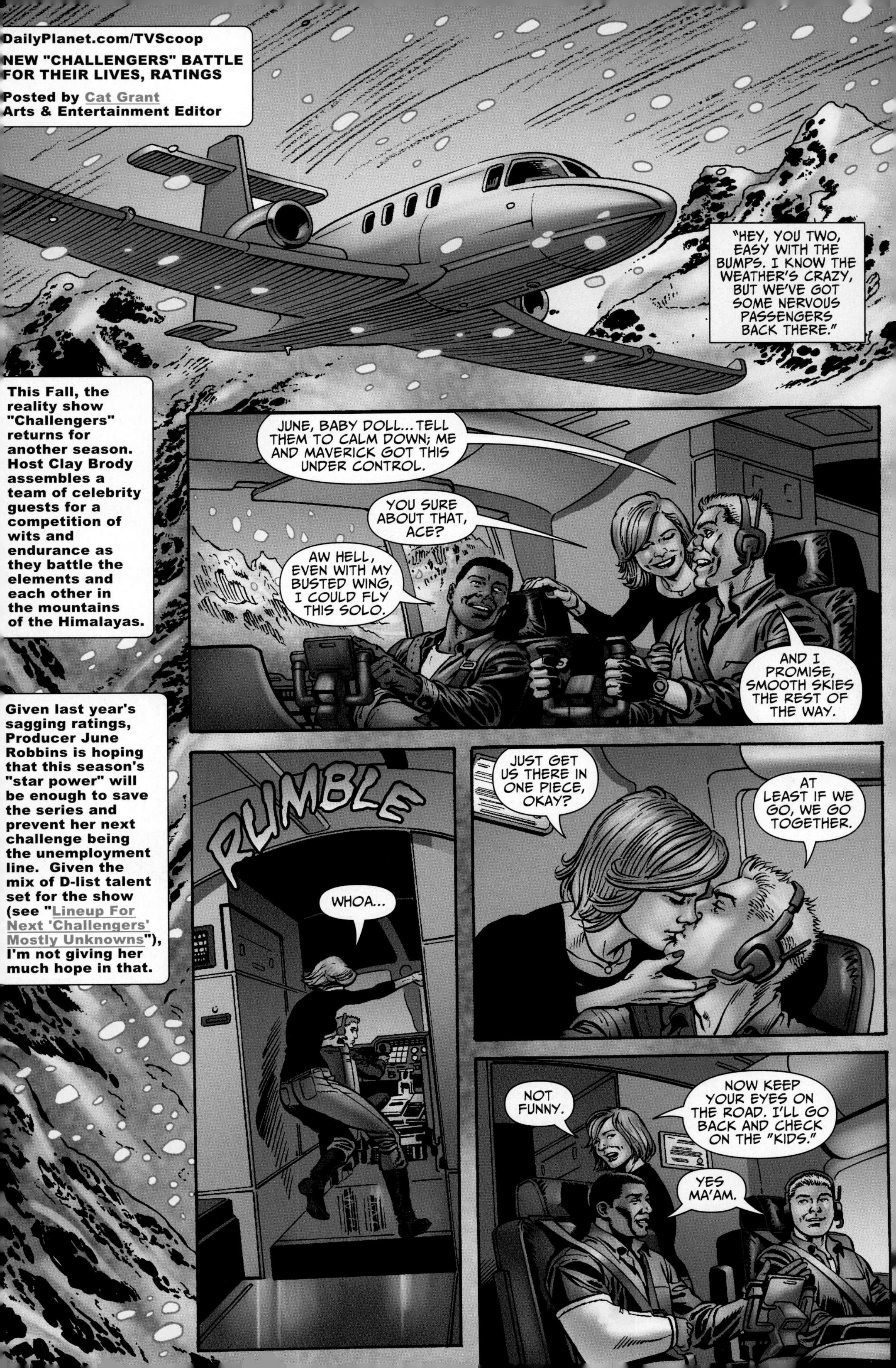
DailyPlanet.com/TVScoop
NEW "CHALLENGERS" BATTLE FOR THEIR LIVES, RATINGS
Posted by Cat Grant
Arts & Entertainment Editor
"HEY, YOU TWO, EASY WITH THE BUMPS. I KNOW THE WEATHER'S CRAZY, BUT WE'VE GOT SOME NERVOUS PASSENGERS BACK THERE."
This Fall, the reality show "Challengers" returns for another season. Host Clay Brody assembles a team of celebrity guests for a competition of wits and endurance as they battle the elements and each other in the mountains of the Himalayas.
JUNE, BABY DOLL... TELL THEM TO CALM DOWN; ME AND MAVERICK GOT THIS UNDER CONTROL.
YOU SURE ABOUT THAT, ACE?
AW HELL, EVEN WITH MY BUSTED WING, I COULD FLY THIS SOLO.
AND I PROMISE, SMOOTH SKIES THE REST OF THE WAY.
Given last year's sagging ratings, Producer June Robbins is hoping that this season's "star power" will be enough to save the series and prevent her next challenge being the unemployment line. Given the mix of D-list talent set for the show (see "Lineup For Next 'Challengers' Mostly Unknowns"), I'm not giving her much hope in that.
RUMBLE
WHOA...
JUST GET US THERE IN ONE PIECE, OKAY?
AT LEAST IF WE GO, WE GO TOGETHER.
NOT FUNNY.
NOW KEEP YOUR EYES ON THE ROAD. I'LL GO BACK AND CHECK ON THE "KIDS."
YES MA'AM.

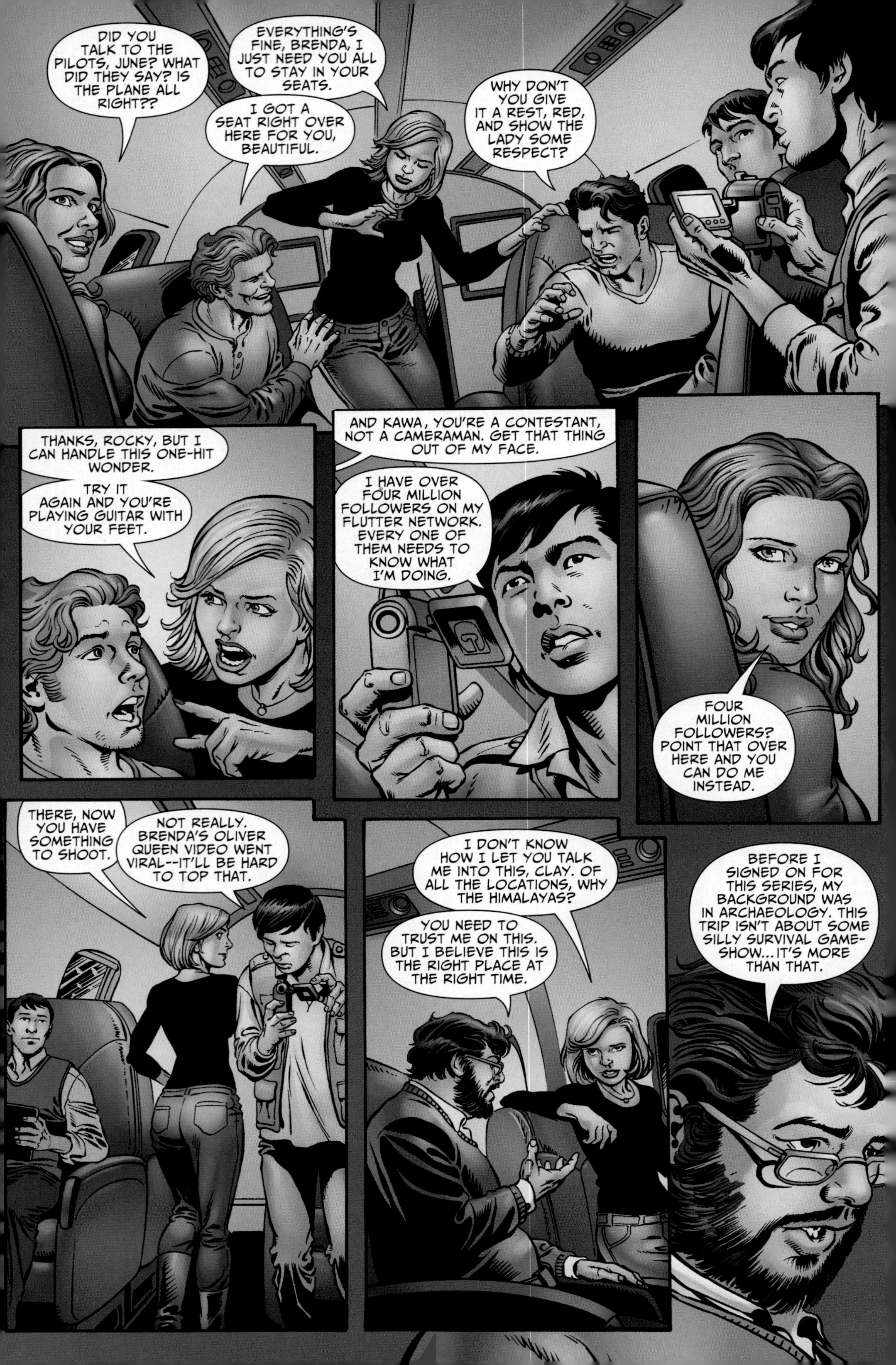
DID YOU TALK TO THE PILOTS, JUNE? WHAT DID THEY SAY? IS THE PLANE ALL RIGHT??
EVERYTHING'S FINE, BRENDA, I JUST NEED YOU ALL TO STAY IN YOUR SEATS.
I GOT A SEAT RIGHT OVER HERE FOR YOU, BEAUTIFUL.
WHY DON'T YOU GIVE IT A REST, RED, AND SHOW THE LADY SOME RESPECT?
THANKS, ROCKY, BUT I CAN HANDLE THIS ONE-HIT WONDER.
TRY IT AGAIN AND YOU'RE PLAYING GUITAR WITH YOUR FEET.
AND KAWA, YOU'RE A CONTESTANT, NOT A CAMERAMAN. GET THAT THING OUT OF MY FACE.
I HAVE OVER FOUR MILLION FOLLOWERS ON MY FLUTTER NETWORK. EVERY ONE OF THEM NEEDS TO KNOW WHAT I'M DOING.
FOUR MILLION FOLLOWERS? POINT THAT OVER HERE AND YOU CAN DO ME INSTEAD.
THERE, NOW YOU HAVE SOMETHING TO SHOOT.
NOT REALLY. BRENDA'S OLIVER QUEEN VIDEO WENT VIRAL--IT'LL BE HARD TO TOP THAT.
I DON'T KNOW HOW I LET YOU TALK ME INTO THIS, CLAY. OF ALL THE LOCATIONS, WHY THE HIMALAYAS?
YOU NEED TO TRUST ME ON THIS. BUT I BELIEVE THIS IS THE RIGHT PLACE AT THE RIGHT TIME.
BEFORE I SIGNED ON FOR THIS SERIES, MY BACKGROUND WAS IN ARCHAEOLOGY. THIS TRIP ISN'T ABOUT SOME SILLY SURVIVAL GAME-SHOW...IT'S MORE THAN THAT.

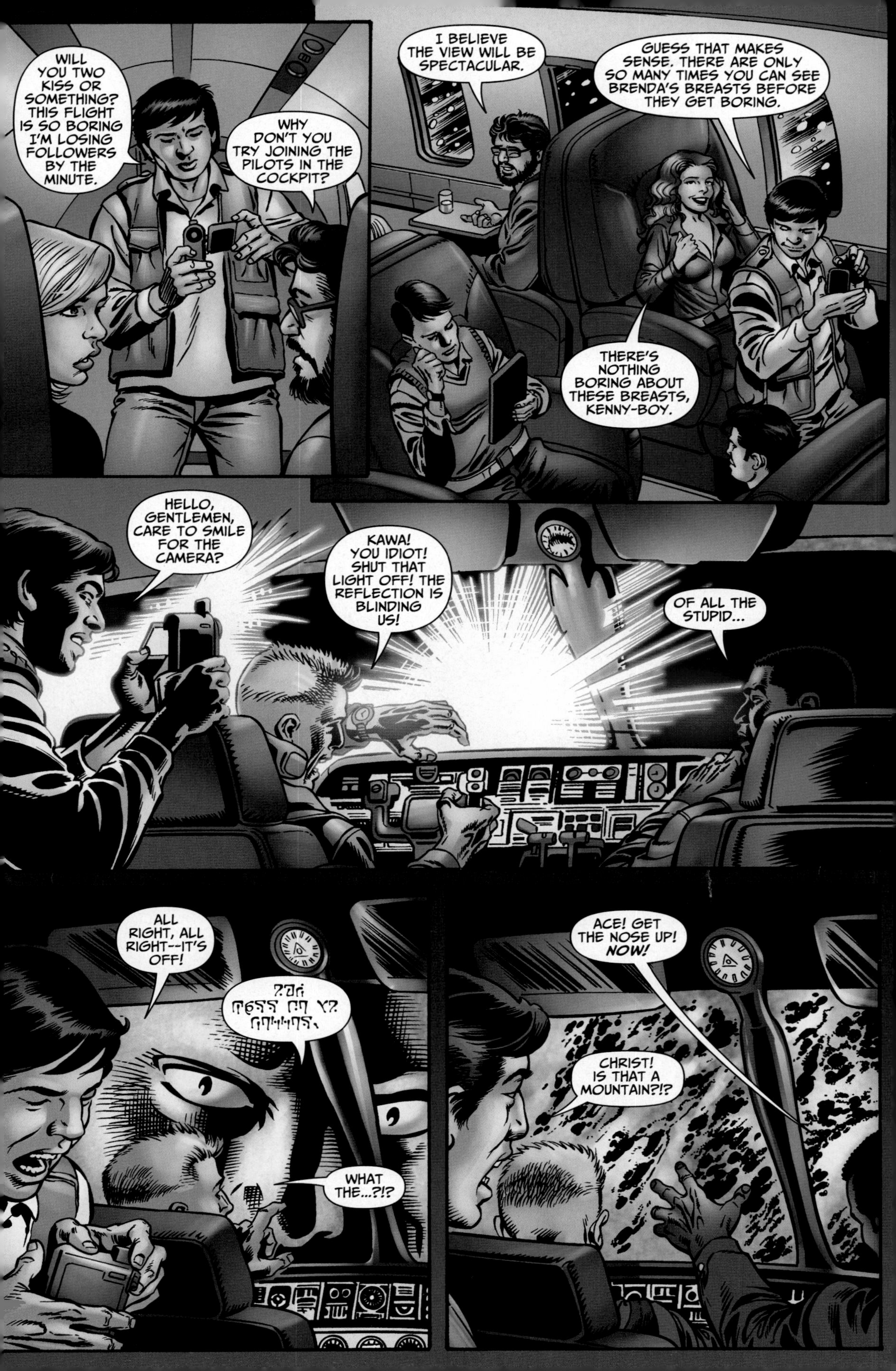

WILL YOU TWO KISS OR SOMETHING? THIS FLIGHT IS SO BORING I'M LOSING FOLLOWERS BY THE MINUTE.
WHY DON'T YOU TRY JOINING THE PILOTS IN THE COCKPIT?
I BELIEVE THE VIEW WILL BE SPECTACULAR.
GUESS THAT MAKES SENSE. THERE ARE ONLY SO MANY TIMES YOU CAN SEE BRENDA'S BREASTS BEFORE THEY GET BORING.
THERE'S NOTHING BORING ABOUT THESE BREASTS, KENNY-BOY.
HELLO, GENTLEMEN, CARE TO SMILE FOR THE CAMERA?
KAWA! YOU IDIOT! SHUT THAT LIGHT OFF! THE REFLECTION IS BLINDING US!
OF ALL THE STUPID...
ALL RIGHT, ALL RIGHT--IT'S OFF!
WHAT THE...?!?
ACE! GET THE NOSE UP! NOW!
CHRIST! IS THAT A MOUNTAIN?!?

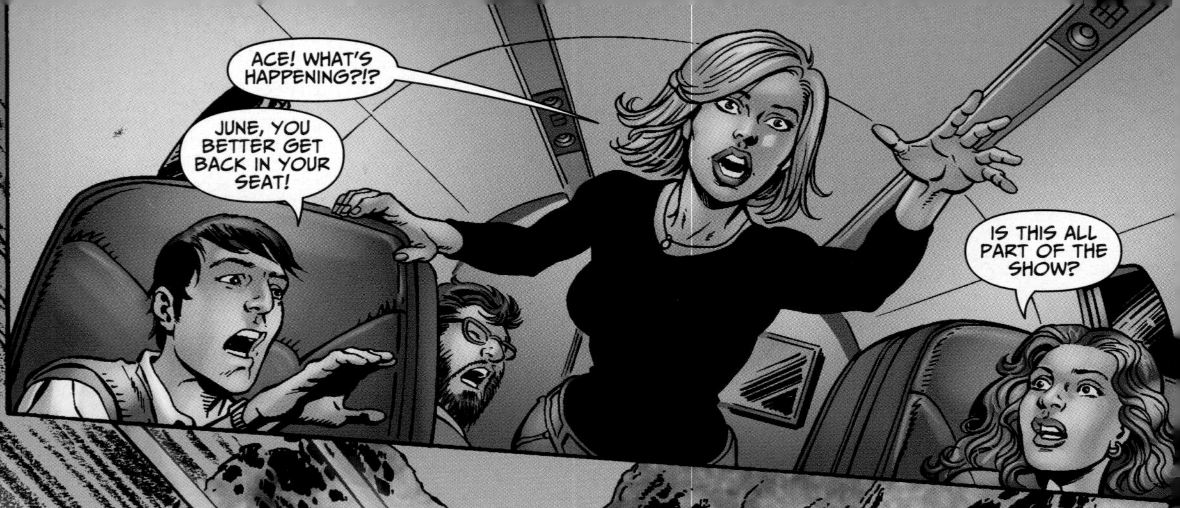
ACE! WHAT'S HAPPENING?!?
JUNE, YOU BETTER GET BACK IN YOUR SEAT!
IS THIS ALL PART OF THE SHOW?
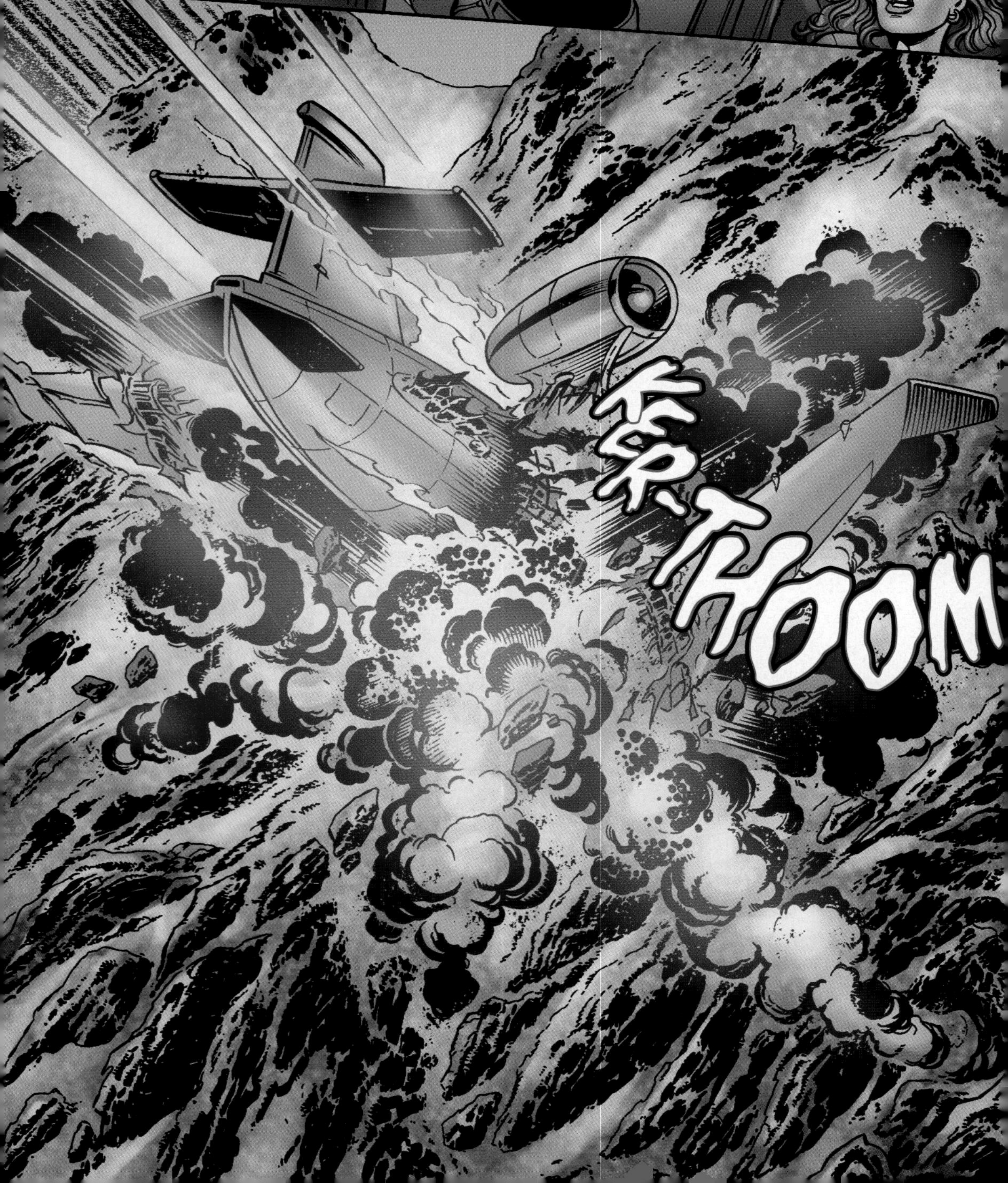
KER-THOOM

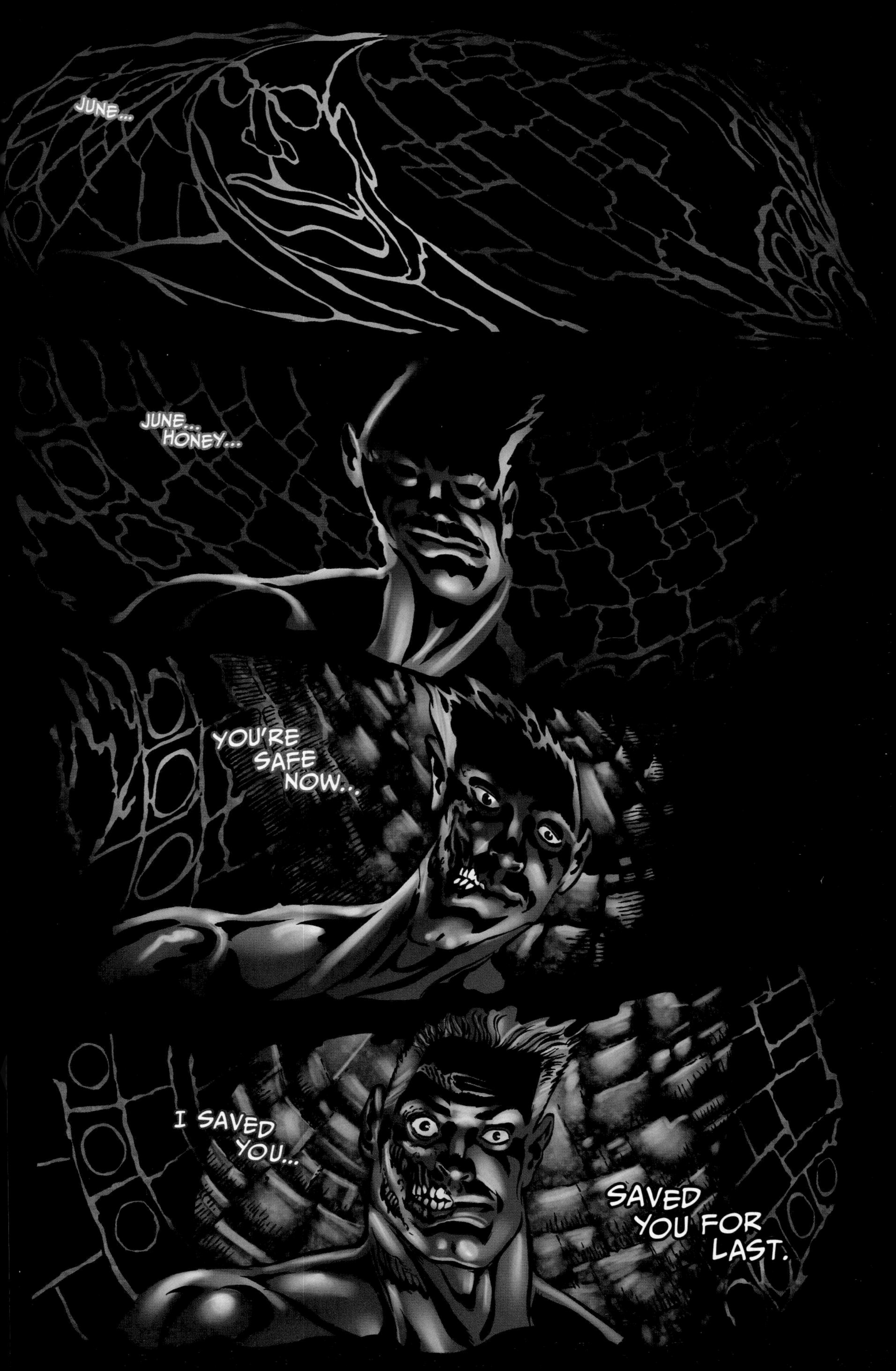
JUNE...
JUNE... HONEY...
YOU'RE SAFE NOW...
I SAVED YOU...
SAVED YOU FOR LAST.

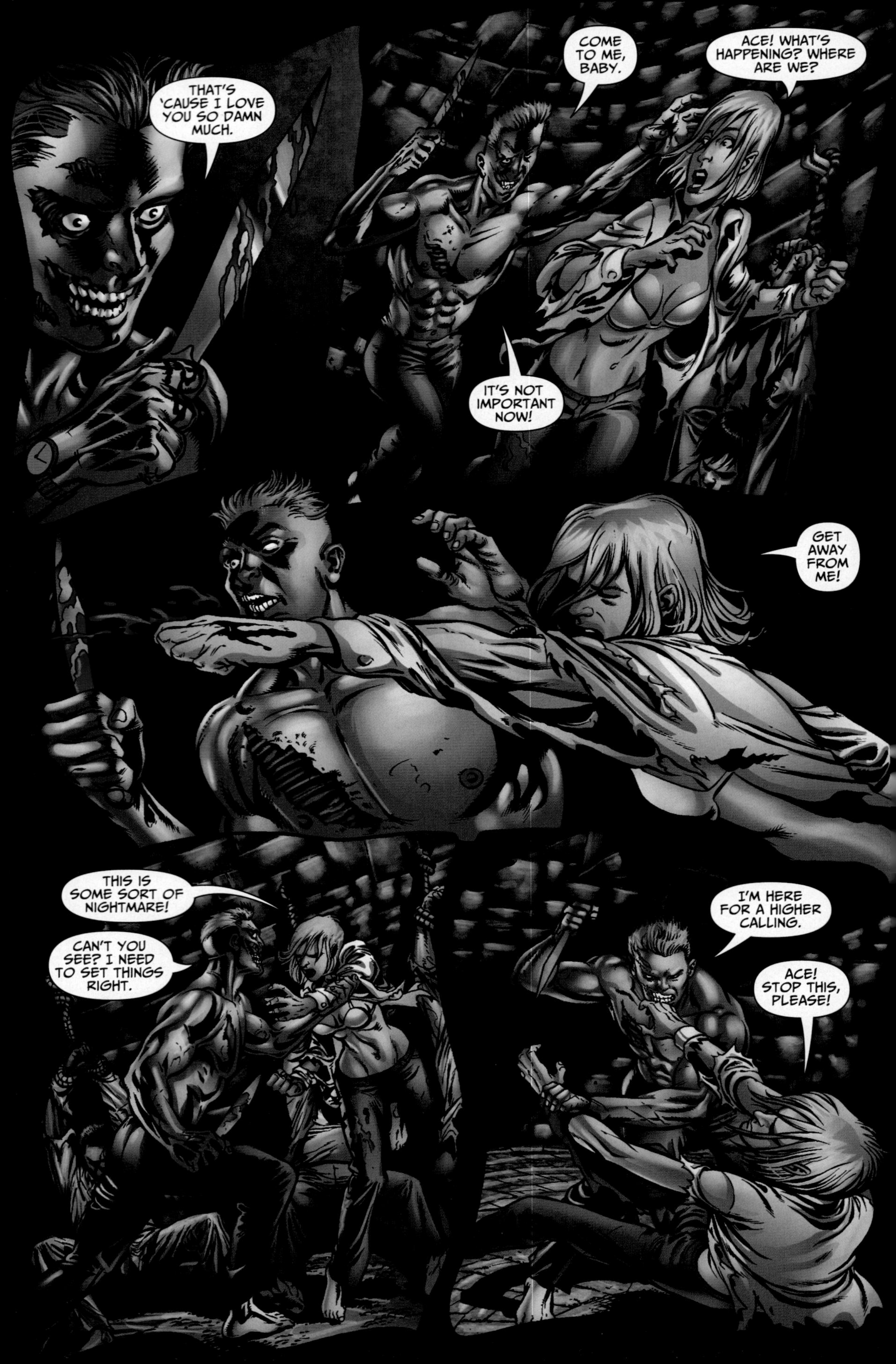
THAT'S 'CAUSE I LOVE YOU SO DAMN MUCH.
COME TO ME, BABY.
ACE! WHAT'S HAPPENING? WHERE ARE WE?
IT'S NOT IMPORTANT NOW!
GET AWAY FROM ME!
THIS IS SOME SORT OF NIGHTMARE!
CAN'T YOU SEE? I NEED TO SET THINGS RIGHT.
I'M HERE FOR A HIGHER CALLING.
ACE! STOP THIS, PLEASE!

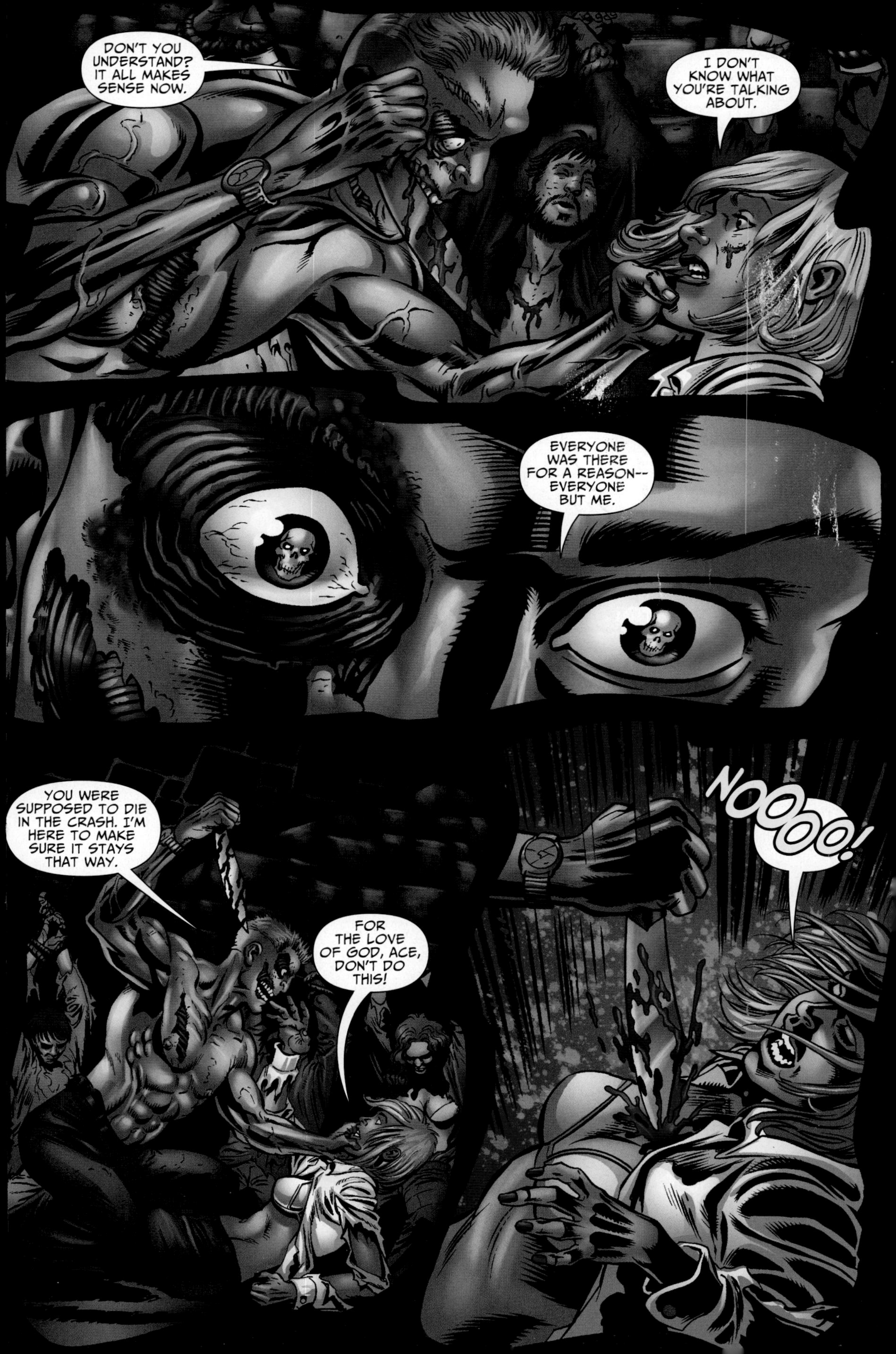
DON'T YOU UNDERSTAND? IT ALL MAKES SENSE NOW.
I DON'T KNOW WHAT YOU'RE TALKING ABOUT.
EVERYONE WAS THERE FOR A REASON-- EVERYONE BUT ME.
YOU WERE SUPPOSED TO DIE IN THE CRASH. I'M HERE TO MAKE SURE IT STAYS THAT WAY.
FOR THE LOVE OF GOD, ACE, DON'T DO THIS!
NOOOO!

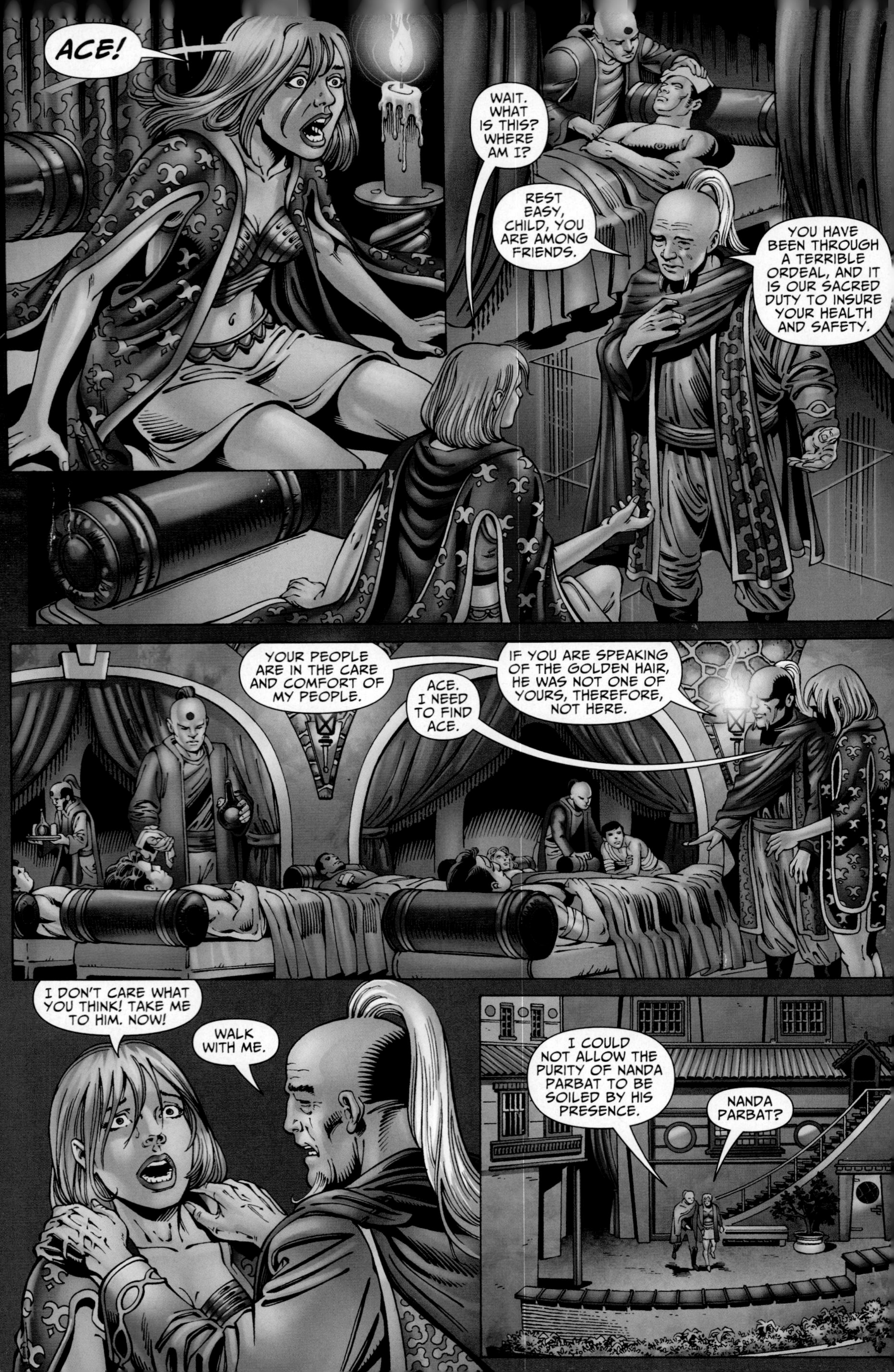
ACE!
WAIT. WHAT IS THIS? WHERE AM I?
REST EASY, CHILD, YOU ARE AMONG FRIENDS.
YOU HAVE BEEN THROUGH A TERRIBLE ORDEAL, AND IT IS OUR SACRED DUTY TO INSURE YOUR HEALTH AND SAFETY.
YOUR PEOPLE ARE IN THE CARE AND COMFORT OF MY PEOPLE.
ACE. I NEED TO FIND ACE.
IF YOU ARE SPEAKING OF THE GOLDEN HAIR, HE WAS NOT ONE OF YOURS, THEREFORE, NOT HERE.
I DON'T CARE WHAT YOU THINK! TAKE ME TO HIM. NOW!
WALK WITH ME.
I COULD NOT ALLOW THE PURITY OF NANDA PARBAT TO BE SOILED BY HIS PRESENCE.
NANDA PARBAT?

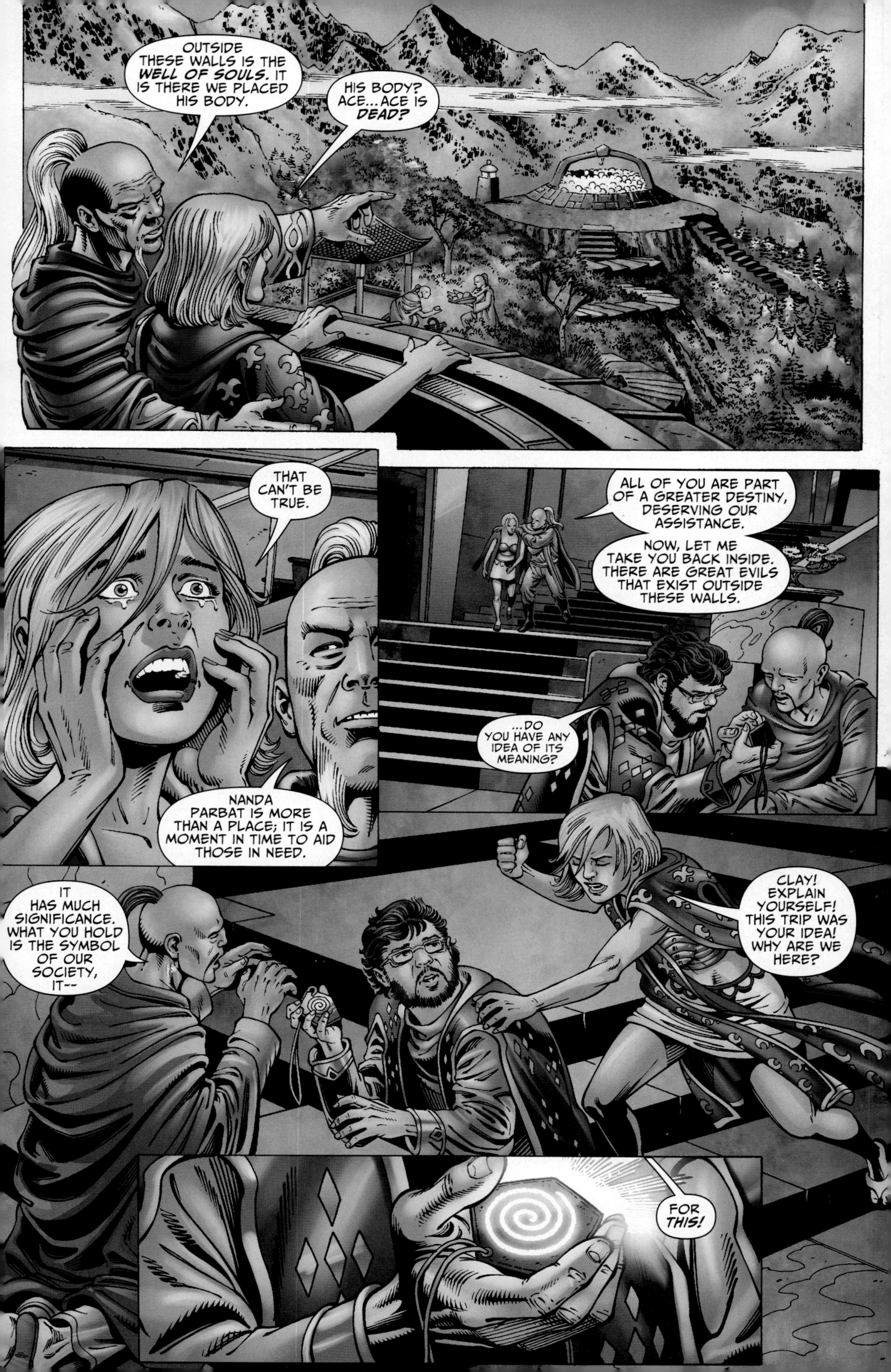

OUTSIDE THESE WALLS IS THE WELL OF SOULS. IT IS THERE WE PLACED HIS BODY.
HIS BODY? ACE...ACE IS DEAD?
THAT CAN'T BE TRUE.
NANDA PARBAT IS MORE THAN A PLACE; IT IS A MOMENT IN TIME TO AID THOSE IN NEED.
ALL OF YOU ARE PART OF A GREATER DESTINY, DESERVING OUR ASSISTANCE.
NOW, LET ME TAKE YOU BACK INSIDE. THERE ARE GREAT EVILS THAT EXIST OUTSIDE THESE WALLS.
...DO YOU HAVE ANY IDEA OF ITS MEANING?
IT HAS MUCH SIGNIFICANCE. WHAT YOU HOLD IS THE SYMBOL OF OUR SOCIETY, IT--
CLAY! EXPLAIN YOURSELF! THIS TRIP WAS YOUR IDEA! WHY ARE WE HERE?
FOR THIS!

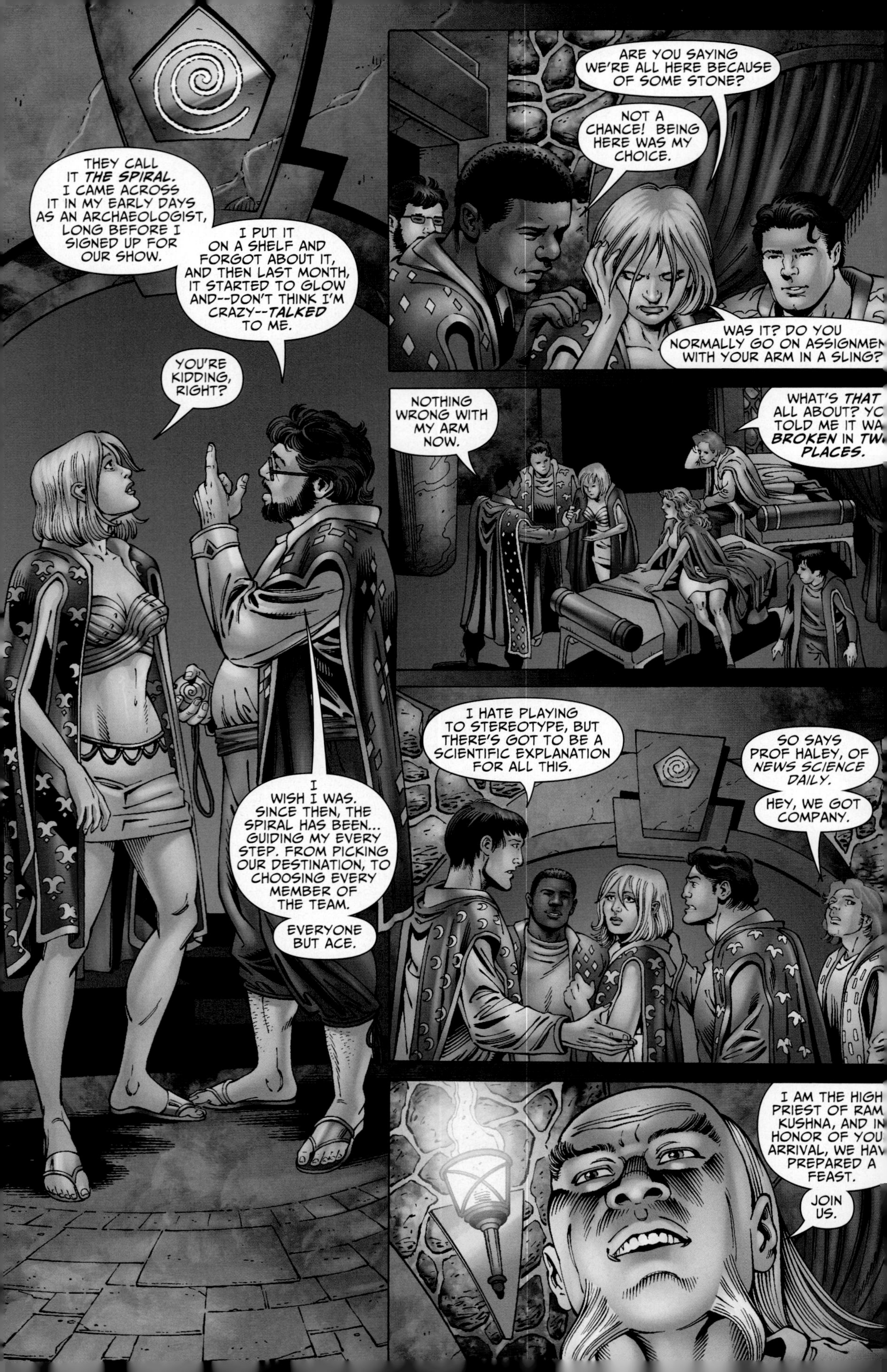
THEY CALL IT THE SPIRAL. I CAME ACROSS IT IN MY EARLY DAYS AS AN ARCHAEOLOGIST, LONG BEFORE I SIGNED UP FOR OUR SHOW.
I PUT IT ON A SHELF AND FORGOT ABOUT IT, AND THEN LAST MONTH, IT STARTED TO GLOW AND--DON'T THINK I'M CRAZY--TALKED TO ME.
YOU'RE KIDDING, RIGHT?
I WISH I WAS. SINCE THEN, THE SPIRAL HAS BEEN... GUIDING MY EVERY STEP. FROM PICKING OUR DESTINATION, TO CHOOSING EVERY MEMBER OF THE TEAM.
EVERYONE BUT ACE.
ARE YOU SAYING WE'RE ALL HERE BECAUSE OF SOME STONE?
NOT A CHANCE! BEING HERE WAS MY CHOICE.
WAS IT? DO YOU NORMALLY GO ON ASSIGNMEN WITH YOUR ARM IN A SLING?
NOTHING WRONG WITH MY ARM NOW.
WHAT'S THAT ALL ABOUT? YO TOLD ME IT WA BROKEN IN TW PLACES.
I HATE PLAYING TO STEREOTYPE, BUT THERE'S GOT TO BE A SCIENTIFIC EXPLANATION FOR ALL THIS.
SO SAYS PROF HALEY, OF NEWS SCIENCE DAILY.
HEY, WE GOT COMPANY.
I AM THE HIGH PRIEST OF RAM KUSHNA, AND IN HONOR OF YOU ARRIVAL, WE HAV PREPARED A FEAST.
JOIN US.

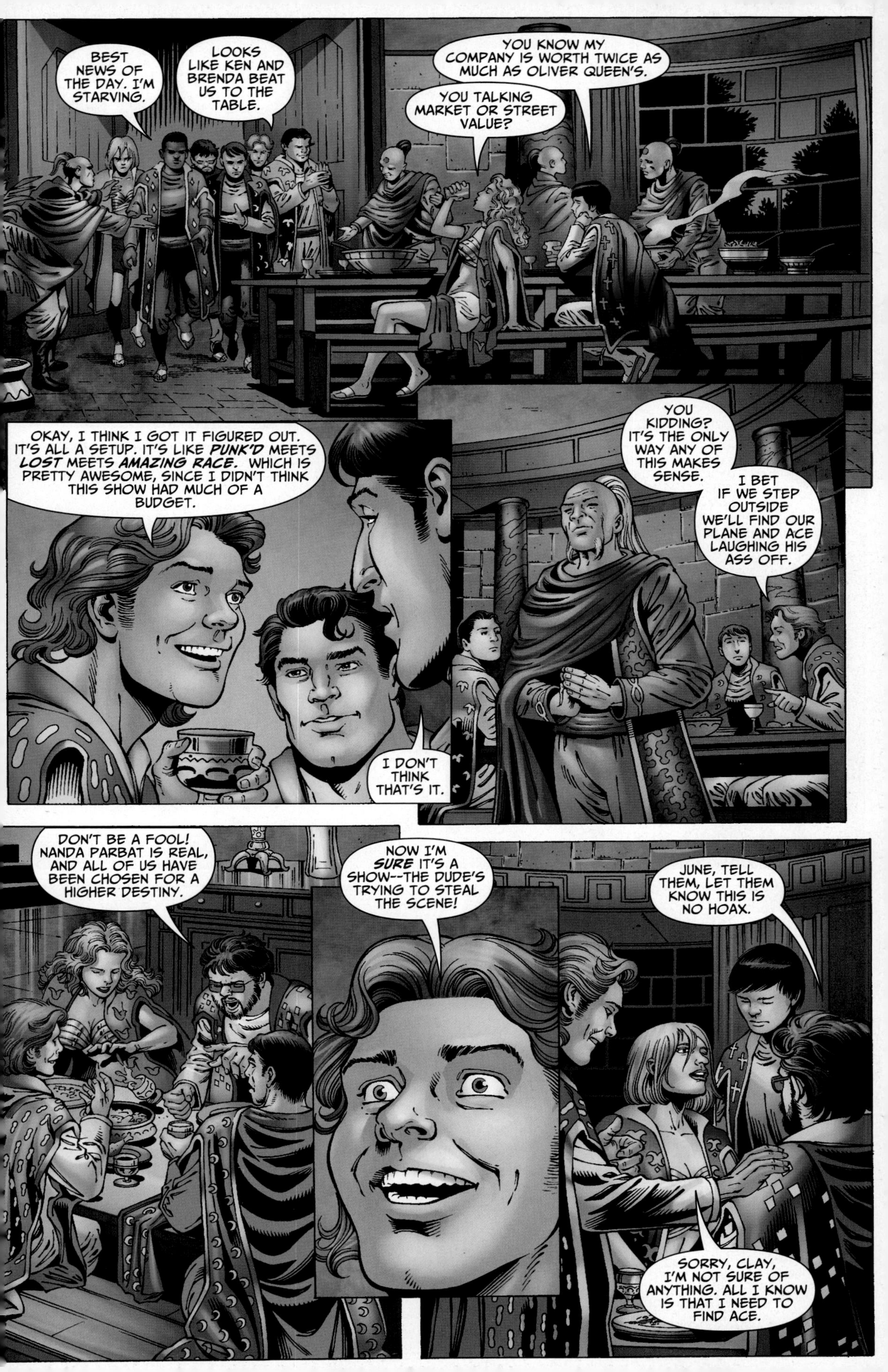
BEST NEWS OF THE DAY. I'M STARVING.
LOOKS LIKE KEN AND BRENDA BEAT US TO THE TABLE.
YOU KNOW MY COMPANY IS WORTH TWICE AS MUCH AS OLIVER QUEEN'S.
YOU TALKING MARKET OR STREET VALUE?
OKAY, I THINK I GOT IT FIGURED OUT. IT'S ALL A SETUP. IT'S LIKE PUNK'D MEETS LOST MEETS AMAZING RACE. WHICH IS PRETTY AWESOME, SINCE I DIDN'T THINK THIS SHOW HAD MUCH OF A BUDGET.
I DON'T THINK THAT'S IT.
YOU KIDDING? IT'S THE ONLY WAY ANY OF THIS MAKES SENSE.
I BET IF WE STEP OUTSIDE WE'LL FIND OUR PLANE AND ACE LAUGHING HIS ASS OFF.
DON'T BE A FOOL! NANDA PARBAT IS REAL, AND ALL OF US HAVE BEEN CHOSEN FOR A HIGHER DESTINY.
NOW I'M SURE IT'S A SHOW--THE DUDE'S TRYING TO STEAL THE SCENE!
JUNE, TELL THEM, LET THEM KNOW THIS IS NO HOAX.
SORRY, CLAY, I'M NOT SURE OF ANYTHING. ALL I KNOW IS THAT I NEED TO FIND ACE.

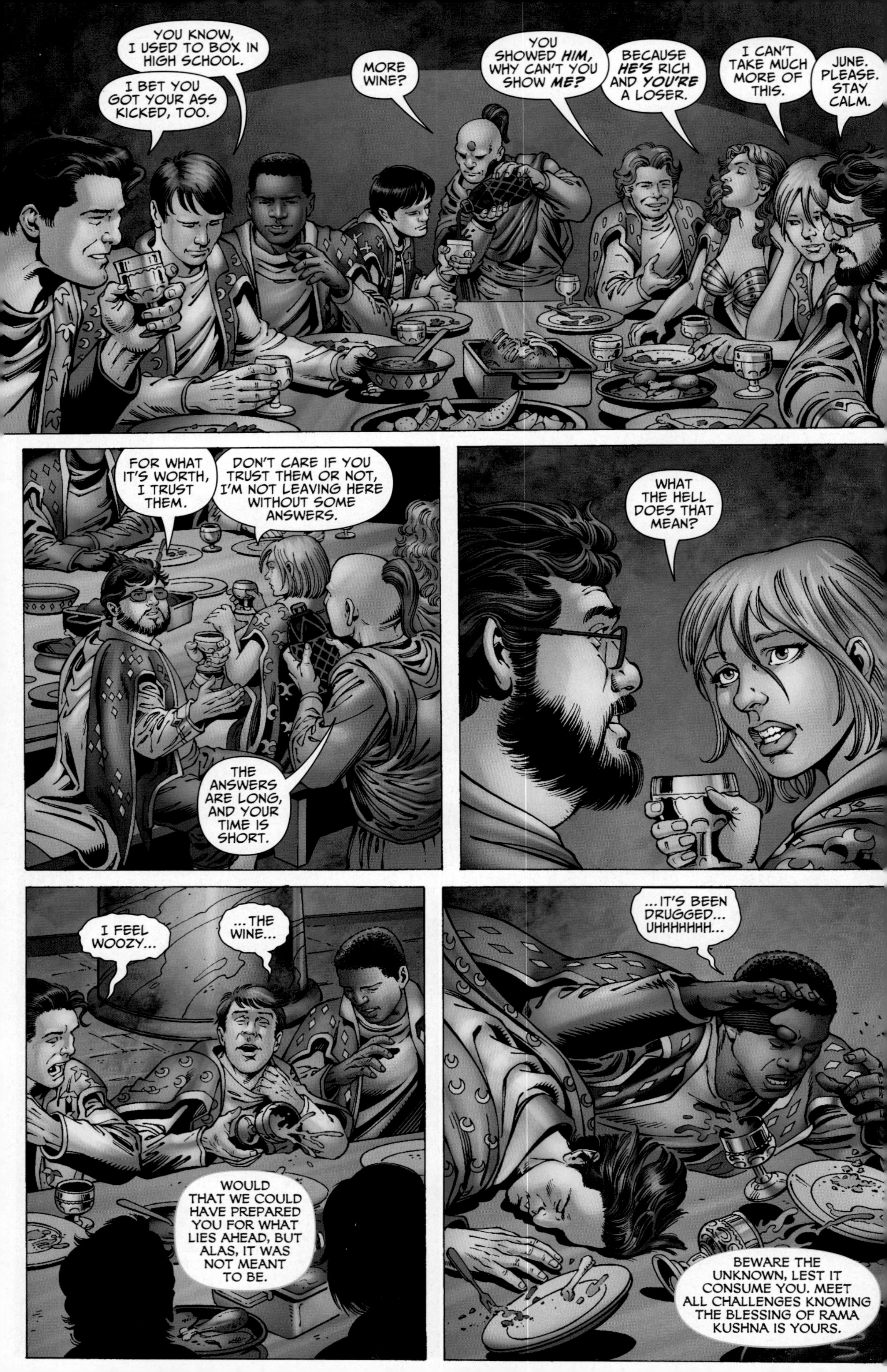
YOU KNOW, I USED TO BOX IN HIGH SCHOOL.
I BET YOU GOT YOUR ASS KICKED, TOO.
MORE WINE?
YOU SHOWED *HIM*, WHY CAN'T YOU SHOW *ME?*
BECAUSE *HE'S* RICH AND *YOU'RE* A LOSER.
I CAN'T TAKE MUCH MORE OF THIS.
JUNE. PLEASE. STAY CALM.
FOR WHAT IT'S WORTH, I TRUST THEM.
DON'T CARE IF YOU TRUST THEM OR NOT, I'M NOT LEAVING HERE WITHOUT SOME ANSWERS.
THE ANSWERS ARE LONG, AND YOUR TIME IS SHORT.
WHAT THE HELL DOES THAT MEAN?
I FEEL WOOZY...
...THE WINE...
WOULD THAT WE COULD HAVE PREPARED YOU FOR WHAT LIES AHEAD, BUT ALAS, IT WAS NOT MEANT TO BE.
...IT'S BEEN DRUGGED... UHHHHHHH...
BEWARE THE UNKNOWN, LEST IT CONSUME YOU. MEET ALL CHALLENGES KNOWING THE BLESSING OF RAMA KUSHNA IS YOURS.

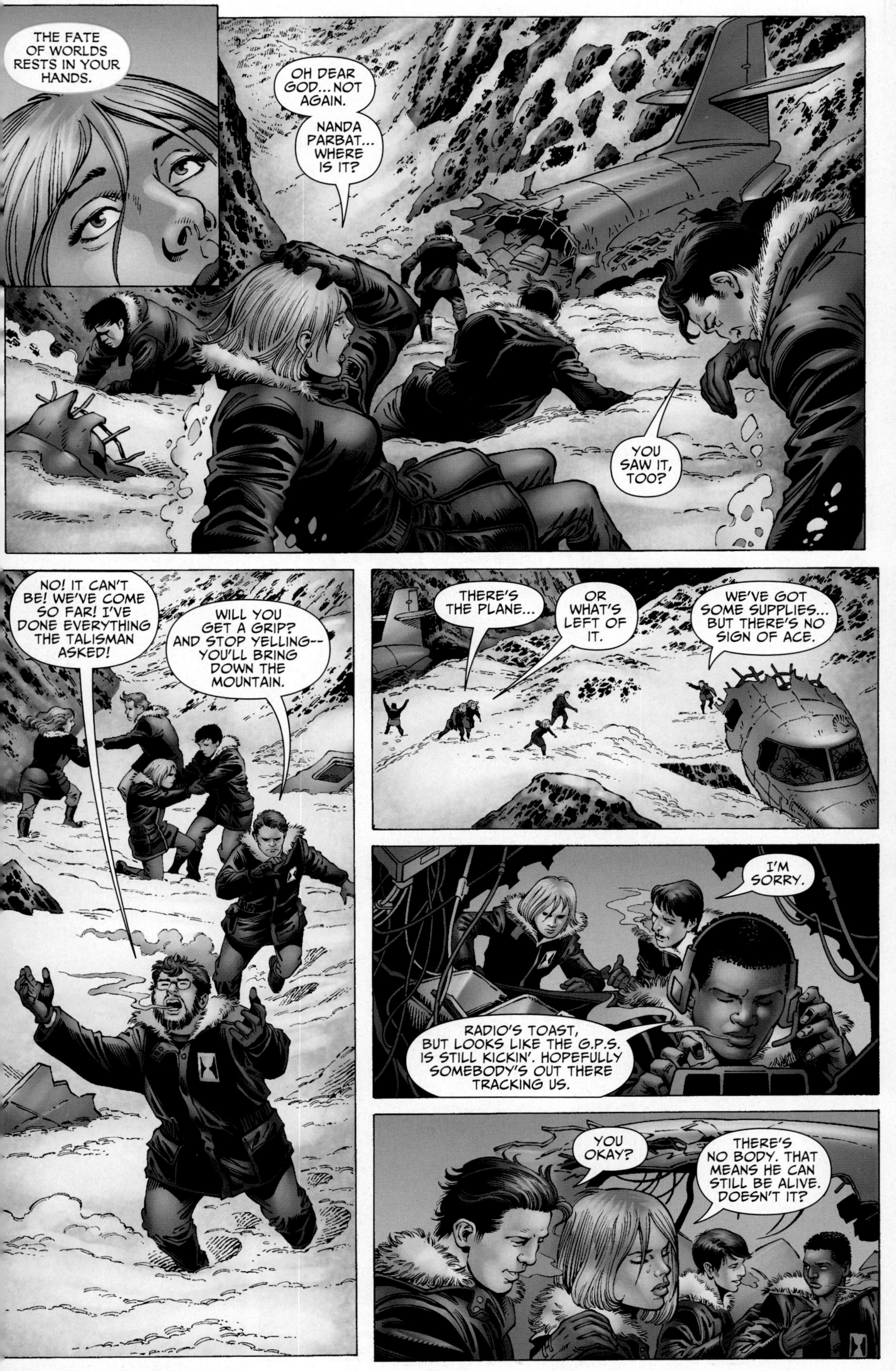
THE FATE OF WORLDS RESTS IN YOUR HANDS.
OH DEAR GOD...NOT AGAIN.
NANDA PARBAT... WHERE IS IT?
YOU SAW IT, TOO?
NO! IT CAN'T BE! WE'VE COME SO FAR! I'VE DONE EVERYTHING THE TALISMAN ASKED!
WILL YOU GET A GRIP? AND STOP YELLING--YOU'LL BRING DOWN THE MOUNTAIN.
THERE'S THE PLANE...
OR WHAT'S LEFT OF IT.
WE'VE GOT SOME SUPPLIES... BUT THERE'S NO SIGN OF ACE.
I'M SORRY.
RADIO'S TOAST, BUT LOOKS LIKE THE G.P.S. IS STILL KICKIN'. HOPEFULLY SOMEBODY'S OUT THERE TRACKING US.
YOU OKAY?
THERE'S NO BODY. THAT MEANS HE CAN STILL BE ALIVE. DOESN'T IT?

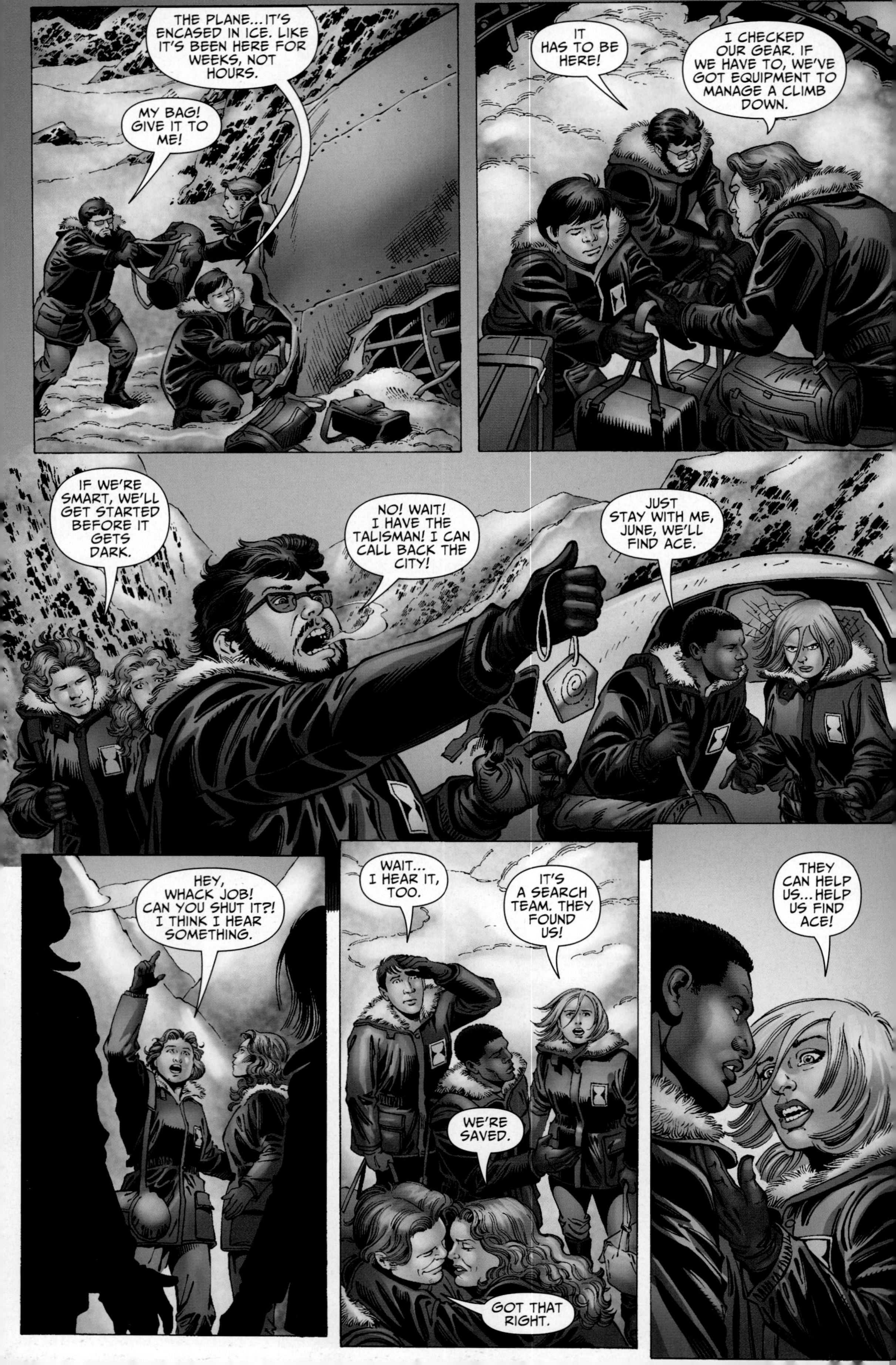
THE PLANE...IT'S ENCASED IN ICE. LIKE IT'S BEEN HERE FOR WEEKS, NOT HOURS.
MY BAG! GIVE IT TO ME!
IT HAS TO BE HERE!
I CHECKED OUR GEAR. IF WE HAVE TO, WE'VE GOT EQUIPMENT TO MANAGE A CLIMB DOWN.
IF WE'RE SMART, WE'LL GET STARTED BEFORE IT GETS DARK.
NO! WAIT! I HAVE THE TALISMAN! I CAN CALL BACK THE CITY!
JUST STAY WITH ME, JUNE, WE'LL FIND ACE.
HEY, WHACK JOB! CAN YOU SHUT IT?! I THINK I HEAR SOMETHING.
WAIT... I HEAR IT, TOO.
IT'S A SEARCH TEAM. THEY FOUND US!
WE'RE SAVED.
GOT THAT RIGHT.
THEY CAN HELP US...HELP US FIND ACE!

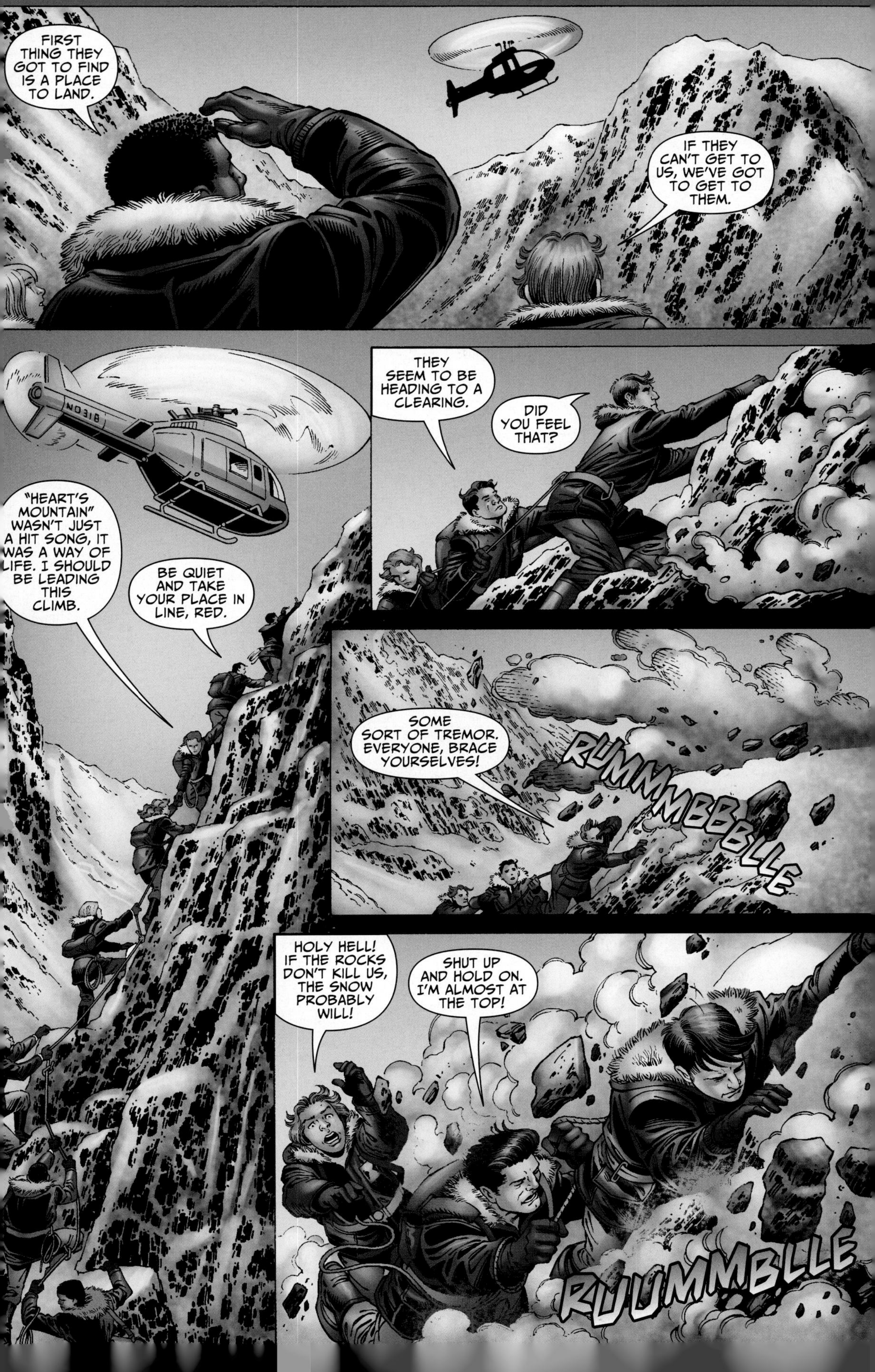
FIRST THING THEY GOT TO FIND IS A PLACE TO LAND.
IF THEY CAN'T GET TO US, WE'VE GOT TO GET TO THEM.
NO318
"HEART'S MOUNTAIN" WASN'T JUST A HIT SONG, IT WAS A WAY OF LIFE. I SHOULD BE LEADING THIS CLIMB.
BE QUIET AND TAKE YOUR PLACE IN LINE, RED.
THEY SEEM TO BE HEADING TO A CLEARING.
DID YOU FEEL THAT?
SOME SORT OF TREMOR. EVERYONE, BRACE YOURSELVES!
RUMMMBBBLLE
HOLY HELL! IF THE ROCKS DON'T KILL US, THE SNOW PROBABLY WILL!
SHUT UP AND HOLD ON. I'M ALMOST AT THE TOP!
RUUMMBLLE

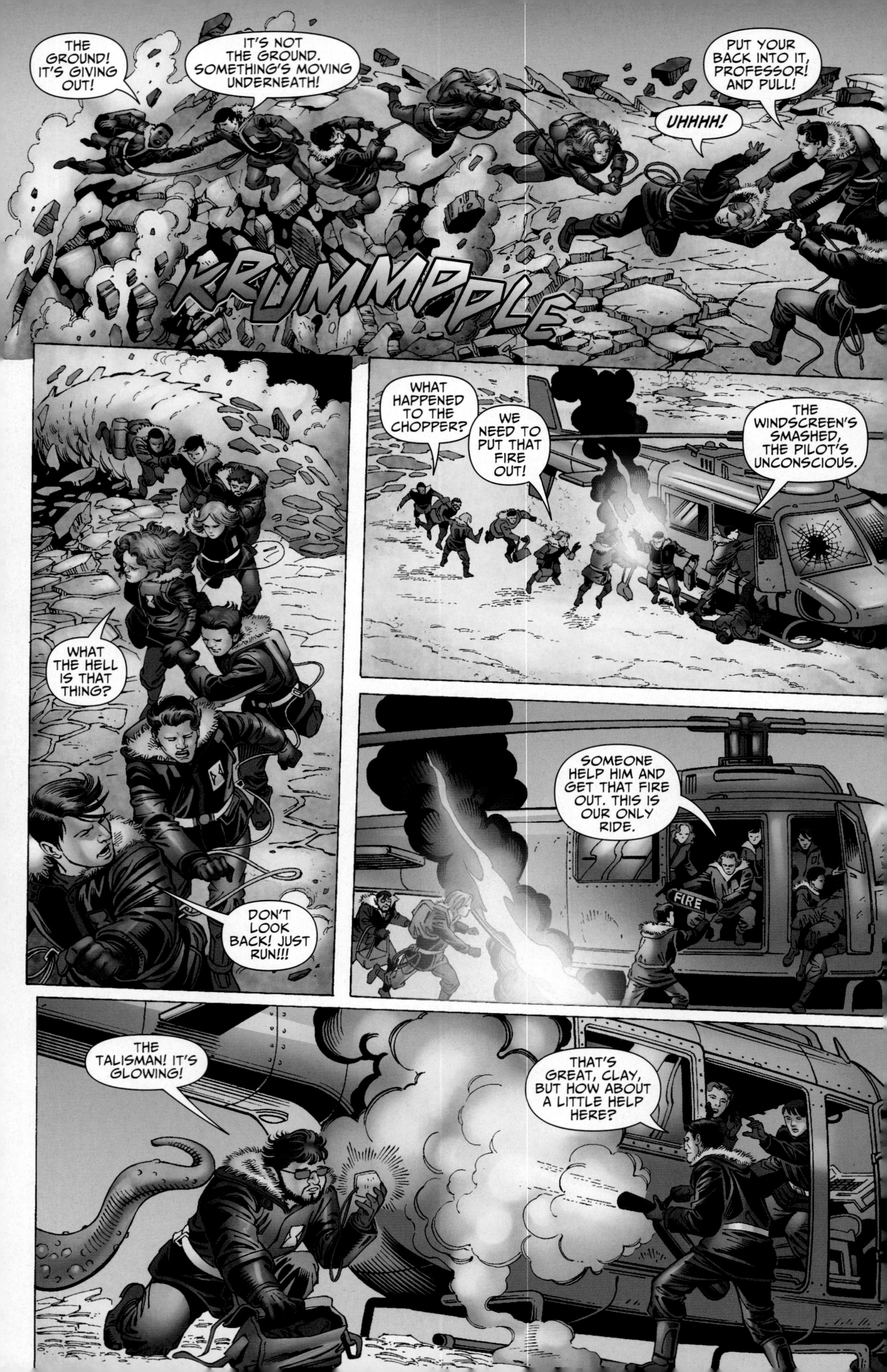
THE GROUND! IT'S GIVING OUT!
IT'S NOT THE GROUND. SOMETHING'S MOVING UNDERNEATH!
UHHHH!
PUT YOUR BACK INTO IT, PROFESSOR! AND PULL!
KRUMMBBLE
WHAT THE HELL IS THAT THING?
DON'T LOOK BACK! JUST RUN!!!
WHAT HAPPENED TO THE CHOPPER?
WE NEED TO PUT THAT FIRE OUT!
THE WINDSCREEN'S SMASHED, THE PILOT'S UNCONSCIOUS.
SOMEONE HELP HIM AND GET THAT FIRE OUT. THIS IS OUR ONLY RIDE.
FIRE
THE TALISMAN! IT'S GLOWING!
THAT'S GREAT, CLAY, BUT HOW ABOUT A LITTLE HELP HERE?

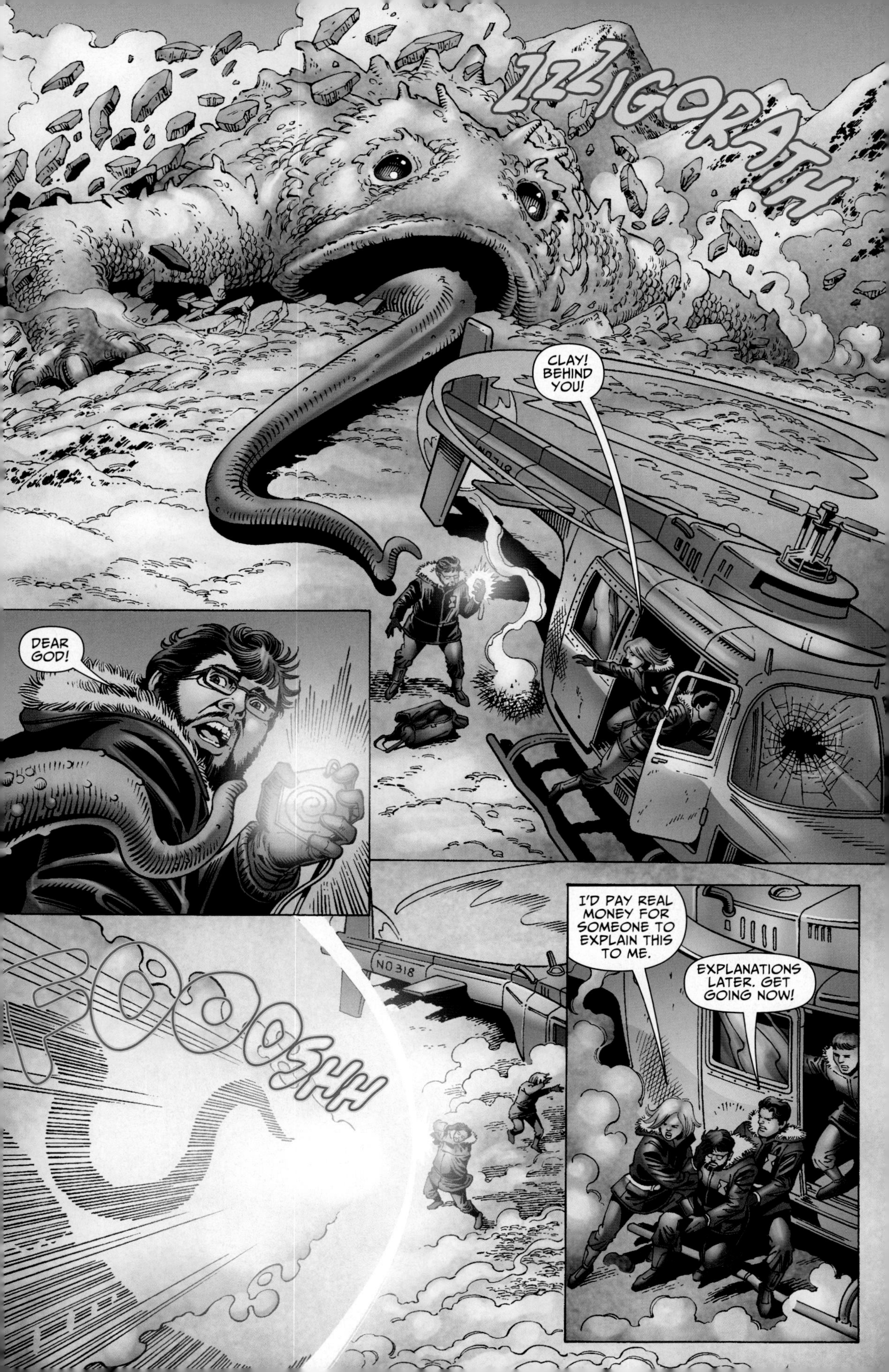
ZZZIGORATH
CLAY! BEHIND YOU!
DEAR GOD!
NO 318
FOOOOSHH
I'D PAY REAL MONEY FOR SOMEONE TO EXPLAIN THIS TO ME.
EXPLANATIONS LATER. GET GOING NOW!

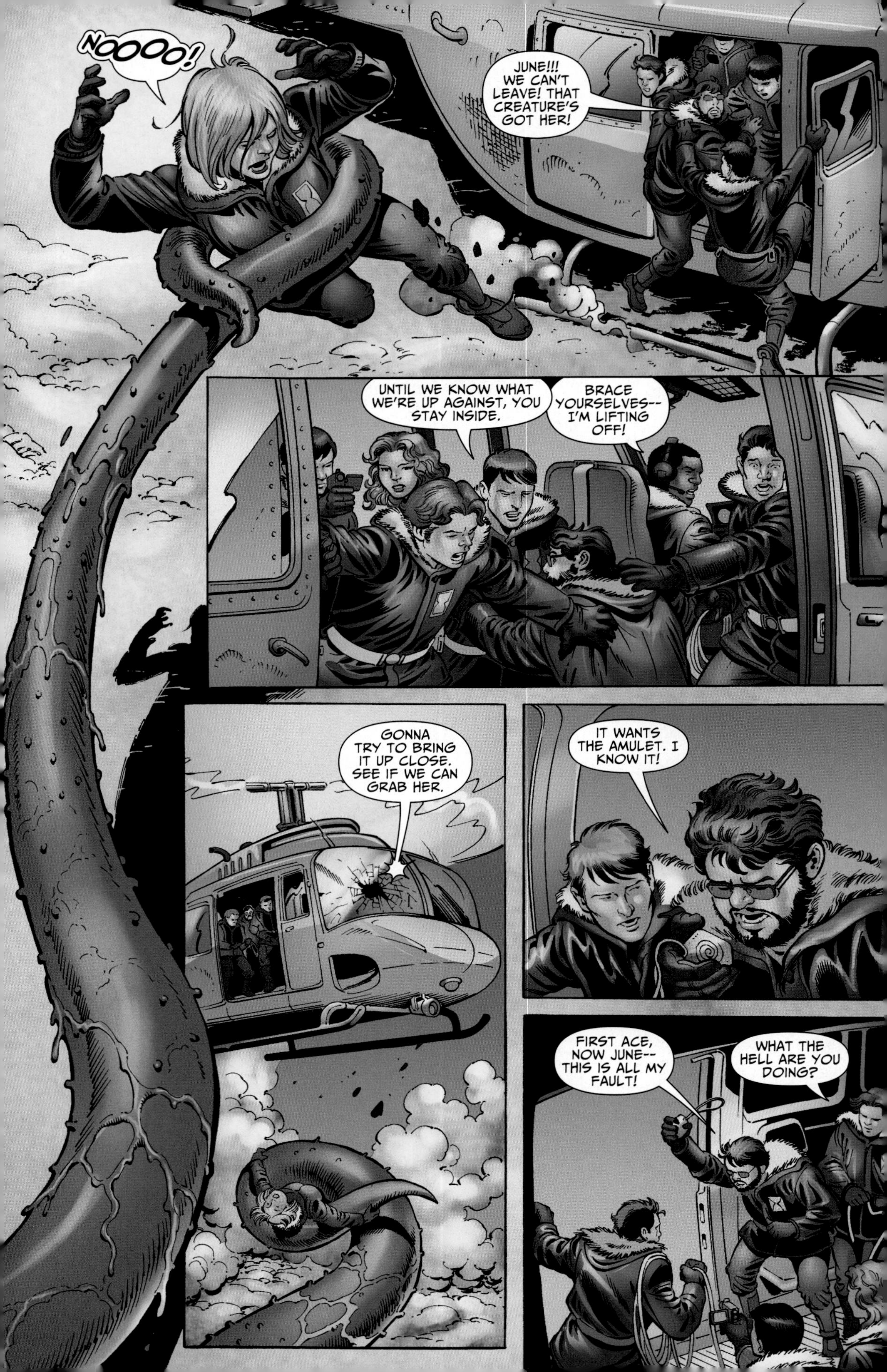
NOOOO!
JUNE!!! WE CAN'T LEAVE! THAT CREATURE'S GOT HER!
UNTIL WE KNOW WHAT WE'RE UP AGAINST, YOU STAY INSIDE.
BRACE YOURSELVES-- I'M LIFTING OFF!
GONNA TRY TO BRING IT UP CLOSE. SEE IF WE CAN GRAB HER.
IT WANTS THE AMULET. I KNOW IT!
FIRST ACE, NOW JUNE-- THIS IS ALL MY FAULT!
WHAT THE HELL ARE YOU DOING?

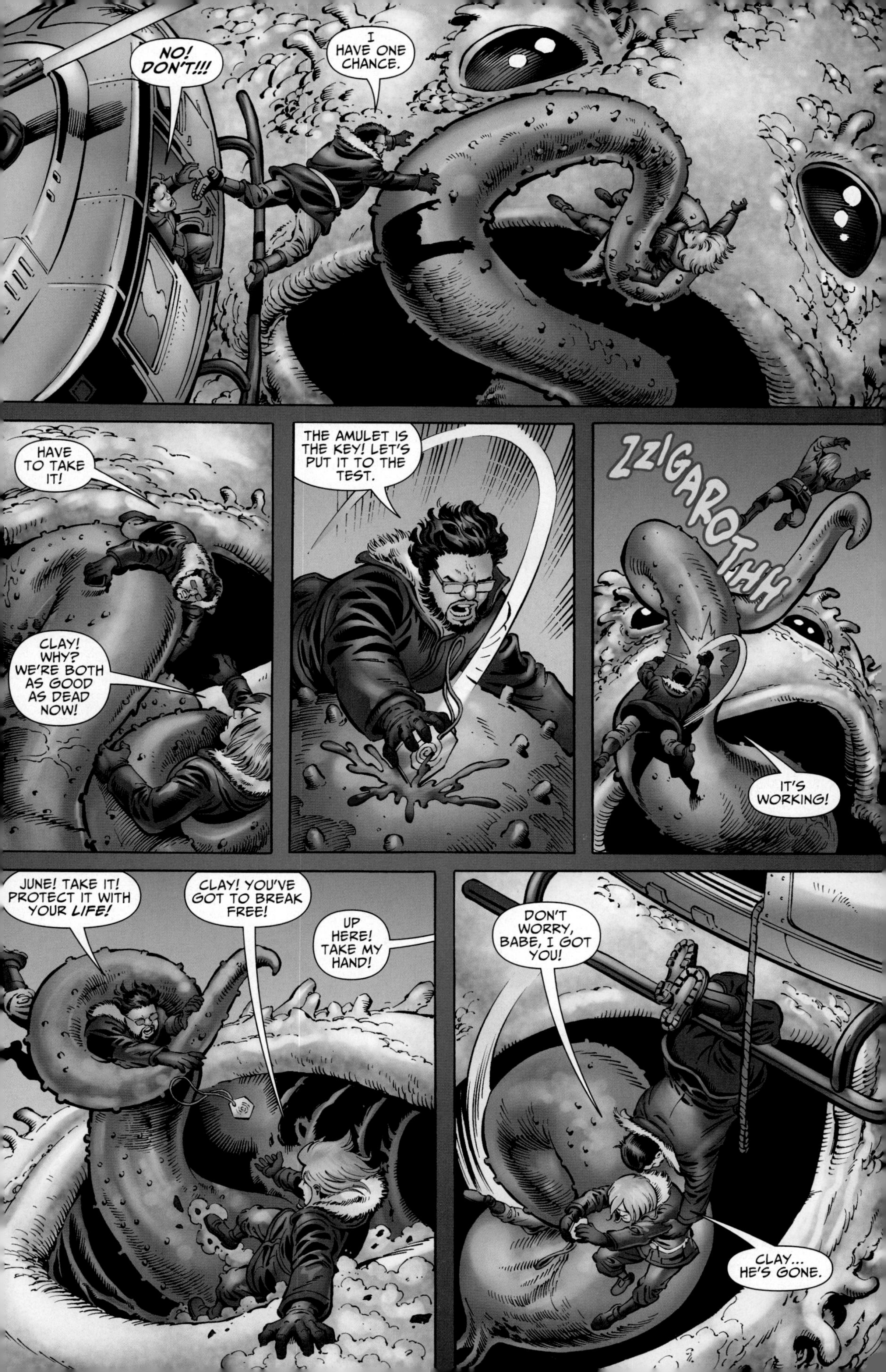
NO! DON'T!!!
I HAVE ONE CHANCE.
HAVE TO TAKE IT!
CLAY! WHY? WE'RE BOTH AS GOOD AS DEAD NOW!
THE AMULET IS THE KEY! LET'S PUT IT TO THE TEST.
ZZIGAROTHH
IT'S WORKING!
JUNE! TAKE IT! PROTECT IT WITH YOUR *LIFE!*
CLAY! YOU'VE GOT TO BREAK FREE!
UP HERE! TAKE MY HAND!
DON'T WORRY, BABE, I GOT YOU!
CLAY... HE'S GONE.

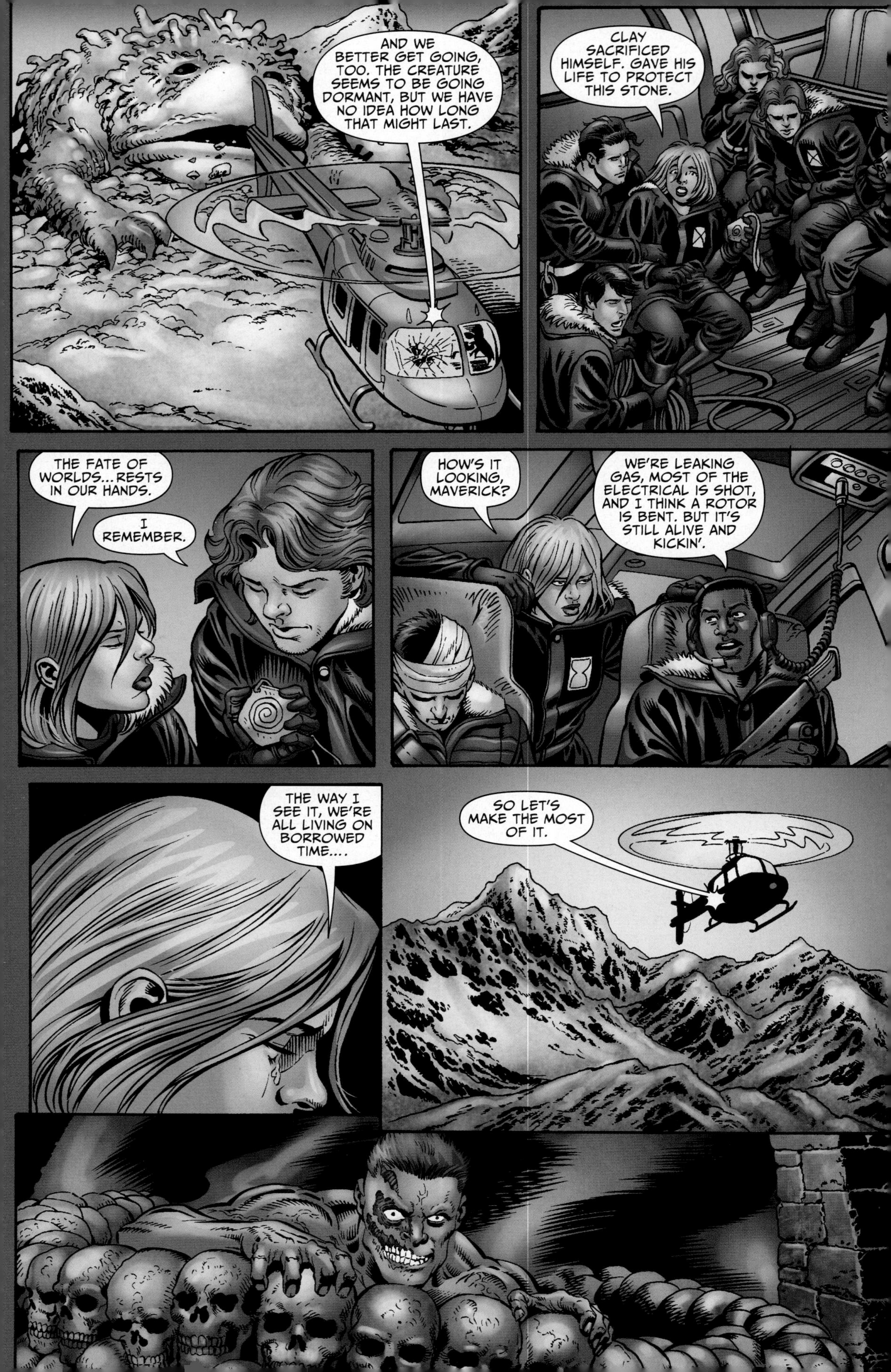
AND WE BETTER GET GOING, TOO. THE CREATURE SEEMS TO BE GOING DORMANT, BUT WE HAVE NO IDEA HOW LONG THAT MIGHT LAST.
CLAY SACRIFICED HIMSELF. GAVE HIS LIFE TO PROTECT THIS STONE.
THE FATE OF WORLDS...RESTS IN OUR HANDS.
I REMEMBER.
HOW'S IT LOOKING, MAVERICK?
WE'RE LEAKING GAS, MOST OF THE ELECTRICAL IS SHOT, AND I THINK A ROTOR IS BENT. BUT IT'S STILL ALIVE AND KICKIN'.
THE WAY I SEE IT, WE'RE ALL LIVING ON BORROWED TIME....
SO LET'S MAKE THE MOST OF IT.

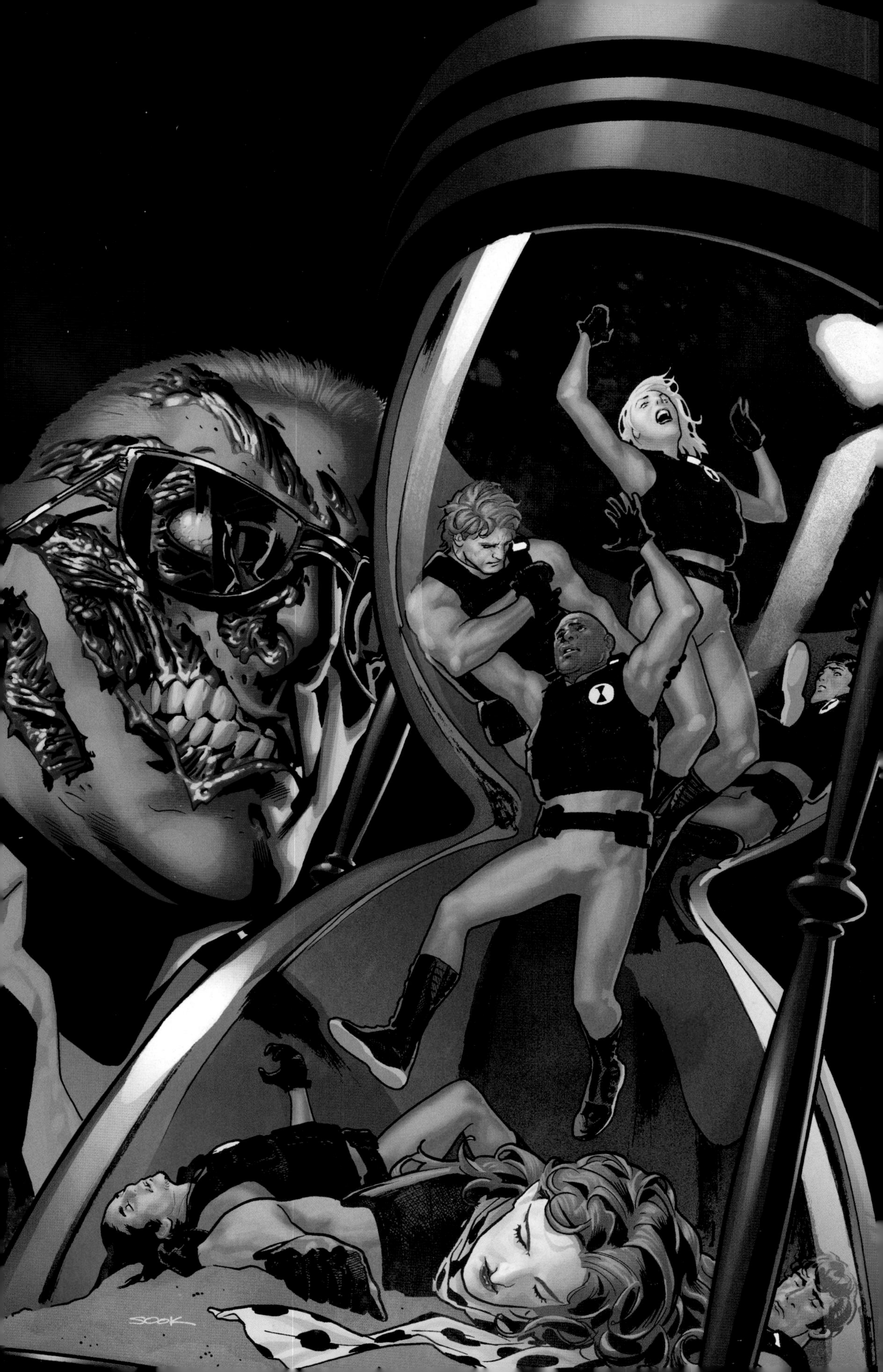
SOOK

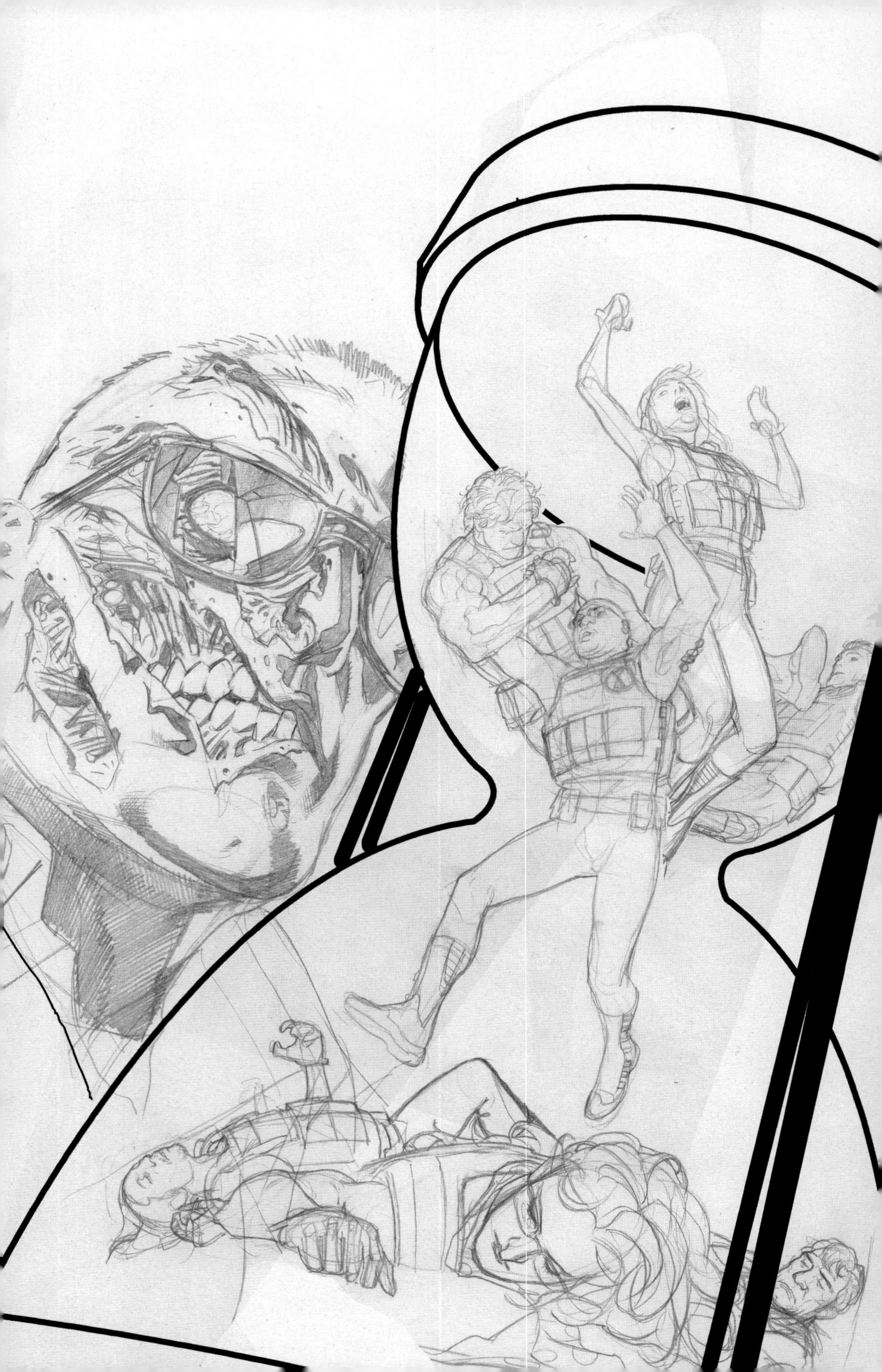

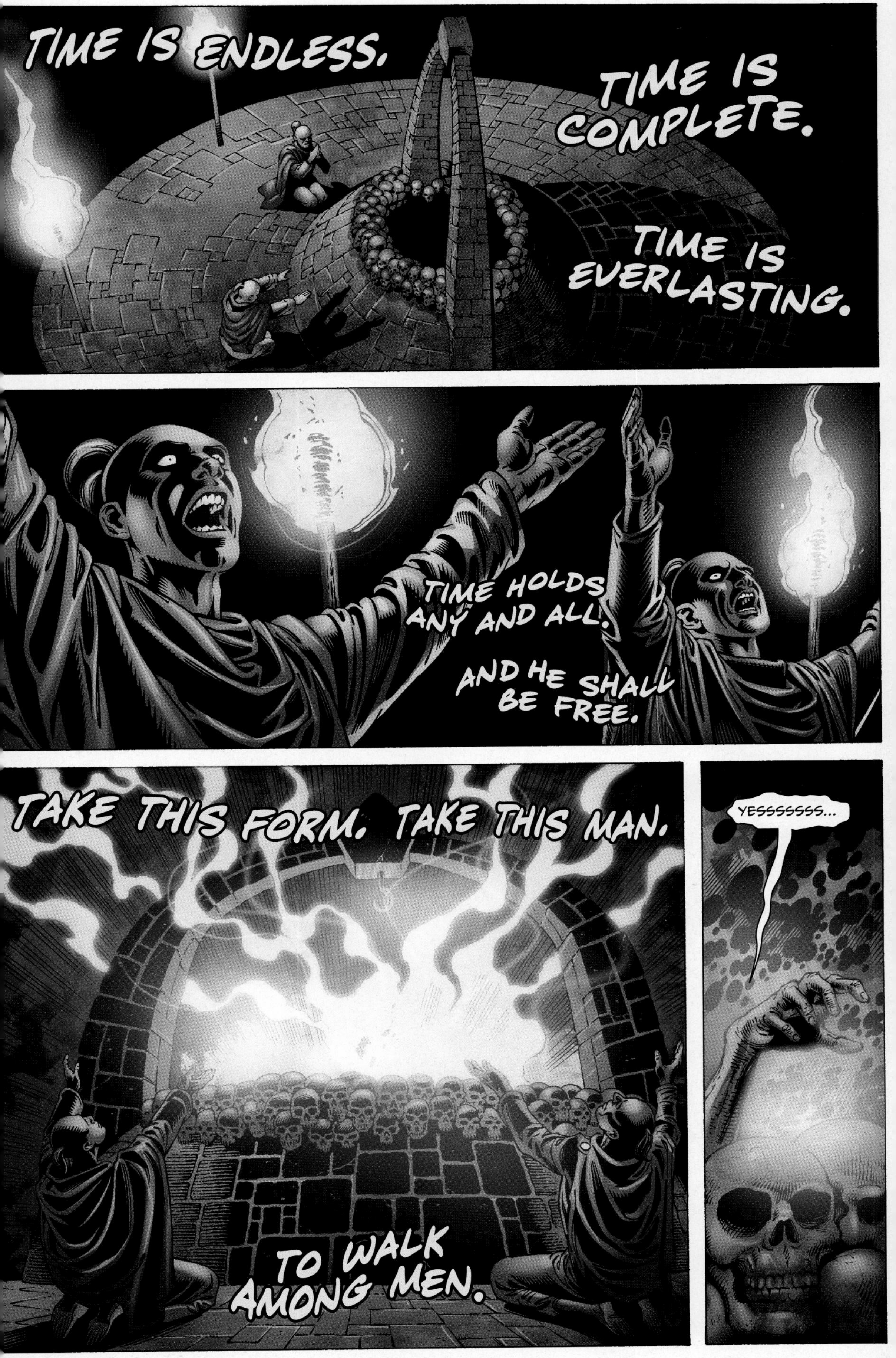
TIME IS ENDLESS.
TIME IS COMPLETE.
TIME IS EVERLASTING.
TIME HOLDS ANY AND ALL.
AND HE SHALL BE FREE.
TAKE THIS FORM. TAKE THIS MAN.
TO WALK AMONG MEN.
YESSSSSSSS...

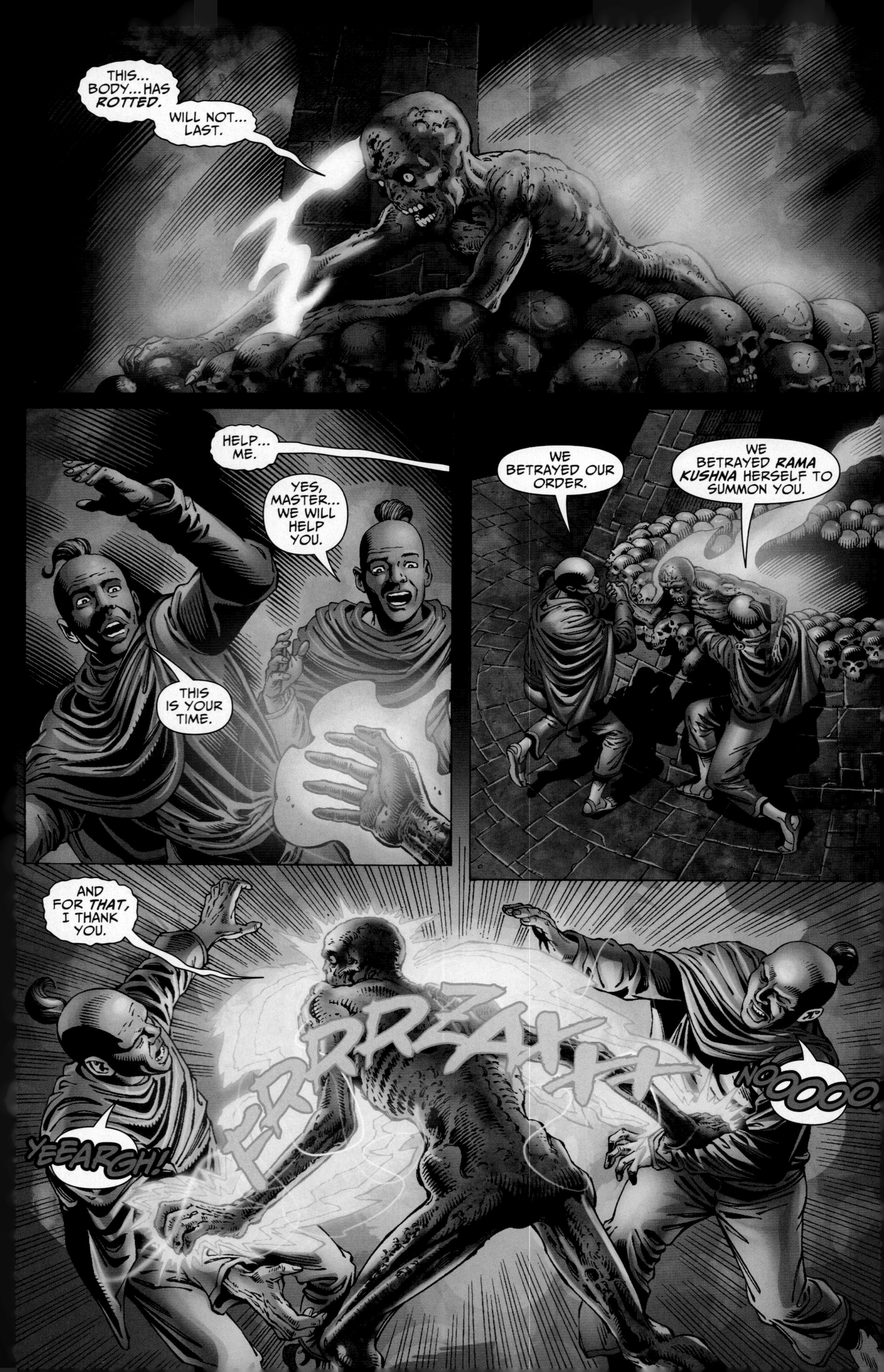
THIS... BODY...HAS ROTTED.
WILL NOT... LAST.
HELP... ME.
YES, MASTER... WE WILL HELP YOU.
THIS IS YOUR TIME.
WE BETRAYED OUR ORDER.
WE BETRAYED RAMA KUSHNA HERSELF TO SUMMON YOU.
AND FOR THAT, I THANK YOU.
FRRZAKK
YEEARGH!
NOOOOO!

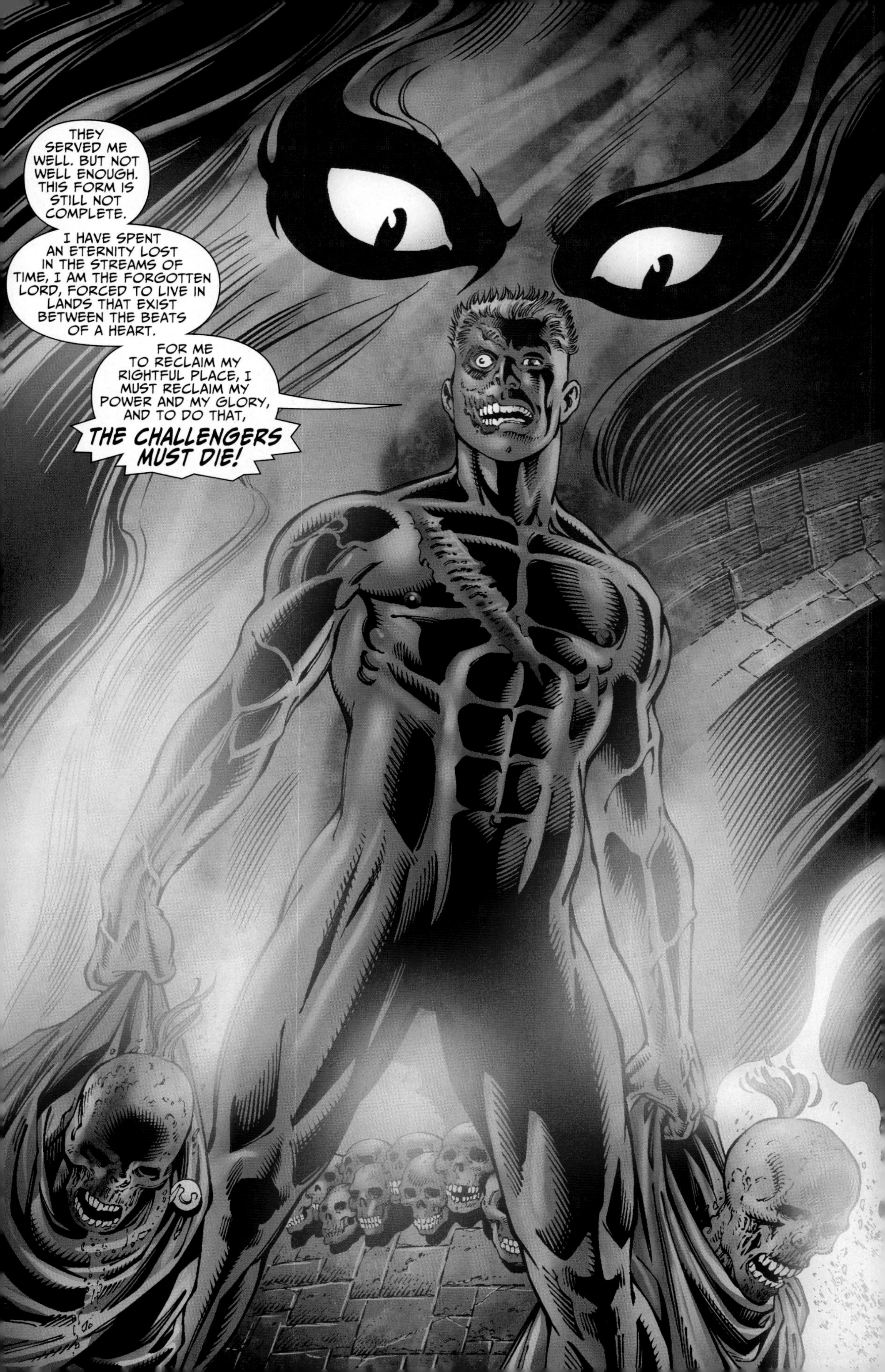
THEY SERVED ME WELL. BUT NOT WELL ENOUGH. THIS FORM IS STILL NOT COMPLETE.
I HAVE SPENT AN ETERNITY LOST IN THE STREAMS OF TIME, I AM THE FORGOTTEN LORD, FORCED TO LIVE IN LANDS THAT EXIST BETWEEN THE BEATS OF A HEART.
FOR ME TO RECLAIM MY RIGHTFUL PLACE, I MUST RECLAIM MY POWER AND MY GLORY, AND TO DO THAT,
THE CHALLENGERS MUST DIE!

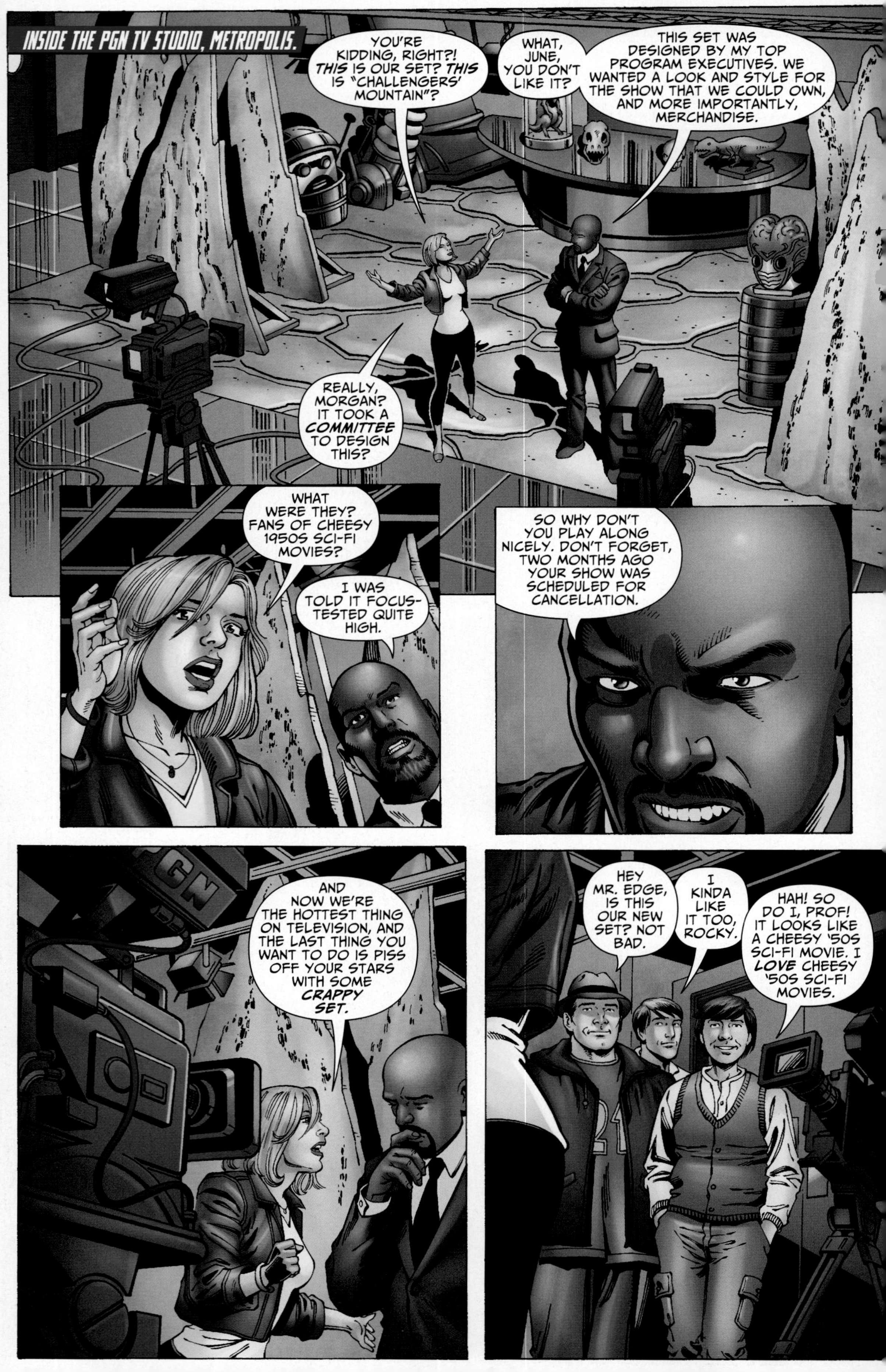
INSIDE THE PGN TV STUDIO, METROPOLIS.
YOU'RE KIDDING, RIGHT?! THIS IS OUR SET? THIS IS "CHALLENGERS' MOUNTAIN"?
WHAT, JUNE, YOU DON'T LIKE IT?
THIS SET WAS DESIGNED BY MY TOP PROGRAM EXECUTIVES. WE WANTED A LOOK AND STYLE FOR THE SHOW THAT WE COULD OWN, AND MORE IMPORTANTLY, MERCHANDISE.
REALLY, MORGAN? IT TOOK A COMMITTEE TO DESIGN THIS?
WHAT WERE THEY? FANS OF CHEESY 1950S SCI-FI MOVIES?
I WAS TOLD IT FOCUS-TESTED QUITE HIGH.
SO WHY DON'T YOU PLAY ALONG NICELY. DON'T FORGET, TWO MONTHS AGO YOUR SHOW WAS SCHEDULED FOR CANCELLATION.
AND NOW WE'RE THE HOTTEST THING ON TELEVISION, AND THE LAST THING YOU WANT TO DO IS PISS OFF YOUR STARS WITH SOME CRAPPY SET.
HEY MR. EDGE, IS THIS OUR NEW SET? NOT BAD.
I KINDA LIKE IT TOO, ROCKY.
HAH! SO DO I, PROF! IT LOOKS LIKE A CHEESY '50S SCI-FI MOVIE. I LOVE CHEESY '50S SCI-FI MOVIES.

THANK YOU, KEN.

SEE, JUNE? THE FOCUS GROUPS WERE RIGHT AGAIN.

OH BROTHER.

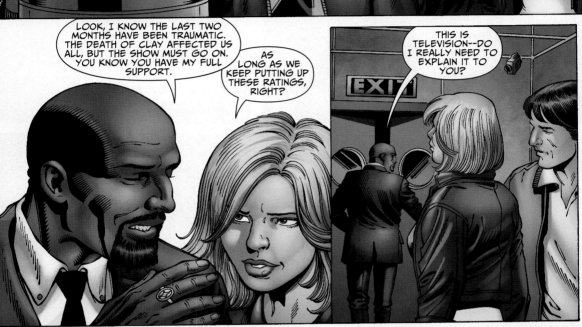

LOOK, I KNOW THE LAST TWO MONTHS HAVE BEEN TRAUMATIC. THE DEATH OF CLAY AFFECTED US ALL, BUT THE SHOW MUST GO ON. YOU KNOW YOU HAVE MY FULL SUPPORT.

AS LONG AS WE KEEP PUTTING UP THESE RATINGS, RIGHT?

THIS IS TELEVISION--DO I REALLY NEED TO EXPLAIN IT TO YOU?

I BET THINGS WERE EASIER WITH YOUR OLD SERIES, PROF.

IT WAS A CHILDREN'S SCIENCE SHOW ON PUBLIC TELEVISION. WE COULDN'T EVEN AFFORD A MICROSCOPE.

YEAH WELL, WE NEED TO GET OUR HANDS ON SOME EQUIPMENT TO ANALYZE THE TALISMAN.

IT HAS TO HOLD THE ANSWER AS TO WHY WE'RE ALL STILL ALIVE.

HEY, JUNE--

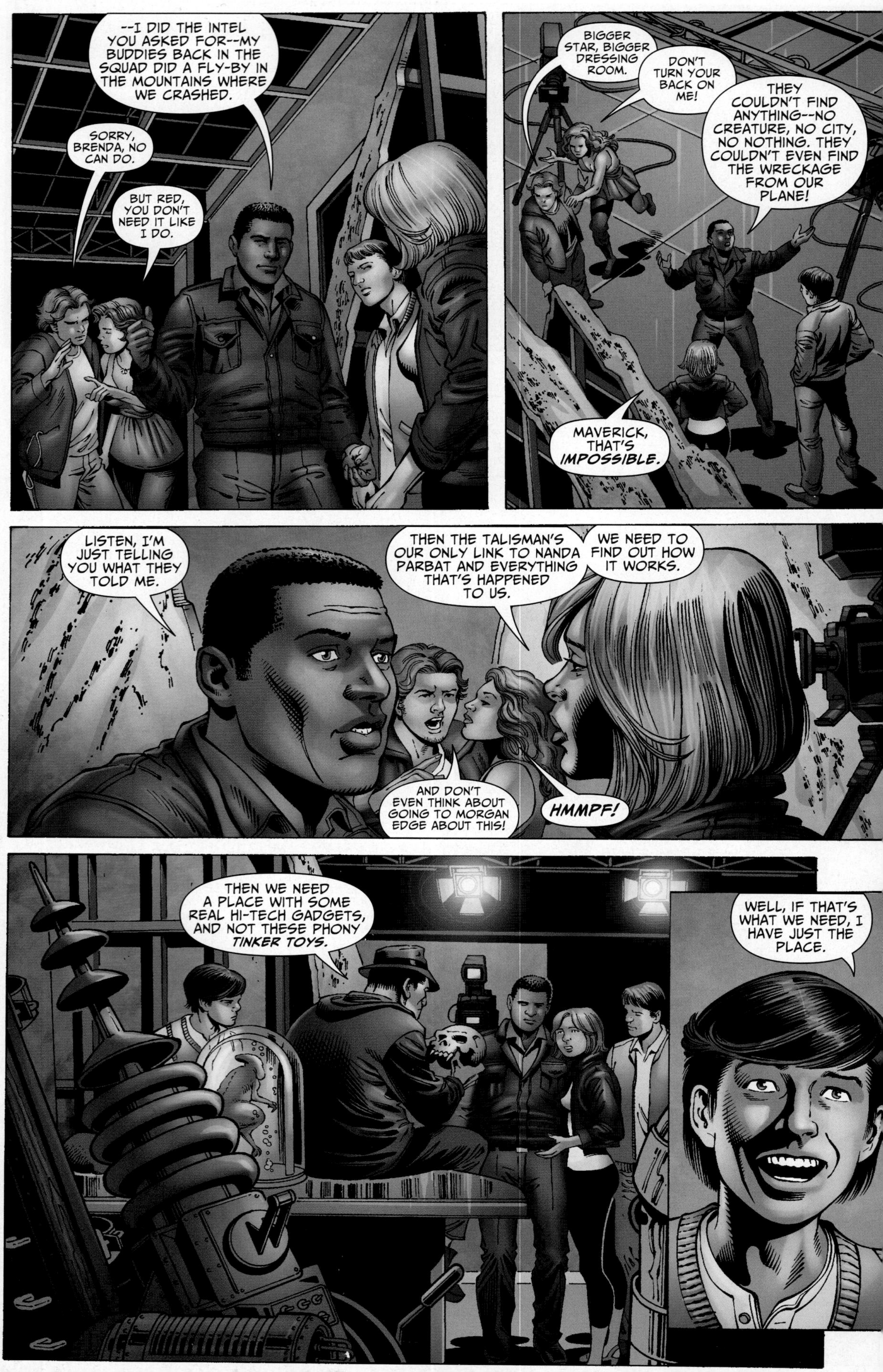
--I DID THE INTEL YOU ASKED FOR--MY BUDDIES BACK IN THE SQUAD DID A FLY-BY IN THE MOUNTAINS WHERE WE CRASHED.
SORRY, BRENDA, NO CAN DO.
BUT RED, YOU DON'T NEED IT LIKE I DO.
BIGGER STAR, BIGGER DRESSING ROOM.
DON'T TURN YOUR BACK ON ME!
THEY COULDN'T FIND ANYTHING--NO CREATURE, NO CITY, NO NOTHING. THEY COULDN'T EVEN FIND THE WRECKAGE FROM OUR PLANE!
MAVERICK, THAT'S *IMPOSSIBLE.*
LISTEN, I'M JUST TELLING YOU WHAT THEY TOLD ME.
THEN THE TALISMAN'S OUR ONLY LINK TO NANDA PARBAT AND EVERYTHING THAT'S HAPPENED TO US.
WE NEED TO FIND OUT HOW IT WORKS.
AND DON'T EVEN THINK ABOUT GOING TO MORGAN EDGE ABOUT THIS!
HMMPF!
THEN WE NEED A PLACE WITH SOME REAL HI-TECH GADGETS, AND NOT THESE PHONY *TINKER TOYS.*
WELL, IF THAT'S WHAT WE NEED, I HAVE JUST THE PLACE.

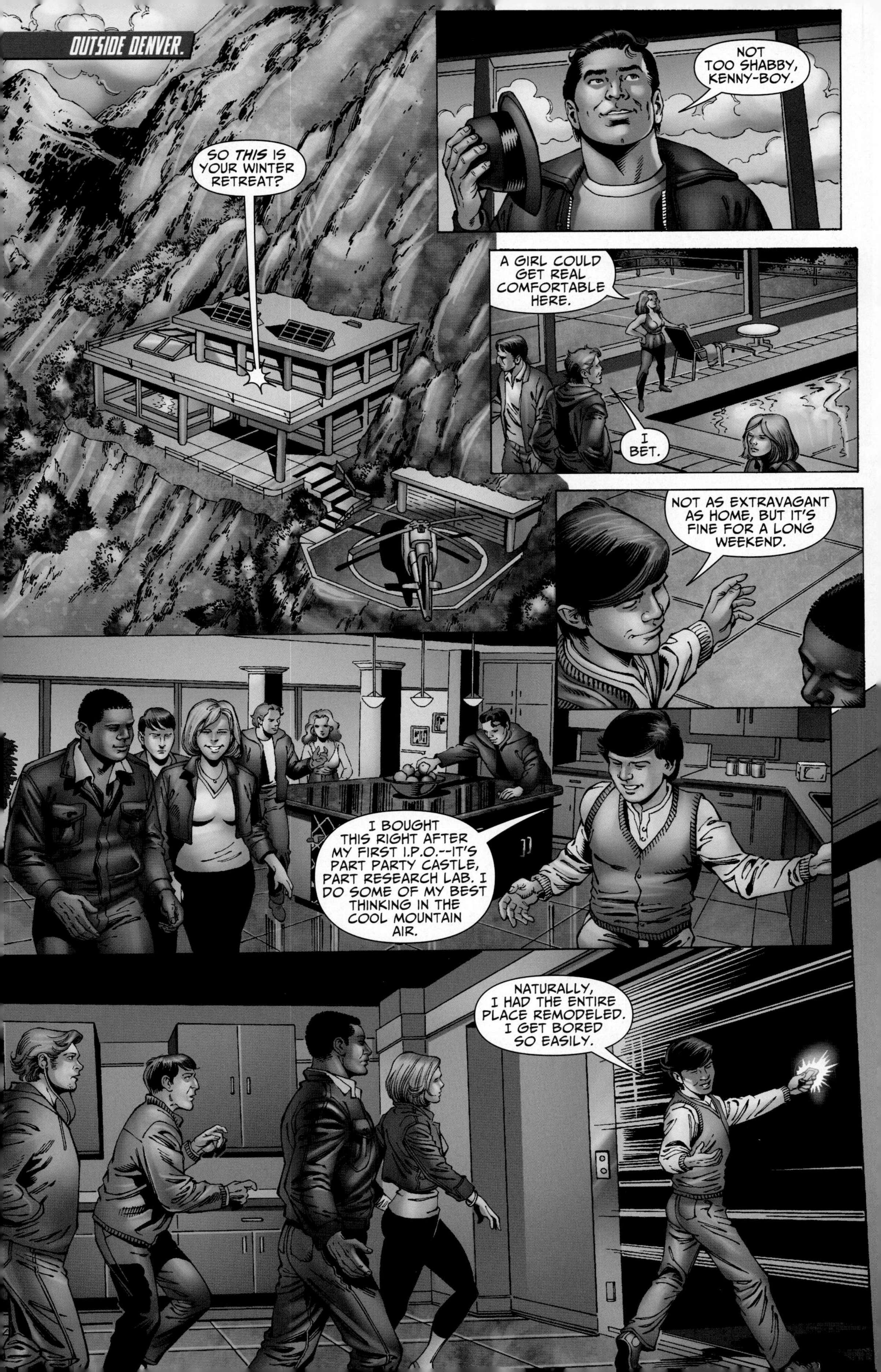
OUTSIDE DENVER.
SO THIS IS YOUR WINTER RETREAT?
NOT TOO SHABBY, KENNY-BOY.
A GIRL COULD GET REAL COMFORTABLE HERE.
I BET.
NOT AS EXTRAVAGANT AS HOME, BUT IT'S FINE FOR A LONG WEEKEND.
I BOUGHT THIS RIGHT AFTER MY FIRST I.P.O.--IT'S PART PARTY CASTLE, PART RESEARCH LAB. I DO SOME OF MY BEST THINKING IN THE COOL MOUNTAIN AIR.
NATURALLY, I HAD THE ENTIRE PLACE REMODELED. I GET BORED SO EASILY.

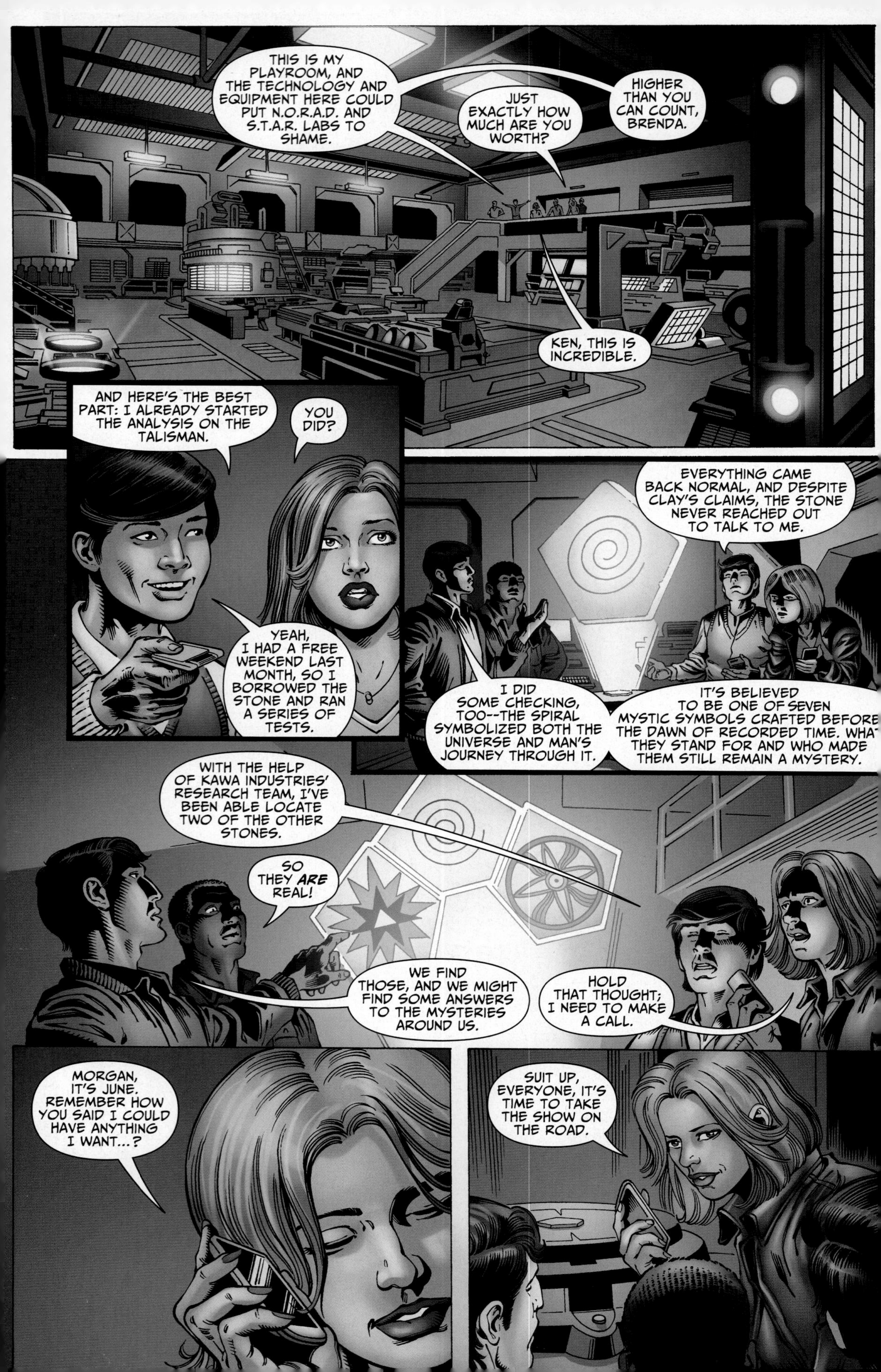
THIS IS MY PLAYROOM, AND THE TECHNOLOGY AND EQUIPMENT HERE COULD PUT N.O.R.A.D. AND S.T.A.R. LABS TO SHAME.
JUST EXACTLY HOW MUCH ARE YOU WORTH?
HIGHER THAN YOU CAN COUNT, BRENDA.
KEN, THIS IS INCREDIBLE.
AND HERE'S THE BEST PART: I ALREADY STARTED THE ANALYSIS ON THE TALISMAN.
YOU DID?
YEAH, I HAD A FREE WEEKEND LAST MONTH, SO I BORROWED THE STONE AND RAN A SERIES OF TESTS.
EVERYTHING CAME BACK NORMAL, AND DESPITE CLAY'S CLAIMS, THE STONE NEVER REACHED OUT TO TALK TO ME.
I DID SOME CHECKING, TOO--THE SPIRAL SYMBOLIZED BOTH THE UNIVERSE AND MAN'S JOURNEY THROUGH IT.
IT'S BELIEVED TO BE ONE OF SEVEN MYSTIC SYMBOLS CRAFTED BEFORE THE DAWN OF RECORDED TIME. WHAT THEY STAND FOR AND WHO MADE THEM STILL REMAIN A MYSTERY.
WITH THE HELP OF KAWA INDUSTRIES' RESEARCH TEAM, I'VE BEEN ABLE LOCATE TWO OF THE OTHER STONES.
SO THEY *ARE* REAL!
WE FIND THOSE, AND WE MIGHT FIND SOME ANSWERS TO THE MYSTERIES AROUND US.
HOLD THAT THOUGHT; I NEED TO MAKE A CALL.
MORGAN, IT'S JUNE. REMEMBER HOW YOU SAID I COULD HAVE ANYTHING I WANT...?
SUIT UP, EVERYONE, IT'S TIME TO TAKE THE SHOW ON THE ROAD.

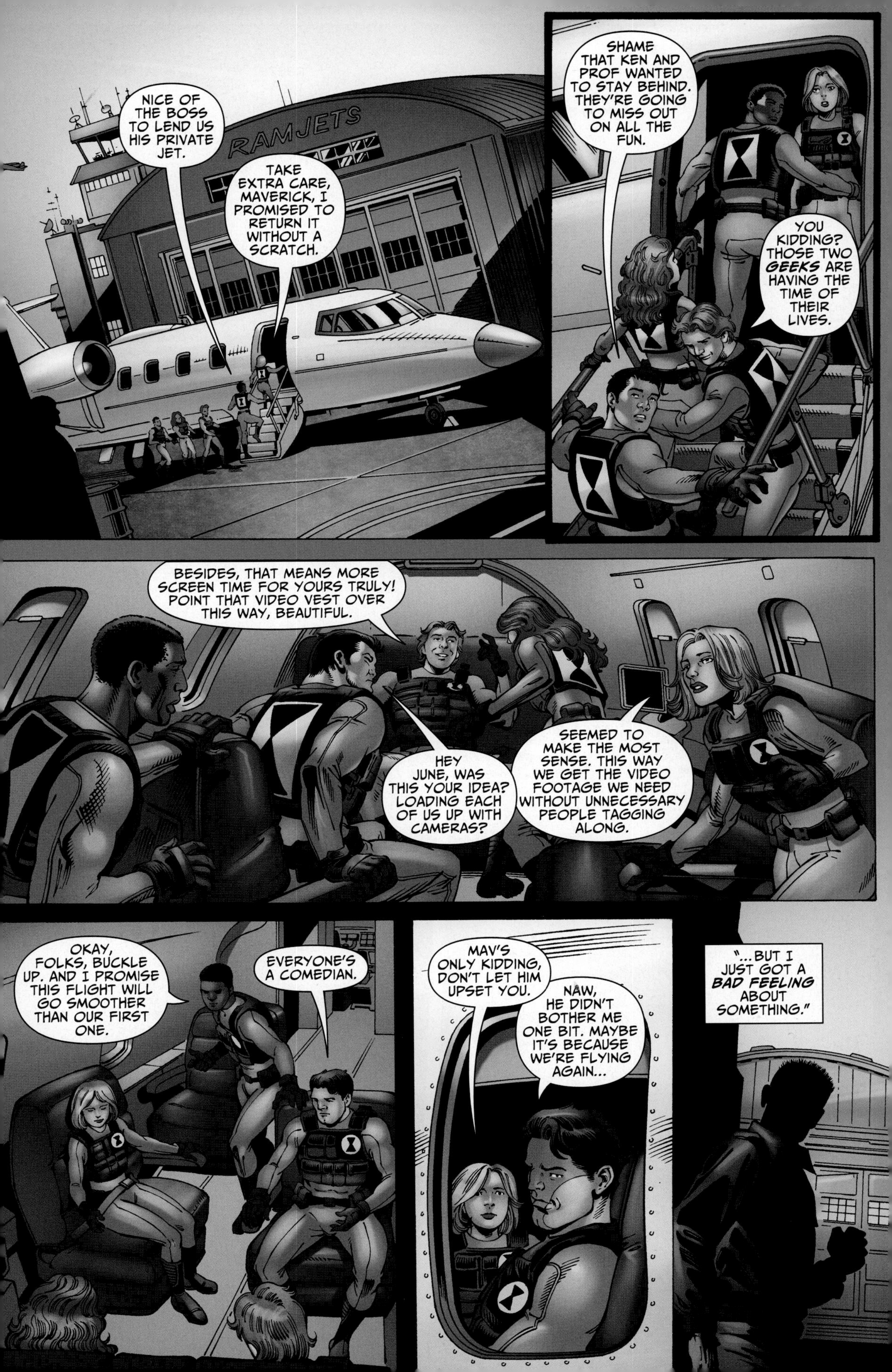
RAMJETS
NICE OF THE BOSS TO LEND US HIS PRIVATE JET.
TAKE EXTRA CARE, MAVERICK, I PROMISED TO RETURN IT WITHOUT A SCRATCH.
SHAME THAT KEN AND PROF WANTED TO STAY BEHIND. THEY'RE GOING TO MISS OUT ON ALL THE FUN.
YOU KIDDING? THOSE TWO *GEEKS* ARE HAVING THE TIME OF THEIR LIVES.
BESIDES, THAT MEANS MORE SCREEN TIME FOR YOURS TRULY! POINT THAT VIDEO VEST OVER THIS WAY, BEAUTIFUL.
HEY JUNE, WAS THIS YOUR IDEA? LOADING EACH OF US UP WITH CAMERAS?
SEEMED TO MAKE THE MOST SENSE. THIS WAY WE GET THE VIDEO FOOTAGE WE NEED WITHOUT UNNECESSARY PEOPLE TAGGING ALONG.
OKAY, FOLKS, BUCKLE UP. AND I PROMISE THIS FLIGHT WILL GO SMOOTHER THAN OUR FIRST ONE.
EVERYONE'S A COMEDIAN.
MAV'S ONLY KIDDING, DON'T LET HIM UPSET YOU.
NAW, HE DIDN'T BOTHER ME ONE BIT. MAYBE IT'S BECAUSE WE'RE FLYING AGAIN...
"...BUT I JUST GOT A *BAD FEELING* ABOUT SOMETHING."

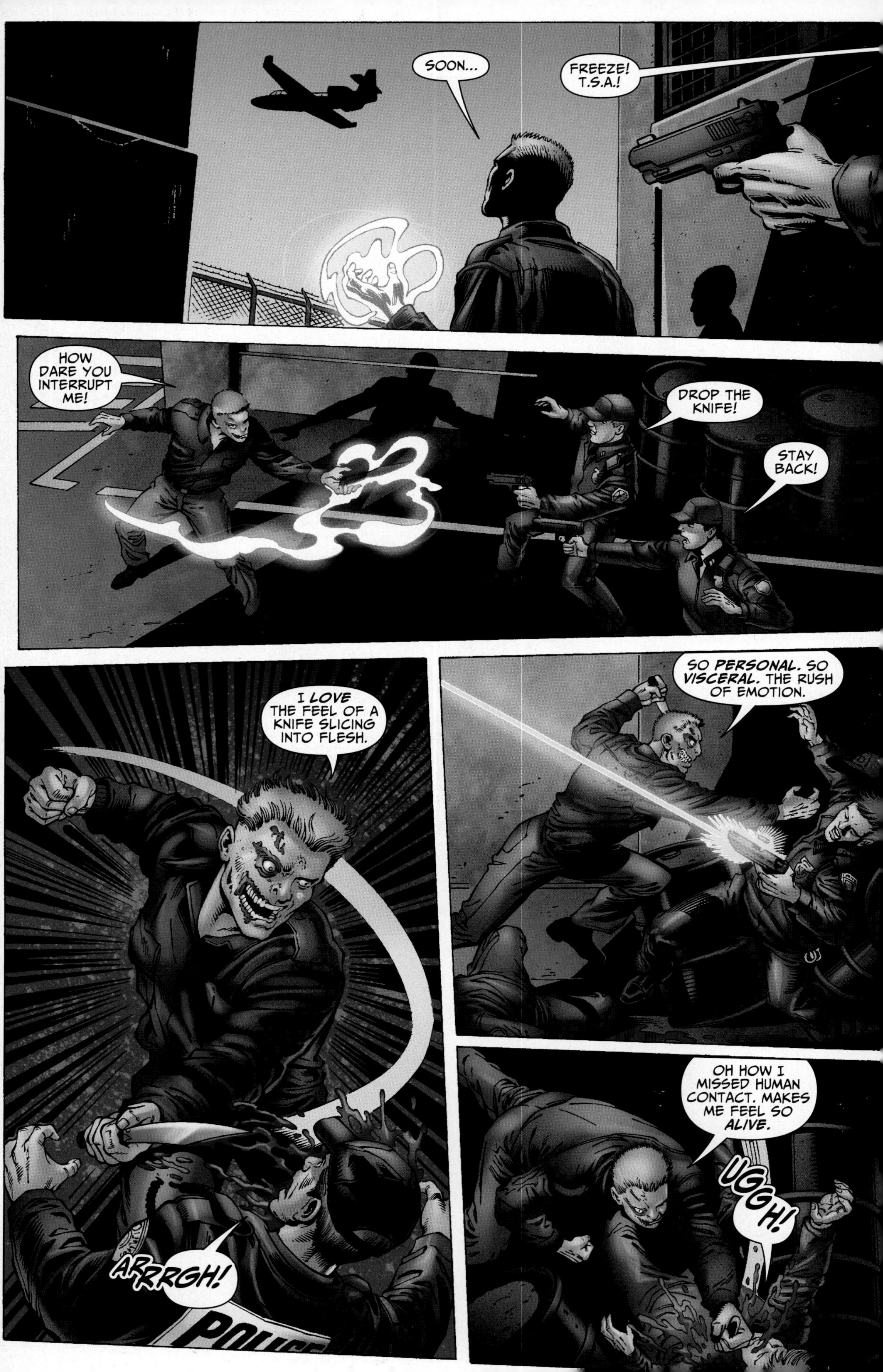
SOON...
FREEZE! T.S.A.!
HOW DARE YOU INTERRUPT ME!
DROP THE KNIFE!
STAY BACK!
I LOVE THE FEEL OF A KNIFE SLICING INTO FLESH.
ARRRGH!
SO PERSONAL. SO VISCERAL. THE RUSH OF EMOTION.
OH HOW I MISSED HUMAN CONTACT. MAKES ME FEEL SO ALIVE.
UGGH!

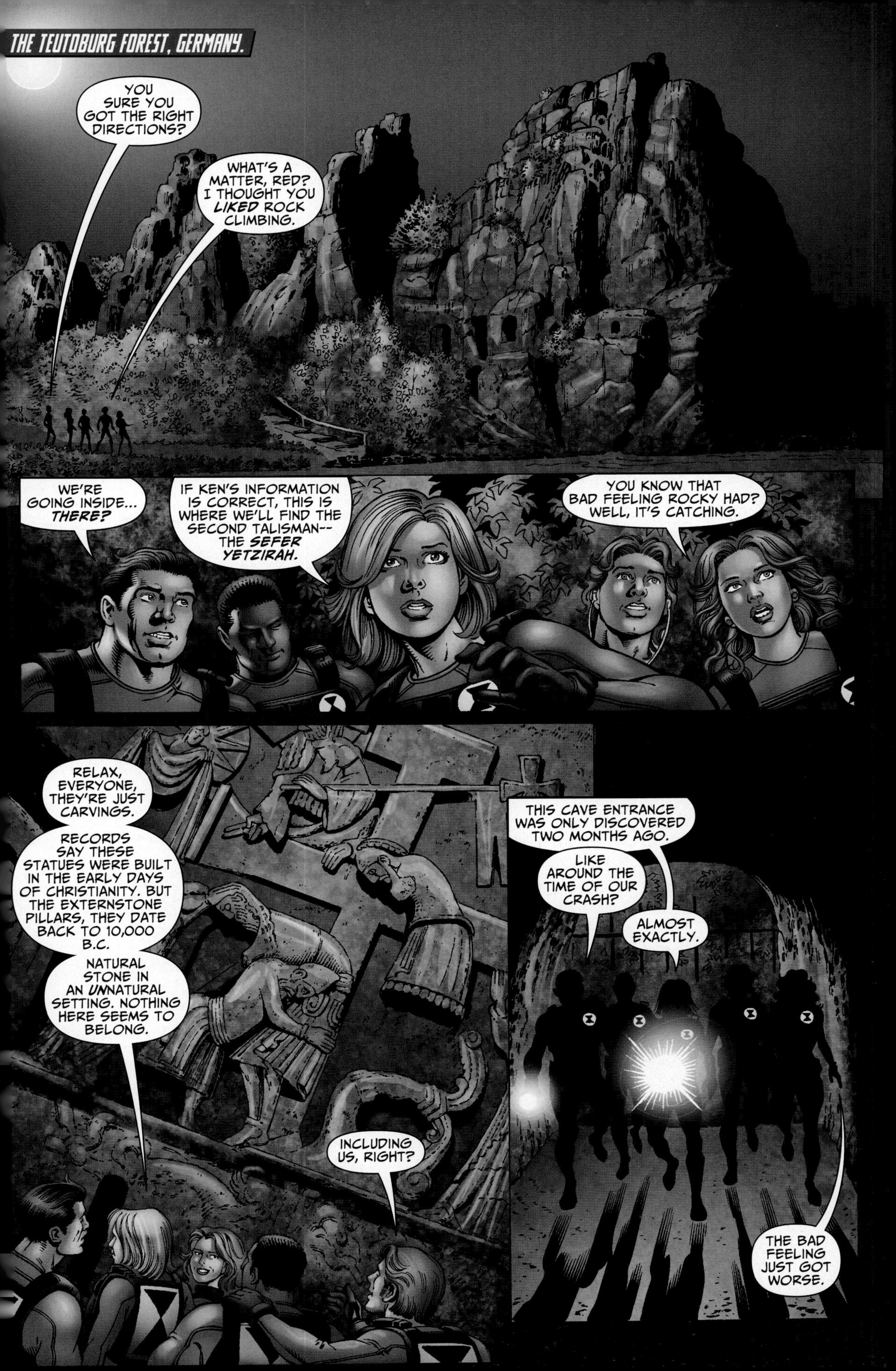
THE TEUTOBURG FOREST, GERMANY.
YOU SURE YOU GOT THE RIGHT DIRECTIONS?
WHAT'S A MATTER, RED? I THOUGHT YOU LIKED ROCK CLIMBING.
WE'RE GOING INSIDE... THERE?
IF KEN'S INFORMATION IS CORRECT, THIS IS WHERE WE'LL FIND THE SECOND TALISMAN-- THE SEFER YETZIRAH.
YOU KNOW THAT BAD FEELING ROCKY HAD? WELL, IT'S CATCHING.
RELAX, EVERYONE, THEY'RE JUST CARVINGS.
RECORDS SAY THESE STATUES WERE BUILT IN THE EARLY DAYS OF CHRISTIANITY. BUT THE EXTERNSTONE PILLARS, THEY DATE BACK TO 10,000 B.C.
NATURAL STONE IN AN UNNATURAL SETTING. NOTHING HERE SEEMS TO BELONG.
INCLUDING US, RIGHT?
THIS CAVE ENTRANCE WAS ONLY DISCOVERED TWO MONTHS AGO.
LIKE AROUND THE TIME OF OUR CRASH?
ALMOST EXACTLY.
THE BAD FEELING JUST GOT WORSE.

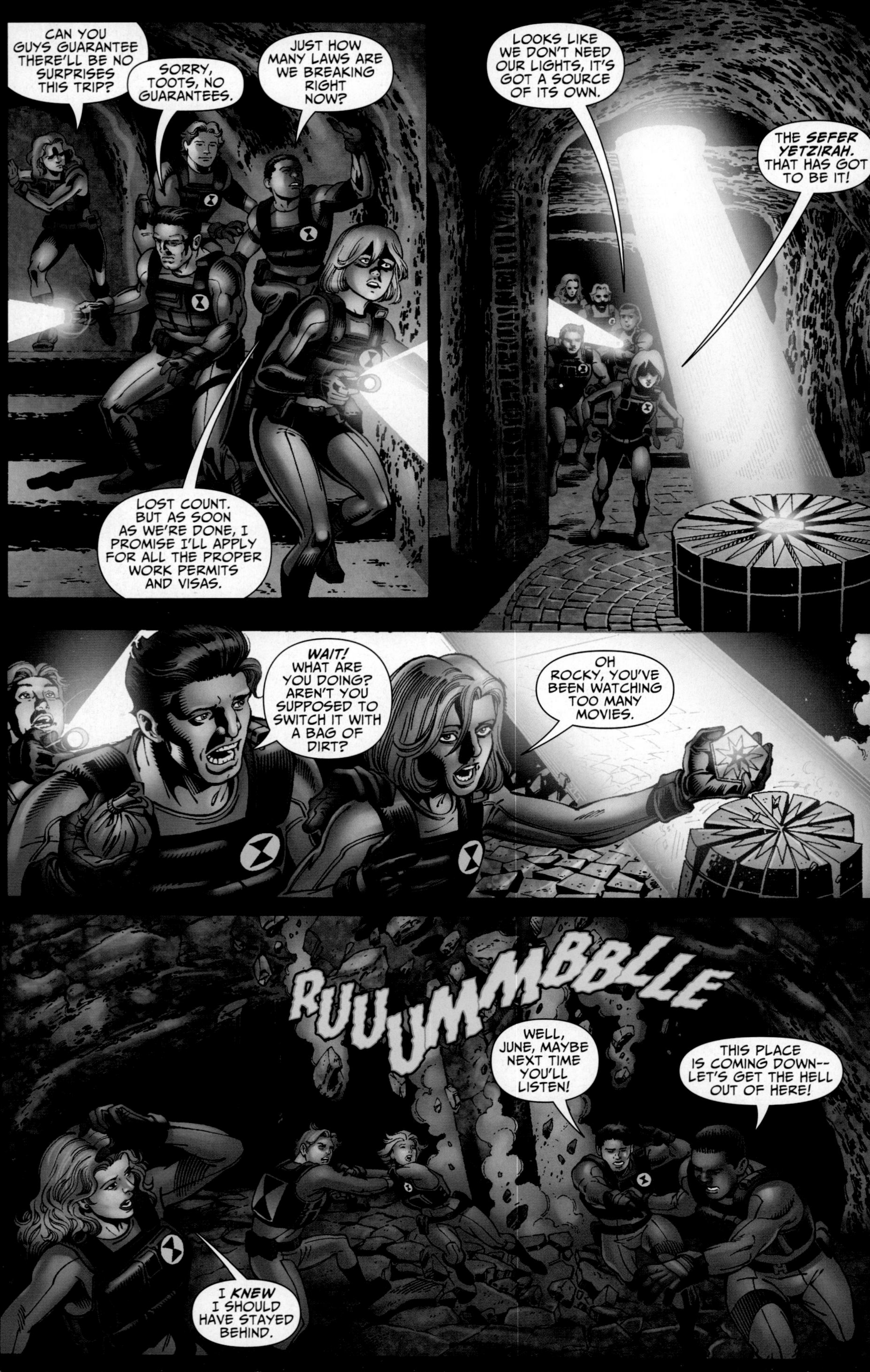
CAN YOU GUYS GUARANTEE THERE'LL BE NO SURPRISES THIS TRIP?
SORRY, TOOTS, NO GUARANTEES.
JUST HOW MANY LAWS ARE WE BREAKING RIGHT NOW?
LOST COUNT. BUT AS SOON AS WE'RE DONE, I PROMISE I'LL APPLY FOR ALL THE PROPER WORK PERMITS AND VISAS.
LOOKS LIKE WE DON'T NEED OUR LIGHTS, IT'S GOT A SOURCE OF ITS OWN.
THE SEFER YETZIRAH. THAT HAS GOT TO BE IT!
WAIT! WHAT ARE YOU DOING? AREN'T YOU SUPPOSED TO SWITCH IT WITH A BAG OF DIRT?
OH ROCKY, YOU'VE BEEN WATCHING TOO MANY MOVIES.
RUUUMMBBLLE
WELL, JUNE, MAYBE NEXT TIME YOU'LL LISTEN!
THIS PLACE IS COMING DOWN-- LET'S GET THE HELL OUT OF HERE!
I KNEW I SHOULD HAVE STAYED BEHIND.

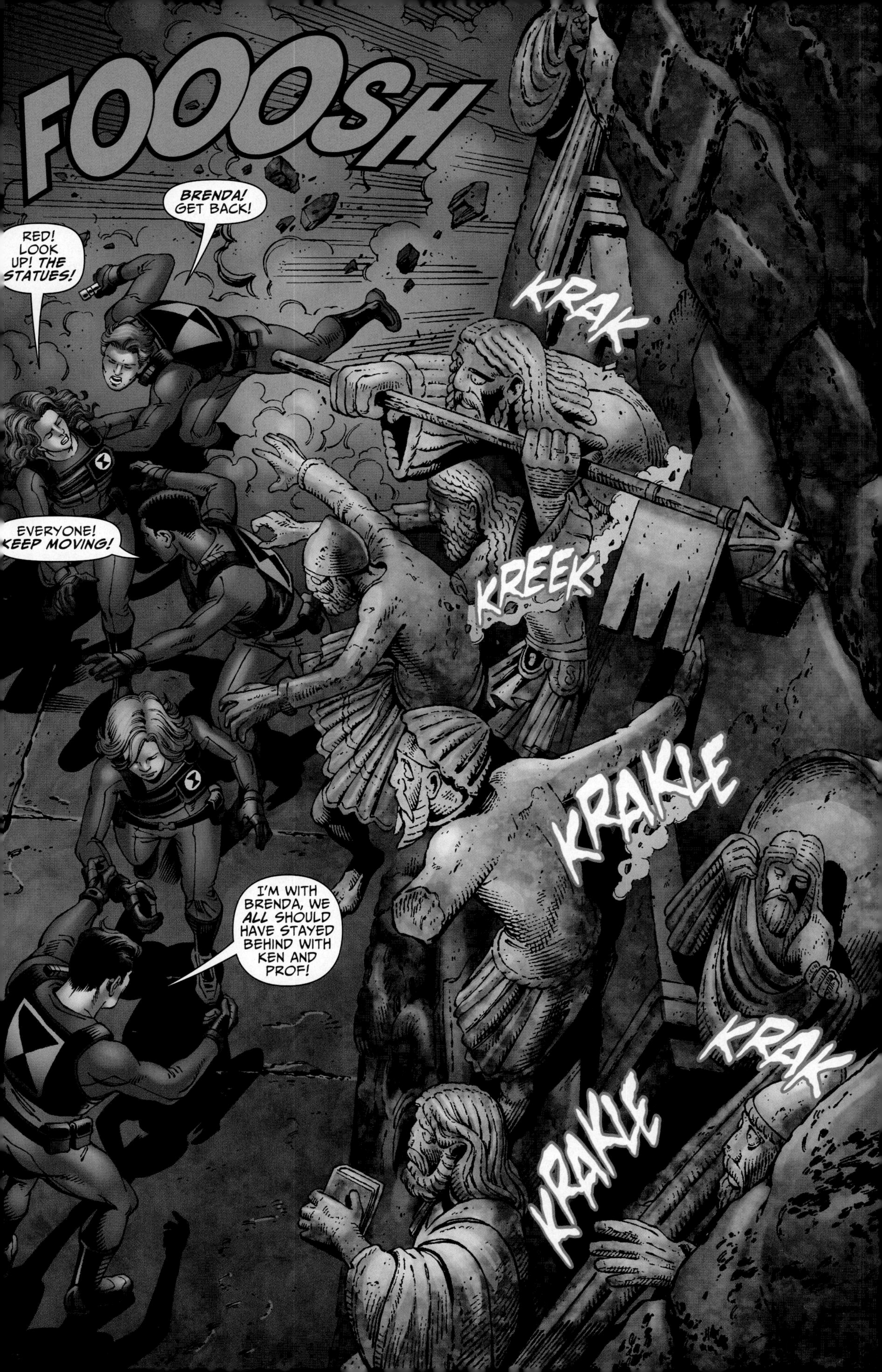
FOOOSH
BRENDA! GET BACK!
RED! LOOK UP! THE STATUES!
KRAK
EVERYONE! KEEP MOVING!
KREEK
KRAKLE
I'M WITH BRENDA, WE ALL SHOULD HAVE STAYED BEHIND WITH KEN AND PROF!
KRAK
KRAKLE

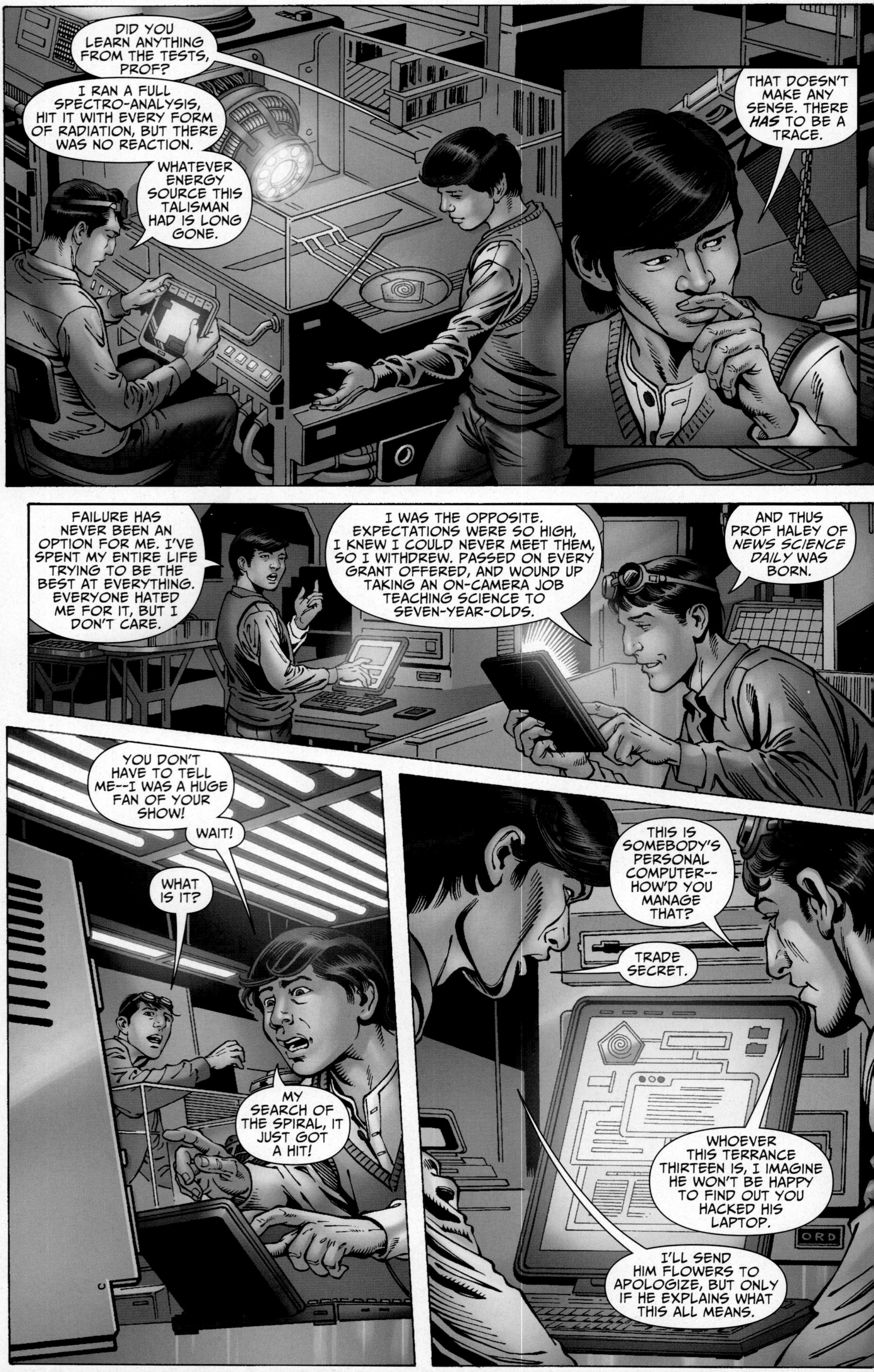
DID YOU LEARN ANYTHING FROM THE TESTS, PROF?
I RAN A FULL SPECTRO-ANALYSIS, HIT IT WITH EVERY FORM OF RADIATION, BUT THERE WAS NO REACTION.
WHATEVER ENERGY SOURCE THIS TALISMAN HAD IS LONG GONE.
THAT DOESN'T MAKE ANY SENSE. THERE HAS TO BE A TRACE.
FAILURE HAS NEVER BEEN AN OPTION FOR ME. I'VE SPENT MY ENTIRE LIFE TRYING TO BE THE BEST AT EVERYTHING. EVERYONE HATED ME FOR IT, BUT I DON'T CARE.
I WAS THE OPPOSITE. EXPECTATIONS WERE SO HIGH, I KNEW I COULD NEVER MEET THEM, SO I WITHDREW. PASSED ON EVERY GRANT OFFERED, AND WOUND UP TAKING AN ON-CAMERA JOB TEACHING SCIENCE TO SEVEN-YEAR-OLDS.
AND THUS PROF HALEY OF NEWS SCIENCE DAILY WAS BORN.
YOU DON'T HAVE TO TELL ME--I WAS A HUGE FAN OF YOUR SHOW!
WAIT!
WHAT IS IT?
MY SEARCH OF THE SPIRAL, IT JUST GOT A HIT!
THIS IS SOMEBODY'S PERSONAL COMPUTER--HOW'D YOU MANAGE THAT?
TRADE SECRET.
WHOEVER THIS TERRANCE THIRTEEN IS, I IMAGINE HE WON'T BE HAPPY TO FIND OUT YOU HACKED HIS LAPTOP.
I'LL SEND HIM FLOWERS TO APOLOGIZE, BUT ONLY IF HE EXPLAINS WHAT THIS ALL MEANS.

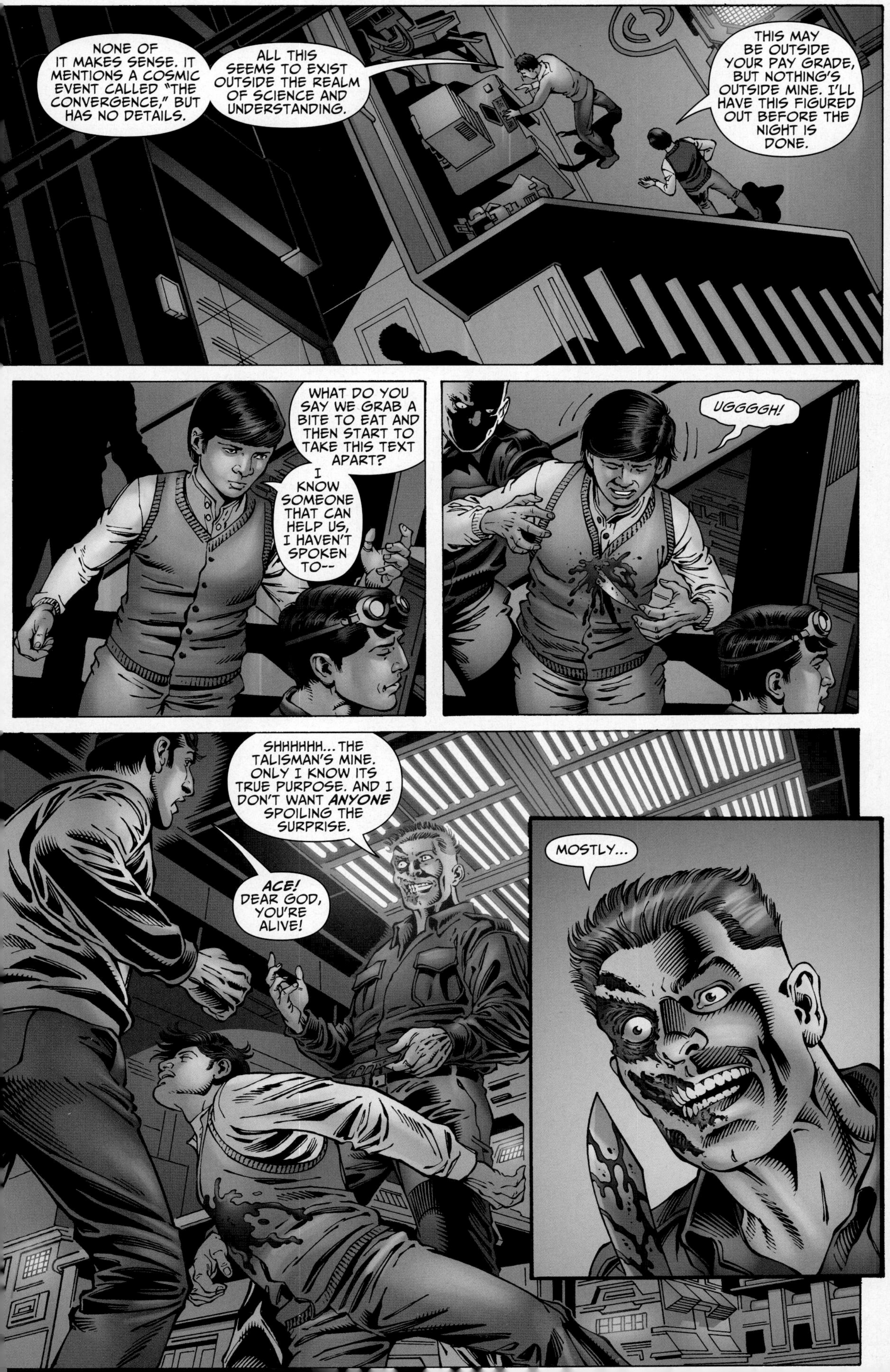
NONE OF IT MAKES SENSE. IT MENTIONS A COSMIC EVENT CALLED "THE CONVERGENCE," BUT HAS NO DETAILS.
ALL THIS SEEMS TO EXIST OUTSIDE THE REALM OF SCIENCE AND UNDERSTANDING.
THIS MAY BE OUTSIDE YOUR PAY GRADE, BUT NOTHING'S OUTSIDE MINE. I'LL HAVE THIS FIGURED OUT BEFORE THE NIGHT IS DONE.
WHAT DO YOU SAY WE GRAB A BITE TO EAT AND THEN START TO TAKE THIS TEXT APART?
I KNOW SOMEONE THAT CAN HELP US, I HAVEN'T SPOKEN TO--
UGGGGH!
SHHHHHH... THE TALISMAN'S MINE. ONLY I KNOW ITS TRUE PURPOSE. AND I DON'T WANT ANYONE SPOILING THE SURPRISE.
ACE! DEAR GOD, YOU'RE ALIVE!
MOSTLY...

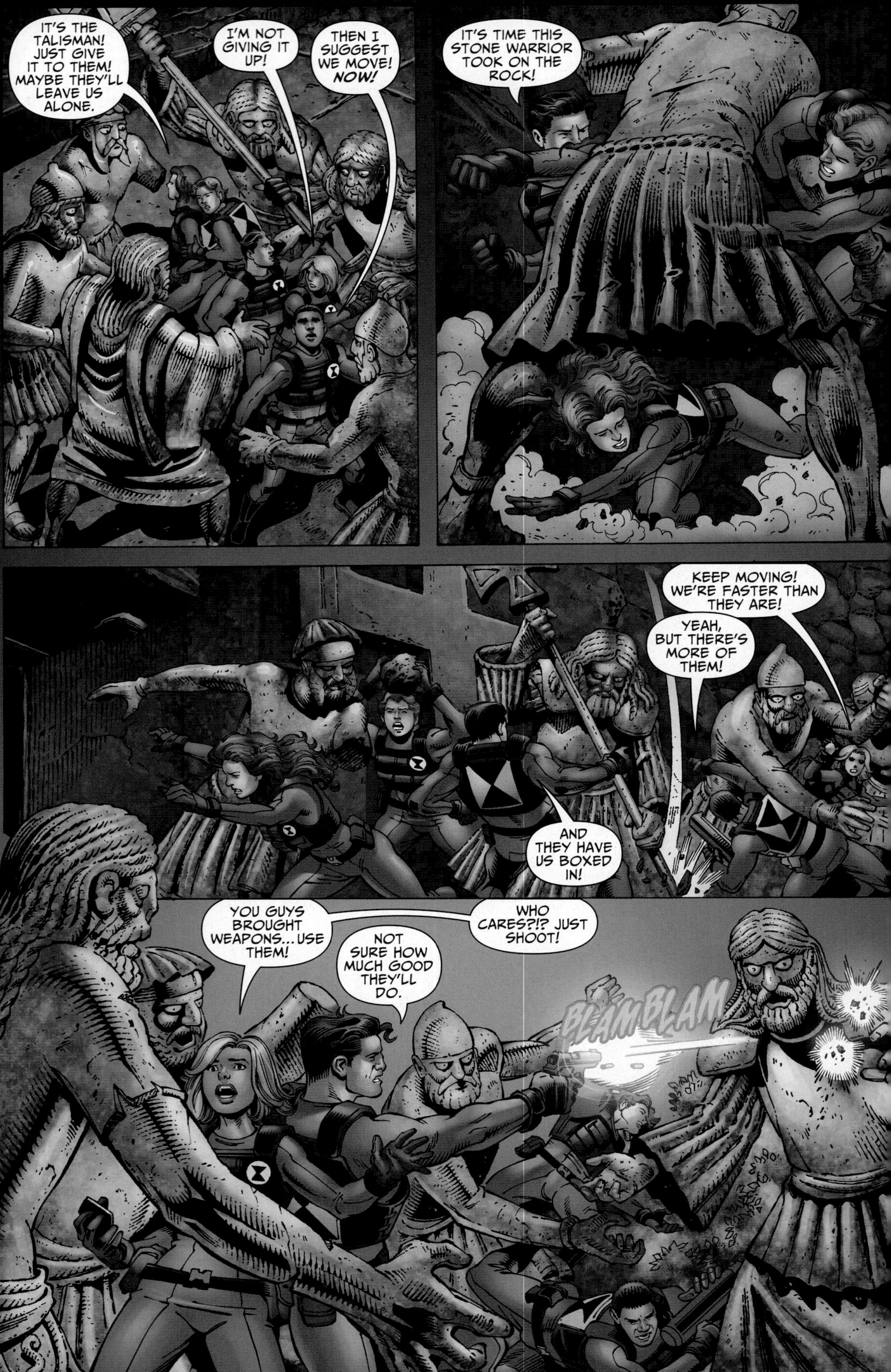

IT'S THE TALISMAN! JUST GIVE IT TO THEM! MAYBE THEY'LL LEAVE US ALONE.
I'M NOT GIVING IT UP!
THEN I SUGGEST WE MOVE! *NOW!*
IT'S TIME THIS STONE WARRIOR TOOK ON THE ROCK!
KEEP MOVING! WE'RE FASTER THAN THEY ARE!
YEAH, BUT THERE'S MORE OF THEM!
AND THEY HAVE US BOXED IN!
YOU GUYS BROUGHT WEAPONS... USE THEM!
NOT SURE HOW MUCH GOOD THEY'LL DO.
WHO CARES?!? JUST SHOOT!
BLAM BLAM

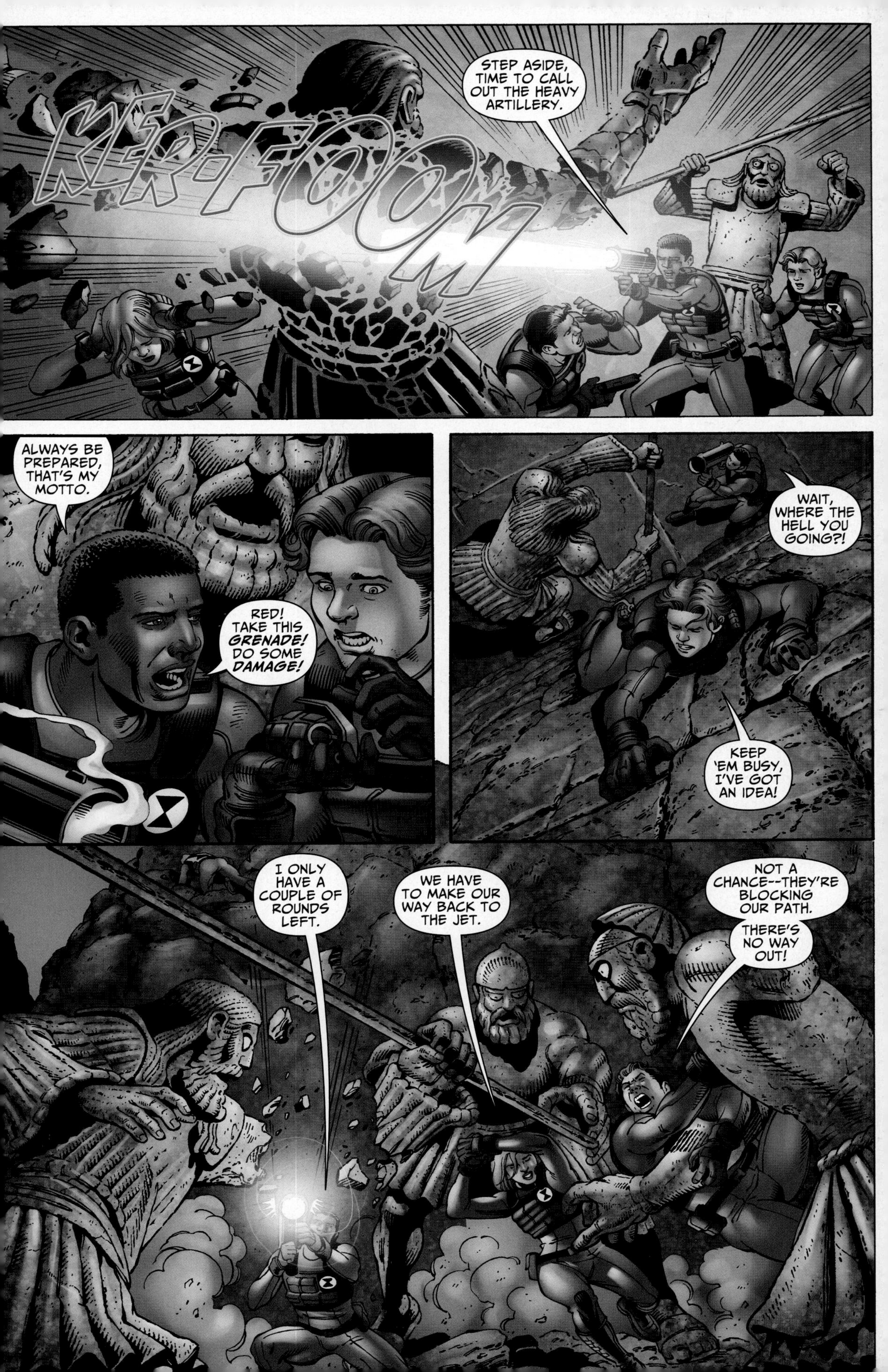
KER-FOOOM
STEP ASIDE, TIME TO CALL OUT THE HEAVY ARTILLERY.
ALWAYS BE PREPARED, THAT'S MY MOTTO.
RED! TAKE THIS GRENADE! DO SOME DAMAGE!
WAIT, WHERE THE HELL YOU GOING?!
KEEP 'EM BUSY, I'VE GOT AN IDEA!
I ONLY HAVE A COUPLE OF ROUNDS LEFT.
WE HAVE TO MAKE OUR WAY BACK TO THE JET.
NOT A CHANCE--THEY'RE BLOCKING OUR PATH.
THERE'S NO WAY OUT!

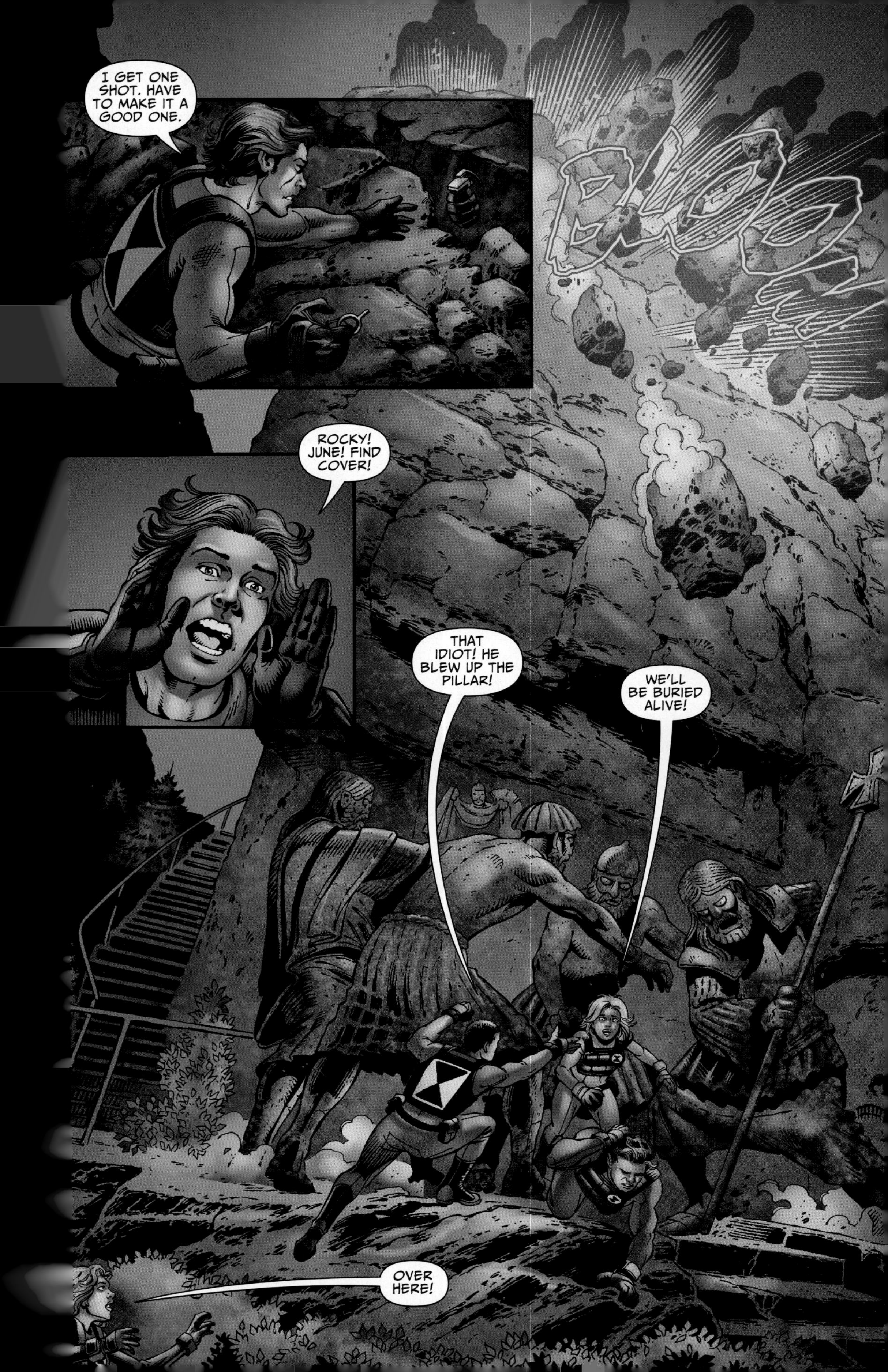
I GET ONE SHOT. HAVE TO MAKE IT A GOOD ONE.
ROCKY! JUNE! FIND COVER!
THAT IDIOT! HE BLEW UP THE PILLAR!
WE'LL BE BURIED ALIVE!
OVER HERE!

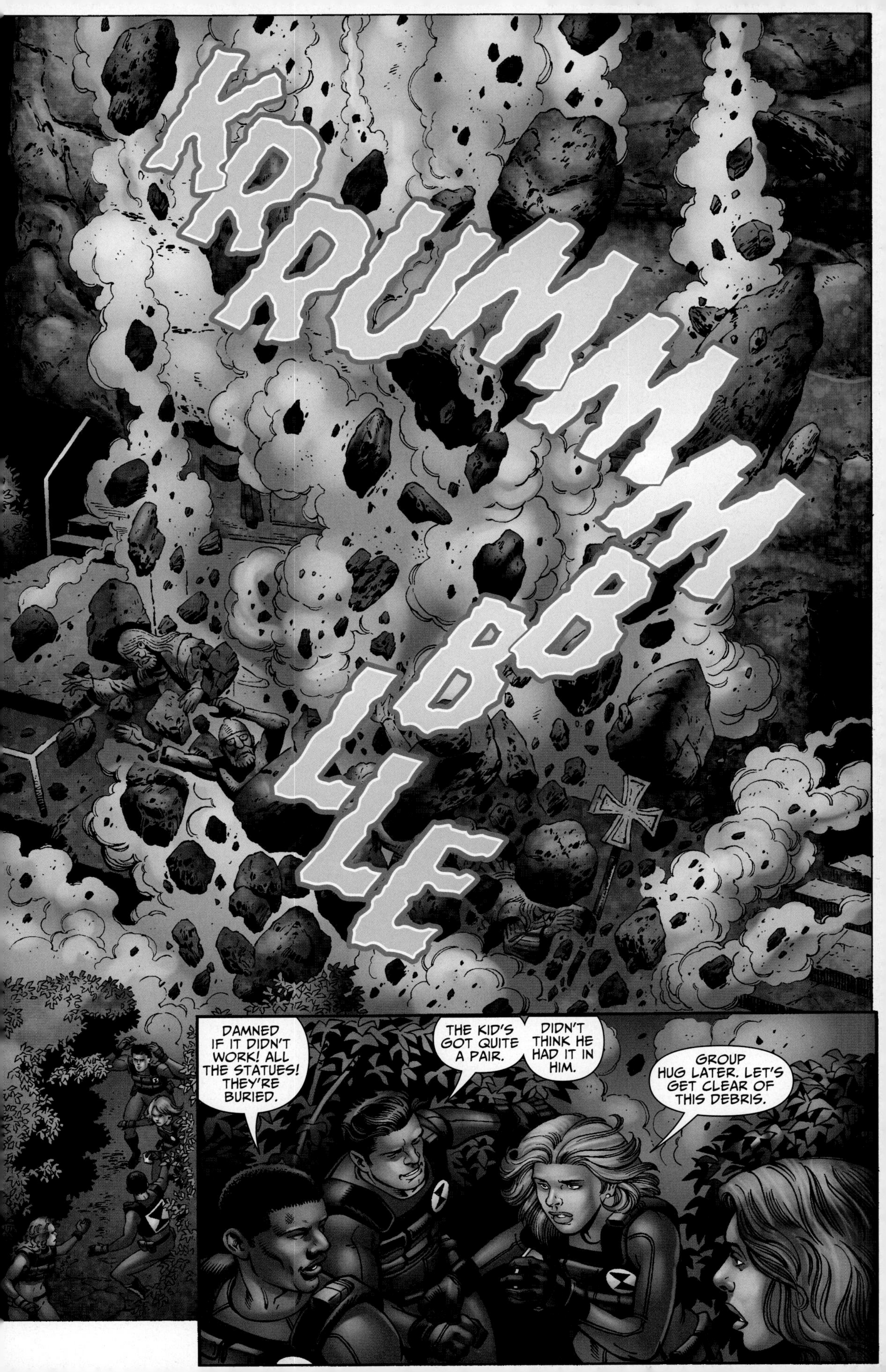
KRUMMMBBLE
DAMNED IF IT DIDN'T WORK! ALL THE STATUES! THEY'RE BURIED.
THE KID'S GOT QUITE A PAIR.
DIDN'T THINK HE HAD IT IN HIM.
GROUP HUG LATER. LET'S GET CLEAR OF THIS DEBRIS.

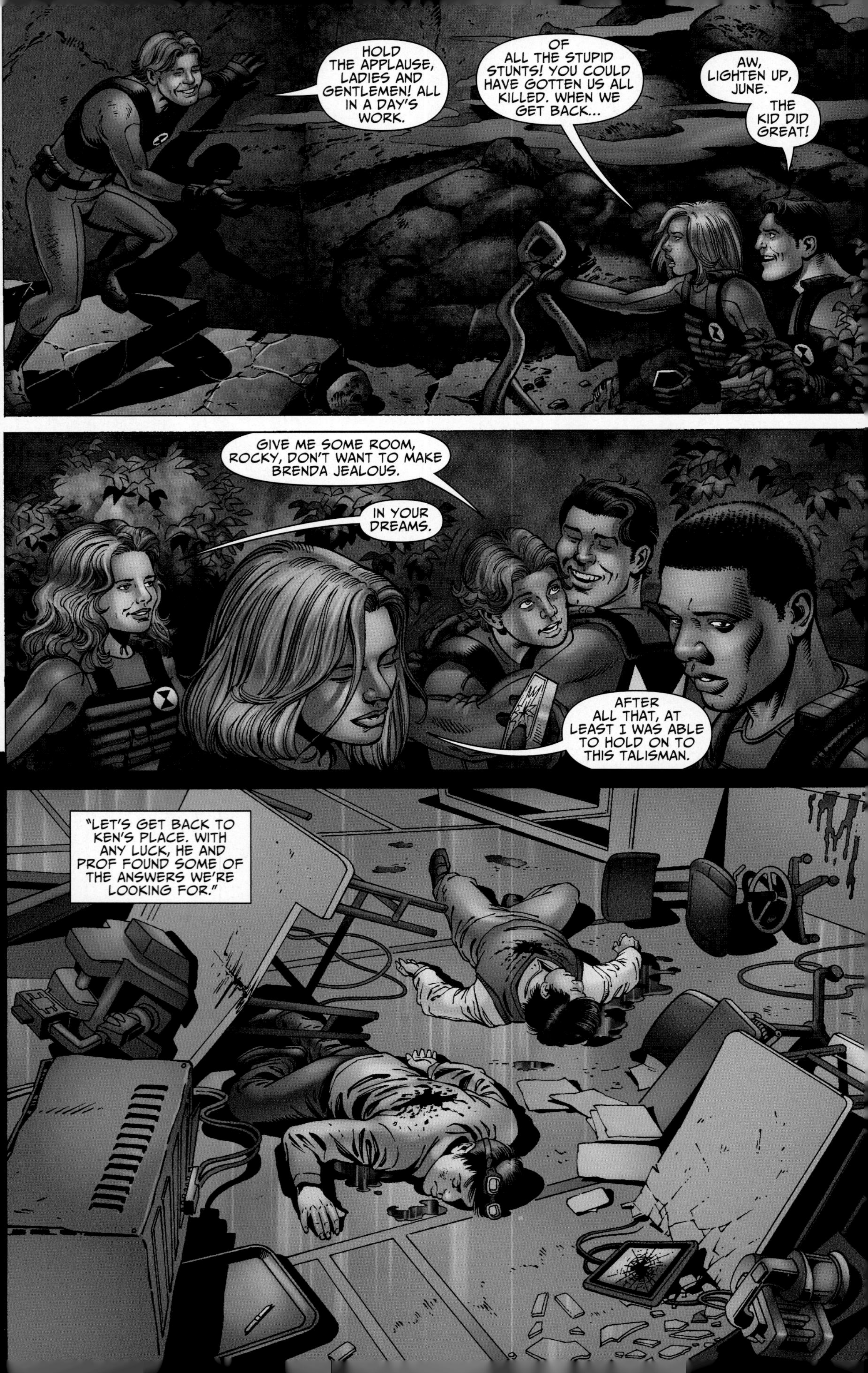
HOLD THE APPLAUSE, LADIES AND GENTLEMEN! ALL IN A DAY'S WORK.
OF ALL THE STUPID STUNTS! YOU COULD HAVE GOTTEN US ALL KILLED. WHEN WE GET BACK...
AW, LIGHTEN UP, JUNE.
THE KID DID GREAT!
GIVE ME SOME ROOM, ROCKY, DON'T WANT TO MAKE BRENDA JEALOUS.
IN YOUR DREAMS.
AFTER ALL THAT, AT LEAST I WAS ABLE TO HOLD ON TO THIS TALISMAN.
"LET'S GET BACK TO KEN'S PLACE. WITH ANY LUCK, HE AND PROF FOUND SOME OF THE ANSWERS WE'RE LOOKING FOR."

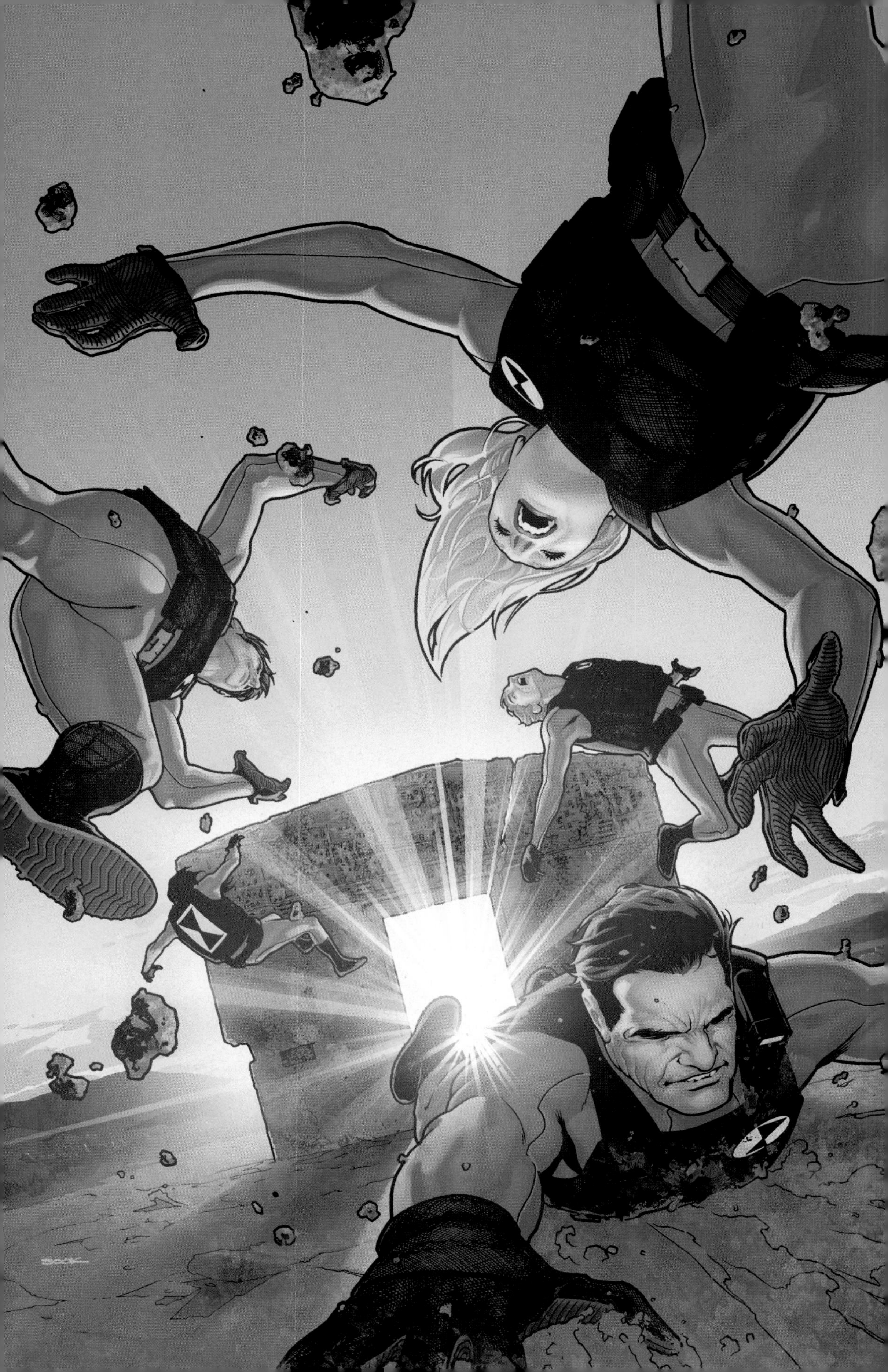
SOOK

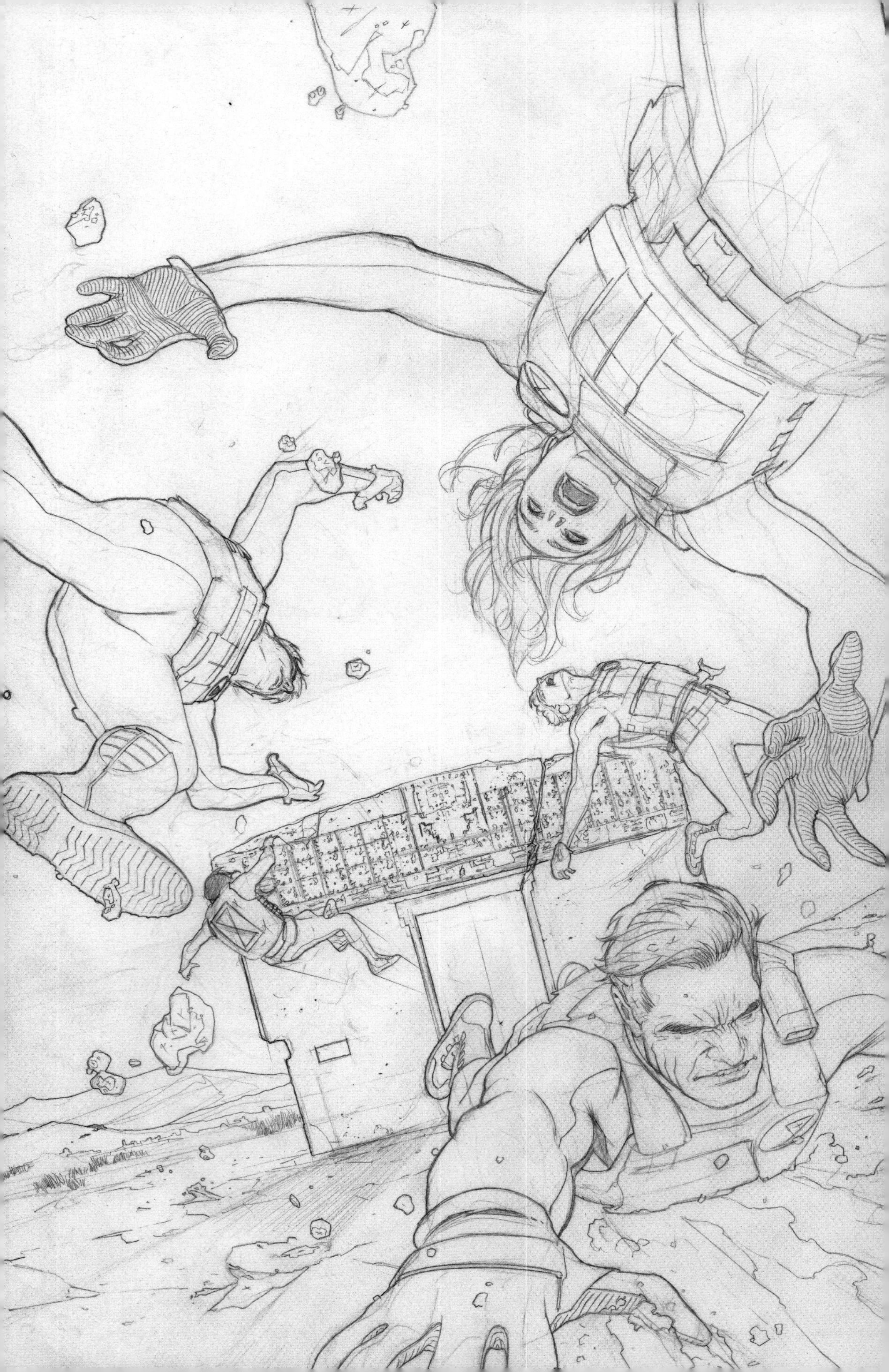

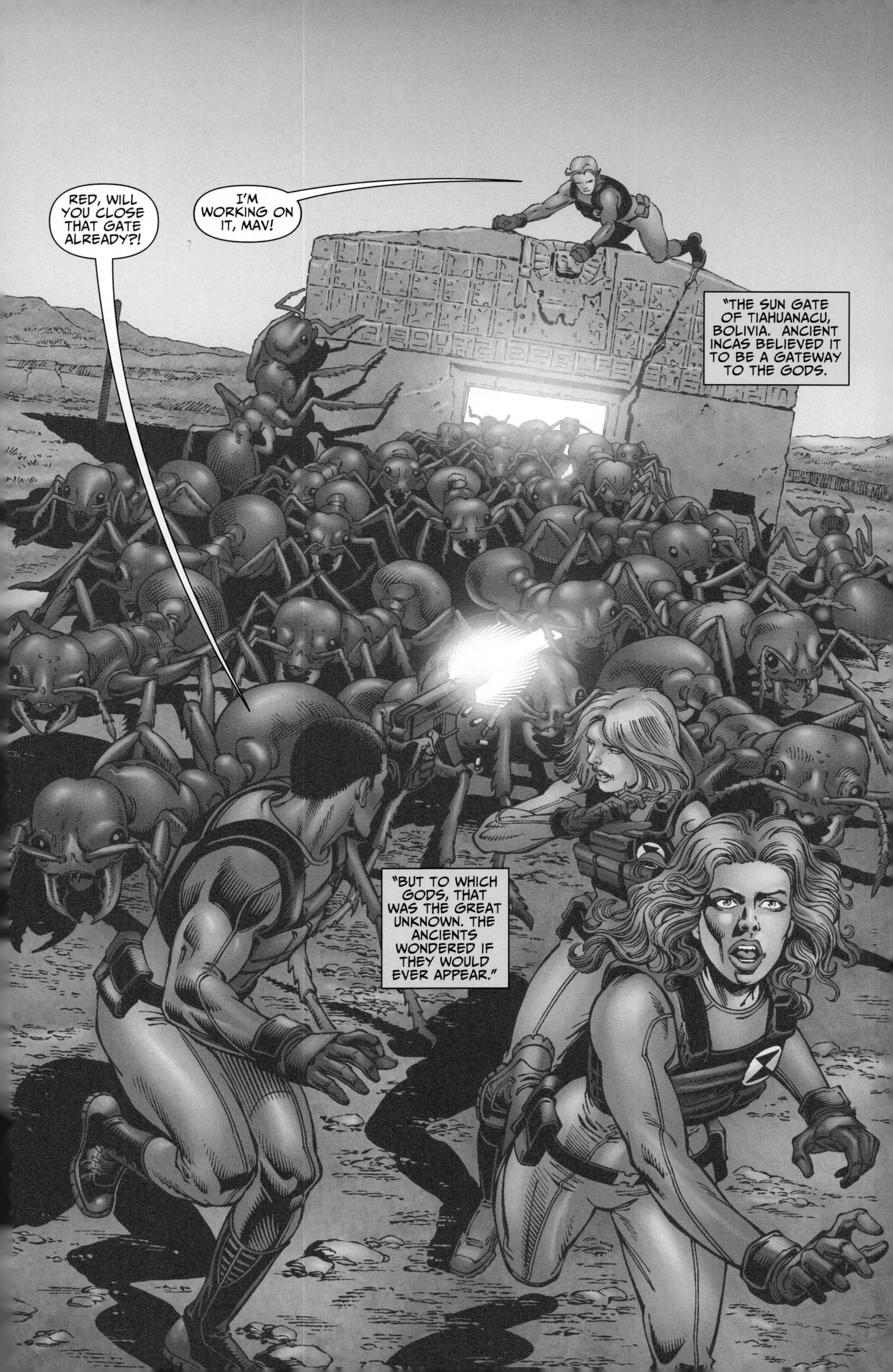
RED, WILL YOU CLOSE THAT GATE ALREADY?!
I'M WORKING ON IT, MAV!
"THE SUN GATE OF TIAHUANACU, BOLIVIA. ANCIENT INCAS BELIEVED IT TO BE A GATEWAY TO THE GODS.
"BUT TO WHICH GODS, THAT WAS THE GREAT UNKNOWN. THE ANCIENTS WONDERED IF THEY WOULD EVER APPEAR."

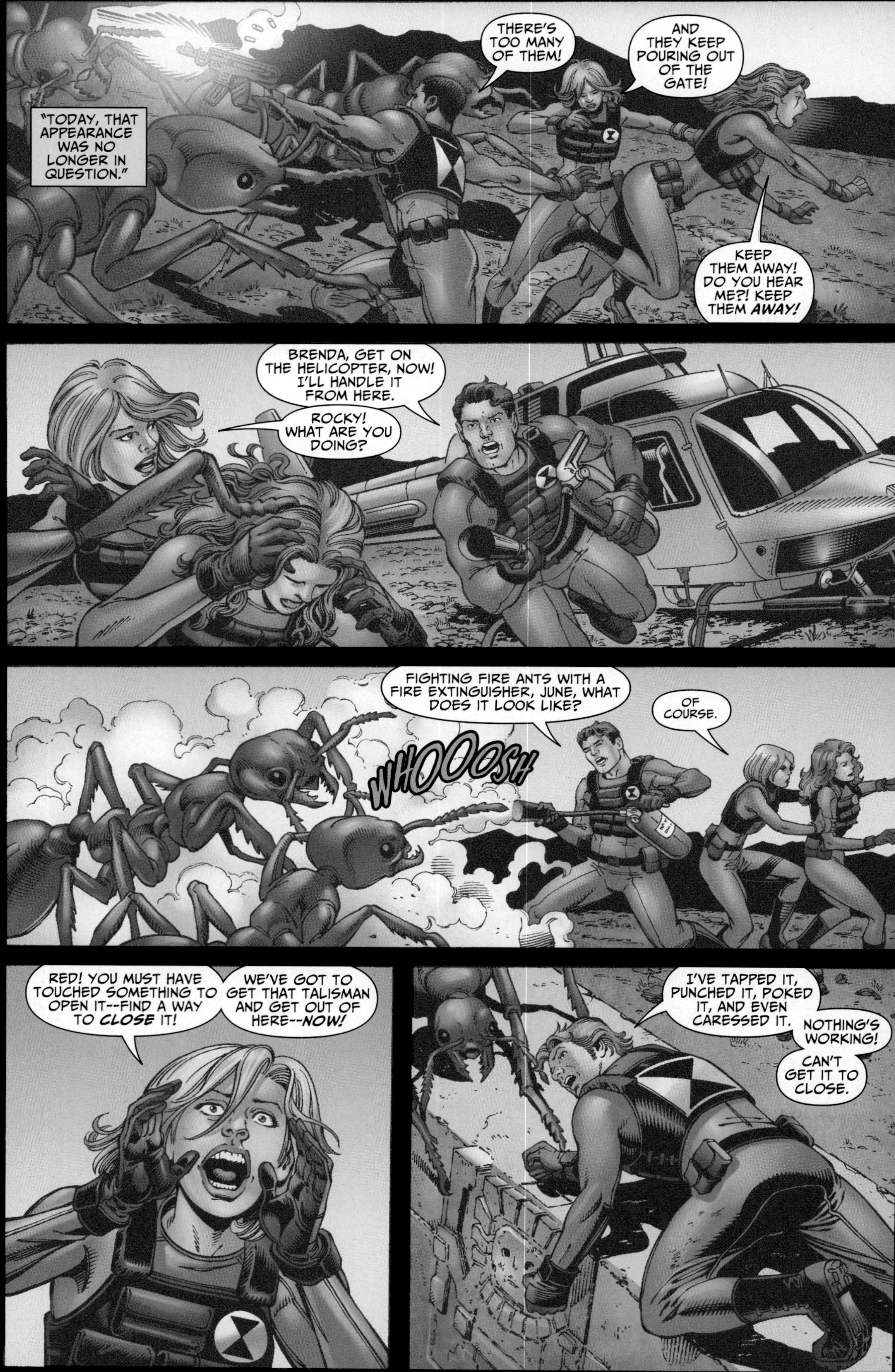
"TODAY, THAT APPEARANCE WAS NO LONGER IN QUESTION."
THERE'S TOO MANY OF THEM!
AND THEY KEEP POURING OUT OF THE GATE!
KEEP THEM AWAY! DO YOU HEAR ME?! KEEP THEM *AWAY!*
BRENDA, GET ON THE HELICOPTER, NOW! I'LL HANDLE IT FROM HERE.
ROCKY! WHAT ARE YOU DOING?
FIGHTING FIRE ANTS WITH A FIRE EXTINGUISHER, JUNE, WHAT DOES IT LOOK LIKE?
OF COURSE.
WHOOOOSH
RED! YOU MUST HAVE TOUCHED SOMETHING TO OPEN IT--FIND A WAY TO *CLOSE* IT!
WE'VE GOT TO GET THAT TALISMAN AND GET OUT OF HERE--*NOW!*
I'VE TAPPED IT, PUNCHED IT, POKED IT, AND EVEN CARESSED IT.
NOTHING'S WORKING!
CAN'T GET IT TO CLOSE.

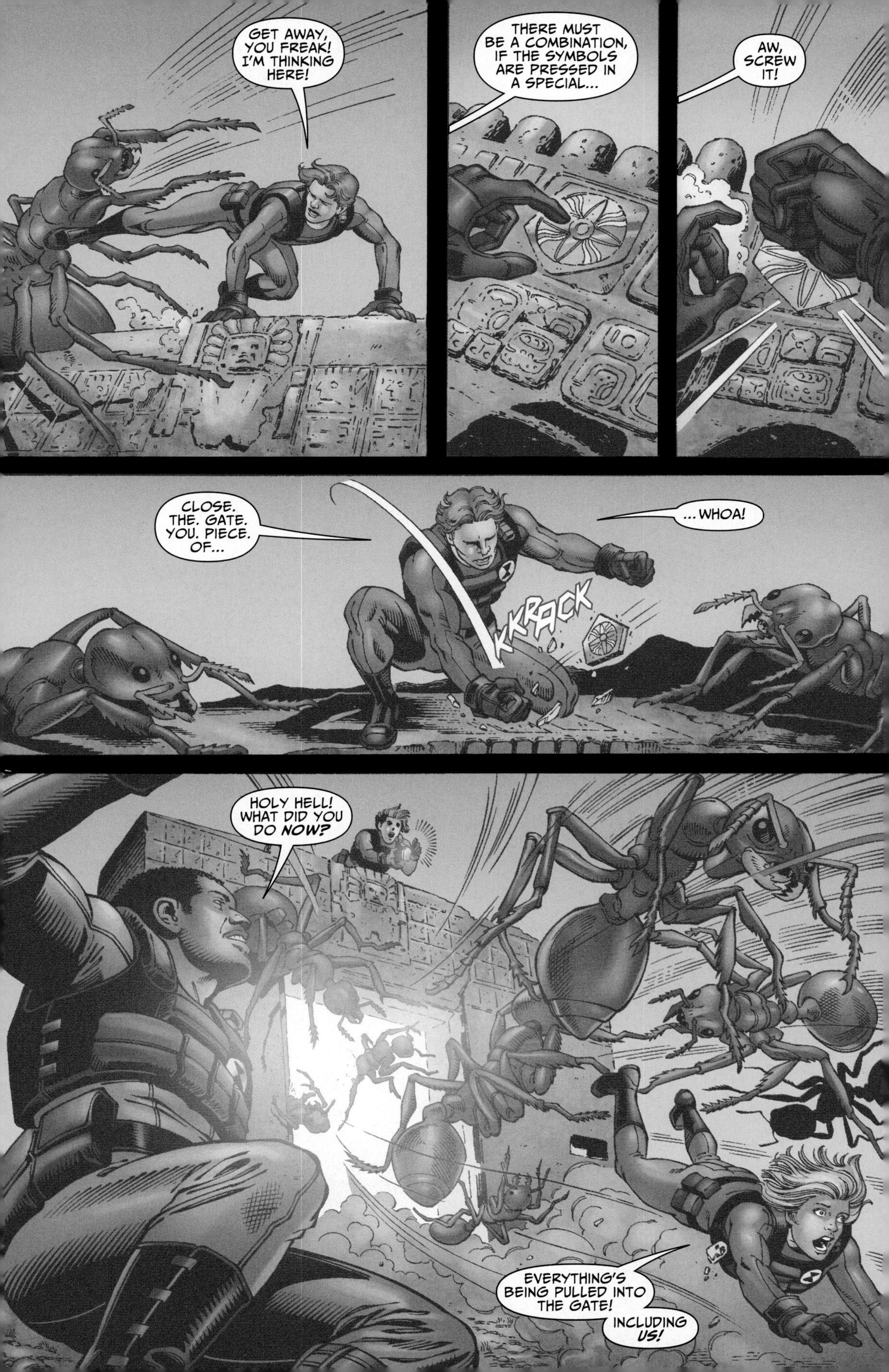
GET AWAY, YOU FREAK! I'M THINKING HERE!
THERE MUST BE A COMBINATION, IF THE SYMBOLS ARE PRESSED IN A SPECIAL...
AW, SCREW IT!
CLOSE. THE. GATE. YOU. PIECE. OF...
KKRACK
...WHOA!
HOLY HELL! WHAT DID YOU DO NOW?
EVERYTHING'S BEING PULLED INTO THE GATE!
INCLUDING US!

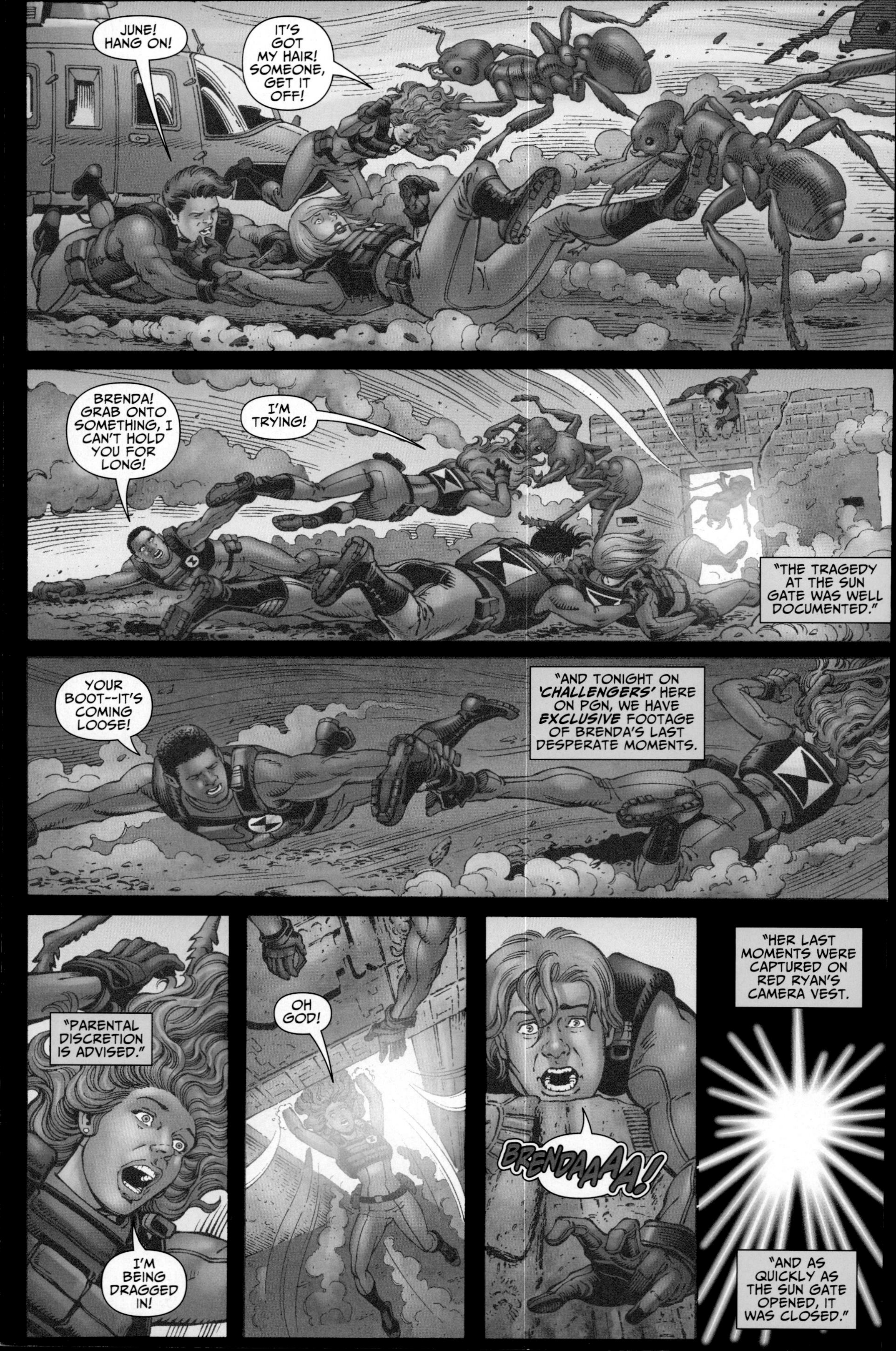
JUNE! HANG ON!
IT'S GOT MY HAIR! SOMEONE, GET IT OFF!
BRENDA! GRAB ONTO SOMETHING, I CAN'T HOLD YOU FOR LONG!
I'M TRYING!
"THE TRAGEDY AT THE SUN GATE WAS WELL DOCUMENTED."
YOUR BOOT--IT'S COMING LOOSE!
"AND TONIGHT ON 'CHALLENGERS' HERE ON PGN, WE HAVE EXCLUSIVE FOOTAGE OF BRENDA'S LAST DESPERATE MOMENTS.
"PARENTAL DISCRETION IS ADVISED."
I'M BEING DRAGGED IN!
OH GOD!
BRENDAAAAA!
"HER LAST MOMENTS WERE CAPTURED ON RED RYAN'S CAMERA VEST.
"AND AS QUICKLY AS THE SUN GATE OPENED, IT WAS CLOSED."

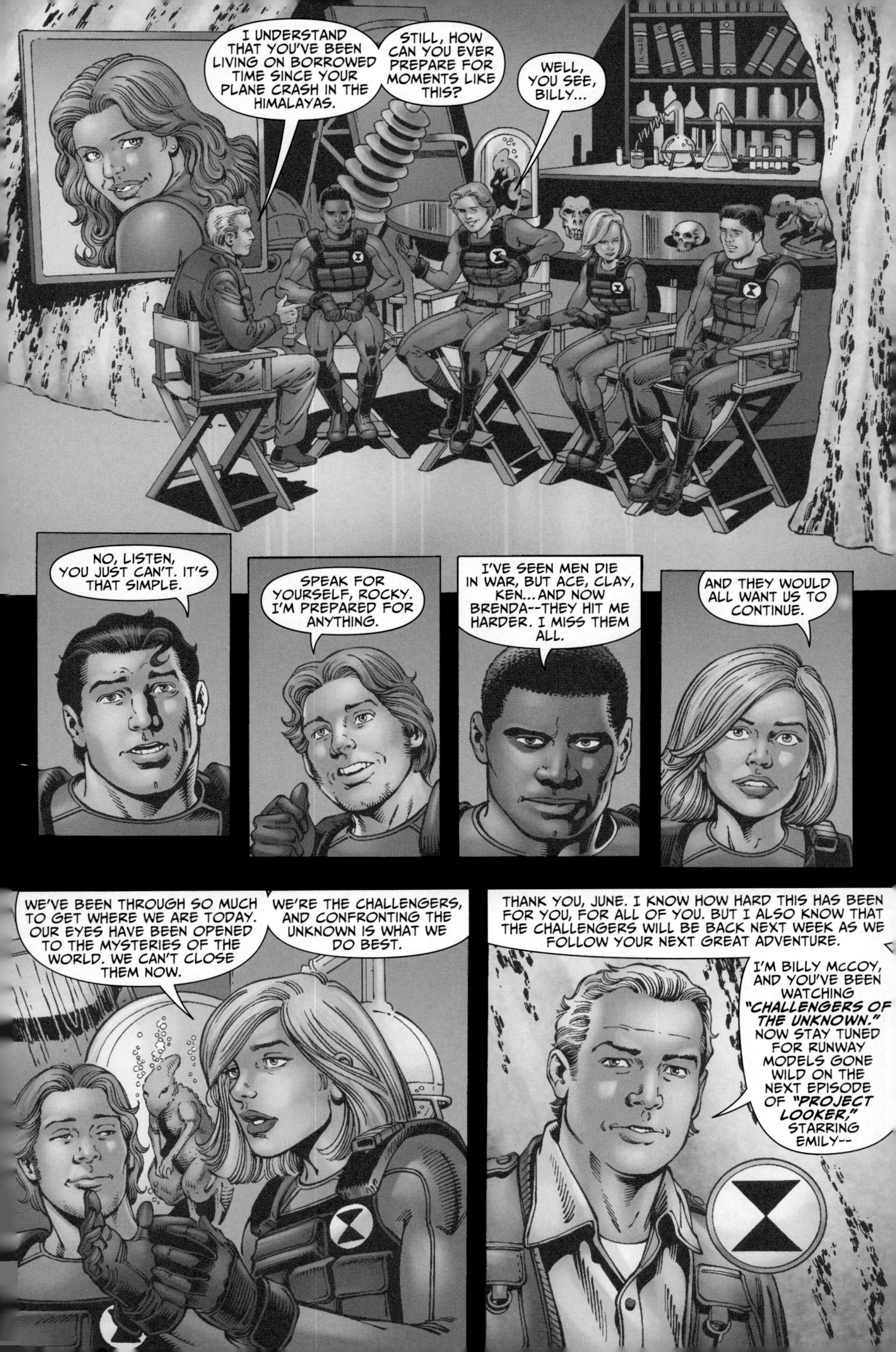
I UNDERSTAND THAT YOU'VE BEEN LIVING ON BORROWED TIME SINCE YOUR PLANE CRASH IN THE HIMALAYAS.
STILL, HOW CAN YOU EVER PREPARE FOR MOMENTS LIKE THIS?
WELL, YOU SEE, BILLY...
NO, LISTEN, YOU JUST CAN'T. IT'S THAT SIMPLE.
SPEAK FOR YOURSELF, ROCKY. I'M PREPARED FOR ANYTHING.
I'VE SEEN MEN DIE IN WAR, BUT ACE, CLAY, KEN...AND NOW BRENDA--THEY HIT ME HARDER. I MISS THEM ALL.
AND THEY WOULD ALL WANT US TO CONTINUE.
WE'VE BEEN THROUGH SO MUCH TO GET WHERE WE ARE TODAY. OUR EYES HAVE BEEN OPENED TO THE MYSTERIES OF THE WORLD. WE CAN'T CLOSE THEM NOW.
WE'RE THE CHALLENGERS, AND CONFRONTING THE UNKNOWN IS WHAT WE DO BEST.
THANK YOU, JUNE. I KNOW HOW HARD THIS HAS BEEN FOR YOU, FOR ALL OF YOU. BUT I ALSO KNOW THAT THE CHALLENGERS WILL BE BACK NEXT WEEK AS WE FOLLOW YOUR NEXT GREAT ADVENTURE.
I'M BILLY McCOY, AND YOU'VE BEEN WATCHING "CHALLENGERS OF THE UNKNOWN." NOW STAY TUNED FOR RUNWAY MODELS GONE WILD ON THE NEXT EPISODE OF "PROJECT LOOKER," STARRING EMILY--

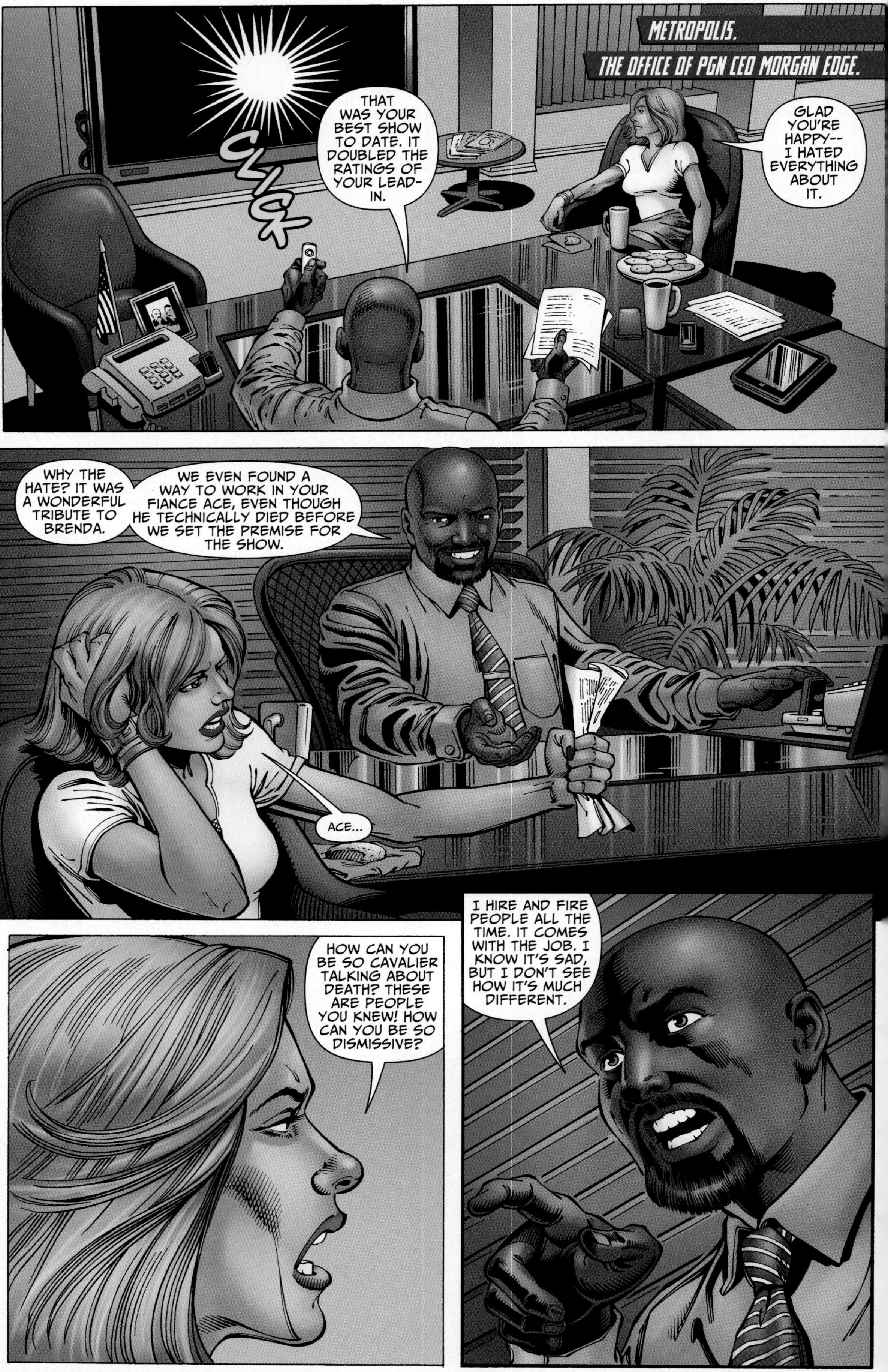
METROPOLIS.
THE OFFICE OF PGN CEO MORGAN EDGE.
THAT WAS YOUR BEST SHOW TO DATE. IT DOUBLED THE RATINGS OF YOUR LEAD-IN.
CLICK
GLAD YOU'RE HAPPY-- I HATED EVERYTHING ABOUT IT.
WHY THE HATE? IT WAS A WONDERFUL TRIBUTE TO BRENDA.
WE EVEN FOUND A WAY TO WORK IN YOUR FIANCE ACE, EVEN THOUGH HE TECHNICALLY DIED BEFORE WE SET THE PREMISE FOR THE SHOW.
ACE...
HOW CAN YOU BE SO CAVALIER TALKING ABOUT DEATH? THESE ARE PEOPLE YOU KNEW! HOW CAN YOU BE SO DISMISSIVE?
I HIRE AND FIRE PEOPLE ALL THE TIME. IT COMES WITH THE JOB. I KNOW IT'S SAD, BUT I DON'T SEE HOW IT'S MUCH DIFFERENT.

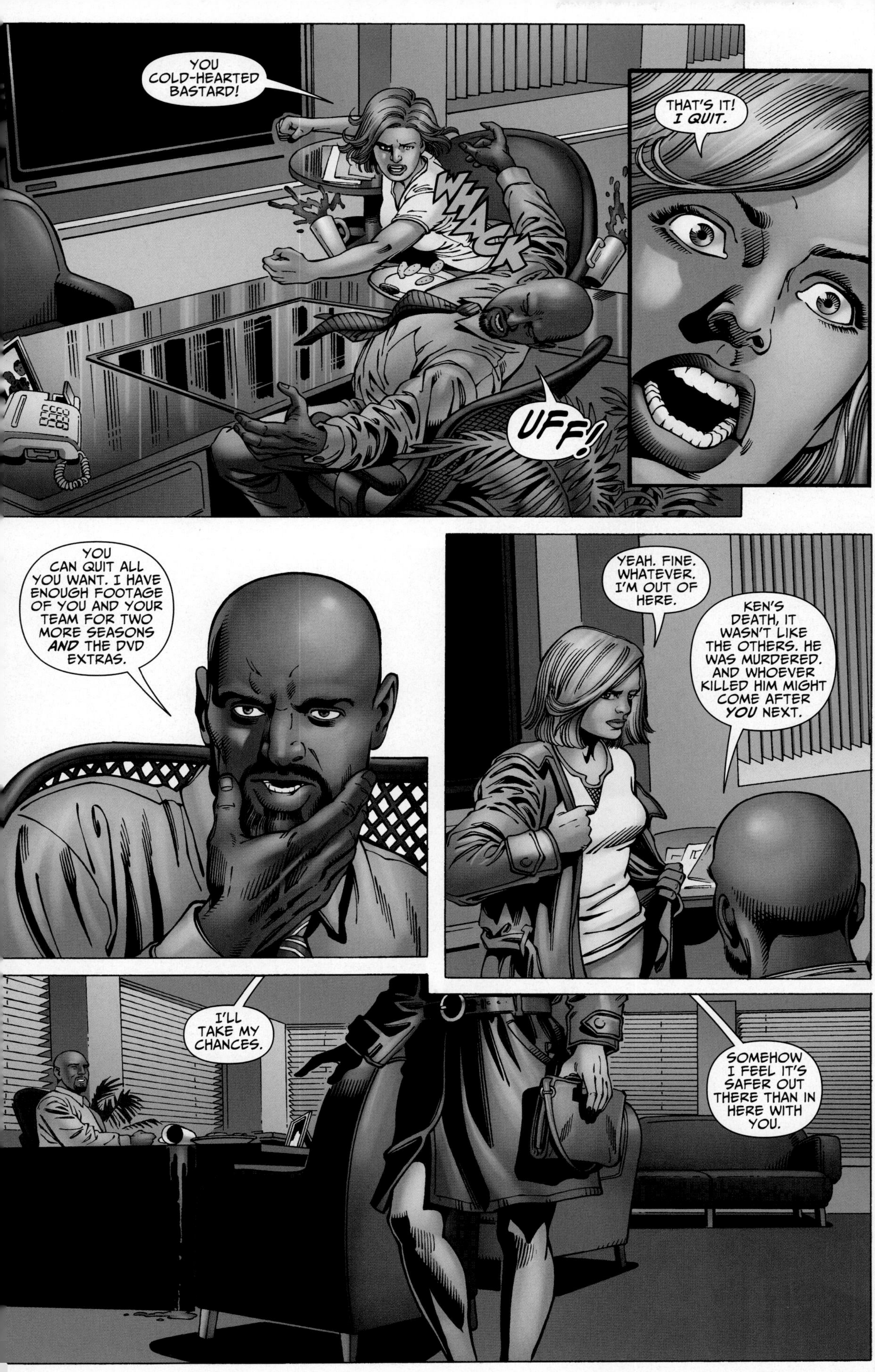
YOU COLD-HEARTED BASTARD!
WHACK
UFF!
THAT'S IT! I QUIT.
YOU CAN QUIT ALL YOU WANT. I HAVE ENOUGH FOOTAGE OF YOU AND YOUR TEAM FOR TWO MORE SEASONS AND THE DVD EXTRAS.
YEAH. FINE. WHATEVER. I'M OUT OF HERE.
KEN'S DEATH, IT WASN'T LIKE THE OTHERS. HE WAS MURDERED. AND WHOEVER KILLED HIM MIGHT COME AFTER YOU NEXT.
I'LL TAKE MY CHANCES.
SOMEHOW I FEEL IT'S SAFER OUT THERE THAN IN HERE WITH YOU.

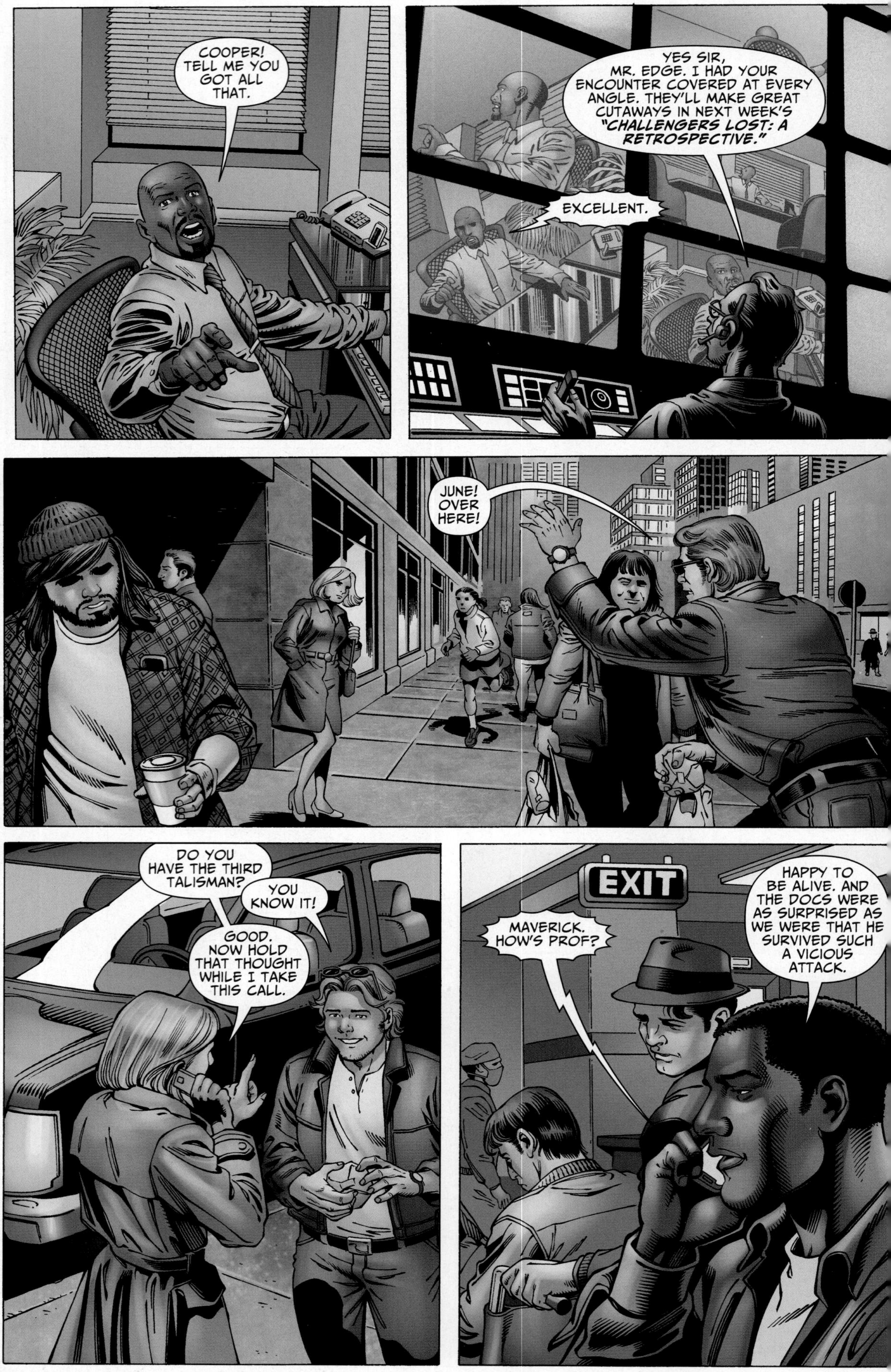
COOPER! TELL ME YOU GOT ALL THAT.
YES SIR, MR. EDGE. I HAD YOUR ENCOUNTER COVERED AT EVERY ANGLE. THEY'LL MAKE GREAT CUTAWAYS IN NEXT WEEK'S "CHALLENGERS LOST: A RETROSPECTIVE."
EXCELLENT.
JUNE! OVER HERE!
DO YOU HAVE THE THIRD TALISMAN?
YOU KNOW IT!
GOOD. NOW HOLD THAT THOUGHT WHILE I TAKE THIS CALL.
EXIT
MAVERICK. HOW'S PROF?
HAPPY TO BE ALIVE. AND THE DOCS WERE AS SURPRISED AS WE WERE THAT HE SURVIVED SUCH A VICIOUS ATTACK.

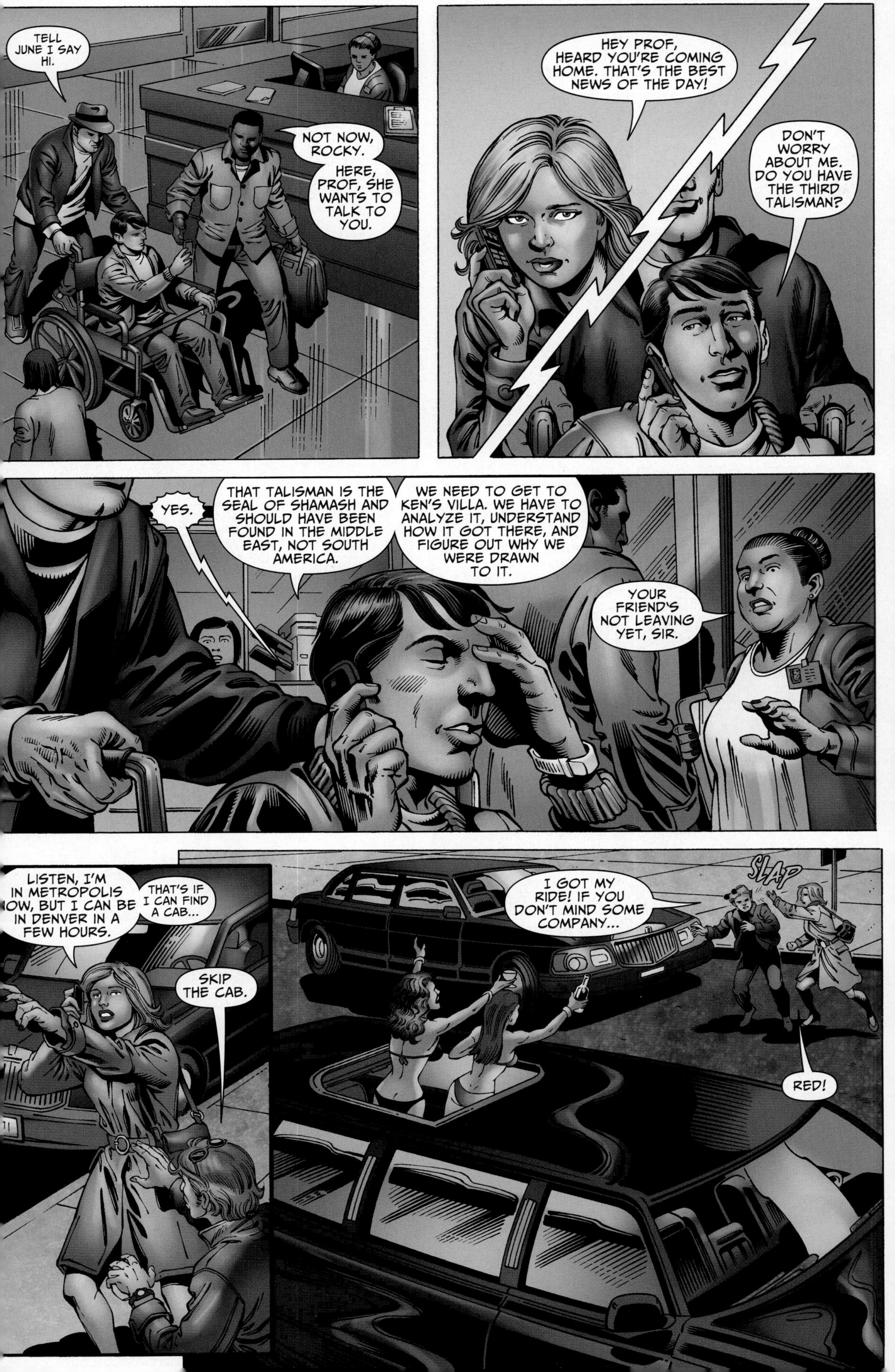
TELL JUNE I SAY HI.
NOT NOW, ROCKY.
HERE, PROF, SHE WANTS TO TALK TO YOU.
HEY PROF, HEARD YOU'RE COMING HOME. THAT'S THE BEST NEWS OF THE DAY!
DON'T WORRY ABOUT ME. DO YOU HAVE THE THIRD TALISMAN?
YES.
THAT TALISMAN IS THE SEAL OF SHAMASH AND SHOULD HAVE BEEN FOUND IN THE MIDDLE EAST, NOT SOUTH AMERICA.
WE NEED TO GET TO KEN'S VILLA. WE HAVE TO ANALYZE IT, UNDERSTAND HOW IT GOT THERE, AND FIGURE OUT WHY WE WERE DRAWN TO IT.
YOUR FRIEND'S NOT LEAVING YET, SIR.
LISTEN, I'M IN METROPOLIS OW, BUT I CAN BE IN DENVER IN A FEW HOURS.
THAT'S IF I CAN FIND A CAB...
SKIP THE CAB.
SLAP
I GOT MY RIDE! IF YOU DON'T MIND SOME COMPANY...
RED!

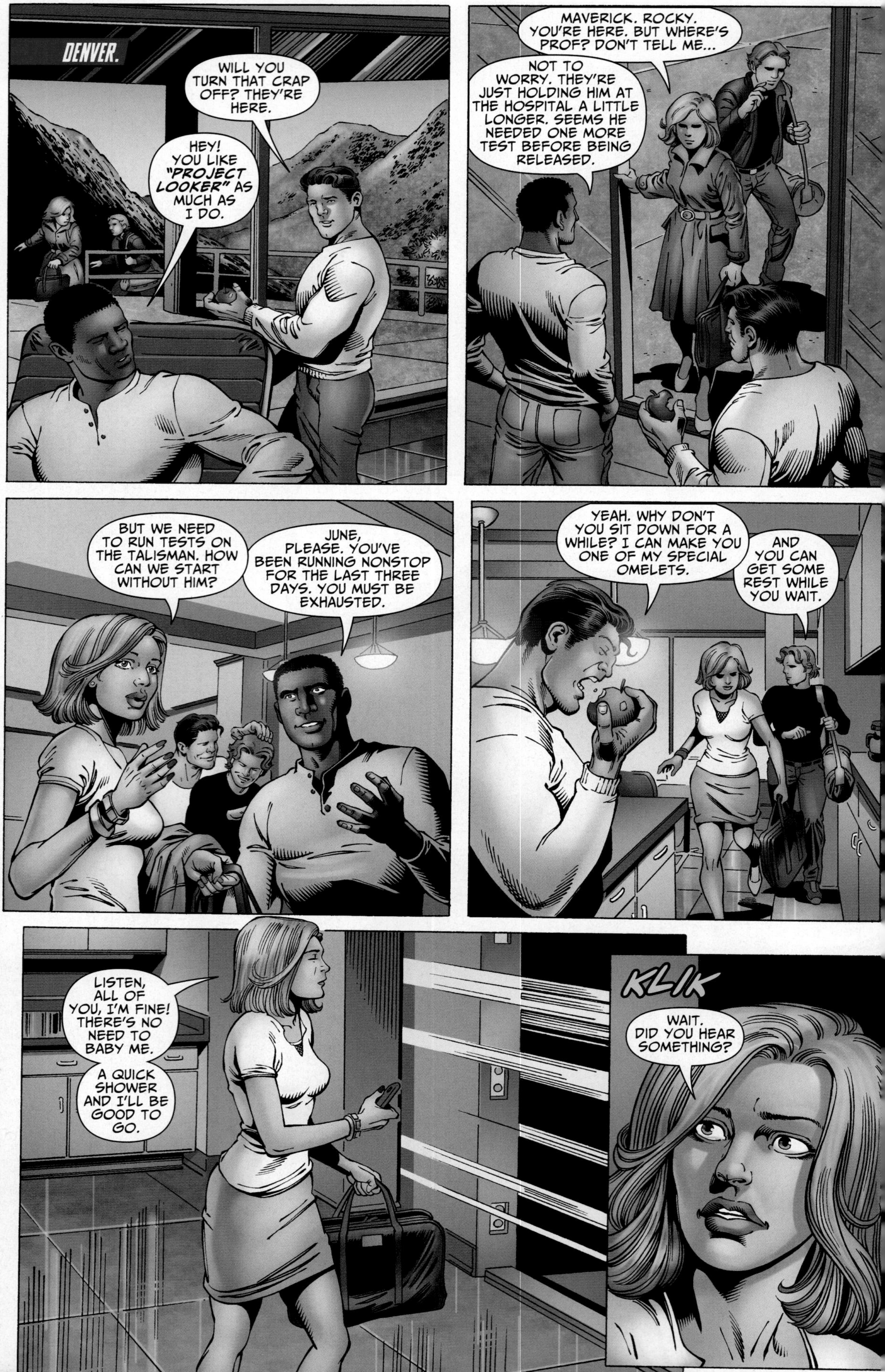
DENVER.
WILL YOU TURN THAT CRAP OFF? THEY'RE HERE.
HEY! YOU LIKE "PROJECT LOOKER" AS MUCH AS I DO.
MAVERICK. ROCKY. YOU'RE HERE. BUT WHERE'S PROF? DON'T TELL ME...
NOT TO WORRY. THEY'RE JUST HOLDING HIM AT THE HOSPITAL A LITTLE LONGER. SEEMS HE NEEDED ONE MORE TEST BEFORE BEING RELEASED.
BUT WE NEED TO RUN TESTS ON THE TALISMAN. HOW CAN WE START WITHOUT HIM?
JUNE, PLEASE. YOU'VE BEEN RUNNING NONSTOP FOR THE LAST THREE DAYS. YOU MUST BE EXHAUSTED.
YEAH. WHY DON'T YOU SIT DOWN FOR A WHILE? I CAN MAKE YOU ONE OF MY SPECIAL OMELETS.
AND YOU CAN GET SOME REST WHILE YOU WAIT.
LISTEN, ALL OF YOU, I'M FINE! THERE'S NO NEED TO BABY ME.
A QUICK SHOWER AND I'LL BE GOOD TO GO.
KLIK
WAIT. DID YOU HEAR SOMETHING?

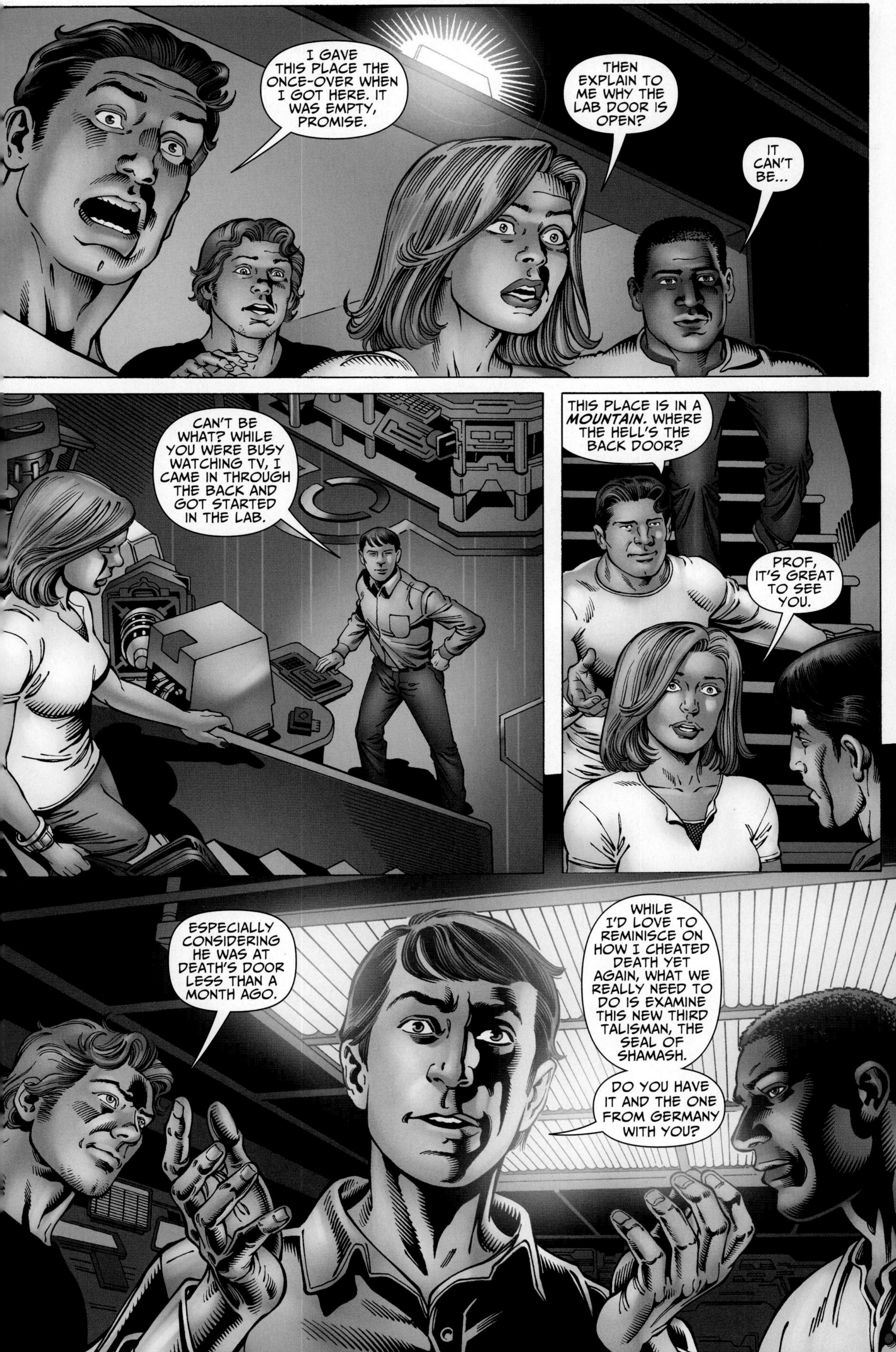
I GAVE THIS PLACE THE ONCE-OVER WHEN I GOT HERE. IT WAS EMPTY, PROMISE.
THEN EXPLAIN TO ME WHY THE LAB DOOR IS OPEN?
IT CAN'T BE...
CAN'T BE WHAT? WHILE YOU WERE BUSY WATCHING TV, I CAME IN THROUGH THE BACK AND GOT STARTED IN THE LAB.
THIS PLACE IS IN A *MOUNTAIN.* WHERE THE HELL'S THE BACK DOOR?
PROF, IT'S GREAT TO SEE YOU.
ESPECIALLY CONSIDERING HE WAS AT DEATH'S DOOR LESS THAN A MONTH AGO.
WHILE I'D LOVE TO REMINISCE ON HOW I CHEATED DEATH YET AGAIN, WHAT WE REALLY NEED TO DO IS EXAMINE THIS NEW THIRD TALISMAN, THE SEAL OF SHAMASH.
DO YOU HAVE IT AND THE ONE FROM GERMANY WITH YOU?

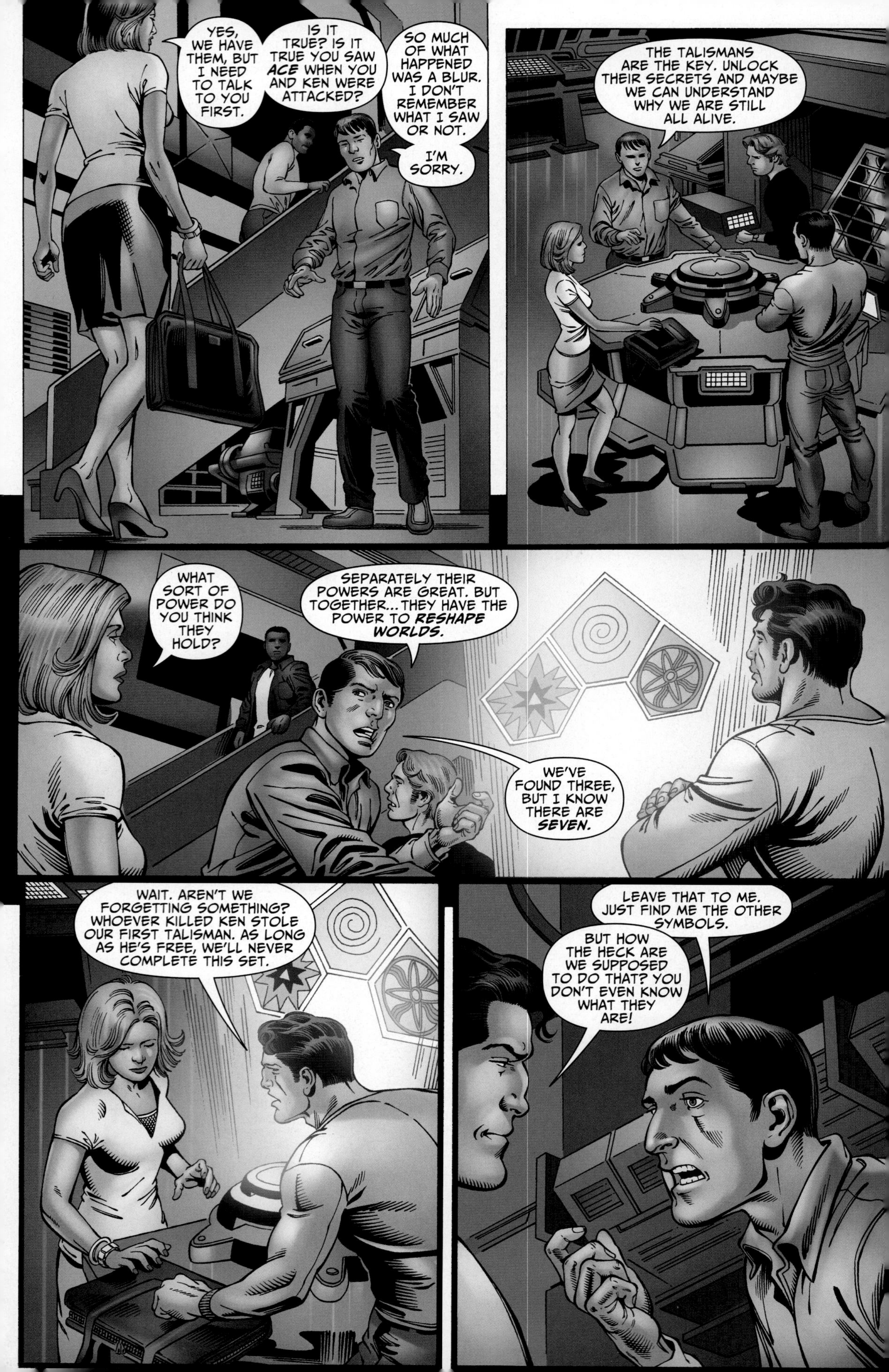
YES, WE HAVE THEM, BUT I NEED TO TALK TO YOU FIRST.
IS IT TRUE? IS IT TRUE YOU SAW ACE WHEN YOU AND KEN WERE ATTACKED?
SO MUCH OF WHAT HAPPENED WAS A BLUR. I DON'T REMEMBER WHAT I SAW OR NOT.
I'M SORRY.
THE TALISMANS ARE THE KEY. UNLOCK THEIR SECRETS AND MAYBE WE CAN UNDERSTAND WHY WE ARE STILL ALL ALIVE.
WHAT SORT OF POWER DO YOU THINK THEY HOLD?
SEPARATELY THEIR POWERS ARE GREAT. BUT TOGETHER... THEY HAVE THE POWER TO RESHAPE WORLDS.
WE'VE FOUND THREE, BUT I KNOW THERE ARE SEVEN.
WAIT. AREN'T WE FORGETTING SOMETHING? WHOEVER KILLED KEN STOLE OUR FIRST TALISMAN. AS LONG AS HE'S FREE, WE'LL NEVER COMPLETE THIS SET.
LEAVE THAT TO ME. JUST FIND ME THE OTHER SYMBOLS.
BUT HOW THE HECK ARE WE SUPPOSED TO DO THAT? YOU DON'T EVEN KNOW WHAT THEY ARE!

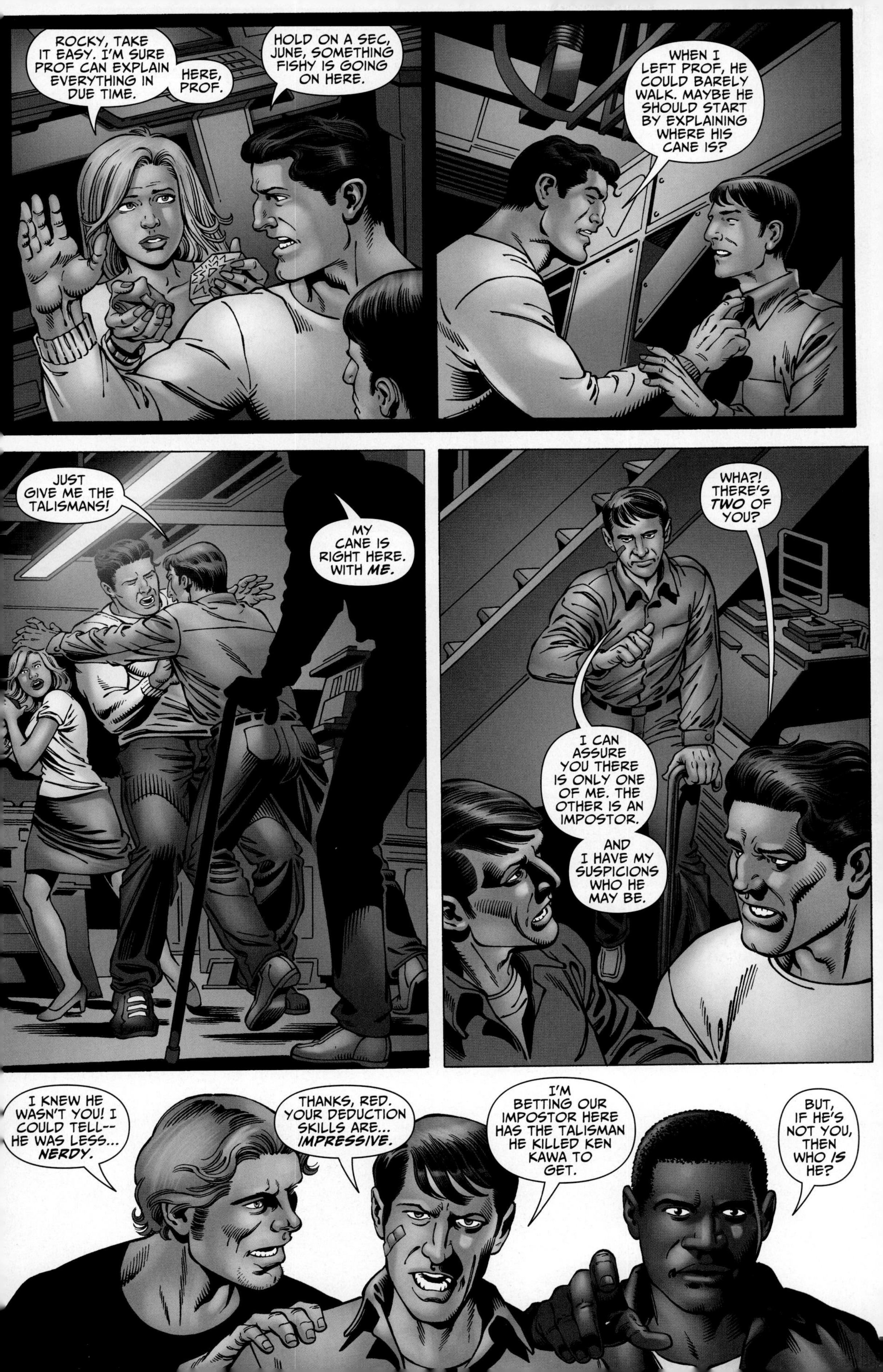
ROCKY, TAKE IT EASY. I'M SURE PROF CAN EXPLAIN EVERYTHING IN DUE TIME.
HERE, PROF.
HOLD ON A SEC, JUNE, SOMETHING FISHY IS GOING ON HERE.
WHEN I LEFT PROF, HE COULD BARELY WALK. MAYBE HE SHOULD START BY EXPLAINING WHERE HIS CANE IS?
JUST GIVE ME THE TALISMANS!
MY CANE IS RIGHT HERE. WITH *ME.*
WHA?! THERE'S *TWO* OF YOU?
I CAN ASSURE YOU THERE IS ONLY ONE OF ME. THE OTHER IS AN IMPOSTOR.
AND I HAVE MY SUSPICIONS WHO HE MAY BE.
I KNEW HE WASN'T YOU! I COULD TELL-- HE WAS LESS... *NERDY.*
THANKS, RED. YOUR DEDUCTION SKILLS ARE... *IMPRESSIVE.*
I'M BETTING OUR IMPOSTOR HERE HAS THE TALISMAN HE KILLED KEN KAWA TO GET.
BUT, IF HE'S NOT YOU, THEN WHO *IS* HE?

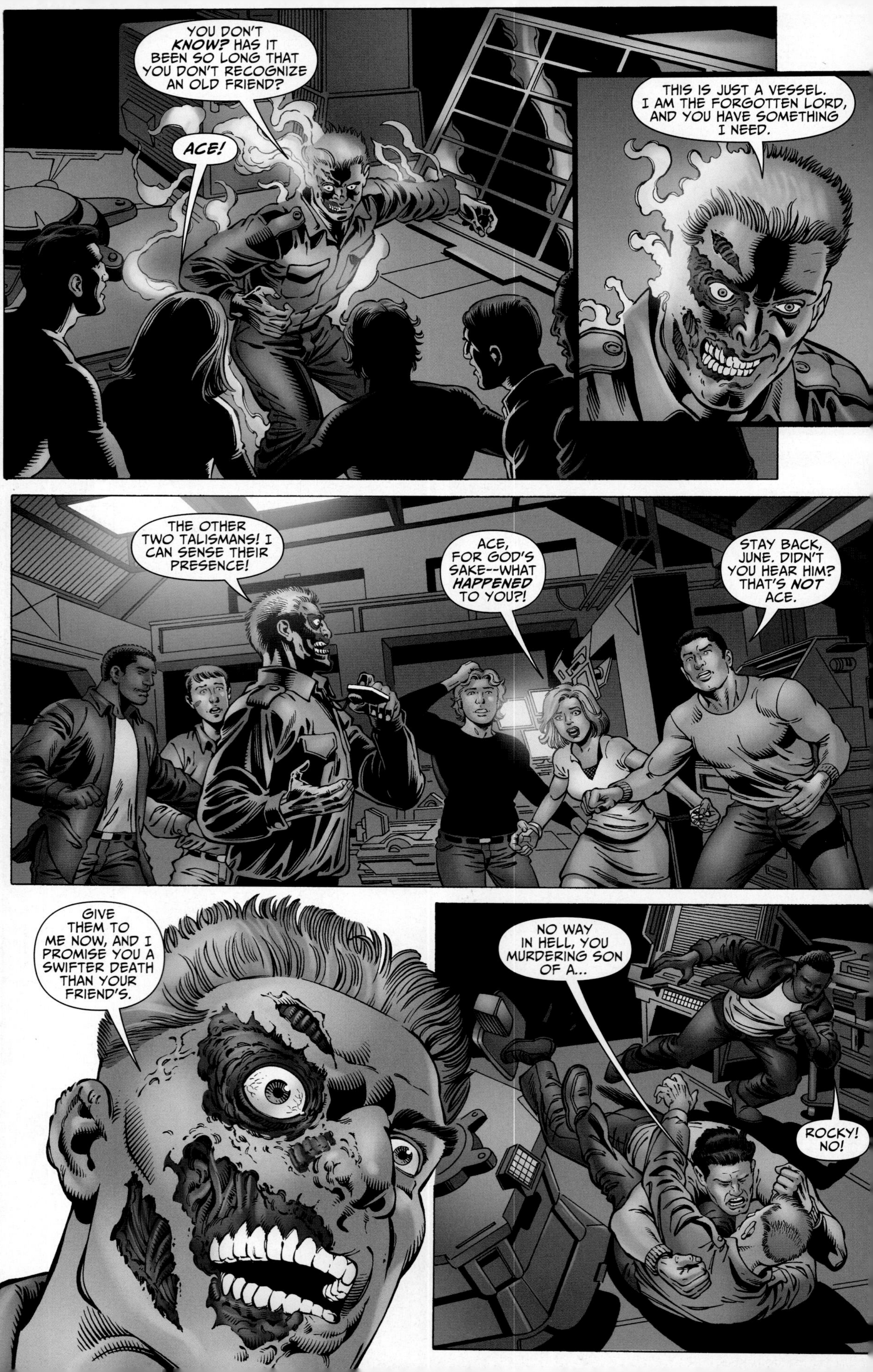
YOU DON'T *KNOW?* HAS IT BEEN SO LONG THAT YOU DON'T RECOGNIZE AN OLD FRIEND?
ACE!
THIS IS JUST A VESSEL. I AM THE FORGOTTEN LORD, AND YOU HAVE SOMETHING I NEED.
THE OTHER TWO TALISMANS! I CAN SENSE THEIR PRESENCE!
ACE, FOR GOD'S SAKE--WHAT *HAPPENED* TO YOU?!
STAY BACK, JUNE. DIDN'T YOU HEAR HIM? THAT'S *NOT* ACE.
GIVE THEM TO ME NOW, AND I PROMISE YOU A SWIFTER DEATH THAN YOUR FRIEND'S.
NO WAY IN HELL, YOU MURDERING SON OF A...
ROCKY! NO!

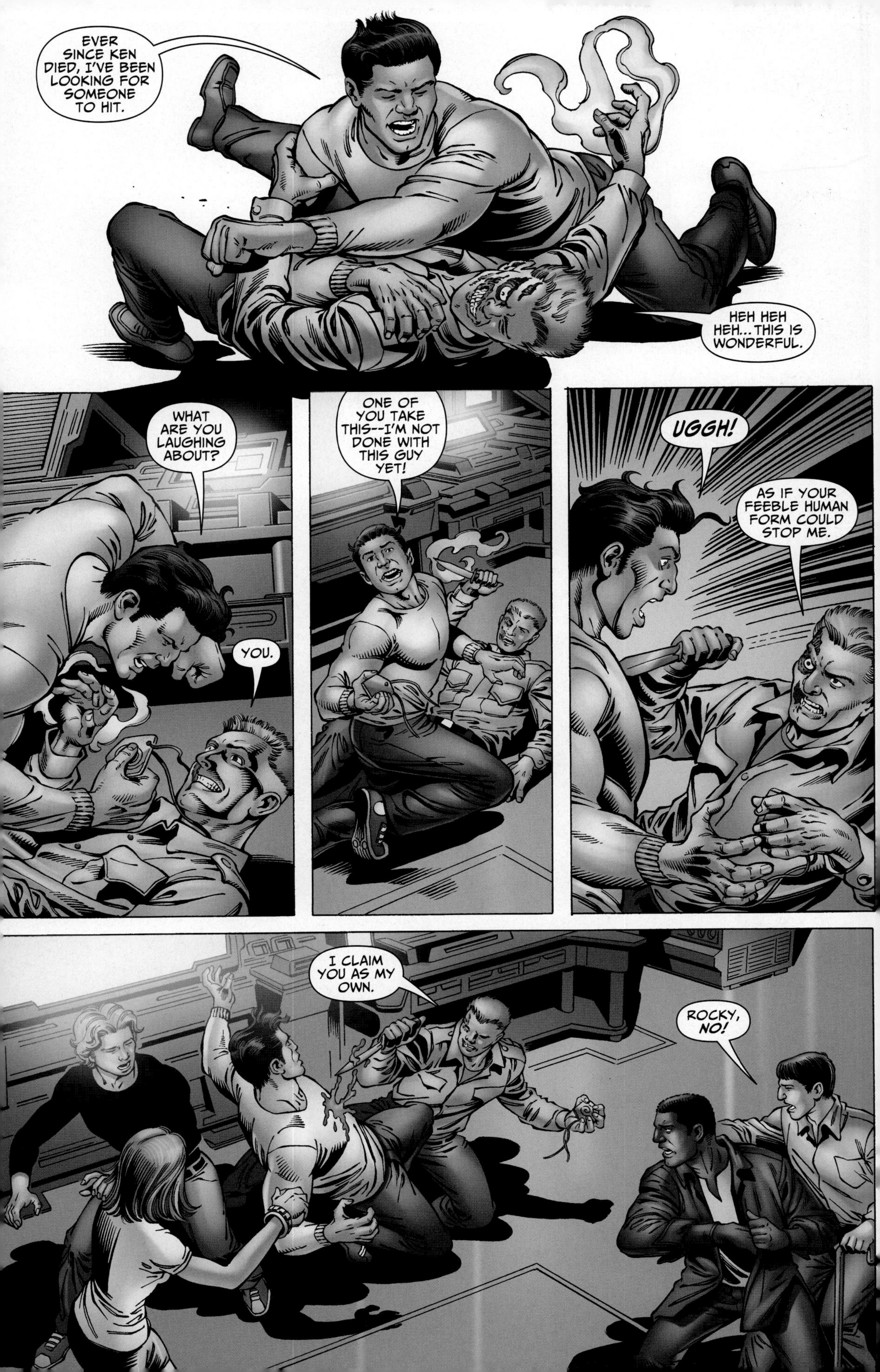
EVER SINCE KEN DIED, I'VE BEEN LOOKING FOR SOMEONE TO HIT.
HEH HEH HEH... THIS IS WONDERFUL.
WHAT ARE YOU LAUGHING ABOUT?
YOU.
ONE OF YOU TAKE THIS--I'M NOT DONE WITH THIS GUY YET!
UGGH!
AS IF YOUR FEEBLE HUMAN FORM COULD STOP ME.
I CLAIM YOU AS MY OWN.
ROCKY, NO!

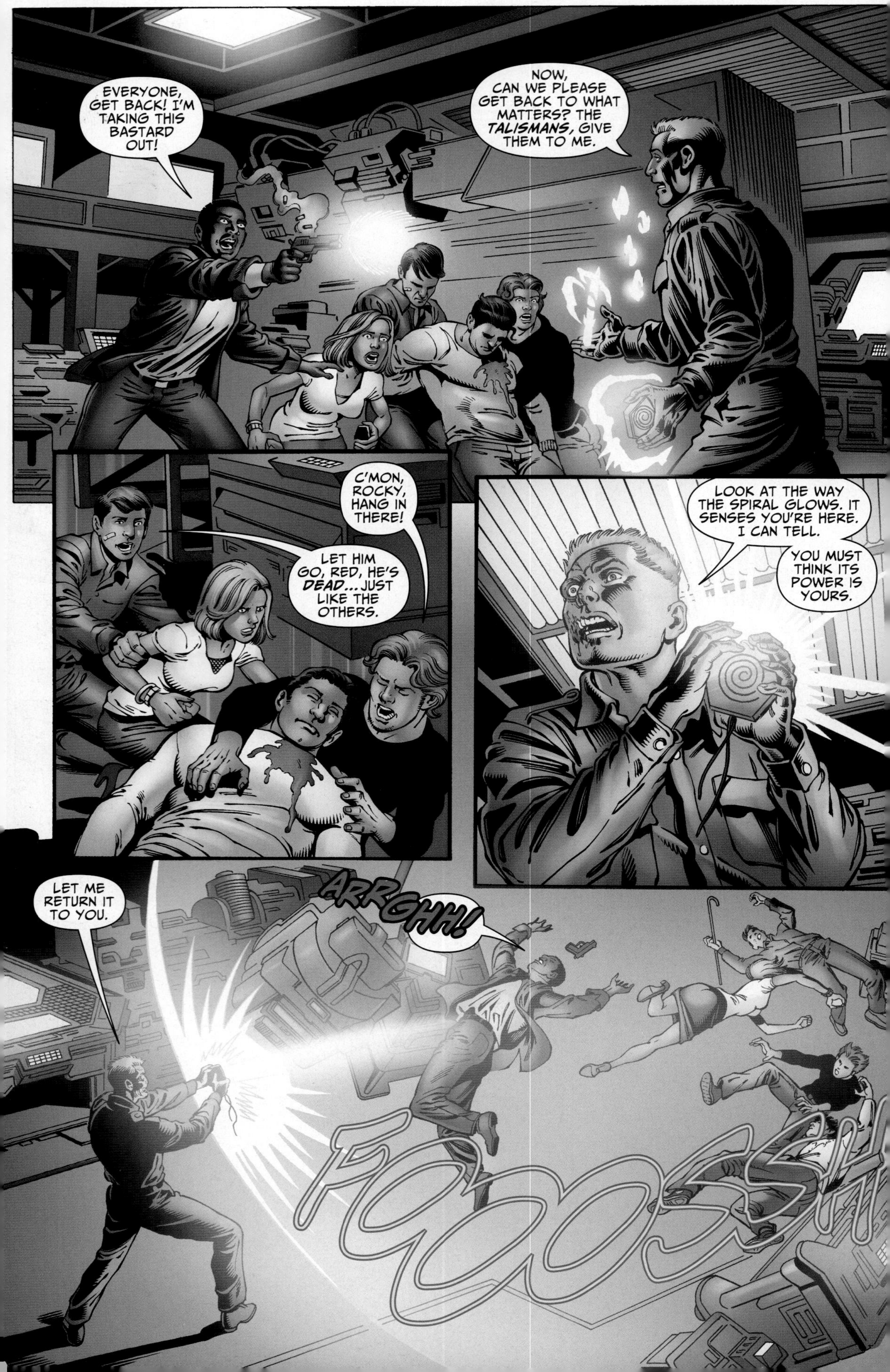
EVERYONE, GET BACK! I'M TAKING THIS BASTARD OUT!
NOW, CAN WE PLEASE GET BACK TO WHAT MATTERS? THE *TALISMANS*, GIVE THEM TO ME.
C'MON, ROCKY, HANG IN THERE!
LET HIM GO, RED, HE'S *DEAD*... JUST LIKE THE OTHERS.
LOOK AT THE WAY THE SPIRAL GLOWS. IT SENSES YOU'RE HERE. I CAN TELL.
YOU MUST THINK ITS POWER IS YOURS.
LET ME RETURN IT TO YOU.
ARRGHH!
FOOOSSH!

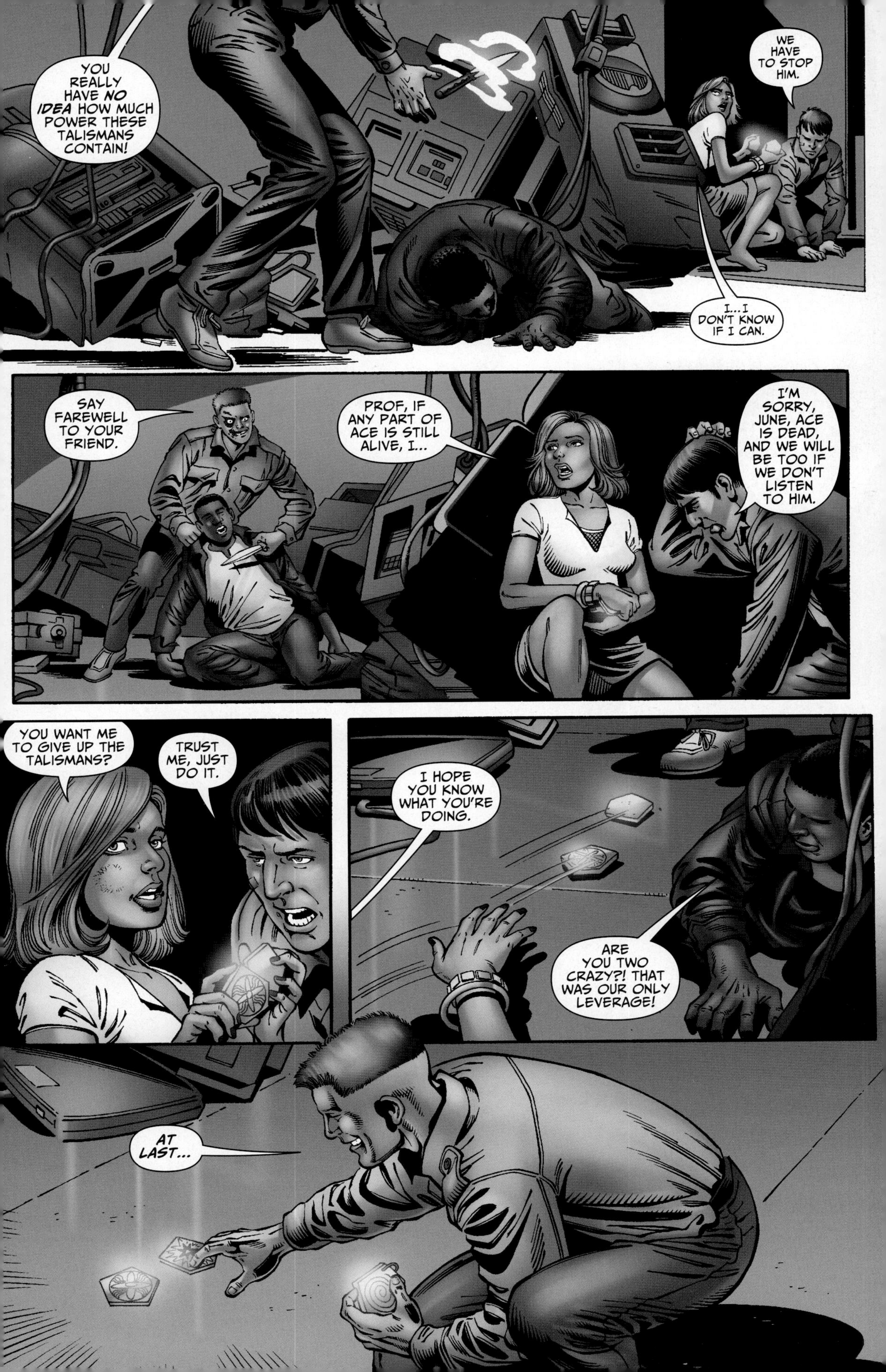
YOU REALLY HAVE NO IDEA HOW MUCH POWER THESE TALISMANS CONTAIN!
WE HAVE TO STOP HIM.
I...I DON'T KNOW IF I CAN.
SAY FAREWELL TO YOUR FRIEND.
PROF, IF ANY PART OF ACE IS STILL ALIVE, I...
I'M SORRY, JUNE, ACE IS DEAD, AND WE WILL BE TOO IF WE DON'T LISTEN TO HIM.
YOU WANT ME TO GIVE UP THE TALISMANS?
TRUST ME, JUST DO IT.
I HOPE YOU KNOW WHAT YOU'RE DOING.
ARE YOU TWO CRAZY?! THAT WAS OUR ONLY LEVERAGE!
AT LAST...

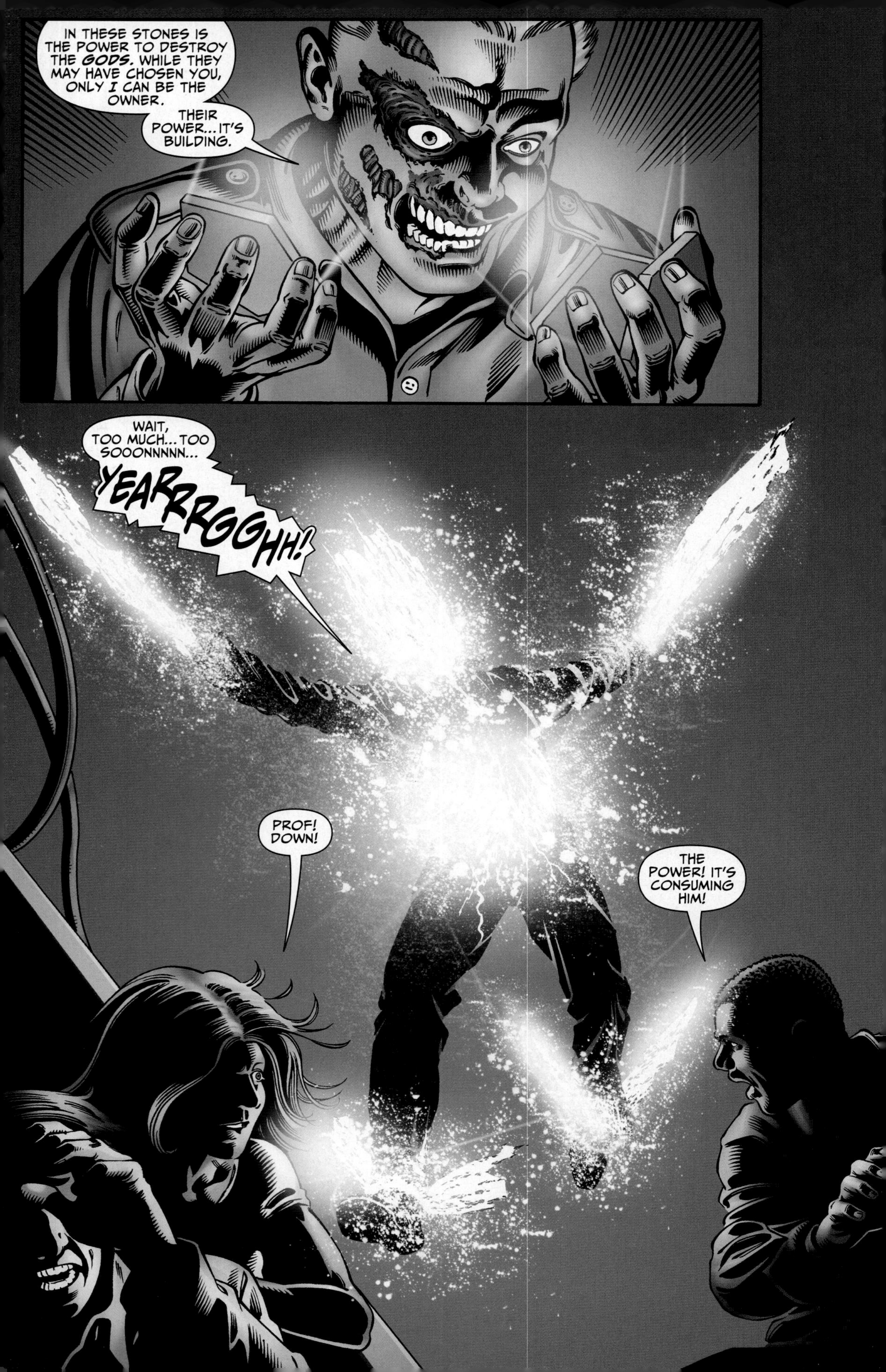
IN THESE STONES IS THE POWER TO DESTROY THE GODS. WHILE THEY MAY HAVE CHOSEN YOU, ONLY I CAN BE THE OWNER.
THEIR POWER...IT'S BUILDING.
WAIT, TOO MUCH...TOO SOOONNNNN...
YEARRRGGHH!
PROF! DOWN!
THE POWER! IT'S CONSUMING HIM!

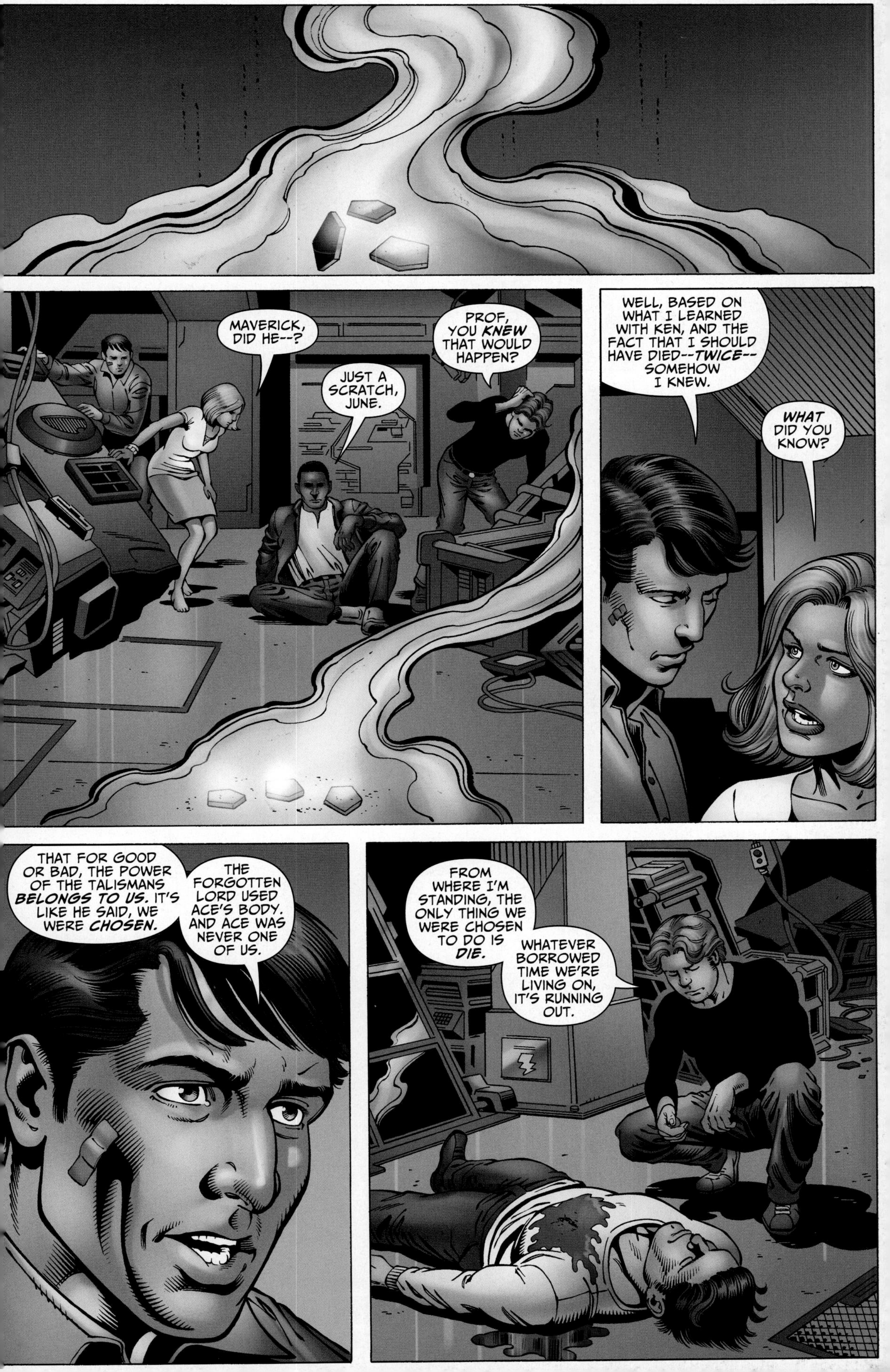
MAVERICK, DID HE--?
JUST A SCRATCH, JUNE.
PROF, YOU KNEW THAT WOULD HAPPEN?
WELL, BASED ON WHAT I LEARNED WITH KEN, AND THE FACT THAT I SHOULD HAVE DIED--TWICE--SOMEHOW I KNEW.
WHAT DID YOU KNOW?
THAT FOR GOOD OR BAD, THE POWER OF THE TALISMANS BELONGS TO US. IT'S LIKE HE SAID, WE WERE CHOSEN.
THE FORGOTTEN LORD USED ACE'S BODY. AND ACE WAS NEVER ONE OF US.
FROM WHERE I'M STANDING, THE ONLY THING WE WERE CHOSEN TO DO IS DIE.
WHATEVER BORROWED TIME WE'RE LIVING ON, IT'S RUNNING OUT.

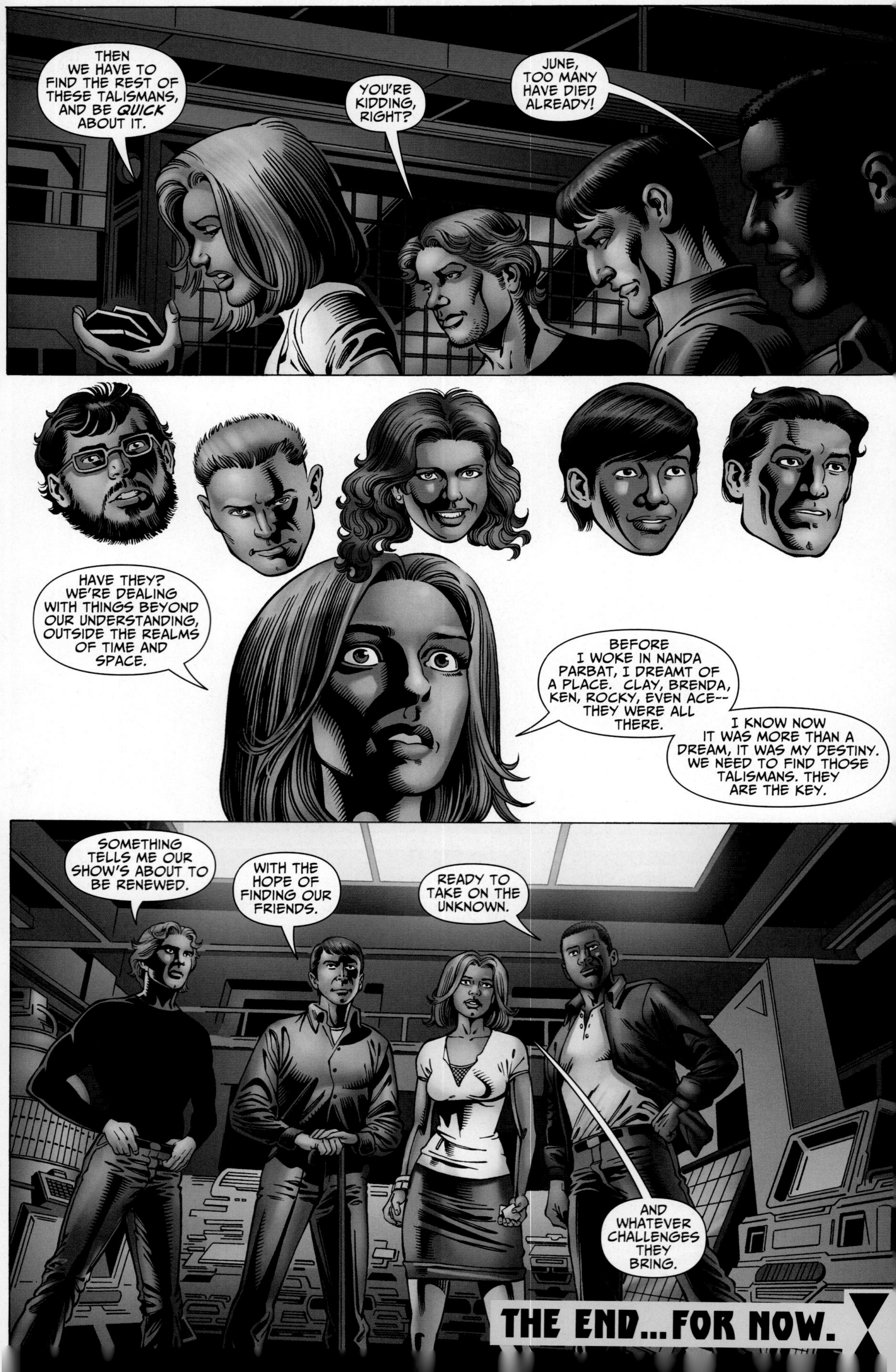
THEN WE HAVE TO FIND THE REST OF THESE TALISMANS, AND BE *QUICK* ABOUT IT.
YOU'RE KIDDING, RIGHT?
JUNE, TOO MANY HAVE DIED ALREADY!
HAVE THEY? WE'RE DEALING WITH THINGS BEYOND OUR UNDERSTANDING, OUTSIDE THE REALMS OF TIME AND SPACE.
BEFORE I WOKE IN NANDA PARBAT, I DREAMT OF A PLACE. CLAY, BRENDA, KEN, ROCKY, EVEN ACE-- THEY WERE ALL THERE.
I KNOW NOW IT WAS MORE THAN A DREAM, IT WAS MY DESTINY. WE NEED TO FIND THOSE TALISMANS. THEY ARE THE KEY.
SOMETHING TELLS ME OUR SHOW'S ABOUT TO BE RENEWED.
WITH THE HOPE OF FINDING OUR FRIENDS.
READY TO TAKE ON THE UNKNOWN.
AND WHATEVER CHALLENGES THEY BRING.
THE END...FOR NOW.

COVER SKETCHES & ROUGHS BY RYAN SOOK

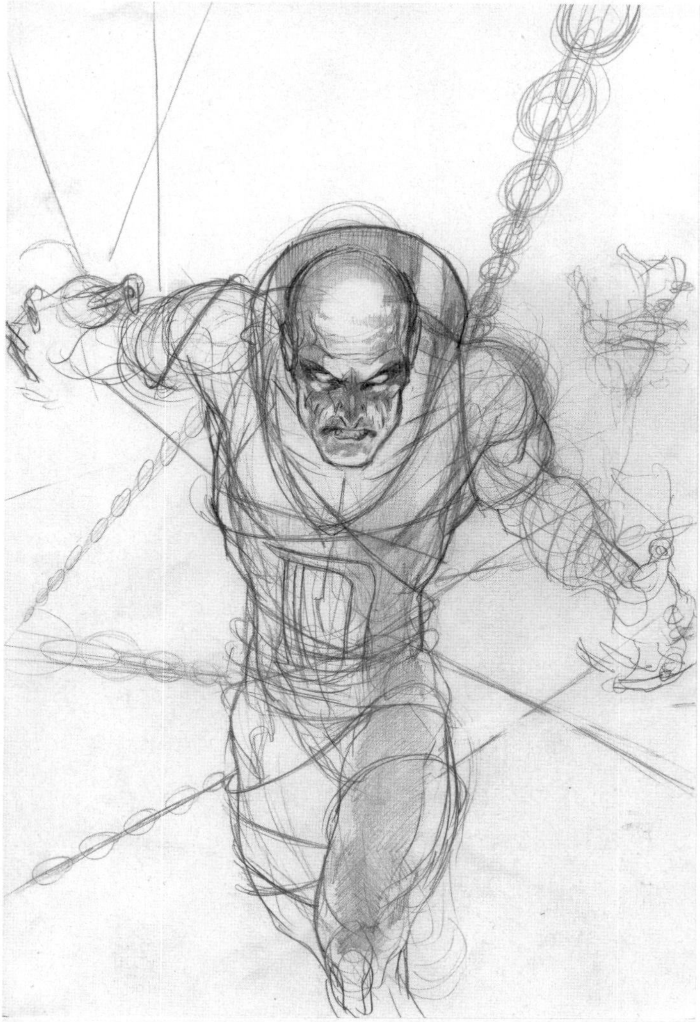

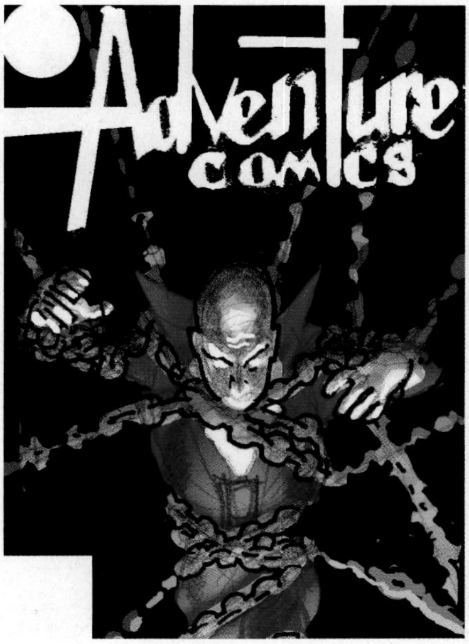
Adventure
COMICS

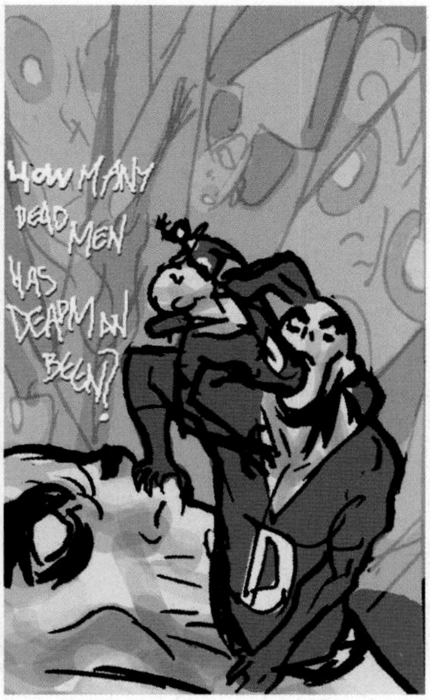
HOW MANY DEAD MEN HAS DEADMAN BEEN?

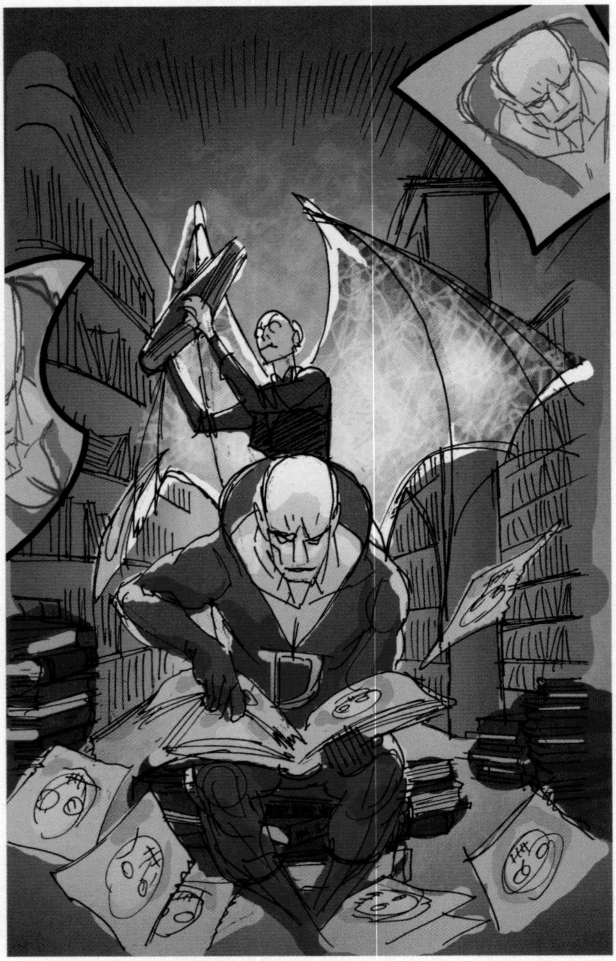

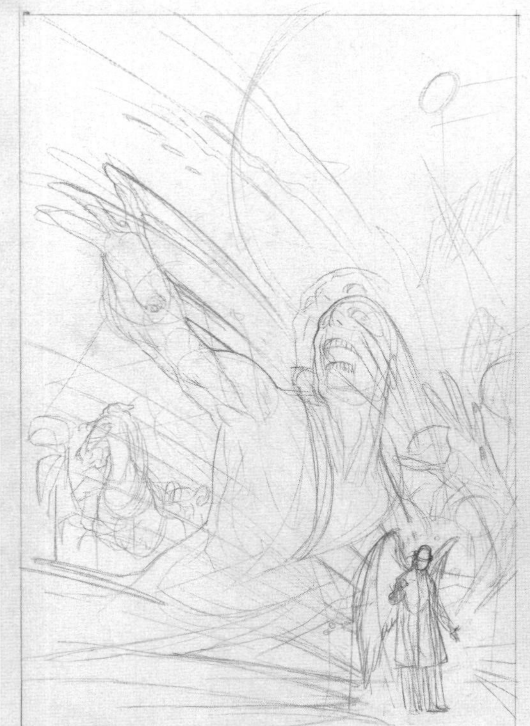

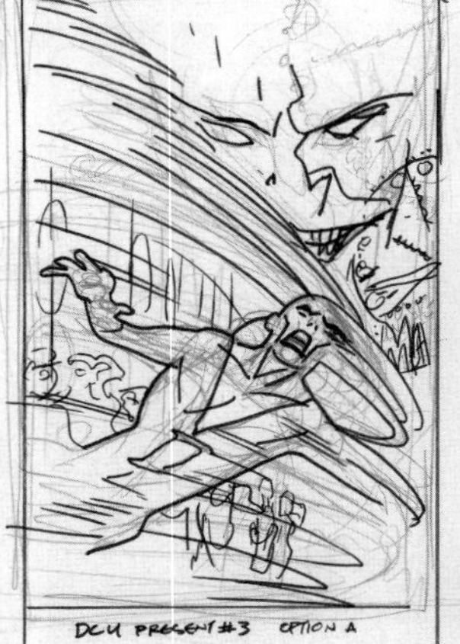
DCU PRESENT #3 OPTION A

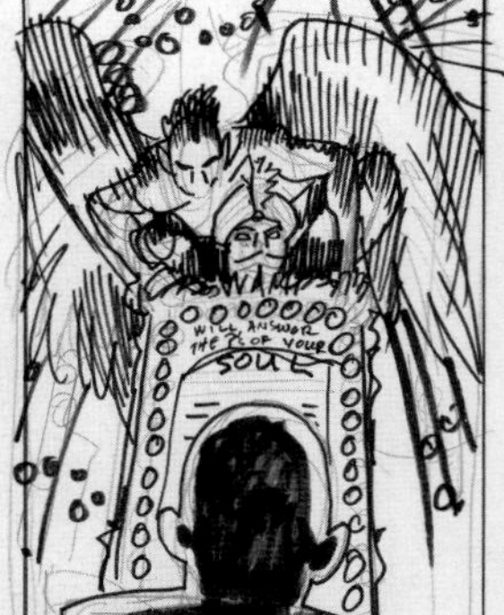
WILL ANSWER
SOUL
DCU PRESENT #3 OPTION B

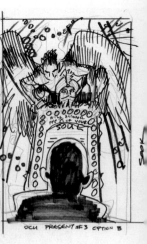

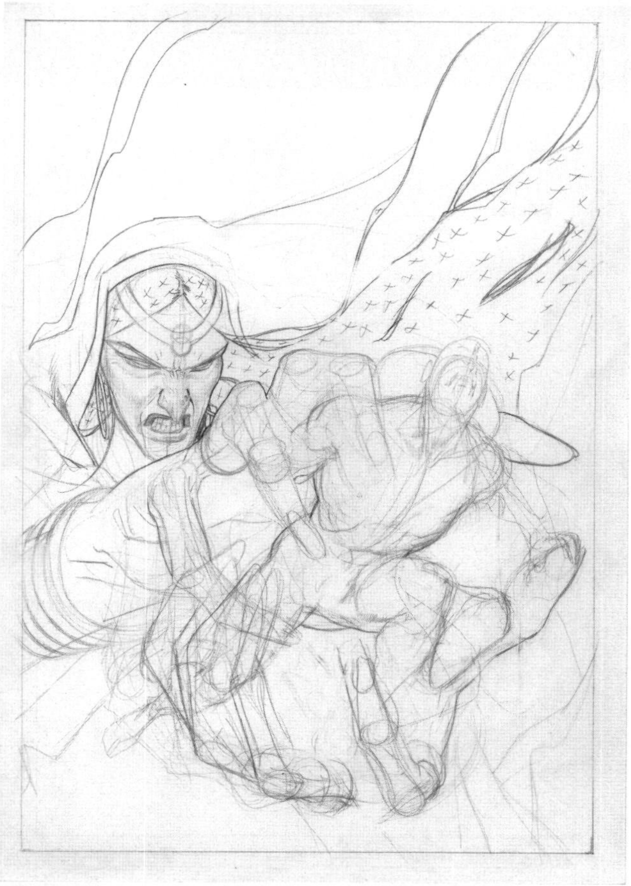

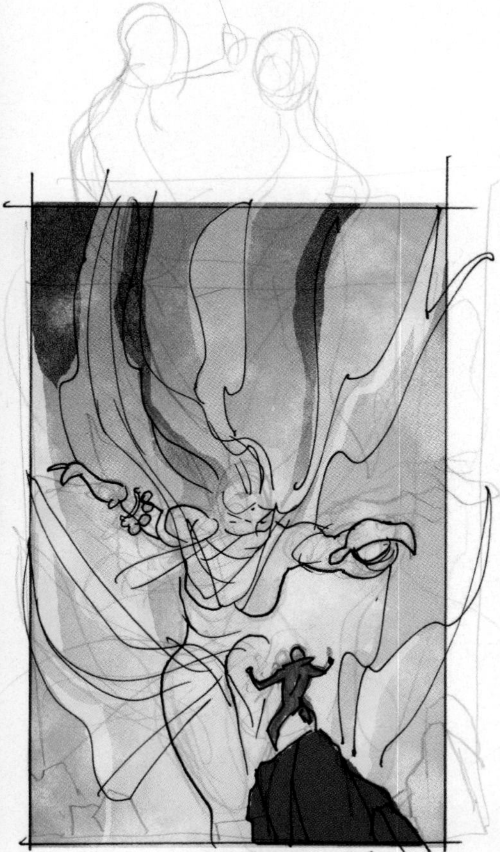

A DCU PRESENTS #5

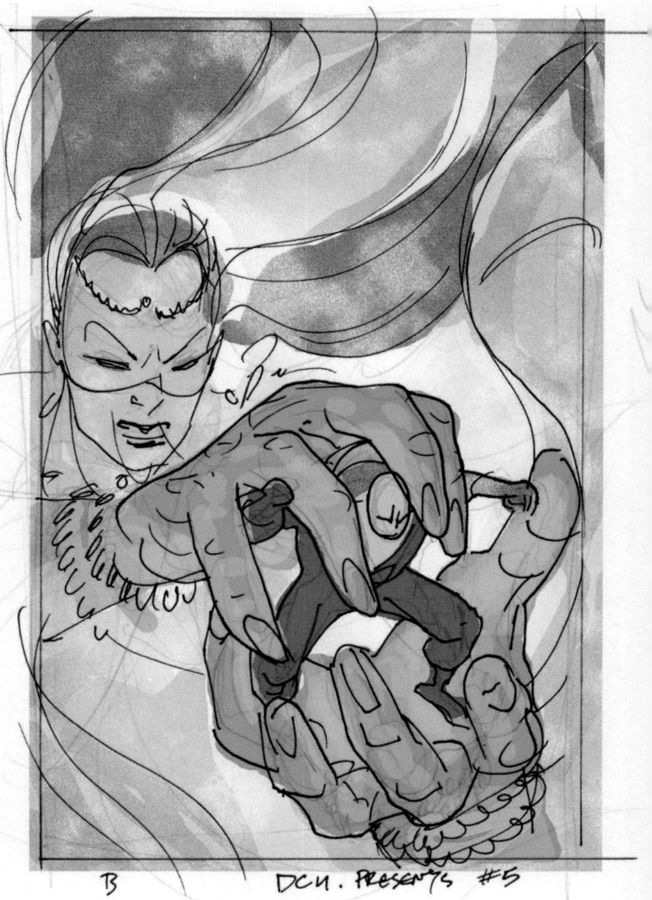

B DCU. PRESENTS #5

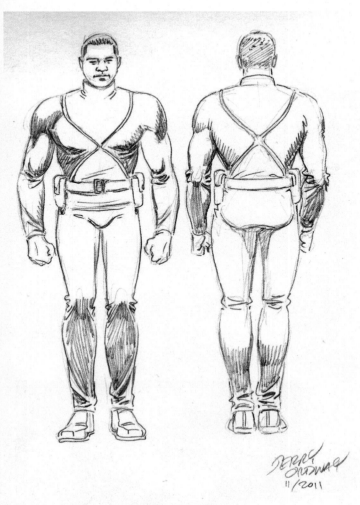

Challenger costume by Jerry Ordway

Challenger costume by Ryan Sook

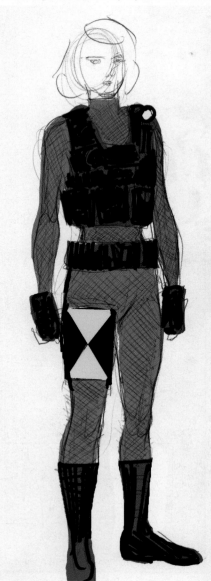

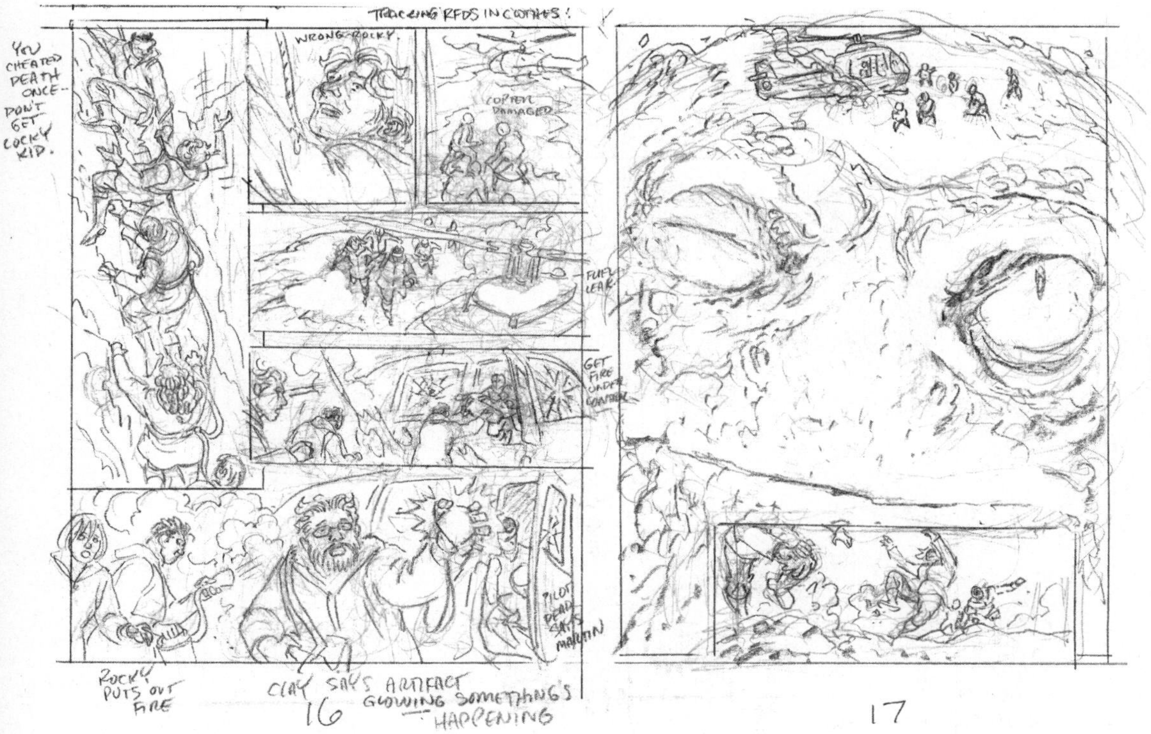
YOU CHEATED DEATH ONCE-- DON'T GET COCKY KID.
WRONG ROCKY.
COPTER DAMAGED
FUEL LEAK
GET FIRE UNDER CONTROL
PILOT DEAD SAYS MARTIN
ROCKY PUTS OUT FIRE
CLAY SAYS ARTIFACT GLOWING SOMETHING'S HAPPENING
16
17

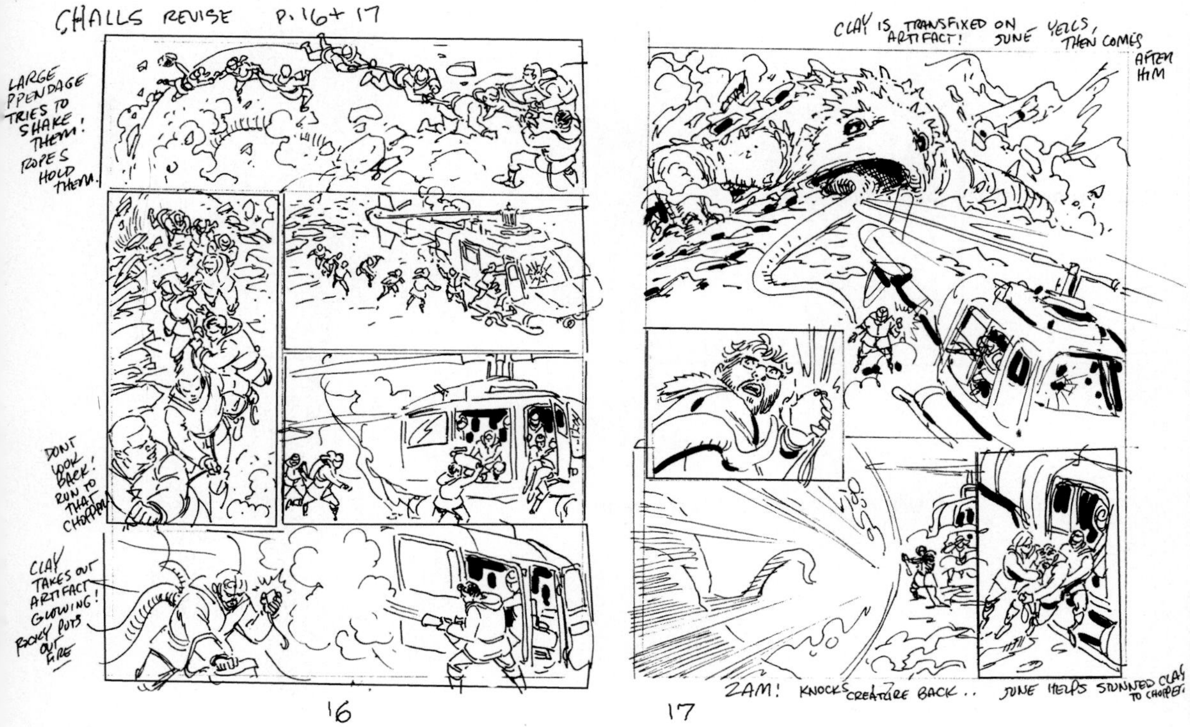
CHALLS REVISE P. 16 + 17
LARGE APPENDAGE TRIES TO SHAKE THEM! ROPES HOLD THEM.
DON'T LOOK BACK! RUN TO THAT CHOPPER!
CLAY TAKES OUT ARTIFACT GLOWING! ROCKY PUTS OUT FIRE
CLAY IS TRANSFIXED ON ARTIFACT! JUNE YELLS, THEN COMES AFTER HIM
ZAM! KNOCKS CREATURE BACK..
JUNE HELPS STUNNED CLAY TO CHOPPER.
16
17

Early rough and revised version of DC UNIVERSE PRESENTS #6 pages 16 & 17

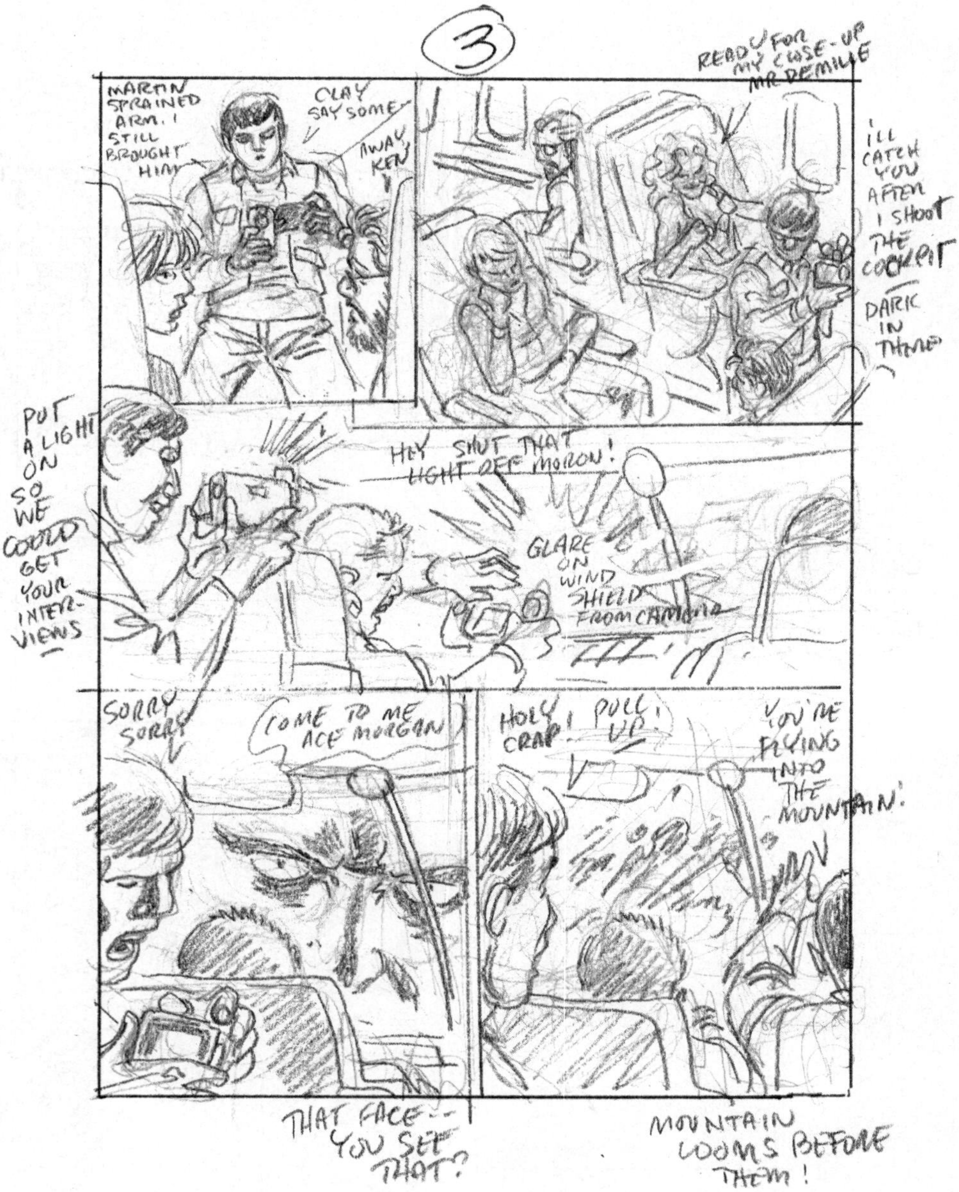
3
MARTIN SPRAINED ARM. I STILL BROUGHT HIM
CLAY SAY SOME-
AWAY KEN
READY FOR MY CLOSE-UP MR DEMILLE
I'LL CATCH YOU AFTER I SHOOT THE COCKPIT
DARK IN
PUT A LIGHT ON SO WE COULD GET YOUR INTERVIEWS
HEY SHUT THAT LIGHT OFF MORON!
GLARE ON WIND SHIELD FROM CAMERA
SORRY SORRY
COME TO ME ACE MORGAN
HOLY CRAP! PULL UP!
YOU'RE FLYING INTO THE MOUNTAIN!
THAT FACE.. YOU SEE THAT?
MOUNTAIN LOOMS BEFORE THEM!

DC UNIVERSE PRESENTS #6 page 3

Early unused layout for DC UNIVERSE PRESENTS #6 pages 4 & 5

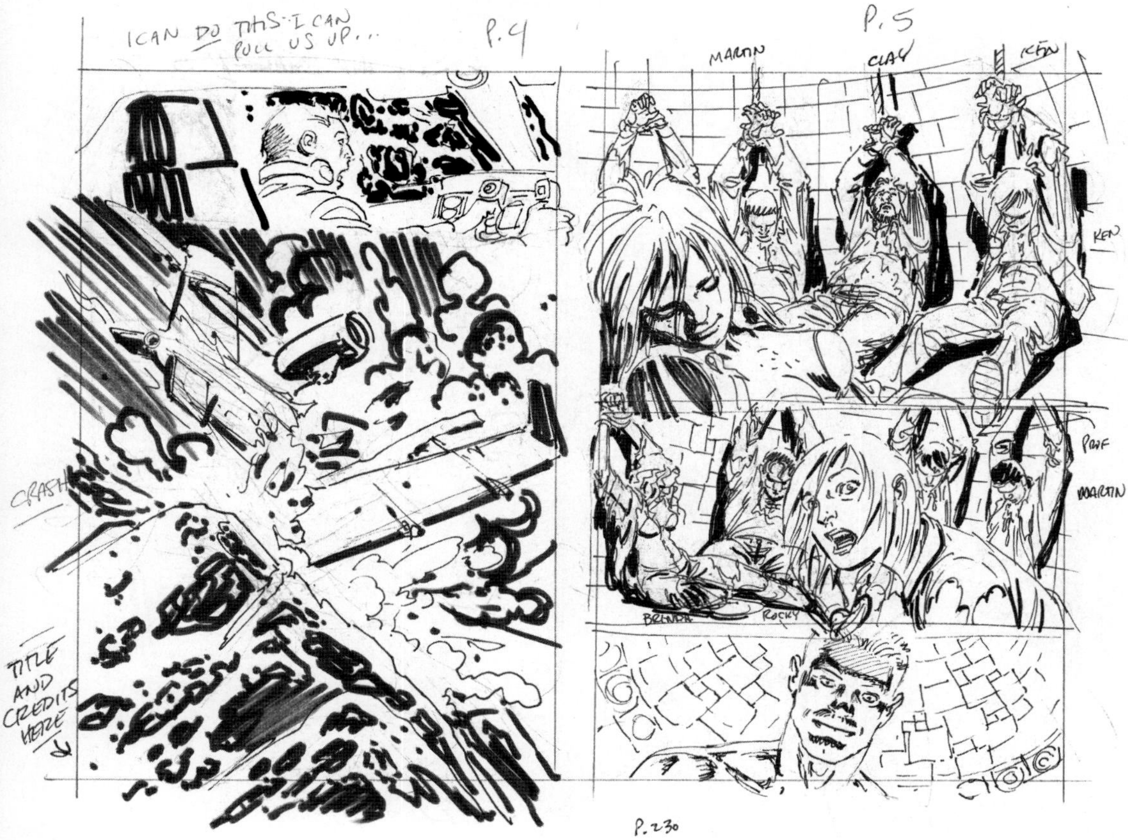
I CAN DO THIS·I CAN PULL US UP...
P.4
P.5
MARTIN
CLAY
KEN
KEN
CRASH
TITLE AND CREDITS HERE
PROF
MARTIN
BRENDA
ROCKY
P.230

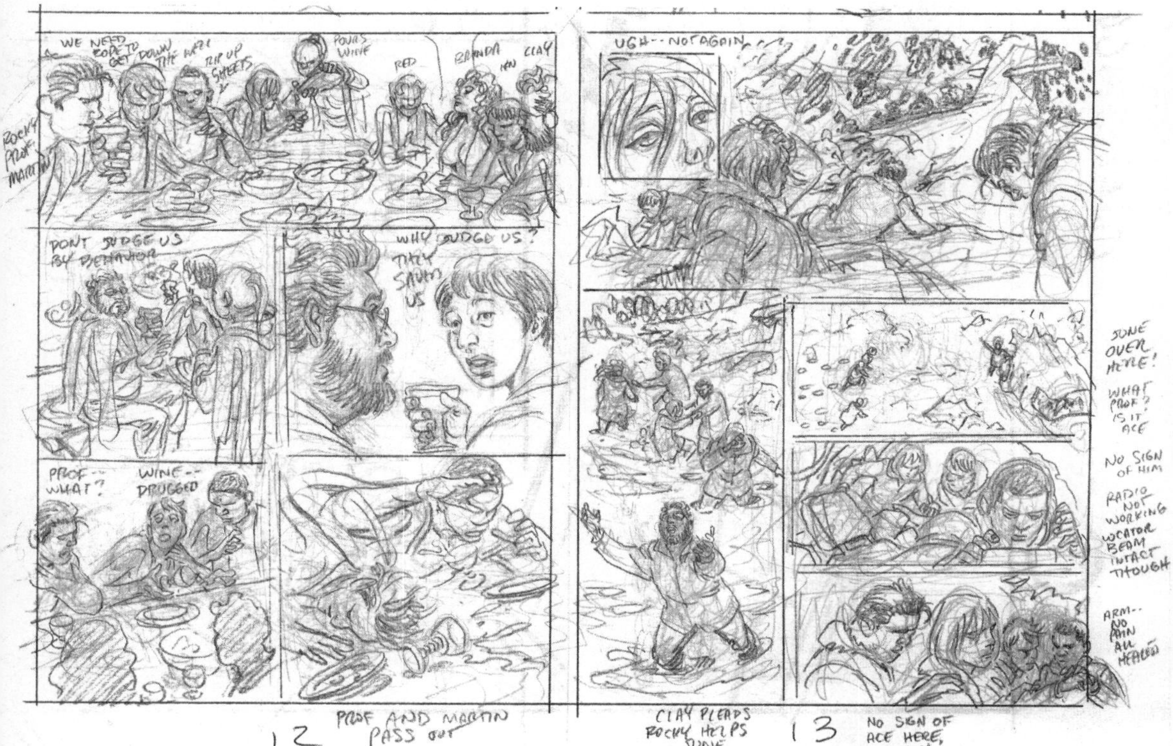
RIP UP SHEETS
POURS WINE
RED
BRENDA
KEN
CLAY
ROCKY PROF MARTIN
DON'T JUDGE US BY BEHAVIOR
PROF— WHAT?
WINE— DRUGGED
UGH— NOT AGAIN
JUNE OVER HERE!
WHAT PROF? IS IT ACE
NO SIGN OF HIM
RADIO NOT WORKING
LOCATOR BEAM INTACT THOUGH
ARM— NO PAIN ALL HEALED
12
PROF AND MARTIN PASS OUT
CLAY PLEADS ROCKY HELPS JUNE
ACE & BRENDA IN BACK
13
NO SIGN OF ACE HERE, SORRY

DC UNIVERSE PRESENTS #6 pages 12 & 13

DC UNIVERSE PRESENTS #7 pages 13 & 14

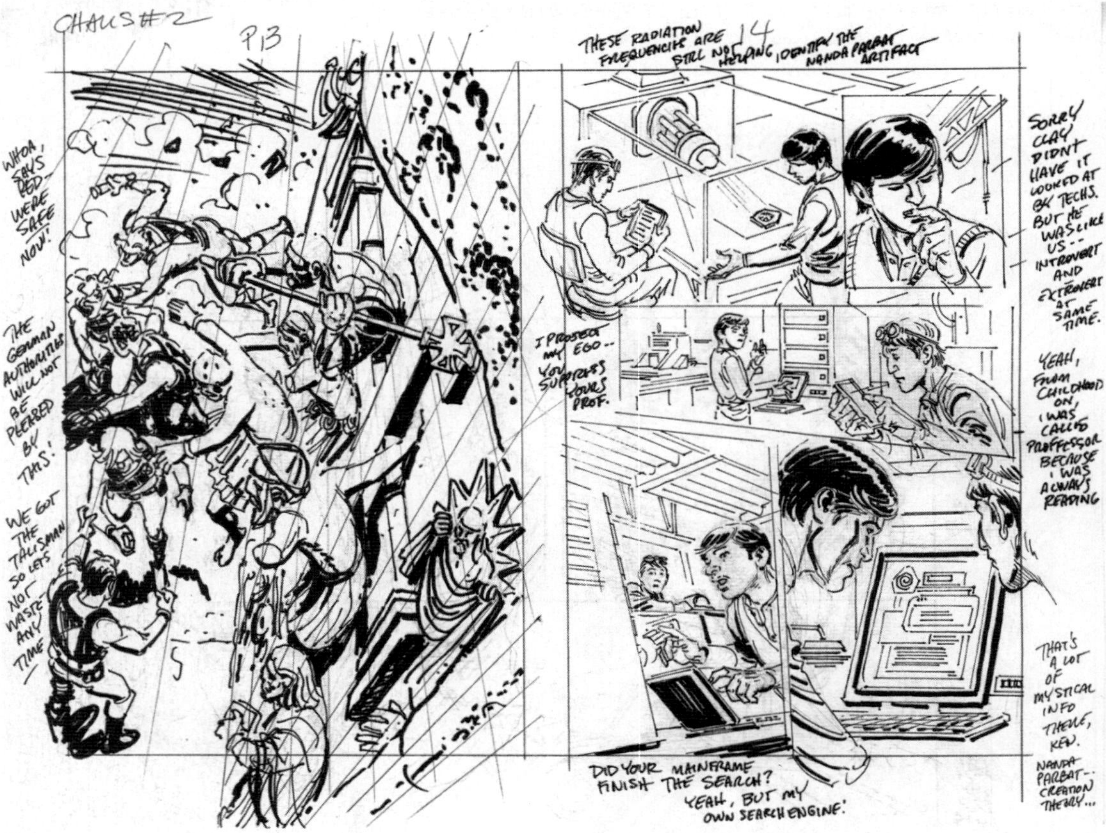
CHAUS #2
P13
14
WHOA, SAYS RED-- WE'RE SAFE NOW!
THE GERMAN AUTHORITIES WILL NOT BE PLEASED BY THIS!
WE GOT THE TALISMAN SO LETS NOT WASTE ANY TIME
THESE RADIATION FREQUENCIES ARE STILL NOT HELPING IDENTIFY THE NANDA PARBAT ARTIFACT
SORRY CLAY DIDNT HAVE IT LOOKED AT BY TECHS. BUT HE WAS LIKE US-- INTROVERT AND EXTROVERT AT SAME TIME.
I PROJECT MY EGO... YOU SUPPRESS YOURS PROF.
YEAH, FROM CHILDHOOD ON, I WAS CALLED PROFESSOR BECAUSE I WAS ALWAYS READING
THAT'S A LOT OF MYSTICAL INFO THERE, KEN. NANDA PARBAT-- CREATION THEORY...
DID YOUR MAINFRAME FINISH THE SEARCH?
YEAH, BUT MY OWN SEARCH ENGINE!

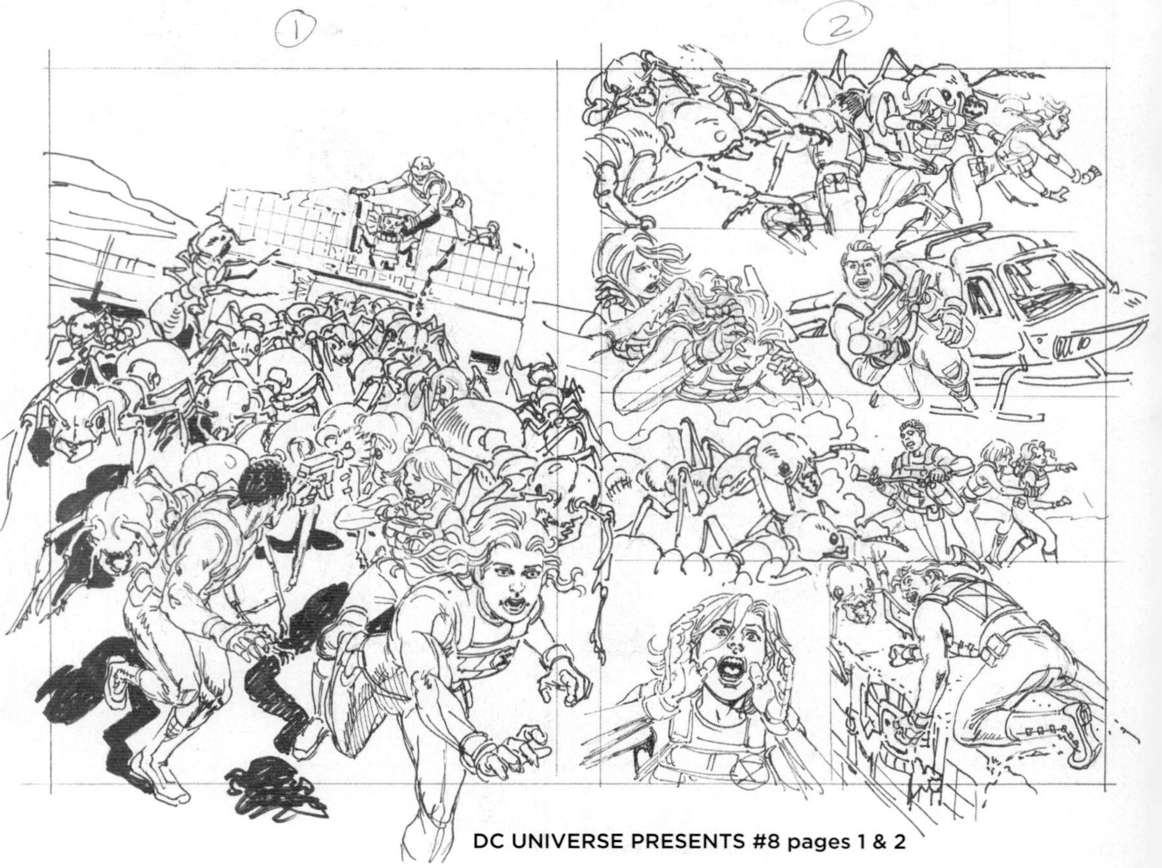
1
2

DC UNIVERSE PRESENTS #8 pages 1 & 2

COVER SKETCHES & ROUGHS BY RYAN SOOK

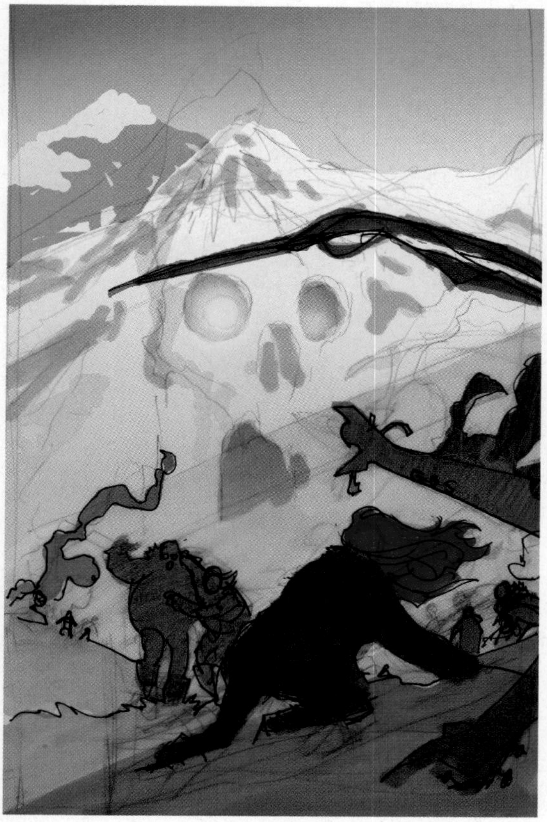

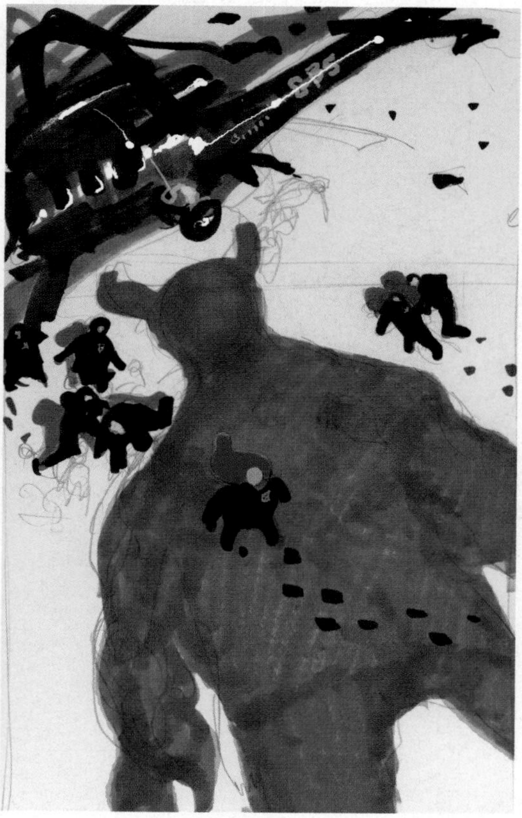

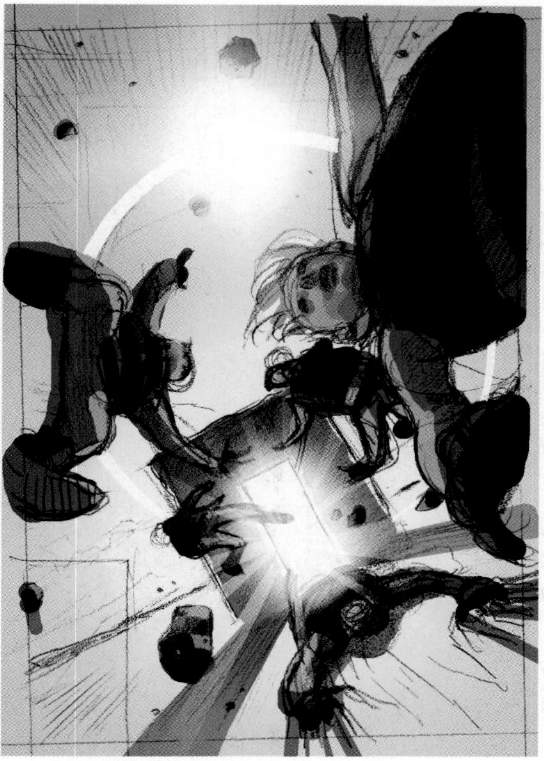

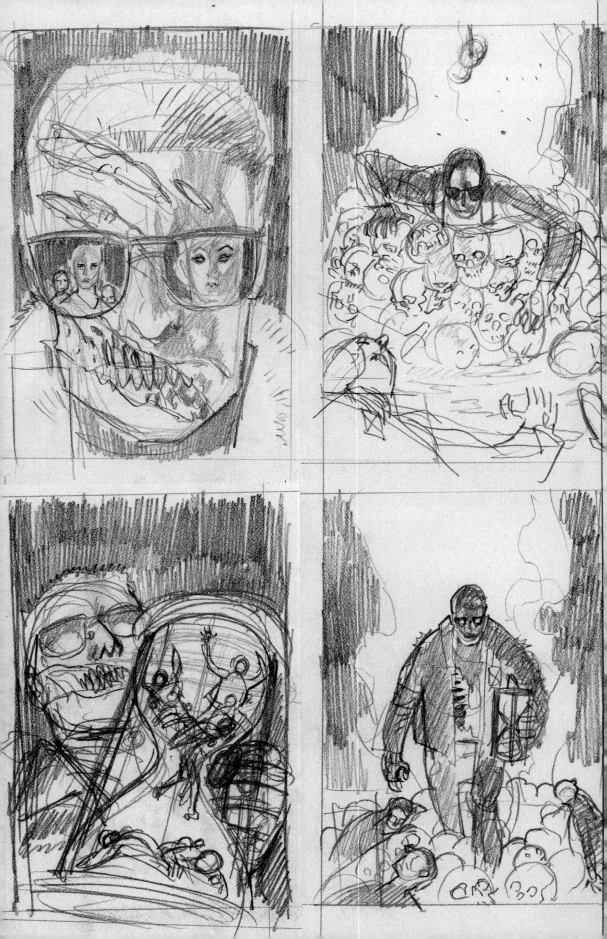